Psychotherapy in the Third Reich:
The Göring Institute

Psychotherapy in the Third Reich

THE GÖRING INSTITUTE

GEOFFREY COCKS

New York   Oxford
OXFORD UNIVERSITY PRESS
1985

The following journals have kindly granted permission to include in this
book articles that were first published in their pages in somewhat different
form:

Journal of the History of the Behavioral Sciences—"Psychotherapy in the
Third Reich: A Research Note," 14 (1978): 33–36.

Spring—"C. G. Jung and German Psychotherapy, 1933–1940: A Research
Note," 10 (1979): 221–27.

Psyche—"Psychoanalyse, Psychotherapie und Nationalsozialismus," 37
(1983): 1057–1106.

Library of Congress Cataloging in Publication Data
Cocks, Geoffrey, 1948–
Psychotherapy in the Third Reich.
Bibliography: p.   Includes index.
1. Psychotherapy—Germany—History—20th century.
2. Germany—History—1933–1945. I. Title. [DNLM:
1. Political systems—Germany. 2. Psychotherapy—
History—Germany.   WM 11 GG4 C6p]
RC438.C63   1985   362.2   83-26830
ISBN 0-19-503461-9

Printing (last digit): 9 8 7 6 5 4 3 2

Printed in the United States of America

To Sarah and Emily

PREFACE

The idea for this book sprang, quite simply, from curiosity. As a student of German history and of psychoanalysis, I came to wonder what had happened in the new, dynamic field of medical psychology in Germany with the advent of Hitler. The very use of the preposition "in" marked a departure from previous thought on the subject since the traditional—and limited—historical view employed the preposition "to" in a declarative sentence: The Nazis did to the field of medical psychology what they did to science and knowledge in general in Germany; that is, they polluted and destroyed it. This traditional judgment was based primarily on the spectacle and testimony of those in the field who had emigrated from Germany to escape Nazi persecution.

Such a judgment had, and still has, considerable merit. The psychoanalytic movement that had revolutionized the treatment of mental disorders was forced to move the foci of its activities from Vienna and Berlin to London and New York. Jewish psychoanalysts who did not flee were tortured and murdered in Nazi concentration camps. The fist of Nazi totalitarianism closed around the Freudian movement so tightly as to squeeze out light and life.

But there were several interesting shards of evidence that pointed to the possibility that one could reconstruct a history of developments in German medical psychology, as well as the damage done to it, beginning in 1933: the existence of a journal for psychotherapy published continuously from 1928 to 1944; accounts of a psychotherapist who assumed leadership of his colleagues and who was a relative of the powerful Nazi leader Hermann Göring; the fact of a strong psychotherapeutic lobby in German medicine that was impoverished but apparently not destroyed by the expulsion of the prominent and predominantly Jewish psychoanalytic movement; and research into the domestic history of the Third Reich, which revealed the seams, cracks, and niches that marked the facets of an order that its Nazi masters had proclaimed as smooth as the rally of stones at Nuremberg.

Fortunately, the leads for the pursuit of this history were not as cold as Speer's blocks piled up in Dutzendteich. From psychoanalysts who had emigrated to the United States in the 1930s, I learned of colleagues who had remained in Germany and who, together with non-Freudian psychotherapists, had pursued their profession under the aegis of the so-called Göring Institute. My research in Germany thus began with interviews and hours of research in libraries and archives. The institute building itself had been destroyed in 1945, so from the beginning this research took me to a wide variety of sources and locales. With time, of course, resources and recourses multiplied. As a result, the list of those to whom I must express my gratitude is long, but such gratitude is anything but a burden and, moreover, it is a special pleasure for a historian to look back over the history of a project in order to thank the many organizations, institutions, and individuals whose assistance was so generously given.

A fellowship from the Deutscher Akademischer Austauschdienst provided for the first year of indispensable and timely research in Europe. An additional grant from the National Endowment for the Humanities enabled me to see this project through to its completion. A major grant from the Faculty Development Committee, out of funds awarded Albion College by the Andrew W. Mellon Foundation, assisted in the final revision of the manuscript. In addition, two smaller grants from the same source were forthcoming—one making possible a quick trip to Germany in 1979 to tape a crucial interview and the other helping cover the cost of preparing an index. I am also indebted to Julian Rammelkamp, former chairman of the Department of History at Albion College; to Neil Thorburn, former Dean of the Faculty at Albion; and to the latter's successor, Russell Aiuto, for their support of my work. I also wish to thank the Department of History at UCLA and its chair, Hans Rogger, for a term of university teaching that made possible, and complemented, some of the final stages of research. The department at UCLA was also generous in the provision of funds for some technical costs in the reproduction of illustrations.

I also extend my appreciation to the following institutions whose resources and staffs were instrumental in the completion of the research. The Berlin Document Center in Berlin-Zehlendorf, under its late director Richard Bauer, present chief Daniel Simon, and with the assistance of Werner Pix, served as a consistently exciting source of documentation. I am also grateful to the Bundesarchiv and Bundesarchiv-Bildarchiv at Coblenz; the Bundesarchiv-Militärarchiv and Militärgeschichtliches Forschungsamt in Freiburg im Breisgau; the Institut für Zeitgeschichte in Munich; the Institute of Contemporary History and Wiener Library in London; the National Archives in Washington, D.C.; the Geheimes Staatsarchiv in Berlin-Dahlem; the Hoover Institution on War, Revolution and Peace at Stanford University; to Hadassah Modlinger of the Central Archives for the Disaster and the Heroism at Yad Vashem in Jerusalem; the Sigmund Freud-Gesellschaft in Vienna; the Bundesärztekammer and Kassenärztliche Bundesvereinigung in Cologne; the Bundesminister der Verteidigung and Sanitätsamt der Bundeswehr in Bonn; the Niedersächsisches Hauptsaatsarchiv in Hanover; the Institut für Geschichte der Medizin der Freien Universität Berlin; the Staatsbibliothek Berlin, the Landesarchiv Berlin, and the Bildarchiv Preussischer Kulturbesitz in West Berlin; the Institut für Medizinische Psychologie und Psychotherapie der Technischen Universität München; and, to a lesser extent, the Zentrales Staatsarchiv in Potsdam. The research and Medical libraries of the Free University of Berlin, the Friedrich-Alexander University in Erlangen, the University of California at Los Angeles, and the University of Michigan provided efficient access to a wide range of primary and secondary sources. The libraries of Occidental College, Albion College (with special thanks to Judy Johnson), Portland State University, Stanford University, and the Monterey Institute of International Studies, along with the Carmel (California) Public Library, also served as valuable sources of material. Finally, I am grateful to the National Library of Medicine for an off-line bibliographic citation list generated by Medlars II.

Apart from those men and women who consented to be interviewed about their roles in, and perspectives on, the history of psychotherapy in the Third Reich and whose contributions are credited in the bibliography, I must thank Gerhard Adler, M.D.; Thomas Aichhorn; Ellen Bartens; Bruno Bettelheim; Dr. med. Adolf-Martin Däumling; Lloyd deMause; Dr. med. Annemarie Dührssen; Judith Elkin; Ernst Federn; Dietmar Frenzel of the Embassy of the Federal Republic of Germany in Washington, D.C.; Daniel Goleman of the *New York Times;* Martin Grotjahn, M.D.; David Heron of the Hoover Institution; Dr. med. Johanna Herzog-Dürck; Zoe Heyer; James Hillman; Dr. med. Wolfgang Hochheimer; Dr. sc. med. Kurt Höck of the Haus der Gesundheit in East Berlin; Klaus Hoppe, M.D.; Wolfgang Huber; Aniela Jaffé; Dr. med. Heinz Knoche, director of the Arbeitsgruppe "Geschichte der Deutschen Luft- und Raumfahrtmedizin" of the Deutschen Gesellschaft für Luft- und Raumfahrtmedizin in Bonn; Dr. med. Gisela Krichhauf; Bernhard Kroner; Peter Loewenberg; Hans-Martin Lohmann; William McGuire; Dr. med. C. A. Meier; Dr. med. Adolf-Ernst Meyer; William Miller; Paul Moor; Dr. med. Hans Müller-Braunschweig; Herman O. Pineas, M.D.; Monika Richarz; Diane Snell and Stella Restropo of CEUCA in Bogotá, Colombia; George Rosenwald; Albert Speer; Rose Spiegel, M.D.; James Steakley; Sanford Thatcher; John Toland; and Robert Wolfe of the National Archives. I am also grateful to the editors of *Psyche* and *Zeitschrift für klinische Psychologie und Psychotherapie;* to the staffs of the Consulate General of the Federal Republic of Germany in Detroit, the Leo Baeck Institute in New York, the Landgericht Lüneburg, and the Amt für Einwohnerwesen in Düsseldorf; and to Charles Scribner's Sons of New York. Special appreciation goes to two colleagues formerly at the Free University of Berlin, Ulfried Geuter (Psychological Institute) and Regine Lockot (Institute for Medical Psychology).

The original thesis on which this work is based was ably directed by Peter Loewenberg and read by Albert Hutter and Hans Rogger. More than anyone else, Peter Loewenberg taught me by word and by deed the skills, the responsibilities, and the joys of the historian, a process so capably begun by John Rodes and Andrew Rolle.

In Germany, Michael and Gwen Wolff of Fürth were more than generous with their hospitality. In the task of revising the thesis into a book, I am grateful to good friends in Los Angeles for joyful and scholarly sanctuary at St. Albans. The production of the final manuscript owes a great deal to the kind and patient expertise of Sara Blackburn of New York City. Grace Waterbury, Carole Steinaway, and Gwen Fellenberger of Ann Arbor typed the final copy. At Oxford University Press, Nancy Lane proved to be an able and generous editor and was efficiently aided by a number of associates, in particular, Joan Knizeski. The index was prepared by Dorothy Hoffman. I am grateful to all these fine professionals. Finally, I thank my wife Sarah for her assistance, her support, and, all too often, her tolerance.

All translations are my own unless otherwise noted. And, of course, in spite of the help I have received, the responsibility for any errors of fact or interpretation is mine alone.

Albion, Michigan   G.C.
June 1984

CONTENTS

ILLUSTRATIONS

ABBREVIATIONS

BDC   Berlin Document Center
DAF   Deutsche Arbeitsfront
DFG   Deutsche Forschungsgemeinschaft
DGPT   Deutsche Gesellschaft für Psychotherapie und Tiefenpsychologie
DPG   Deutsche Psychoanalytische Gesellschaft
NSDAP   Nationalsozialistische Deutsche Arbeiterpartei
NSV   Nationalsozialistische Volkswohlfahrt
OKW   Oberkommando der Wehrmacht
RFR   Reichsforschungsrat
SA   Sturmabteilung
SD   Sicherheitsdienst
SS   Schutzstaffel
ZfP   *Zentralblatt für Psychotherapie und ihre Grenzgebiete einschliesslich der medizinischen Psychologie und psychischen Hygiene*

Psychotherapy in the Third Reich:
The Göring Institute

CHAPTER I

Psychotherapy and National Socialism: An Overview

The advent of Hitler in Germany in 1933 had, as in almost all realms of German life, a dramatic effect on the field of medical psychology. For the profession as a whole, the most obvious and distressing consequence of the Nazi seizure of power was the exodus of doctors who were Jews or simply opponents of the new regime. The Berlin Psychoanalytic Institute, the first in the world, suffered a crippling loss of staff members and students, and in 1936 disappeared as an independent entity. With the German annexation of Austria in 1938 came the destruction of the Vienna Psychoanalytic Society and Institute and the exile of Freud himself to one last year of life in London. In place of the rich and often disputatious environment produced by psychoanalysts, psychotherapists, psychologists, and psychiatrists in Germany, there emerged strident and intellectually shallow affirmations of professional loyalty to National Socialism and a dedication to the creation of a "new German psychotherapy" (*neue deutsche Seelenheilkunde*).

What has heretofore escaped notice, however, was the surprising opportunity for those who remained in Germany. A number of lesser-known physicians and laypersons involved in the practice and propagation of all types of psychotherapy, including psychoanalysis, were now, through a confluence of conditions, in a position to foster its professional exercise and promulgation. Even at the zenith of Nazi persecution, an important degree of professional continuity was maintained. And furthermore, the particular conditions that prevailed beginning in 1933 allowed these psychotherapists to achieve an institutional status and capacity for practice that has been unrivaled in Germany before or since.

Studies in intellectual history generally concentrate on those landmark thinkers and systems through which the development of the respective fields can be charted. Yet a measure of historical concentration on those periods and individuals who fill the interstices beside and between the giants and milestones can be enormously revealing, not only for our understanding of how a system of thought evolved but in providing an expanded perspective from which to perceive it.

This is, to say the least, ironic since in the case of psychotherapy in the Third Reich, of course, we are dealing with another instance of a disastrous enforced caesura in the established conduct of professional and intellectual activity in Germany and, ultimately, in Nazi-occupied Europe. It is a reasonable hypothesis that had the Nazis never come to power, psychotherapy, led by the brilliant psychoanalytic movement in Central Europe, would have achieved a prestige and position beyond what was dug out by psychotherapists in the Third Reich.

But the Nazis did come to power and it is remarkable that their intrusion, while certainly destructive, did not spell an end to serious and substantive change in the field of medical psychology in Germany. It is of course true that nothing worthwhile could flourish under a dictatorship such as Hitler's, and it is manifestly *not* the thesis of this book that Nazi Germany provided a positive environment for the practice of medical psychology, for the advancement of science, knowledge, and human services in general, or that psychotherapists in the Third Reich were unsung heroes and martyrs. It *is* the thesis of this book, however, that the Third Reich witnessed not only the survival but also the professional and institutional development of psychotherapy in Germany—and thus that medical psychology *as an institutional and professional entity* fared much better under National Socialism than might have been expected and has been assumed. This continuity with the preceding and succeeding developments in the field occurred alongside the destruction of individual careers, the compromise of professional, private, and public ethics, and within the general malaise that settled over human affairs under Hitler. Thus, the history of psychotherapy in the Third Reich is not an inspirational tale of advances in sophisticated theory and the alleviation of mental suffering, but rather of a morally and intellectually ambiguous accommodation to the established powers of Nazi Germany, on both the individual and collective level, in pursuit of professional and institutional status.

Those few German psychotherapists who, on the basis of a Romantic and politically naive cultural chauvinism, genuinely and fervently believed in National Socialism as a force for the development of ideas came away from the engagement empty-handed. In terms of ideas, Hitler's Reich generated sparse light, but it threw shadows, shapes of little substance that could darken but not transform. The Nazis did not display the sharp, skillfully wielded scalpel of ideas, but the blunt, clumsy truncheon of racism: the witches' hammer in place of Occam's razor. The situation was memorably formulated in the words of Franz

Wirz, the Nazi party's Chief Administrator for University Affairs (Dezernent für Hochschulangelegenheiten der NSDAP). On this occasion Wirz was responding to traditional yet also newly anxious and "loyal" criticism of Freud from some German psychotherapists at a meeting on 26 April 1936. He noted that he and the party were not so much opposed to the science of psychoanalysis as to its practice by Jews, saying, "We all know that the Wassermann reaction was discovered by a Jew. But no one in Germany would be so foolish as to no longer make use of this reaction."[1]

There transpired no battle, much less a victory, for ideas in Nazi Germany, but rather the fervent mobilization of existing social, economic, and institutional resources, all within the nimbus of the vague and subjective notions of militant racial destiny. This pragmatism was born of the absence of specific reforms based on a rational ideology, raised amid the scramble of former "outs" making the most of being "ins"—along with the squabbles of Hitler's paladins, vassals, sycophants, and servants—and elaborately cloaked in the "German spirit."

The history of psychotherapy in the Third Reich is notable because it offered its participants the opportunity for professional development. This study is only partially one of "Nazi psychotherapy," just as it is only to a limited extent a study, like so many others, of those acts of omission and commission that spawned, supported, and tolerated National Socialism. It is not the intent of this book to attempt to justify or condemn the morals and ethics of psychotherapists in the Third Reich, or to assess the degree of their historical responsibility for the advent and actions of the Nazis. Rather, it means to demonstrate and explain the psychotherapists' success within, and often against, the medical establishment in Germany between 1933 and 1945, and to record the sometimes perilous course they navigated between the chaotic features of Nazi party and state.

The study of German psychotherapists under National Socialism, moving as occupational outsiders to define and demonstrate their professional identity, offers a dynamic view of professional life in Nazi Germany. The perspective is much broader than the one offered by the comparatively static portraits of larger and more established professions, framed in the flatter dimensions of collaboration with and resistance to Nazi ignorance and oppression. Earlier studies of the Third Reich, especially when they touched on the fate of intellectuals, academics, and professionals, stressed discontinuity—that is, in effect, the end of any significantly worthwhile or autonomous work or thought.[2] However, to understand this era in the history of psychotherapy, the traditional historical focus on the corrosive Nazi effect on ideas and people will not suffice.

With the establishment of the Berlin Psychoanalytic Institute in 1920, Germany's capital had joined Vienna at the forefront of the movement in modern medical psychology created by Freud and his school. The progress psychoanalysis made in the ensuing decade was in large part due to the success of its practitioners during World War I in treating the cases of neurosis that so baffled the traditionally trained psychiatrists employed by the military. The war experience had also inspired a number of young physicians in Germany to pursue psychotherapy and encourage its development as a profession within the ranks of the medical establishment that was still, by and large, oriented to purely somatic diagnoses and cures. This campaign on behalf of psychotherapy had originally been inspired by the psychoanalytic movement that had revived the medical and philosophical ideals of German Romantic natural philosophy, ideals that sharply opposed the materialist and positivist tradition of German medicine and university psychiatry.

In 1926 psychiatrists Robert Sommer and Wladimir Eliasberg founded the General Medical Society for Psychotherapy. This international organization sought to rally all physicians dedicated to the use of various modes of psychotherapy in medical practice. With the formal chartering of the society in 1928, a journal was initiated; in 1930 it became the *Zentralblatt für Psychotherapie*. Prominent members of the society included Alfred Adler, Carl Jung, Frieda Fromm-Reichmann, Karen Horney, Ernst Kretschmer, Erwin Liek, Felix Deutsch, Georg Groddeck, Kurt Lewin, Ernst Simmel, Johannes Heinrich Schultz, Viktor von Weizsäcker, and Harald Schultz-Hencke. The German Psychoanalytic Society refused to recognize the General Medical Society for Psychotherapy, since its international membership included "wild psychoanalysts," anathematized by Freud himself, and contained proponents of other nonorthodox psychotherapeutic orientations whose tenets were not acceptable to the psychoanalysts.

When the Nazis came to power in 1933, the members of the General Medical Society for Psychotherapy were confronted by the new regime's persistent charge that psychology was "Jewish," as well as by the Nazis' efforts to extend their control over all realms of activity in Germany. The psychotherapists responded by forming in September 1933, the German General Medical Society for Psychotherapy, a separate national group to fall within the international umbrella organization now headed by Carl Jung. As leader of the German contingent the psychotherapists chose Matthias Heinrich Göring, a neuropathologist from Wuppertal who had long been active as a psychotherapist. This was a wise choice for its members and one that was approved of without incident by the National Socialist party and the state medical bureaucracy, since Göring was a cousin of Hermann Göring, the Nazi vizier of Prussia. It was under the protection of the Göring name that the German psychotherapists were to function, and even fatten, until 1945.

The psychotherapists under M. H. Göring were eager to provide a protected institutional base for the teaching, practice, and propagation of the new profession of psychotherapy. Göring himself, along with a number of his colleagues, also had naïve visions of some sort of synthesis of the reigning systems in the field of medical psychology into a nominally "German" psychotherapy. Ironically, in a process that we will explore in Chapter 4, the health department of the Reich Interior Ministry suggested that the Göring-led group merge with the now badly crippled Berlin Psychoanalytic Institute. Such an amalgamation would allow the remaining non-Jewish psychoanalysts there to continue to function, as well as to provide the psychotherapists of the financially strapped General Medical Society with offices in which to operate an institute. The irony was actually a double one: Not only was a Nazi agency facilitating the survival of psychoanalysis, the "Jewish science" they so despised, but the General Medical Society psychotherapists were to benefit from association with their newly stigmatized old rivals, the psychoanalysts. As we will see, this forced association would provide shared benefits far beyond the convenience of shared quarters.

Thus it was that in the early summer of 1936 Göring managed to establish an institute in Berlin: The German Institute for Psychological Research and Psychotherapy came into being and was quickly dubbed the Göring Institute. For the first three years it received its primary financial support from contributions by its members, but with the onset of war in 1939, it began receiving significant funding from the wealthy German Labor Front, which, aside from its generally acquisitive and imperialistic organizational ethos, was interested in the institute's potential professional capacities in the realm of industrial psychology. The Göring Institute's work in the teaching, practice, and study of psychotherapy was also supported by the Luftwaffe (we will be surveying that association in Chapter 6). Added to this were working relationships with a number of party and state welfare agencies and mental health institutions. The institute and various of its members had ongoing professional contact with the Hitler Youth, the League of German Girls, the Reich Criminal Police Office, the SS-Lebensborn, and individual members of the Nazi hierarchy. This growing network of service and reciprocal support allowed the institute eventually to establish branches in Munich, Stuttgart, Düsseldorf, Wuppertal, and Frankfurt am Main.

The Labor Front, however, for all its wealth, was a flabby and uncertain source of supervision and money. As a result, in 1943 Göring managed to have the funding of the institute supplemented to a significant degree by contributions from the Reich Research Council, which, not coincidentally, had in June 1942 come under the direction of Hermann Göring. In January 1944 the institute was renamed the Reich Institute for Psychological Research and Psychotherapy in the Reich Research Council. The formal affiliation happened as a result of the Reich Marshal Göring's attempt to shore up the bastions of his personal empire against the incursions of Goebbels's Total War program. But with this step, the Göring Institute achieved a quasi-governmental status that was the peak of psychotherapy's professional identity in the Third Reich. While it was to last only until 1945, the Göring Institute represented a unique and significant step in the development of psychotherapy in Central Europe. Before we begin to examine the details of this unusual history, it is necessary to survey briefly the general conditions that allowed it to develop.

Conditions That Allowed the Profession to Develop

Broadly defined, psychotherapy is the treatment, alleviation, and cure of mental disorders, and ranges in technique from simple modes of advice and encouragement to complex cultural rituals and sophisticated scientific theories. More narrowly defined, psychotherapy historically includes those theories and methods which see mental disorders as a range of crises of the psychological and physiological totality of the human organism within its environment rather than as manifestations of a physical malfunction of the brain or nervous system. It is this latter definition that serves this study. This is the case because the theoretical and methodological conflicts over the nature of mind and body became particularly sharp during the nineteenth century, when scientific positivism inspired and informed much of the research into the operations of the brain and nervous system.

These conflicts were especially sharp in Germany, where various physicians and laymen, in great measure inspired by a Freudian movement that had revived and greatly expanded the old Romantic notion of the psyche (see Chapter 2), were extremely critical of the somatic orientation of the reigning university psychiatrists. This rising challenge was intensified by World War I, which, as we observed earlier, confronted military psychiatrists with cases their physicalistic theories could not explain and their laboratory methods could not treat. Psychoanalysis in particular was boosted by its successful use in the treatment of war neuroses. As a result, the 1920s in Germany nurtured a variety of groups that campaigned for physicians to recognize the existence of the crucial interaction between mind and body. Chief among these was the General Medical Society for Psychotherapy. As it amalgamated and institutionalized itself under the leadership of Matthias Heinrich Göring, and worked to promote psychotherapy as an independent profession, it encompassed both medicine and general psychology, drawing its theories and methods from a wide range of disciplines in the natural (medical) sciences (*Naturwissenschaften*) and the so-called human sciences (*Geisteswissenschaften*).

We have noted that the establishment of what became known as the Göring Institute was all the more important at the time because the Nazi terror had forced the emigration of many of the best minds in the field of medical psychology. As a result, instead of spectacular theoretical advances by the discipline's great (and predominantly Jewish) intellectual pioneers, there transpired for psychotherapy under National Socialism a process of settling into a significant degree of established practice, and a concomitant positive recognition by both the public and, more slowly, the medical profession.

We have already noted the Romantic tradition that prevailed among German medical psychologists, an intellectual and cultural bent that was shared by the Nazis. Even more important in the development of psychotherapy as a profession in Germany in the three decades before mid-century was the Göring Institute's commitment to psychotherapy over psychoanalysis as it pursued its charge of harmonizing the interests of the individual and the prevailing social order. The psychotherapists who gathered under the roof of the Göring Institute offered a variety of supportive and generally short-term therapies designed to further the integration of a happy and productive individual into society. Such an emphasis was clearly congruent with the Nazi design for the subordination of the individual to the community (*"Gemeinnutz geht vor Eigennutz."*), and thus conferred immediate advantages on the newly institutionalized psychotherapists. It also brought psychotherapy into closer contact with a greater number of general medical practitioners who wished to incorporate such simpler modes of psychotherapy into their own practices. Psychoanalysis, more didactic, of longer duration, and by nature committed to support the individual in his struggle against society, was simply not as accessible to them— even if they wished to ignore the traditional objections to it common within the German medical profession and to defy the newer racial condemnations propounded by the Nazis.

But as Franz Wirz so unabashedly pointed out, although Freud was officially disavowed by German psychotherapists under Hitler, Freudian theory and practice was too important a part of the new medical psychology to be discarded. Psychoanalysis, too, preserved through the departure of Jewish analysts and by the cover of the Göring name, established a significant position within an institute that was largely successful not only in protecting but in promoting almost all types of medical and nonmedical psychotherapy.

And so the Nazis did not destroy psychotherapy, either by efficient and ruthless suppression or by transforming it into a mute slave to their own muddled ideology. Instead, a kaleidoscope of four major conditions, produced out of the historical evolution of medical psychology in Germany and modified by the institutional dynamics of Nazism in power, combined to create a unique opportunity for psychotherapy to continue to develop as a profession after 1933. The first condition was the very fact of a group of psychotherapists looking toward the growth and expanded practice of this new profession within the field of medicine. The second was the ongoing organizational disorder that characterized the untutored and often frenzied Nazi mobilization of state and society. The third condition was the Nazis' ideological and pragmatic interest in psychotherapy and psychology in general. Powerfully concerned with the "care and control" (*Betreuung*) of the populace, they, through a crude combination of racism, behavioralism, and Romantic notions of the "soul," regarded a properly Aryanized psychology and psychotherapy as an important means of ensuring the loyalty and productivity of the German people (*Volk*). The intriguing young profession offered the Nazis an appealing synthesis of a Romantic heritage and what they regarded as basic to the task of medical psychology: dealing with the *internal qualities* of human beings. Obsessed as they were by the external determinants of race, the Nazis believed that the true Aryan was distinguished not only by his blood, bone structure, and coloring, but also by the internal and intangible qualities of character.

The fourth condition that allowed the successful development of psychotherapy in the Third Reich was the presence of Matthias Heinrich Göring. It was primarily the result of Göring's influence that for the first time public funds were made available for the teaching and practice of psychotherapy. The fact that for nine years psychotherapists in Germany enjoyed professional success and status unsurpassed either before or since stemmed from the unique institutional base that was developed, above all, from the influence and protection bestowed by the Göring name. Göring, although he was impelled—as we will see—by his own ideas concerning a "German" psychotherapy, by family loyalty to his cousin Hermann, and by his conservative nationalist allegiance to the state and to Hitler, never served as a mere appointed *Gauleiter* for psychotherapy. Indeed, because of who he was, psychotherapists were allowed an autonomy that went far beyond that created for them by the superficial, if often damaging, nature of the Nazi mobilization of Germany's professional resources. Göring, a rather shy man who had long been dedicated to the development of psychotherapy, by and large allowed the institute to pursue serious work along all avenues of medical psychology, including psychoanalysis.

Given the confluence of all these conditions, it is understandable that Karl Jaspers observed after the war that in 1936 "something vitally new occurred when the German Institute for Psychological Research and Psychotherapy was founded in Berlin under the direction of M. H. Göring."[3]

In Chaos, Survival:
Mental Health in the Third Reich

Why has this particular story heretofore remained untold? Most early studies of the Third Reich were undertaken in direct response to Hitler's tyranny and aggression.[4] The result was an emphasis on the spectacularly brutal means by which Hitler and the Nazis sought to assert their control over Germany and Europe. Only as the shock over the horrors of Nazism fades at last has the avalanche of books on the Nazi police state and Hitler's foreign policy and military campaigns given way to studies of the domestic history of Nazi Germany.

Nazi aggression and oppression, both at home and abroad, offered the historian a fairly clear line of intent and action. Matters of governance and of social and economic policy in the Third Reich have presented a different picture, however. Rather than presenting any direct confrontation between old and new, between status quo and reform, or between state and party, the result of the Nazi "revolution" was a confused tangle of issues, offices, influences, and ideas. Given the hollow Nazi pretensions to substantive reform, pre-Nazi era issues and power centers (army, industry, bureaucracy) played significant roles in the ebb and flow of administration and governance in the Third Reich. Such was certainly the case, to cite one prominent example, with the concerns of bureaucrats in the Reich Interior Ministry.[5] And, as we will see in Chapter 5, the confusions of Hitler's Reich were to land the Göring Institute in a position somewhere between a party and a state bureaucracy that were simultaneously in flux and in conflict.

In the wake of an abiding emphasis on experimentation and euthanasia, the subject of health care in Nazi Germany has received scant attention.[6] This is understandable and justified in light of the way the Nazis dealt with those they pronounced as their enemies, but the result has been misleading. It has long been assumed that the Nazi attitude toward mental illness was based solely on biological grounds. According to this view, mental illness for the Nazis was a sign of inferior racial stock; a pure Aryan would be free of such taint, and a policy defending the mental health of the German people would thus consist only of selection and regulation rather than care. It is true that German psychiatrists were mobilized to some degree to espouse and exercise Nazi eugenics, that is, the merciless treatment of those deemed for biological reasons unfit for inclusion in the racial community (*Volksgemeinschaft*). The Nazis did attempt to single out, exclude, sterilize, and finally exterminate all those individuals suffering from severe incurable or congenital mental illnesses—those whom they defined, like the Jews, as biological enemies. They exercised the same brutality toward many mental patients as they did toward their political opponents. For Hitler and the Nazis, the life of races was one of struggle for survival; no quarter was asked or given.

This ruthless logic also accounted for why the Nazis never utilized the asylum as a repository for political opponents, as the Soviets have so notoriously done, whereby simply and systematically "protest against society can be explained away as a neurotic symptom."[7] Such a perspective, in spite of its essential violation of individual human dignity and generally abusive application, implies, like all manner of authoritarian and totalitarian effort at mind control, the possibility and desirability of correction. To be sure, many under such a system are simply locked away forever in a sad and savage parody of medical care, but the distinction raised here between Nazi and Soviet methods helps to illuminate a heretofore unexamined sphere of public and professional life in the Third Reich. Whatever the similarities between Nazi Germany and Soviet Russia as totalitarian systems, their ideologies are fundamentally different. Marxism, in its materialism, is inherently rational and looks to scientific strategies—in this case, a psychiatry originally based on Pavlovian psychology and now characterized by an organic chemical bias—to build and secure a well-ordered egalitarian society.[8] National Socialism, for its part, had no ideology worthy of the name; it was a movement founded on a charismatic, not an ideological, basis.[9] For the Nazis, "feeling with the blood" was sufficient reason for letting the blood of their enemies flow freely. Unlike the Soviets, the rational determinism of whose psychiatric system in theory excludes no one save a very few completely hopeless cases from treatment or from inclusion within the socialist order, the Nazis embraced an exclusionary biological and racial determinism that robbed psychiatry of any officially recognized reparative function at all.

But while psychiatry under National Socialism was thus assigned a defensive role by the irrational Nazi concern with racial biology, psychotherapy could exploit the complementary Nazi desire to exert "care and control" over the deep-seated irrational elements of superior will and character possessed by the racially pure "Aryans" who comprised the majority of the people living in Germany. Aside from those psychiatrically defined cases of genetic disorder already in asylums, and the flagrant cases of homosexuality and other officially deviant behavior among those the Nazis labeled "asocials"—who were also to be eliminated through sterilization and extermination—the Nazis could not apply a racial-biological standard to Aryans who exhibited lesser, and more common, neurotic conflict; by ideological as well as psychological definition, mental disorder within the master race could not be genetic or essentially organic. It followed that, given the proper guidance of an innate German will, any such mental distress a member of the German *Volksgemeinschaft* suffered was correctable.

The Nazis pretended to an opposite reality, originally to oppose the "Jewish science" of psychology and to promote the concept of Aryan racial superiority, propaganda that has also helped obscure the existence of the Third Reich's recourse to psychology and psychotherapy. But the truth is that the Nazis simply could not ignore the need for psychological care and adjustment, both inside and outside their own ranks. Their pragmatic stance was strengthened by the totalitarian Nazi emphasis on leadership, control, and education to duty, and by their concern with human productivity in both the civilian and military realms. Indeed, the Nazi use of applied psychology in inspiring and bolstering the enthusiasm and will of the populace was in a sense psychotherapy before the fact. At any rate, since no combination of Nazi institutions, propaganda, and the use of applied psychology could completely preempt maladjustment and neurosis, the need for the resources offered by medical psychology was clear. We must also remember that the Nazis were by no means immune to an almost childish delight in the technical achievements of German scientists. And added to all of this was the exhortative vagueness of National Socialism, which arose out of the genuine Nazi ideological obsession with deep-seated elemental and irrational forces of collective and individual will and which was of fundamental importance to the institutional growth of psychotherapy.

Taken together, these factors allowed for a much greater role for psychotherapy during the Nazi years than has so far been realized. Psychotherapists and psychologists were in fact mobilized to promote the psychological health and effectiveness of the great bulk of Germans who were seen by the regime to constitute the hardy stock of a warrior people. As a result, psychiatry and psychotherapy occupied distinct and important realms in the Nazi scheme of things. Alongside, however, ran an emphasis on the complementary relationship between genetics, or hereditary biology (*Erbbiologie*), which formed the pseudoscientific basis for the Nazi concept of immutable racial characteristics, and what the Nazis called psychological education and some psychotherapists termed "psychagogy" (*Psychagogik*). This was precisely the division of labor within the general mobilization of medicine made clear on one occasion to a 1940 meeting of child psychiatrists by Hans Reiter, a medical official from the Ministry of the Interior.[10]

There is a case to be made, however, that any such emphasis on the subordination of the individual to the state and to society, whether communist or fascist, is antithetical to effective physical and mental health care. It is certainly true that those people in Germany branded as politically and racially undesirable (*rassenfremd*)—pursued, harried, molested, and persecuted—were particularly vulnerable to strain and breakdown. Also susceptible were those sensitive and perceptive individuals, including many psychiatrists, psychoanalysts, and psychotherapists, who labored under a terrible awareness of the morally noxious nature of the regime under which they lived and worked.[11] Martin Gumpert, a German émigré homeopath, argued from exile that the very effort to mobilize the health of all those *"völkisch"* Germans was "opposed to the fundamental tenets of all civilized health welfare work, the substance of which is that care and consideration are the essential presuppositions of social achievement." He sought to characterize and document what he saw as the "general nervous breakdown which hangs like a dark cloud over Germany."[12] But Gumpert's analysis was limited by its subscribing to the common wartime illusion about the total efficiency and regimentation of the Nazi state.

The fact was that two realities prevented the complete, heartless regimentation of minds and bodies under Hitler. Nazi Germany, particularly before the outbreak of war, could boast of not simply an economy, but a whole society, of butter as well as guns. As a necessary prelude and accompaniment to the actions aimed at political and military superiority in Europe, Hitler had sought to cast an amalgam of social welfare, public works, industrial expansion, military regeneration, and patriotic rhetoric. He did so out of a fear that morale would collapse on the home front as he had witnessed it during World War I. It was this concern, along with the inherent inefficiency of Nazi governance, that allowed room for health services to function.

With the terrible exceptions we have noted, it seems Nazi Germany did manage to provide some degree of health and contentment for that large number of Germans who, save perhaps under the impact of the war, were not overly sensitive to the regime's policies. Even late in the war, the British Foreign Office reported that Nazi health organizations showed a remarkable resilience.[13] The Göring Institute not only treated a great number of the mental casualties produced by the war, it also provided psychotherapy for a large number of homosexuals, many from the Nazi youth organizations, and was involved in at least two research projects connected with certain crucial psychological dysfunctions. (See Chapter 6.) It is true that the effectiveness of the psychotherapy offered must certainly have been diminished by the overall strain of those years, given the mutual fear for medical confidentiality and the limited personal options available within a totalitarian social order. For instance, to whatever extent Hitler's order in 1942 that medical confidentiality be lifted in cases involving national security (see Chapter 4) became known, that very knowledge could only serve to damage the necessary "therapeutic alliance" between therapist and patient. Still, there is no clinical evidence that individual neurosis and psychosis were especially prevalent during the Third Reich,[14] either in terms of popular pathological support for Nazi brutalities or, tragically, as mental "protest" against them; personal problems, however aggravated or not by totalitarianism, seem to have taken precedence over direct and adverse mental reactions to the political environment.

The history of psychotherapy as a whole has tended to be obscured by the attention paid to the vigorous psychoanalytic movement, and especially by the appalled conviction that the Nazis managed to destroy psychoanalysis in Central Europe.[15] The silent assumption in this has been that the Nazi phenomenon constituted an end to all medical psychology in Germany, or that all other psychotherapeutic orientations met the same fate. The historical reality is more complex than that.

The Nazis did not succeed in destroying the practice of psychoanalysis in Germany, much less that of psychotherapy in general. The advent of Hitler did eliminate Berlin and then Vienna as centers of psychoanalysis, and shifted the loci of the movement to London and New York.[16] But psychoanalysis as a method did survive among professionals and, under compulsion, to be sure, shared in the mutual benefit its enforced cooperation bestowed on all the psychotherapeutic schools of thought, as we will see in Chapter 6.

Within a fractious and fissured Reich that actually promoted the growth of psychotherapy in general, psychoanalysis presents us with a particularly dramatic instance of survival. That psychoanalysis survived is important in itself, but why it survived reveals the furious, haphazard nature of Nazi postures, plans, and programs. Psychoanalysis was officially banned from the public domain in 1938, and in February 1936 the Ministry of the Interior had already made it plain that an independent psychoanalytic institute would never receive a license to teach or practice.[17] Since psychoanalysis was the creation of a—or the—Jew, it could not be tolerated as an independent entity. It would, however, be given over to "reliable" experts in the field, under the auspices of the Göring Institute.

Perhaps the Nazis hoped, since they themselves had little or no such expertise, that Matthias Heinrich Göring (especially a Göring!) would create a Nazified psychotherapy for them, an expectation that was fulfilled only to a very limited extent. For "new German psychotherapy" remained essentially a label for the cosmetic assemblage of extant psychotherapeutic orientations. Psychoanalysis was able to adopt a secure, if somewhat defensive and subordinate, position within the institute, where differences, however extreme, by and large remained professional and personal, not political.

Perhaps it is superfluous to observe that, whatever the differences among schools of psychotherapeutic thought, Freud was an indispensable common source for all of them. And the other schools of theory gathered safely within the institute proved receptive to the practice of psychoanalysis insofar as they all represented opposition to the attempts by such psychiatrists as Ernst Kretschmer to make psychotherapy the exclusive prerogative of medically trained psychiatrists. The campaign of Kretschmer and others raised the specter of one of Freud's greatest fears, the primary reason for his specific defense of lay analysis. In addition, as Hannah Decker has shown, the traditional view that psychoanalysis from the beginning met with massive resistance from the German medical profession is only partly the case. And since the response to psychoanalysis was in fact not uniformly hostile, with only certain exceptions taken to Freud's thought, there existed before 1933 a substantial basis for physicians' interest in, and cooperation with, psychoanalysts. Freudian theory and practice, though loudly condemned in Nazi Germany, thus actually survived by two means. The first was the sheer fact that psychoanalytic thought had already penetrated into almost all systems of psychotherapeutic theory and praxis; the second was the persistence of the practice of psychoanalysis itself in both its orthodox and neo-Freudian forms. The growing neo-Freudian orientation was of particular importance, for by 1933 psychoanalysis had not only been attacked, accepted, and adapted from without, but altered from within in such a way as to provide some lines of congruence with the approved psychotherapy of the Nazi era.

This ongoing process of just how the acceptance of Freud came into being has generally been overlooked by those psychoanalytic hagiographers concerned with purity of doctrine. Given their insistence that the independent superiority of psychoanalytic doctrine was hopelessly compromised by its forced association with other models of psychotherapy, the traditional view of a uniform rejection of psychoanalysis before 1933 and a uniform oppression of its practice and practitioners after 1933 was thus only strengthened in an inability to acknowledge its survival as a method and as a powerful influence between 1933 and 1945. The attitude of compromise by association became manifest after the war, when the German psychoanalysts were confronted with opposition when they attempted to rejoin the international association, not because of any stigma of collaboration with the Nazis but because of concern about whether the psychoanalysts had been adversely influenced by their collaboration with the other psychotherapeutic schools.[18]

In the same way, divisions among psychotherapists in general have contributed to the lack of knowledge concerning the history of psychotherapy in general during the Nazi period. Aside from psychotherapists' fear of professional guilt by association, a number of psychiatrically oriented psychotherapists have seen the direction taken by the psychotherapists in the Göring Institute as a step backwards. This attitude has led to the self-serving judgment that "political events following 1933 pushed German psychotherapy, and especially analytic psychotherapy, into the background for a long time."[19]

The oppressive intellectual environment created by the Nazis did in fact have the effect of reducing both the amount and the quality of academic discourse. There was a concomitant decline in interdisciplinary contact, discussion, and debate. The seventh congress of the General Medical Society for Psychotherapy, scheduled for 6–9 April 1933 in Vienna, was canceled and held a year later in Germany at Bad Nauheim, with a telling reduction in the quantity and quality of participants.

Alongside the profession's preoccupation with assuming a loyal profile—which the psychotherapist and Nazi enthusiast Walter Cimbal, in explaining the interruption of publication of the *Zentralblatt,* quaintly called "participation in the national revolution"[20]—came either the fear of guilt by association with a group or discipline that had not put its own house in ideological and organizational order to the satisfaction of the authorities, or absorption by a stronger and more loyal competitor or opponent. One result of these conditions was a decline during the first three years of the Third Reich in the number of articles, reviews, and reports on psychotherapy in German medical journals. *Fortschritte der Neurologie,* for one, did not publish a review relating to the field of psychotherapy in 1934; Hans von Hattingberg wrote one the following year, and only lead time had allowed Arthur Kronfeld's to appear in 1933. Discussions of psychoanalysis, of course, suffered an even sharper decline: The *Zeitschrift für Kinderforschung,* for example, was not the only journal simply to drop the word from its index.

Such cautious "cauterization" was not uniform, but nonetheless characteristic, especially of the first stormy years of the regime. Psychotherapy in the Third Reich also suffered from a decline, and then an almost complete cessation, in international scientific dialogue. Amid the incalculable spiritual and intellectual damage wreaked by the Third Reich, it is remarkable that anything resembling the kind of survival and professional development of psychotherapy already sketched out could have emerged from these twelve years of turmoil, terror, and war.

Questions of Responsibility and Ethics

Given the destructive nature of Nazism, and the ethical standards that accompany medical practice, we must examine, in general terms at least, the cultural and historical conditions that affected the response of German intellectuals, professionals, and academics to National Socialism. We will also briefly consider some of the ethical questions involved in the choice by psychotherapists to pursue the practice of psychotherapy in the Third Reich.

Psychotherapists, as learned individuals and products of the German university system, reflected the peculiar intellectual tradition Fritz Stern has labeled the "unpolitical German," breeding within the educated elite in government, education, and the professions a conservative, and even reactionary, cultural and social arrogance peculiar in strength and kind to those Fritz Ringer has portrayed as the "German mandarins."[21] This intellectual tradition clouded the ethical issues raised by collaboration with, or merely toleration of, National Socialism beyond the gray complexities of any modern state.

Responses in the medical profession ranged from emigration, particularly the forced emigration of Jews, to joyous collaboration. Most individual reactions, especially over time, fell somewhere in between. Ernst Kretschmer opted for withdrawal into the relative backwaters of a university clinic. John Rittmeister, who returned from exile in Switzerland to become director of the Göring Institute's outpatient clinic, died in the resistance. There were degrees and styles of collaboration: Johannes Heinrich (I. H.) Schultz, always "correct," maintained a rigidly professional and apolitical profile while promoting psychotherapy in the context of his own militant German patriotism. Gustav Richard Heyer, possessed of a more volatile personality, joined the Nazi party in 1937 out of what seems a mixture of opportunism, some degree of ideological agreement, and an altruistic desire to effect the values inherent in psychotherapy.

Furthermore, the general enthusiasm of 1933 had its special effect on the "unpolitical German." Psychoanalyst Werner Kemper, for one, has admitted that had he been "political" he might well have supported the Nazis in 1933.[22] If not enthusiasm, then patriotism—especially after 1939, and after the defeat at Stalingrad in 1943—could and did stifle criticism. From the beginning, moreover, Hitler's government could be regarded as legal, and though the purge of Ernst Röhm's SA in 1934 might have raised questions about the continuing barbarity of the new rulers, this action also seemed to mark the defeat of party radicals.[23] The purge thus reinforced the convenient conviction of many Germans that if the Nazis were not to be temporary, at least their extreme rhetoric and behavior was.

In any case, the individual German's subordination to the state in the practice of his profession proved of great value to the Nazis in taming potential critics. At the same time, the perceived and propagandized image of Hitler as being above politics appealed to a large number of intelligent Germans distressed and disgusted by what they saw as a materialistic and ineffectual experiment with Western democracy attempted by the Weimar Republic. The Nazi party, its membership and support socially and politically heterogeneous in nature,[24] seemed by contrast to represent a national, rather than a purely political, movement. Even Nazi policy toward the Jews was characterized by starts and stops.[25] With all this, it was difficult at the time to see that the defeat of the left wing in the party began a process whereby the right wing, in the form of the SS, could establish itself within the institutions of the German state in order to supervise Hitler's policy of territorial expansion and racial extermination.[26] This policy, preparations for whose implementation began between 1936 and 1938, arose in the end from what Klaus Epstein has termed Hitler's "fanatical tenacity."[27]

It might have made a decisive difference had psychotherapists and other German professionals, intellectuals, and academics said *"nein"* or at least *"ohne mich"* ("without me"), but what they did do composes a revealing history of professional development in, as well as the institutional nature of, National Socialist Germany. This history is not as noble, though also not as brief, as that of the Dutch psychoanalytic society, which dissolved itself in 1941 in protest over the ban against Jewish members. But while the Dutch were facing a wartime occupation regime, the Germans were in the position of confronting their own government, and the opportunity not only for professional survival but professional development under the protection of the Göring name made dissolution a less than attractive option.

The good fortune to have as a member of the General Medical Society for Psychotherapy a cousin of Hermann Göring made any decision in favor of a higher morality even more difficult. And the psychotherapists' decision was made even easier by the "voluntary" resignation of Jewish members, who also wished to preserve psychoanalysis and psychotherapy. The "Aryan" psychoanalysts of the Berlin Psychoanalytic Institute, on the other hand, faced a most difficult choice with the persecution and forced departure of so many important colleagues who were Jewish. While the proffered incorporation into the Göring Institute seemed a surrender to the Nazification of the discipline, it also represented an opportunity at least to maintain psychoanalytic practice in the interest of present and future patients and medical science in general. In addition, a dissolution of the Berlin Psychoanalytic Institute, or an underground existence, did not seem practical, especially for the lay analysts, who could not rely on a medical practice for their livelihood.[28]

Although the Nazis made much of the "coordination" or "synchronization" (*Gleichschaltung*) of German society, the nature of their governance and the all-embracing vagueness of their programs permitted and even encouraged what might be termed "autocoordination." This process augmented the terror that for most Germans hovered only in the background by encouraging doubt over not belonging to a compelling movement of fellow citizens.[29]

Among the psychotherapists, this phenomenon was manifested most clearly in the hesitation of the newly renamed German General Medical Society for Psychotherapy to associate itself with the Berlin Psychoanalytic Institute. This might seem to have been simple and sensible prudence, since Freudian psychoanalysis had been officially declared "un-German" by the Nazis. At the time (1936), however, we must remember that the psychotherapists under Göring were seeking facilities for an institute and were very short on funds. It was finally an official in the Medical Office of the Reich Interior Ministry who suggested to the psychoanalysts that they seek out Göring and offer the facilities of the Berlin Institute to the psychotherapists as a means of ensuring the survival of "Aryan" psychoanalysts.[30] Although Göring's initial hesitation was based on his own (and others') vision of a "German" psychotherapy free from Jewish and Freudian influence, it is also revealingly clear that in this instance, at least, the Nazis were less afraid of the psychoanalysts than were the psychotherapists.

Such considerations compel the historian to take account of the fact that in Nazi Germany the individual and group dynamics of the human psyche, like psychotherapy and psychoanalysis, were not banished.[31] In the ethical realm, the process of autocoordination entailed greater personal responsibility for individual actions, since some choice was available; but at the individual level these were not usually choices between "good" and "evil," but among levels of culpability intermixed with considerations of professional responsibility and opportunity. For psychotherapists, as for so many other relatively "good" Germans, the crimes were primarily ones of "unpolitical" omission before and after the fact of Hitler. These individuals were participants in an intellectual and cultural tradition that contributed to an acceptance, however enthusiastic or qualified, of National Socialism in place of either wholehearted support or pure opportunism.

The factors that "created" Hitler and allowed his rise to power transcended what could be done by psychotherapists after 30 January 1933. They were mandarins by philosophical bent, but not in terms of their position, status, or power. They did not, for example, possess the prestige and influence of the holders of high academic chairs within the universities. For the psychotherapists, the universities could serve neither as a refuge nor as a rostrum for resistance. Therefore, unlike, for example, German historians, they are less accountable for their political enthusiasm or quiescence in 1933.[32] This does not make those who opposed Hitler any less heroic or worthy of admiration, nor does it render those who participated or acquiesced in National Socialism any less guilty. Those who emigrated or resisted did so courageously out of the noblest motives, but it is true that for most people it was easiest (and most advantageous) to continue along the path of least resistance, making the daily moral compromises which kept them safe, sane, and comfortable.

Aside from professional motives which, in any case, were to a significant degree informed by a sense of contribution to humanity, psychotherapists under the Hippocratic oath were responsible first of all to their patients. And aside from the number of patients psychotherapists saw and presumably helped during the Third Reich, there were also those, as we will see in Chapter 6, who, but for the intervention of psychotherapists during wartime, would have been declared "malingerers" and shot. Again, as we will see in Chapter 6, the psychotherapists were also engaged on their own initiative and at the behest of the authorities in treating homosexuals, a category of individuals who under the Nazis otherwise faced only persecution.

Psychotherapists at the Göring Institute, of course, were not permitted to treat Jews; some did not wish to, a clear and contemptible violation of the physician's oath. And to assert, as some did, that an Aryan could not help a Jew simply was to festoon unethical conduct with obtuseness. At the same time, however, one former member of the institute claimed that it at least tolerated the regular, if limited, treatment in private practice of Jewish patients. Private practice remained private and, although few, if any, Jews were treated after 1933, one must assume that this situation was an ethical burden for at least some of the psychotherapists. To treat Jews or to protest the Nazi dictum was to risk not only personal professional destruction but also destruction of the profession and practice of psychotherapy itself. And then what of the patients who needed treatment? As a group, however, psychotherapists did much at the behest of the Nazis and compromised the interests of many patients for professional gain. And we do not know the worst that may have happened in some cases, and we probably never will. There are no heroes in this book; it is an unhappy fact that most, if not all, of the psychotherapists in the Third Reich were more concerned about their own, and their profession's, survival than they were about the fate of others. But to dismiss their work on this basis alone would be to ignore common human frailties as well as a significant degree of accomplishment during very difficult times.

Another troubling question exists. To what degree did organized psychotherapy *contribute* to the Nazi regime's goals and programs? Despite the rhetoric and actions of both the Nazi leadership and the psychotherapists themselves (to be examined in the chapters which follow), it seems that the contribution of institutionalized psychotherapy to the functioning of the Nazi state and empire was essentially no greater than that of any other occupational group of Germans on the job during the twelve years of Nazi rule. Psychotherapy, despite its many institutional ties to the regime, never became an efficiently wielded tool for the manipulation of the masses. This was the case for three reasons: the vagueness of Nazi ideas about "the will" and its strengthening; the organizational chaos of the Nazi bureaucracy; and the psychotherapists' own preservation of their professional autonomy. Surely there were individual psychotherapists who directly and indirectly helped instill and buttress ideals of loyalty to the party and to the nation, and surely the work of the Göring Institute in general promoted the general health and subsequent effectiveness of German citizens, soldiers, and workers, thus contributing to the preservation and expansion of Nazi rule; and surely some of the psychotherapists were actually dedicated to just such ends, while others were simply content to enjoy the fruits of German victory while they were in season. It is, however, more accurate to describe the Göring Institute's functions as maintaining the psychological health of its patients than to perceive its activities as having contributed to any genuine sort of systematic Nazified "hardening" sponsored by the regime. This seems to be the case, even though the German Romantic and therapeutic emphasis on community and productivity did tend to violate the line between pure medical assistance and the breeding of social and political conformity. (See Chapter 4.)

The psychotherapists of the Göring Institute were also spared the onerous tasks allotted to those academic psychologists and traditional psychiatrists responsible for, respectively, the general typological definition and biological defense (see Chapter 4) of the race.[33] The former required gross and ephemeral judgments about the alleged characteristics of Aryans and non-Aryans, while the latter involved sentencing the mentally ill to sterilization and euthanasia. The psychotherapists, surrounded by barbarity and by the loathsome political and moral castrati of the Nazi intelligentsia, could at least practice medicine.

The Nature of the
Profession's Development

Compared with other academic groups, such as scholars of classical antiquity, who were not touched at all by the Nazis,[34] or with those historians under Walter Frank who erected a full-blown Nazi institute for history,[35] the psychotherapists occupied the middle ground. In 1933 psychotherapists were still outsiders whose overriding concern was growth and professional recognition within the field of medicine. Still on the margins of the medical and academic establishments, non-Jewish psychotherapists, both individually and as a body, were relatively protected from the very beginning of the regime: The political threat to their discipline was minimized by its very nature as well as by the opportunism of its representatives, and their status and degree of organization gave them little to lose. Although some among them advocated adopting a sort of Nazified psychotherapy, almost all of them shared a commitment to seizing whatever opportunity existed for their profession's development; they were faced by powerful antagonists from inside the medical profession, and the opportunity they were offered by the Göring name minimized the differences over this Nazification issue—as it could not, for example, in the case of the physics community, which suffered considerable harm in the Third Reich.[36] (The contrasting natures of psychotherapy and physics also made a "German" psychotherapy, however objectionable in terms of the universal humanitarian goals of science and medicine, and however limited in therapeutic effect by its own goal of adjusting patients to a repressive social and political order, much less inherently ridiculous than an "Aryan" physics.) In addition, the "cauterization" of contacts with other disciplines and professional groups that prevailed, especially during the first years of the regime—out of fear of being associated with a group that had not passed the Nazi litmus test for loyalty, or of being subordinated to one that had—gave the psychotherapists the chance to organize themselves, submerge their own professional differences, and then initiate their own contacts under the protection and advantage of the Göring name. Ironically, it was precisely their status as outsiders that allowed the psychotherapists to ally themselves early on with Nazi party forces intent on reforming the medical establishment.

Because psychotherapists in Germany, like those throughout the world, still have not achieved full professional status, their experience under the Third Reich hardly represents a resolution of the crucial problems of professional definition that continue to face the field as a whole. That dilemma stems chiefly from the fact that psychotherapy lacks clear definitional and disciplinary boundaries, embracing as it does so many theories and practices strewn across the fields of medicine and psychology as well as throughout the social sciences and humanities. In Germany, this diffuseness was aggravated after 1933 by the attempt of the newly organized psychotherapists to protect and extend their professional control over the entire field of medical psychology— a factor that represented a short-term gain along with some long-term benefits in broadening the influence of their profession. The establishment of the Göring Institute, therefore, constitutes an important part of psychotherapy's past as a landmark in its continuing evolution as a profession in Central Europe and throughout the world.

Since it is in terms of institutional and professional development that the history of psychotherapy in the Third Reich is significant, we must look briefly to the sociology of professions to understand more fully the dynamics at work in the realm of medical psychology in Germany at the time. A. M. Carr-Saunders, perhaps the first social scientist to make a systematic study of professions, provides us with a logical starting point for such an investigation: "A profession may perhaps be defined as an occupation based upon specialized intellectual study and training, the purpose of which is to supply skilled service or advice to others for a definite fee or salary."[37] A profession is distinct from a business occupation with regard to recompense in that "the professional does not work in order to be paid as much as he is paid *in order that he may work.*"[38] The notion of casting vocation in terms of duty and responsibility to those who seek out the professional rather than attributing to them the pecuniary motive that drives the client-seeking business executive is a crucial distinction, and one that is particularly relevant to a study in German culture, with its tradition of the importance of an individual's profession. More specifically, the standards for professional status include a systematic theory, professional responsibility based on a code of ethics, formal professional associations, and community acknowledgment of the profession's authority.[39]

Still, it is as necessary as it is inevitable that the historian will "think of occupations as falling somewhere along a continuum of professions"[40] and be concerned with change and development over time. The historian will also want to know more about how professional development is affected, even defined and determined, by external agencies, a concern that is especially relevant to the study of the professionalization of psychotherapy. By the above criteria, psychotherapy appears well developed as a profession. But Gertrude Blanck, for one, in her analysis of the professional development of psychotherapy in the United States, comes to a less positive conclusion through tracing and comparing four criteria in the cases of medicine and psychotherapy, respectively: differentiation from other professions; evolution of a system of education; development of professional organizations centralized on a national level; and legal recognition in the form of licensure.[41] She found that there are three directions in which psychotherapy might evolve: as a branch of medicine, as a branch of psychology, or as a separate entity. At the present, there seem to be trends in all three directions.[42] According to Blanck, psychotherapy is not yet sufficiently distinct from either medicine or psychology to be judged a profession in its own right, and this is the most crucial difficulty it faces in the way of its professionalization.[43]

Both psychiatrists and clinical psychologists claim psychotherapy as an integral part of their operations, with the former more often concerned with profound mental disturbances, such as schizophrenia, and the latter generally with less severe behavioral problems.[44] The major obstacle to psychotherapy's evolution into a separate, full-fledged profession, however, has been its subordination to the medical profession. Medicine has tended to become all-embracing in its claim to the cure of human illness, and attempts of subsumed disciplines to assert their independence have produced substantial conflict.[45] In Germany, psychiatry had been seriously challenged at the end of the nineteenth century by the rise of a psychodynamic orientation under the leadership of Freudian psychoanalysis. Psychiatry by and large responded with a vigorous defense of its neurological foundations. German psychiatry, closely affiliated with the universities, where there was a strong tendency to slight clinical and therapeutic activities in favor of scientific investigation, was strongly oriented toward research. This scientific bias placed it as a profession firmly within the German medical tradition.

The challenge the psychodynamic movement posed to this essentially nineteenth-century tradition resurrected in the minds of the medical establishment all the uncertainties about the scientific and medical status of psychiatry and psychology that had accompanied the discipline's earlier travails with the alchemy and asylum of the chronically ill. Traditional medicine has always been oriented toward thinking in terms of objective rather than subjective data.[46] During the Nazi years, Oswald Bumke was chief among those psychiatrists who denied the existence of an unconscious and railed against the "dilettantism" he saw as inherent in psychotherapy and psychoanalysis. In 1938 Bumke offered a typical, sweeping condemnation: ". . . Thus does Jung commit the same mistake as before him Freud and even earlier Charcot and Bernheim and many others had: he believes everything that his hysterical patients tell about the innocence of their conscious."[47]

The challenge of the psychodynamic movement to the nosological and neurological establishment of German psychiatry had been raised against the medical profession in general during the 1920s in the form of protests charging a "crisis in medicine." Concern was voiced over a medical profession that was seen to be too distant from its patients as human beings—too scientific, too bureaucratic, and too materialistic by formula and by fee. The General Medical Society for Psychotherapy, founded in 1928, necessarily became part of this campaign. The society declared as its aim the promotion of psychotherapy for the "battle against the national epidemic [*Volksseuche*] of neurosis."[48] It emphasized the need for a medical campaign of social prophylaxis and treatment against neurosis, a diagnosis that seemed to ignore and even belittle the psychiatrist's traditional and academically cloistered classification of diseases of the brain and nervous system. The basis for what one might call an "activist" psychotherapy was to be an appreciation of the human organism in its mental and physical totality as well as a recognition of how it interacted with the environment. Instead of dealing with parts of an object, the psychotherapist—indeed every physician—was to consider the wholeness of the human subject.

The training for such a task had to draw not only on the medical sciences, but on the social sciences and humanities as well. Healing, the medical art, remained the object of all of this, but the broadened perspectives of prevention and rehabilitation engaged psychological and psychotherapeutic techniques that were not continued in the traditional medical sphere of physical repair. In the realm of mental repair—with neurosis regarded as a problem in living for the individual human being—the measures developed to attack these problems and the training necessary to apply them occupied a middle ground between the distinct medical boundaries of sickness and health. All these matters raised a critical question: Is the treatment and cure of neurosis the exclusive prerogative of the physician?

Grosse ("major") psychotherapy, or those theories and techniques dealing with the functioning of the human unconscious, was closer to traditional medicine, stemming for the most part from medical research into the working relationships of the body and the mind. These theories and techniques, such as in the case of psychosomatic medicine, could provide the basis for a psychotherapeutic specialization within the medical profession. Psychoanalysis, however, highly complex and technical in its own right, did not require a medical education for its practice. Psychoanalysts themselves have remained divided on the question of lay analysis, but the whole revolutionary thrust of the Freudian movement was toward the expansion of psychology into the therapeutic realm claimed by medicine. Compromise on the issue of what academic qualifications the psychotherapist, psychoanalyst, or psychologist should possess has rested on medical supervision of nonmedical therapists in order to ensure that no physical ailment has been overlooked. There are, however, problems with this from the medical point of view, as will be explored in Chapter 7.

The other major class of psychotherapy also posed a threat to the exclusive therapeutic claim of the medical profession. *Kleine* ("minor") psychotherapy included all those systematic and unsystematic psychological theories and techniques designed to ease mental suffering at the conscious level. To some degree or other, every doctor knowingly or involuntarily attempts this, but the question again was: Is common psychological sense and empathy, or the ability to comprehend and use various theories of psychology in a medical context, beyond the layperson?

The original aim of most of the doctors in the General Medical Society for Psychotherapy was and continued to be the promotion of training in psychotherapy for every physician—as opposed to entrusting such work only to the specially trained psychotherapist, the expertise of the psychiatrist, or the basic good sense supposedly cultivated among general practitioners through basic medical education. There was also a growing sentiment that the nature of the treatment and cure of mental disorders (*seelische Heilbehandlung*), and the widespread need for it among the populace, called for the training and medical supervision of nonmedical psychotherapists and psychologists. This argument was given added force by the commitment of the General Medical Society for Psychotherapy to control quackery, a commitment of particular concern for two specific groups: physicians who wished to defend scientific medicine, and psychotherapists and psychologists who were eager to avoid that label. In addition, the nineteenth-century Romantic tradition in psychiatry and medicine, with its powerful links to the philosophy of nature (*Naturphilosophie*), was an even stronger force among many influential members of the society. It was this latter group, impelled by professional as well as political fear and emboldened by haphazard opportunities to stake a sweeping professional claim, that was to predominate with the advent of Hitler.

Ernst Kretschmer, who became president of the General Medical Society for Psychotherapy in 1930, was in a distinct minority of those who wished to render psychotherapy a tool to be used only by psychiatrists. When the society was founded in 1928, only doctors could be members, but the trend in the field was changing, and with the setting up in 1933 of the German General Medical Society for Psychotherapy under Göring, the statutes were rewritten to allow special membership for nonmedical psychotherapists. The founding in 1936 of the German Institute for Psychological Research and Psychotherapy brought with it regular membership for all fully trained psychotherapists, whether they were physicians or not. Indeed, in every year of its existence for which there are statistics (1937–1941) except 1938, nonmedical members outnumbered physicians at the institute, and by 1941 nonmedical candidates for certification as "attending psychologists" outnumbered medical candidates.

This prevalence of nonmedical members can be at least partly attributed to a general Nazi encouragement of service to the community and to the state. But the more significant reasons lay within the field of medical psychology itself. While Carl Jung unequivocally favored nonmedical psychotherapists, leading German psychotherapists took a more pragmatic stance. Cimbal saw such recruits as a means to broadening a national psychotherapeutic front against psychiatry. Göring felt that such training was necessary for the emerging field until such time as more physicians undertook psychotherapeutic training and practice.[49]

The second of Blanck's criteria, the evolution of a system of education, delineates five general stages in the case of medicine: from individual practice to the establishment of an apprentice system; the private seminar to the institute; and finally integration into a university system. When psychotherapy is measured against these, its various schools, especially psychoanalysis, are generally found to have passed through all but the final stage. Accomplishing this has been a particularly difficult task in Germany, where the faculties of the universities are securely entrenched behind a massive glacis of knowledge, tradition, prestige, and power. The first official state teaching commission (*staatlicher Lehrauftrag*) for psychotherapy was granted by the medical faculty of the Friedrich Wilhelm University in Berlin to Hans von Hattingberg in August of 1933. The appointment illustrates the growing influence of organized psychotherapy in Germany during the 1920s, primarily under the aegis of the General Medical Society for

Psychotherapy. It was also anticipatory of the more general professional opportunity that was presented by the conjunction of National Socialism with the person and name of Matthias Heinrich Göring. For the most part, however, the universities remained closed to psychotherapy; indeed, they represented a significant potential and actual threat to the profession, since any instruction in psychotherapy remained in the hands of psychiatrists and the newly established academic psychologists.[50]

The threat posed to the independent professional status of psychotherapy by alternative sources of training in the universities was obviated to a significant degree by the essential fulfillment by psychotherapy in the Third Reich of Blanck's third criterion, the centralization of a professional organization on a national basis. Building on the foundation laid by the General Medical Society for Psychotherapy, the Göring Institute achieved this centralization, if imperfectly, for the nine years from 1936 to 1945. The institute's real significance to the professionalization of psychotherapy in Germany beyond 1945, however, lay in its function as a means for survival during that violent and destructive era, the opportunity it occasioned for some degree of constructive communication among the various schools of psychotherapeutic thought, its role as an organizational model for postwar institutes, and its operation as an entity for research, training, and practice in psychotherapy. Many of the leading psychologists and psychotherapists in both postwar Germanies received their training or were professionally active at the Göring Institute.

Blanck's fourth criterion, legal recognition of the profession through licensure, has not yet been met by psychotherapy in Germany. The licensing of a profession restricts the performance of a particular practice to those so licensed. Certification, on the other hand, restricts only the use of a specific title to those who have met certain prescribed standards of training—such as the German title of certified psychologist (*Diplom-Psychologe*), introduced as a result of the demand for psychologists by the Reich's military, and by the combined efforts of university psychologists and the Göring Institute in 1941.[51]

Licensing for psychotherapists and psychologists continues today to be a difficult issue for a number of inherent reasons. In the practice of *kleine* psychotherapy, it is hard to determine exactly what functions a psychotherapist or psychologist performs that are not performed to varying degrees by other professions. While *grosse* psychotherapy is much more specialized, its independent application has generally been restricted to physicians, so that a successful professional delineation has not yet emerged. Finally, the endemic conflicts among psychotherapists, psychoanalysts, and psychologists also stand in the way of establishing standards that might be used to formulate a unified theory or build a professional structure. Nazi Germany saw no resolution of these difficulties, nor any tangible fiscal acknowledgment of professional status by the inclusion of psychotherapists in the state's social insurance scheme, for example. However, as a result of the government support that was afforded the Göring Institute through the German Labor Front, the Reich Research Council, and other organizations, and the absence of any significant professional competition in training or practice, psychotherapy in the Third Reich achieved a significant degree of de facto licensure.

With the question of licensure, we return to the nature of Nazi governance. The Nazi mobilization of German society was effected in the field of medicine, as elsewhere, by the attempted centralization of affairs in the Reich government.[52] Psychotherapy, caught up in the Nazi campaign on behalf of the nation's health (*Volksgesundheit*)—a campaign that exploited the profession's own tendency toward emphasizing the prevention and cure of widespread neurosis—became an officially sanctioned service profession in the new society. Sociologically, professions under fascism in general have been affected in such a way as to "have been forced into patterns which, from the standpoint of modern Western society, are somewhat in between public service and professions . . . the three patterns of business, professions and public service merging into one."[53]

The institutionalization of what Timasheff calls state-inspired "solidaristic motivation," in contrast to motivation based on egoism or altruism, was only imperfectly perpetrated in the Nazi style of highly structured lawlessness. At the fountainhead, Hitler's administrative ignorance and disinterest resulted in almost random gushings of his will through the outlets of various persons and organizations. Coursing from the Führer's juvenile artistic temperament and his political sense of divide and rule, the countercurrents and eddies of the feudal tributaries that composed the mainstream of Nazi leadership diluted the already thin gruel of the movement's ideas. The Nazi aim of *Gleichschaltung* more often meant conformity than revolution.[54] Hitler, bent on his aims of territorial conquest and racial extermination, considered Germany a projectile to be angrily hurled, not an institutional entity to be carefully constructed. This combination of compulsion and chaos, arising from the intellectual and organizational flabbiness of Nazi structures and affairs, allowed psychotherapy under the protection of the Göring Institute to work in a number of different directions, in service both to the regime and to the profession.

Just as the university remained for the most part a closed avenue for the development of psychotherapy as a profession, the state medical bureaucracy was at best ambivalent about the new discipline. It is therefore a mistake to assume that the state served as a relatively rational haven for psychotherapy, while the raging fanatics within the party were its major enemy. It is true, as will be shown in Chapter 4, that in the early years of the Third Reich party radicals did pose a genuine threat to all medical psychology, but for a number of reasons the party bureaucracies concerned with medicine, health, education, and industry were receptive to the idea and practice of a properly loyal psychotherapy. Aside from its formal supervision of the Göring Institute, the Ministry of the Interior did not figure prominently in the affairs of psychotherapists. Indeed, as the official state representative of established medicine, its medical section included no organizational notion of medical psychology apart from the realm of traditional psychiatry. In 1939 Werner Achelis, the psychotherapist director of the Göring Institute's public relations division and an enthusiastic proponent of "German" psychotherapy, decried the materialistic state medical bureaucracy that refused to recognize the advances of the past twenty years, advances that had, in his view, culminated in National Socialism.[55]

Thus, with arriviste confusion on the one hand and traditional skepticism on the other, psychotherapy forged its professional way between the prejudices of both party and state, deriving whatever advantage it could from each but relying fully only on the protections of the seigneurial Göring name and on its confidence in the expertise of its practitioners. By the time Ernst Kretschmer reassumed the presidency of the General Medical Society for Psychotherapy after the war, the substantially broadened field of psychotherapy had received a decided professional boost—even given the great task of reconstruction that would be required of it in the moral and physical rubble left by Hitler's Reich and Hitler's war. In order to show this continuity of development, a history of psychotherapy under National Socialism requires a feature uncommon to other studies of professions and disciplines of that era: the necessity of investigating resultant postwar professional status in the German successor states, a survey of which appears in the final chapter. Although some specific reforms directly or indirectly relevant to the psychotherapy issue from the Nazi era, the development of psychotherapy as a profession in Germany owes nothing to National Socialism in terms of direct systematic sponsorship or reform. But David Schoenbaum has shown how the Nazis transformed German society simply by shaking the tree.[56] The history of psychotherapy in the Third Reich shows that this shaking reached into the branches of German medicine.

CHAPTER 2

Psychotherapy and Medicine: The Rising Challenge

In 1914 Sigmund Freud reflected, in the spirit of Mark Twain, on the "gross exaggerations" of the death of psychoanalysis in Germany before World War I: "After all, to be hailed as a corpse is an advance on being received in dead silence."[1] However much the psychoanalytic movement itself and the accompanying psychotherapeutic schools of thought were to be rent by division, dispute, and even disparagement, Freud remained the indisputable leader of the psychological revolution of the twentieth century. His remark encapsulated both the resistance his ideas had encountered in Germany as well as the growing intellectual ferment they had inspired. The year 1914 did indeed mark a true turning point for the psychoanalytic movement. Carl Jung, the former heir apparent, and Alfred Adler were both declared apostate in a year whose storms were to herald vital opportunity for the acceptance of psychoanalysis by both the medical profession and the general public. But World War I also marked the beginning of a decisive era for all manner of psychotherapy and medical psychology in Germany.

Psychoanalysis, Psychiatry, and World War I

The August 1914 atmosphere in imperial Germany was one of war fever and an eerie feeling of relief. Countries unfurled their young and flung them into battle only to find that the warfare of the new industrial world was a radical departure from their old-fashioned conceptions of heroism. The first year of the war confronted German medicine with a phenomenon labeled "mass psychosis" as young, idealistic, and ill-trained troops came face to face with the grim reality of modern war. The mental casualty rate was increased by the relatively poor monitoring and screening procedures inherent in the rapid and enthusiastic mobilization, a situation that also allowed, among other categories, a high number of epileptics into the ranks. What was typical of these "mass psychoses" was the inverse proportion of their frequency to proximity to the front. They turned out to be caused by the effects of rumor, anxious expectations, and fantasies that were the result of the long periods of waiting behind the lines. Once susceptible personalities had been weeded out, however, and the war had settled into a more individualized mode of trench warfare and small-group operations, these particular psychological manifestations were reduced to almost zero. But by the winter of 1916–17, war neuroses had risen to the point of parity with organic disorders. The effect of incessant artillery bombardment, for example, had led to an increase in traumatic neuroses from 14 percent in 1914 to 45 percent in 1917.[2]

At the famous war session of the German Association for Psychiatry in Munich in September 1916, Robert Gaupp, Max Nonne, Karl Bonhoeffer, and Oswald Bumke, among others, attempted to come to psychiatric terms with the concept of neurosis as symptomatic of psychological, not physical, disorder. Nonne, for one, had had success in using hypnosis to treat war neurotics. (These psychiatrists were not performing a completely unique task; the first studies of war neurosis had been made during the Russo-Japanese War, more than a decade before.[3]) The German psychiatrists at Munich rejected the purely organic thesis advanced by Hermann Oppenhiem, deciding instead on a formula that recognized the psychogenic factor in the cause, or etiology, of war neuroses. Nevertheless, they maintained that it was the body that was the chief source for wish-fantasies, and that it joined together with the psychological disposition to produce a trauma with a subsequent psychogenic recreation.[4]

From the middle of the nineteenth century, German medical psychology had been dominated by a strictly somatological psychiatry.[5] At mid-century, the intellectual confidence of the Enlightenment had begun to take hold in German scientific thought, producing in Germany and Austria physiologists like Johannes Müller, Emil Du Bois-Reymond, and Ernst Brücke, along with pathologist Rudolf Virchow, psychologist Wilhelm Wundt, and the three great psychiatrists Wilhelm Griesinger, Theodor Meynert, and Emil Kraepelin. The work of Du Bois-Reymond and Brücke, as well as that of others, was subsumed under what has been termed the "school of Helmholtz."

Hermann von Helmholtz, a physiologist, espoused a belief in materialism and the primacy of experimentation and observation—to wit, the classic scientific method. Among the psychiatrists, Griesinger turned psychiatry away from the institution and toward the university with the dictum that mental disease was brain disease. Meynert concentrated on disorders of the frontal lobe, mocked his student Freud, and died confessing himself an hysteric to the father of psychoanalysis. Kraepelin's personal impact was especially great: "After he assumed the directorship of a hospital and clinic there was never a question of who was the man in charge. 'Imperial German psychiatry' was said to have gained prominence under the 'chancellorship' of Kraepelin, one of Bismarck's admirers."[6]

Kraepelin's manner reflected a psychiatric doctrine that had imbibed the strutting rigor of the Prussian unification of Germany. Like Bismarck in his critique of the failure of the idealistic liberals of 1848, the *Realpolitik* of the university psychiatric clinic was decreed to be no place for the fuzzy-headed and indulgent notions of psychotherapy. It was this unbending environment that nurtured the work of those, like neurologist Wilhelm Erb, who pioneered the medical use in Germany of electric therapy—a method which Freud was later to find of absolutely no use in a majority of cases of neurosis. Yet within the psychiatric ranks themselves, the "psychological" orientation was beginning to assert itself, as the categories of mental disease worked out by Kraepelin were seen to be yielding no definitive answers to the nature and variety of psychological complaints among patients.

Psychiatrists in the new century, such as Ernst Kretschmer and Robert Gaupp, turned increasingly toward viewing the human being as a psychophysical totality, hence providing some of the impetus for the study of the human psyche that was to bring psychiatry, or at least some of its practitioners, closer to sharing a perspective with psychotherapy.[7] A revealing contrast to the situation in Germany, however, was the leading role in the development of psychoanalysis and psychotherapy assumed by the Swiss psychiatrists Adolf Meyer, Auguste Forel, Eugen Bleuler, and Carl Jung. Another contrast was the inspiration and instruction Freud acquired from the French clinician Jean-Martin Charcot, who, unlike the German psychiatrists, took hysteria seriously.[8]

Yet the psychiatric troops of "imperial German psychiatry" who mobilized for battle in 1914 still went to war against disease, the external invader of a healthy system, not neurosis, the internal imbalance of psychodynamics, environment, and history. Reality would soon challenge psychiatry's reaffirmations of the organic basis of mental illness. "Hysteria," as the terminology then went, became a fact of war. Indeed, the fact that most of those affected came from the rear areas or were afflicted during long pauses in activity at the front cast grave doubt over the early psychiatrically sanguine diagnosis of alterations in the brain's cortex stemming from the shock of battle.

World War I, the phenomenon of war neuroses, and the continuing challenge of psychoanalysis represented the final act in the crisis of nineteenth-century psychiatric medicine. As Gregory Zilboorg notes, "No adequate and equitable appraisal of Freud's contribution is possible unless one takes cognizance of the fact that formal descriptive psychiatry, having reached its peak in the closing years of the past century, stood rather puzzled at the end of the blind alley it had reached."[9] The psychiatric tradition simply did not allow for the conceptualization of such an entity as the unconscious in human behavior, but the inability of the practitioners and theoreticians of psychiatry to deal with the mental symptoms engendered by the experiences of 1914–18 provided a significant chance for an alternative conception of the nature of the human psyche.

In the words of Thomas Kuhn on the shifting of scientific paradigms, "Failure of existing rules is the prelude to a search for new ones."[10] The dramatic final wartime failure of German psychiatry's principles was, according to a contemporary observer, the end of an entire tradition: "Medicine is so deeply imbued with materialism that the majority of its members earnestly proceed with the search for some mythical toxins as the one and only causative factor of mental abnormality, with the result that the human factor, the individual conflict with the environment and the social and biological standpoints are quite lost sight of."[11] Many psychiatrists and neurologists, faced with the psychogenic phenomenon of war neurosis, had asserted that such cases as surfaced in military clinics actually disproved Freudian theory: Where, they asked, was the sexual etiology?[12]

The continuing psychiatric attacks against psychoanalysis were themselves the products of professional anxiety. The dismantling of the scientific scaffolding that surrounded the mental patient, from the heights of which psychiatrists and academic psychologists could study, classify, and prescribe, represented a considerable threat to the comfortable brahmin assessments of severe psychic disarray. No longer could mental disorders be written off simply as matters of mechanics and heredity, and divorced from the pliable emotions and environmental influences common to all human beings. The threat was deeply personal as well as professional. The horror of many segments of the psychiatric profession at the sexual emphasis in Freudian theory revealed its members' own discomfort with the universality of such human drives, and with the painful recognition of human ambivalence.

This division between subject and object also betrayed psychiatry's heavy and longstanding intellectual debt to Cartesian dualism. The psychiatrist was a scientist, wedded to matter through the ceremony of experimentation. The empirical ethos was in the best tradition of eighteenth-century rationalism and nineteenth-century positivism. It also reflected a confidence, brimming over from the Enlightenment, that science was the sure way to the betterment of the human condition. There was no room in this model of the mind for such an "unscientific" notion as the unconscious. Psychiatrists drew from Descartes the dualism of mind and body, and they used the descendant doctrine of psychophysical parallelism to affirm the primacy of organic processes. Thus, any attempt to analyze the mind was simply unscientific.

Du Bois-Reymond had summed up the mechanistic opposition to any attempt to smuggle "philosophical" or "metaphysical" elements into the study of the brain's operations with the words *"ignoramus et ignoramibus*—we do not know and we shall never know."[13] What God had put asunder, let no man join together.

This strict, mechanistic empiricism of the Germans was actually a reaffirmation of the German tradition of idealism. By rigorously excluding all Romantic-rooted medical interest in final cause, teleology, and human attitudes, the psychiatric profession left the realm of the soul to the philosophers and theologians, and proclaimed the impossibility of any attempt to go beyond what could be achieved by physiology. With this approach, medical psychology in the nineteenth century followed Kant in his delineation of what was knowable and what was not. The psychiatrists ventured beyond Kant, however, by seeking to bar any medical iconoclasm that might be so daring as to question the conception of the soul.[14] Freud, whatever materialism was inherent in his theory of psychodynamics, turned the study of human behavior away from the notion of the individual as the sum of his or her physical parts, and toward an understanding of the interactions among mind, body, and environment. That this was not simply otherwordly philosophizing became dramatically evident in the promising potential its practice offered to a hard-pressed Central European officialdom during World War I.

At the Fifth International Psycho-Analytical Congress held in Budapest on 28–29 September 1918, representatives of the German and Austrian governments were in attendance for the first time. They were attracted by the news of the successful use of psychoanalytic techniques in alleviating and curing war neuroses. Such prominent psychoanalysts as Karl Abraham, Max Eitingon, Ernst Simmel, and Sandor Ferenczi had all contributed valuable clinical experience to the problem, and there were plans for establishing psychoanalytic clinics throughout Germany and Austria-Hungary.[15] The November armistice precluded any such program, but the concept of the unconscious life of the individual and its medical treatment had achieved unprecedented public validation and notoriety. Opposition did not, of course, melt away, and Abraham expressed continuing misgivings to Freud regarding the "popularization" of psychoanalysis in 1918.[16]

Psychoanalysis naturally sought to establish itself beyond the "practical" successes of the Great War. Freud's work, beginning with his classic statement of 1900, *The Interpretation of Dreams,* had signaled the onset of a revolution in scientific and medical thought on the matter of mental illness. Operating in the tradition of Charcot and Hippolyte-Marie Bernheim, the great French medical hypnotists, Freud and Josef Breuer discovered the "talking cure." Freud was subsequently to discard hypnosis, replacing it with analysis of the free associations made by the conscious patient. Freud's theories, and the growth of the psychoanalytic movement—from the small coterie in Vienna in 1902, through the founding of the German Psychoanalytic Society (Deutsche Psychoanalytische Gesellschaft) in 1910, to the addition of the Zurich group gathered around C. G. Jung, an international colloquium before World War I, and its institutionalization in Berlin (1920) and Vienna (1922)—aroused tremendous popular and professional opposition. Jones has observed that psychoanalysis lived under the *odium sexicum,* as its theorists and practitioners were depicted as espousing sexual heresies at their Wednesday evening meetings in Vienna.[17]

The rhetoric from psychiatric circles was, as Abraham noted, most heated of all. A notorious example was the virulent opposition of the members of the Vienna Psychiatric Clinic. The authorities, however, continued to express a strong interest in psychoanalysis. Indeed, while there was widespread professional and popular rejection of Freud's ideas, and even outrage over them, they also attracted great interest from both quarters, as the history of psychoanalysis and psychotherapy in Germany shows.[18]

But psychoanalysis itself was not a monolith. Freud himself would revise his thought considerably over his lifetime, and the Freudian epigoni, most significantly the Jungians and the Adlerians and other neo-Freudians, who either broke away or pressed for doctrinal revision from within the classical movement, would alter its theory as well as its practice. While Melanie Klein and her school have reaffirmed the biological determinants of early infantile experience, Freud's own cultivation of ego models—as opposed to his earlier stress on instinctual drive—was elevated by what one might call the Freudian liberal caucus to an exclusive new doctrine:

> The inevitability of anatomy in determining the psychological differences between the sexes, the inevitability of the stages of libido [instinctual] development and the Oedipus complex, were rejected and the importance of interpersonal relations and the cultural background emphasized, and in psychotherapy an attempt was often made to substitute short and active methods for prolonged and passive ones.[19]

Alfred Adler emerged even before the war as the prophet of this cultural/interpersonal orientation. Adler had developed a profound social consciousness in his work with laborers in Vienna. This experience revealed to him the high incidence of somatic defect among his patients. Drawing from his own childhood, which was marred by rickets, pneumonia, and a number of accidents, as well as from his early work with Freud's theory of instincts, Adler evolved his theory that the aggressive drive was a means by which an individual adapted to arduous life tasks. For Adler, the crucial element in the human psyche was the individual's reaction to feelings of inferiority, originating in the child's early relationship to the adult. Sexuality became symbolic of this basic struggle, posing the "masculine protest" against feminine weakness. Adler abandoned causality in favor of teleology, embarking on a campaign to involve the individual psychologist in the process of bringing human beings into harmony with their social environment. This emphasis on the importance of society in the cause and cure of neurosis was shared by all the neo-Freudians.

Aside from Adler, the three principal representatives of the neo-Freudian, or social Freudian, school were Karen Horney, Erich Fromm, and Harry Stack Sullivan. Although each evolved a unique theory, they argued in unison that Freud's biological determinism was inadequate to comprehend the dynamics of humanity's existence as an aggregate of social beings, and that instead of the search for pleasure and the avoidance of pain, the basic human drive was for self-expression and social recognition. Theodor Reik called this "wholeness," and Erik Erikson, "totality." While Horney and the others subscribed to the three basic Freudian precepts of psychic determinism, repression, and the notion of the personality as dynamic and not static, they challenged others they felt were restraining remnants of a nineteenth-century heritage. Those they relegated to the past included Freud's biological orientation; his indifference to contemporary anthropology and sociology, with their emphasis on the relative quality of "human nature"; the dualism of the Freudian theory of life and death instincts; Freud's abstention from moral judgment; and his "mechanistic-evolutionistic" thinking, which denied the "transformation of quantity into quality" (Engels)—and, according to many critics, cast human behavior as nothing but (nichts als) a repetition of childhood patterns.[20] In philosophical terms, Adler and the social Freudians believed that the individual and, ultimately, society could be modified and improved through the active and empathic intervention of the therapist. The desire they shared for short-term, inexpensive modes of psychotherapy and their faith in the prospect of psychosocial engineering were tacks that psychotherapists in Germany were to use to advantage in the Third Reich.

Psychoanalysis also faced a strong challenge from Carl Gustav Jung. In 1900 Jung, who came from a Swiss Reformed religious background, went to the Zürich mental hospital and university psychiatric clinic, the Burghölzli, to study under Bleuler. There he became convinced that dementia praecox (schizophrenia), a common psychotic condition, was treatable by psychotherapeutic means. Jung became an enthusiastic proponent of Freudian theory but broke with Freud over the nature of the instinctual drive, positing a vast area beyond Freud's perception of the unconscious as a "collective unconscious." He rejected Freud's emphasis on neurotic causation in favor of a teleological view: "While for Jung the unconscious is all that consciousness can become, for Freud it is, more simply, all that consciousness is not."[21] Jung scoured the realm of mythology for inspiration from the past to guide the patient's future, while Freud used the patient's unconscious as a guide to myth, as proof of the individual and collective human enslavement to the past. Here, too, the wind that filled Jung's sails was to blow strongly among German psychotherapists.

The Intellectual and Medical Heritage of Psychotherapy in Germany

In a letter to Freud on 6 June 1925, Abraham, then president of the German Psychoanalytic Society, reported that the cultural division of the giant German film studio Ufa wished to produce a film that would explore the dynamics of psychoanalytic theory and practice. The straightforward manner of its proposition recommended it, Abraham thought, in contrast with an earlier offer from Samuel Goldwyn to portray psychoanalytically the great love affairs in history, a proposal Freud had rejected. G. W. Pabst directed Werner Kraus in the 1926 film, *Geheimnisse einer Seele (Secrets of a Soul)*, with the collaboration of Abraham and Hanns Sachs. Freud was not enthusiastic about the venture, and the hyperbole which surrounded the film's release in Germany and abroad only confirmed his reservations. Abraham's view, however, was that agreement to cooperate in its production would preempt its being offered to " 'wild' analysts in Berlin—if only to mention Kronfeld, Schultz, and Hattingberg who would be only too keen to grasp at an offer should we decline."[22] Two of this disdained trio were to be prominent members of the Göring Institute.

Freud himself wrote on the subject of "wild psychoanalysis" and observed that it generally sacrificed depth analysis for initial transference improvements that were based shakily on the early establishment of a positive relationship between doctor and patient, and offered rational help and unspecific guidance under a veil of personal and emotional involvement, along with some limited depth interpretations. These methods, Freud believed, rested more on intuitive inquiry than on proper scientific investigation.[23] Otto Fenichel dismissed these practices by observing that such "methods of psychotherapy . . . have remained the same since the times of the earliest witch doctors, the results were perhaps not bad, but they were not understood and thus were unreliable. You could never tell whether or not they would be achieved at all."[24]

It was true, as Jung had pointed out in his presidential address to the International Psycho-Analytical Congress in 1911,[25] that there were any number of dubious practitioners in the field, especially in Germany, with its lack of legal restrictions on quackery and its turn-of-the-century bourgeois passion for sexology. But the ferment about the varieties of practice also indicated the widespread interest in psychoanalysis that prevailed in Germany among both the general public and doctors. The medical profession's interest in psychoanalysis ranged from enthusiastic reception through various degrees of reservation to outright rejection, reflecting its longstanding concern with the question of the relationship between mind and body. Hattingberg had been secretary of the International Psycho-Analytic Association in 1911,[26] and Abraham's dubbing him a "wild" psychoanalyst stemmed from Hattingberg's idiosyncratic fusion of various psychodynamic models, a melding that was squarely in the German Romantic tradition. Hattingberg's practice typified the great number of German physicians who were evolving their own versions of psychoanalysis and psychotherapy from a rich nineteenth-century heritage that had been brought to startlingly new and fruitful life by Freud and his followers.

This Romantic heritage paved the way not only for advances in medical psychology but for philosophical and practical harmony with National Socialism. Romantic natural philosophy, deriving from Friedrich W. J. von Schelling's mysticism, pantheism, and monism, stressed the basic unity of all life. Early nineteenth-century physicians had become attracted to, and even obsessed with, the realms of the irrational and the emotional, but, as Decker puts it:

> They held beliefs now considered quite sophisticated: the notion of inner conflict; the idea of the human being as a psychobiological entity; that if intense and ungratified "passions" could not find an outlet, the result might be a breakdown of personality function; that ideas can become symbolized and expressed in physical reactions; the belief in an unconscious.[27]

It was this "mentalist" and philosophical preoccupation with the mind that university psychiatrists in Germany rejected during the latter half of the nineteenth century.

The concept of the unity of body and mind and of the unconscious can be traced as far back in medical history as Heraclitus, in the sixth century before Christ. (Carl Haeberlin, a charter member of the General Medical Society for Psychotherapy, identified him as the first in a series of thinkers diverging from a "logocentric science" toward a "biocentric characterology."[28]) Heraclitus, like Rousseau centuries later, believed that though reason was common to persons, it alone could not define the uniqueness of any given individual. During ancient times this conception of the individual as a unitary, biological system rather than as a mechanical object of autonomous parts gained strength, particularly with Galen's notion of the bodily consensus. Yet it was not until the sixteenth century that the two chief orientations in psychology, between which the nineteenth century was to draw distinct battle lines, became manifest. The physiological, descriptive, and empirical approach was espoused by Francis Bacon, while the perspective that attempted to deal with human motivation apart from corporeal determinants was expressed by the Spanish religious humanist Juan Luis Vives and the Basel physician Theophrastus Bombastus von Hohenheim.

The latter Latinized his name to Paracelsus. He became a major critic of witch-hunts and, in a wildly unsystematic way, "envisioned the human personality as a whole, as made up of spiritual and corporeal parts intimately connected with the soul."[29] Paracelsus became somewhat of a legendary figure in Nazi medical circles; the National Socialists heralded his advocacy of natural health and his professional use of written German in place of Latin as part of the cultural and scientific heritage for Nazi ideology. In 1943 the film director Pabst produced a lavish film version of his life.[30]

Paracelsus's notion of each individual as a microcosm mirroring the macrocosm was also implicit in the monadology of Leibniz, who conceived of an irreducible entity of life force. Leibniz's view of the human being as a biological unit contradicted Descartes's conception of human life as a soulless machine.

The figure of Leibniz extends in a direct line to the efforts of those psychotherapists in Germany after 1933 who attempted to fabricate an exclusive German tradition of discovering, exploring, and analyzing the human unconscious. It was not Freud but Leibniz who was credited with recognizing sublimation and repression as mental phenomena, and free association as a valuable method of healing. Matthias Göring himself noted that "had not his work remained completely unknown until 1765 and the later, resulting, work or a better translation of Christian Wolff gone unrecognized, the path toward the research and management of unconscious mental functions would never have been that of Freud and his school."[31] Wolff objected to the Cartesian notion that nothing could be in the mind of which it was not aware, and on a philosophical level, as a step up from the medieval theurgy of Leibniz's thought, "served as a stimulus to the development of neurology and also of the theory of instincts which Freud introduced early in the twentieth century."[32] The supreme irony of Göring's view, of course, is that it was precisely Freud's great contribution to combine the Romantic preoccupation with "hidden forces" in the psyche with the materialism of the late nineteenth-century scientific tradition, to produce a method by which the unconscious could be revealed and treated.[33]

The Romantic movement of the late eighteenth and early nineteenth centuries in Germany celebrated the holistic tradition. While the Englishman Thomas Hobbes believed that any unity of body and soul could be deduced through the application of mathematics and mechanics, Goethe emphasized the sovereign and all-encompassing realm of Nature, of which humanity was the *sensorium commune*. The Romantics resurrected the vitalist tradition of the philosopher Georg Ernst Stahl, which declared that within every living system there exists a substantial entity that imparts to the system powers and qualities not possessed by inanimate bodies. This vital force could not be understood in mechanical terms; it was basic and irreducible, not available to scientific verification.

This unity of the human race with nature had been posited by Schelling; the physician and painter Carl Gustav Carus was another of its advocates. Carus defined psychology as the science of the soul's evolution from the unconscious to the conscious: "The unconscious itself is the subjective expression of that which we must objectively recognize as nature."[34] It followed that the emphasis in curing mental illness had to rest on curing the whole individual, not a particular part or organ. Implicit in this approach, and in its later glorification in the German national and cultural milieu, was also the particular philosophical and religious grandeur it imparted to the human psyche; among other things, it was this quality which was to make Jung's outlook so attractive to twentieth-century German psychotherapists in the Romantic tradition: "The unconscious according to Carus is at a deeper level and at its core not influenced by instinctual drives."[35]

Carus and his most influential work, *Psyche, zur Entwicklungsgeschichte der Seele* (1846), became a chief source of inspiration for Göring and some of the other German psychotherapists under the Third Reich. Other important influences were the works of two Romantic thinkers of the early nineteenth century who were struck from the same mold as Carus: Carl Wilhelm Ideler and Ernst von Feuchtersleben. Feuchtersleben in particular, with his *Diätetik der Seele* (1838), urged the view that mental diseases were diseases of the personality and stressed the need for an "educational" psychotherapy. For M. H. Göring, Feuchtersleben, like Leibniz, Carus, and others, was still another historical witness to the richness of a specifically German psychotherapeutic tradition, and to the consequent relative insignificance of Freud's mechanistic misinterpretation of humanity's unconscious.[36]

The Romantic tradition reached its peak in Eduard von Hartmann's *Philosophie des Unbewussten* (1869). Then it went underground, mining inspiration from the literature of Goethe and Dostoievski and the philosophy of Nietzsche, while overhead reigned the self-assured medical age of scientific positivism and psychiatric nosology. In this way Nietzsche, too, became an important forerunner of modern psychotherapy in Germany.[37]

While university psychiatry dominated medical psychology in late nineteenth-century Germany and Austria, interest in psychotherapy did not wither away completely among physicians. Aside from those few psychiatrists who recognized the value of psychotherapy, a large majority of the doctors interested in psychotherapy came out of the ranks of internists and neuropathologists. Internists came by way of their confrontation with psychosomatic disorders. Neurology, or the science of the human nervous system, had first made its appearance in seventeenth-century England and France, incorporating the Hippocratic dictum that the seat of madness was in the brain. In the nineteenth century, neurologic research brought scientific discipline to the study of mental illness and helped revolutionize asylum care by instigating a reasoned investigation of each patient's mental life. The innovation provided an understanding that was not available from the rigid system of strict psychiatric classification and genetic inquiry. Neurology, as a field of investigation of the brain's functions, also spawned the study of disorders of the nervous system, or neuropathology.

Late in the nineteenth century, psychiatry also benefited from the therapeutic zeal of such pioneering pathologists as Adolf Meyer. Although neurology, especially in Germany, remained a part of, and subordinate to, psychiatry, an increasing number of physicians chose to specialize in neurology on their way to becoming neuropathologists.[38] It is revealing to note here that (allowing for multiple specializations) of twenty-four representative psychotherapists who were prominent, or at least active, before and after 1933, thirteen had become neuropathologists (*Nervenärzte*), four had become specialists in internal medicine, four in psychology, four were general practitioners, and only two specialized in psychiatry.[39]

These men were all veterans of World War I, another factor that extended their own personal experience in the Romantic tradition. Although a full analysis cannot be performed in the present study, it seems useful to speculate whether the membership of the General Medical Society for Psychotherapy as a whole was largely conservative and nationalist and might have displayed some degree of latent anti-Semitism in its views and concerns even before 1933—a possibility the investigation of which would shed further light on the actions of many of its members in the Third Reich. Many of those German doctors who had emerged from the war, and who had campaigned for the medical acceptance of psychotherapy during the years of the Weimar Republic, were intellectually preoccupied with the clash between culture and civilization that the war had represented to them. The phenomenon was particularly widespread among German academics.[40] This German intellectual fixation translated in medical parlance into the struggle between *Geist* ("mind") and *Seele* ("soul"). *Geist* stood for the materialistic Western spirit of the Renaissance, triumphant over the fullness and spirituality of the medieval.[41]

As late as 1944, Heyer, on being considered for the title of professor, eagerly reported on his wartime exploits more than twenty-five years earlier,[42] and Fritz Künkel, who had lost his left arm at Verdun in 1917, integrated the experience of the war directly into his own brand of Adlerian psychology:

> The experience at the front had brought us something new. Through reflection and a turning inward, we no longer found that it was the self at the base of our existence, no longer the private, individual personality, but the group, fellowship and nationality [*Volkstum*].[43]

The average age of these men in 1914 was around twenty-five; the median, twenty-two. So it was that these budding psychotherapists, who by and large represented a young avant-garde in German medicine, determined more than ever after the war to devote themselves to the development of psychotherapy as a profession. They fused their philosophical and professional allegiances into a course of action that would lead those fortunate enough not to be Jews into the surprising opportunities afforded them by the rule of the Third Reich.

A Young Discipline Strives to Expand: The General Medical Society for Psychotherapy, 1926–1933

Despite the hopes of its proponents, the professionalization of psychotherapy in Germany after 1918 reached a stage of significant organization only after the first difficult years of the Weimar period were past. Young doctors had to eat, and amid the chaos of the first postwar years they were impelled to concentrate simply on establishing and maintaining their private practices. Walter Cimbal, albeit with a degree of passionate hyperbole, has recalled how practical psychotherapy had bloomed during World War I, how the German defeat and subsequent inflation had ruined plans for a systematic postwar study of war neuroses and psychoses, and how "German medical science turned ever more sharply toward a mechanistic-materialistic way of thinking."[44]

In 1926 the annual meeting of neurologists and psychiatrists convened in Kassel, and the usual arguments against psychotherapy were aired. But it was only shortly thereafter, in April of that year, that Wladimir Eliasberg of Munich and Robert Sommer of Giessen presided over the first General Medical Congress for Psychotherapy in Baden-Baden, convened "as a kind of spiritual revolution against the materialistic orientation of the German medical profession."[45] The founding of the General Medical Society for Psychotherapy (Allgemeine Ärztliche Gesellschaft für Psychotherapie) followed in 1928, along with the appearance of the *Allgemeine Ärztliche Zeitschrift für Psychotherapie und psychische Hygiene* edited by Eliasberg and Sommer, which became the *Zentralblatt für Psychotherapie und ihre Grenzgebiete* in

1930. Among the co-founders of the society were I. H. Schultz, Heyer, Hattingberg, Arthur Kronfeld, Harald Schultz-Hencke, Haeberlin, Künkel, and Cimbal, most of them members of the young avant-garde in the medical profession whose humanistic and cultural ideals had been sharpened by the war and by Germany's predicaments in the 1920s.

The first congress concerned itself primarily with the antagonistic stance of the psychiatric profession and the incumbent dangers to psychotherapy. This concern stemmed from the desire of these psychotherapeutically inclined physicians to oppose a powerful tradition in German medicine that obstructed physicians' control and development of a scientific and humanistic array of psychotherapeutic techniques. Eliasberg later noted how the psychotherapists conceived of the case histories they presented at the congresses of the General Medical Society for Psychotherapy as an important challenge to the medical establishment: "We wanted to confront the 'systems' with the reality of life as it is seen in the offices of the practitioners, the specialists, and in the hospitals."[46] The primary purpose of the society and its annual congresses from 1926 to 1931 was to minimize the dissension among the various theories of psychotherapy and to encourage its practice in all branches of medicine, as well as to inspire research in the young field.

The first announcement, circulated in 1925, contained an agenda for the 1926 congress that concerned itself not only with the development of psychotherapy as a profession but also with its place in the movement concerned with the so-called "crisis in medicine." The "domestic policies" (as they were termed) for psychotherapy as outlined in this circular were clearly directed toward the general fulfillment of those criteria for professional status that we have described in Chapter 1: definition of a body of knowledge; standards for, and control of, training; professional ethics; and differentiation from neighboring disciplines. The "foreign policies," on the other hand, addressed themselves to psychotherapy's various interfaces with the medical profession and with the social problems and issues that surrounded it. The notion of unity, therefore, was intended not only to further the professional aims of psychotherapy but also to solve the broader problems confronting medicine as a whole.[47]

Critics of the medical establishment, including many psychotherapeutically oriented physicians, saw the reigning "systems" as hopelessly beholden to science, research, classification, and political influence, out of touch with "the reality of life," as Eliasberg put it. The demand for increased attention to what was called "social hygiene" was another front in the challenge to the establishment. August Friedländer, in an address to the third congress of the General Medical Society for Psychotherapy in 1928, claimed that the medical profession as a whole was disunited, that it failed as both a scientific and a social entity. He complained about communistic doctors, overbureaucratization, the warring factions in psychotherapy, the clashes between homeopathy and "school medicine," the overprescription of drugs, and so on. Friedländer demanded a broader kind of academic medicine, a decrease in the prescription of drugs, a concern for social health programs, and, most importantly, physicians who would exhibit more concern for *Volksgesundheit* than for political power.[48]

The General Medical Society for Psychotherapy was particularly concerned with modes of *kleine* psychotherapy that could be used medically and humanistically by all physicians. Its own loyalty to the discipline of medicine was stated clearly and directly on the first page of the first issue of its journal in 1928:

> The most basic orientation of psychotherapy is not that spiritualism should take the place of that materialism under whose flag experimental medicine of the nineteenth century became a rational science. . . . Psychotherapy is a matter for doctors. We are doctors and not laymen.[49]

Its mission, the society announced, was

> to contribute to an inductive, rational, clinical psychotherapy, which stands in exactly the same relationship to special psychotherapeutic methods like psychoanalysis and individual psychology, among others, as the clinic for internal medicine does to physiological chemistry.[50]

Because the society was strongly committed to establishing a place for itself within or alongside the medical profession, many of its members were active in promoting psychotherapy in the pages of the medical journals. Chief among such proselytizers was Schultz, who later noted that it was during the 1920s that psychotherapy became socially and professionally acceptable (*salonfähig*).[51] That it did so was due in no small measure to his own skillful and tireless efforts. Schultz placed articles on psychotherapy in the *Deutsche medizinische Wochenschrift* every year from 1927 through 1930. Before 1926 this journal had published only reports on meetings and reviews—by Schultz, Kronfeld, Gaupp, Kretschmer, and others; the single article on psychotherapy it carried was in 1916, on psychotherapy and traumatic neurosis. The same general pattern held for the *Münchener medizinische Wochenschrift;* in 1930 that journal inaugurated a section heading for psychotherapy with an article by, appropriately, I. H. Schultz.[52] Beginning in 1928, of course, the psychotherapists had their own journal, and in the same year *Hippokrates,* a journal dedicated to "practical medicine" and "the unity of medicine," made its appearance, providing another forum for a sympathetic discussion of psychotherapy and the various social issues facing medical practice.

Mental hygiene had first been professionalized through the work of the American Clifford Beers; in 1909 Beers, Adolf Meyer, and William James were responsible for the foundation of the National Committee for Mental Hygiene. The confluence of the burgeoning appreciation of personality, character, and the unconscious life of the individual, plus a "shift in emphasis of philosophy from the salvation of the individual to the reconstruction of society,"[53] was not restricted to the United States, however. In Germany, Max von Pettenkofer and Robert Koch had pioneered the practice of general social hygiene during the late nineteenth century; soon thereafter, Robert Sommer, who turned from an early traditional opposition to such activism, became the moving spirit behind its evolution. Psychotherapy, of course, was to play a vital role in this enterprise. The General Medical Society for Psychotherapy, in its desire to mobilize all the sciences of the mind into a united front against mental illness, as well as against the skeptics within the medical establishment, claimed a variety of provinces for its potential practice: child care, industrial psychology, clinical practice, and pedagogy were specifically mentioned. On still another front, the psychotherapists were engaged in campaigning against medical quackery (*Kurpfuschertum*), an effort designed to validate psychotherapy as a science and free it from the professional onus of association with fraudulent practitioners.

The congresses, which regularly attracted over 500 participants, proposed to provide psychotherapy as a profession with a solid medical and scientific foundation. The 1927 congress at Bad Nauheim was devoted to four themes: psychoanalysis, health pedagogy, training in psychotherapy, and the fight against quackery.[54] Back at Baden-Baden, the 1928 congress of the now formally licensed society included presentations on individual psychology by Seif, Künkel, and Schultz-Hencke; on character research by Ludwig Klages, Rudolf Allers, Georg Groddeck, Sommer, and Cimbal; and on experimental psychology by Kurt Lewin and Schultz. There was also a session on religion and psychotherapy, including remarks by one M. H. Göring.[55]

The society itself continued to grow and to operate as a forum for a wide range of views, both medical and lay, on psychotherapy and neurosis. In 1928 Sommer was still president, with Cimbal as managing director. The executive committee included Seif, Schultz, Eliasberg, Kronfeld, Kretschmer, and Kurt Goldstein. Carl Jung was listed for the first time as a participant that year, and references to his work multiplied in the 1928 annual report. New members that year included Adler, Hans Prinzhorn, and psychoanalyst Karl Birnbaum. Total membership rose to 399 (Germany 334, Switzerland 18, Austria 16, Holland 15, Czechoslovakia 5, Hungary 4, Sweden 3, France 2, Poland and Spain 1 each). The following year saw the attendance of psychoanalyst Franz Alexander, the presentation of a paper by Jung, and, in line with the group's efforts to build bridges to neighboring disciplines, particularly psychiatry, a paper by Kretschmer. In 1930 Kretschmer was elected president and Jung vice-president.[56]

Sommer had stepped down because of ill health and was named honorary president, although he remained co-editor of the *Zentralblatt* with Kretschmer. The theme for 1930 was compulsion neurosis, and the congress heard papers by Stekel and Karen Horney. J. W. Hauer, who later, as founder of the German Faith Movement (Deutsche Glaubenswewegung), was to become a somewhat celebrated cultural adjunct to National Socialism, spoke on yoga and psychotherapy—a subject that was later pursued within the Göring Institute by Schultz and Gustav Schmaltz. The psychiatrist who was to be closest to the psychotherapists in the Third Reich, Hans Luxenburger, also presented a paper, the subject of which was the heredity and family typology of compulsion. The 1930 congress counted 575 participants, and the society gained eighty new members. The 1931 congress, in Dresden, considered two major issues: somatology (Heyer) and psychology (with Wolfgang Kranefeldt representing Jung). As president, Kretschmer read an address in honor of Freud's seventy-fifth birthday, and it was proposed that the next congress be held in Vienna during 7–10 April 1932, with papers to be given on the relations between neurology and psychology, on child and youth psychotherapy, and on hysteria.[57] This seventh congress did not take place; the economic crisis had become too severe.

Although the aim of the General Medical Society for Psychotherapy was to unify the various tendencies within psychotherapy, the meeting of so many minds in one organization inevitably produced factions. There were Adlerians (including Adler), Jungians (including Jung), Stekelians (including Stekel), and Freudians, such as Groddeck, Horney, Wilhelm Reich, and Sandor Radó (though without, of course, Freud, for orthodox psychoanalysts remained dubious about the society).

Again, it is appropriate to speculate here whether the membership of the General Medical Society for Psychotherapy, despite the breadth of interests, orientations, and branches of medicine it represented, as a whole reflected a conservative, nationalist—and largely Protestant[58]—stance at odds with the generally more liberal, cosmopolitan—and largely Jewish—membership of the DPG. Many of the psychotherapists prominent in the affairs of the General Medical Society for Psychotherapy and the Göring Institute did display a conservative, nationalist and "unpolitical" attitude that was easily transformed into varying degrees of enthusiasm and support for National Socialism beginning in 1933. There is evidence to suggest, furthermore, that, as a whole, physicians in Germany at this time tended toward the political right: Disturbed by socialized medicine, unimpressed with Weimar democracy and "materialism," and ambivalent at best about their Jewish colleagues, of all professional groups in Germany doctors had the highest percentage (45) of Nazi party members within their ranks.[59] Although Käthe Dräger, a young member of the Freudian group at the Göring Institute, has maintained that no more than 5 percent of the institute's members were members of the Nazi party,[60] the percentage of party members among the early spokesmen for psychotherapy in the Third Reich and among the leadership of the German General Medical Society for Psychotherapy and the Göring Institute was much higher. Although membership ultimately conferred no particular advantage, of a group of 47 leading psychotherapists of the time, 17, or 36.17 percent, had joined the party between 1930 and 1938, while only 14 were not members of at least one of the party organizations for doctors, social workers, teachers, and university professors.[61]

The psychiatrists in the society, led by Sommer, Kretschmer, Schultz, and Ernst Speer, were divided among themselves on matters of theory and practice. Sommer, for all of his commitment to a psychotherapeutic campaign against neurosis, had been an early and vociferous critic of Freud's psychogenetic explanation for hysteria. Schultz, a psychiatrist who had turned to neuropathology in 1926, did emerge, along with Speer, as a vigorous proponent of an eclectic psychotherapy under medical control, both during and after the Nazi era. But Kretschmer, who enjoyed great prestige in the medical profession as a whole, and who was steadily gaining influence within the General Medical Society for Psychotherapy, maintained the view that psychotherapy was to be reserved only for medical specialists in psychiatry. It is not unreasonable to suppose that in place of the enforced unity which was soon to prevail within the German General Medical Society for Psychotherapy beginning in 1933, there might well have been one or more genuine splits in, and even secessions from, the society during the process of attempting to resolve the powerful differences in theory, practice, and professionalization that dogged it before the Hitler era. In addition, although several prominent psychoanalysts were members of the society, most of these were revisionists like the neo-Freudian Horney, the almost indefinable Groddeck, the brilliant Reich, and the intensely intellectual rebel Schultz-Hencke. And, as we have noted, the German Psychoanalytic Society did not recognize the General Medical Society for Psychotherapy.[62]

By 1933 the General Medical Society for Psychotherapy had become the major forum in Central Europe for consensus and dissent about the nature and future course of the expanding field of medical psychology. A major challenge to the organic bias of German university psychiatry, arising from the nineteenth-century German philosophy of nature and the *fin de siècle* psychodynamic revival led by Freud, had achieved solid organizational status within the German medical profession. It is impossible to say with certainty, of course, which direction the development of psychotherapy as a profession would have taken had not Hitler come to power. It seems likely, however, that Kretschmer and the traditional university psychiatrists would have been able to exercise far more control over its evolution than they were able to do during the Third Reich. As it was, those who were seeking to establish psychotherapy as an autonomous, eclectic, broadly concerned profession in itself won the opportunity to strengthen its position. Its vehicle for success would be the Göring Institute, the institutionalized monopoly on psychotherapeutic research, training, and practice that would be its province in Hitler's Germany.

Seen in this historical context, the creation of the German General Society for Psychotherapy in 1933, and the German Institute for Psychological Research and Psychotherapy in 1936, represented much more than the Nazi mobilization of medical psychologists, a young profession's collaboration with the Nazis, and an institutional defense against persecution. It represented a seminal episode in the history of a young discipline's continuity with the past. This fact makes the story of psychotherapy during the Third Reich vital to any understanding of the evolution of medical psychology in central Europe.

CHAPTER 3

Psyche and Swastika

Psychotherapists responded to the events of 1933 not only by defending their ideas and their professional identity against both medical and political critics but also by mounting an offensive designed to ride the wave of change that was apparently building to sweep over the German establishment. This response was strengthened by the fact that many of their members believed that the new regime was a realization, or at least the means to a realization, of their own particular professional and cultural ideals; there was an accompanying satisfied conviction, as we shall see, that the times were finally catching up with the revolutionary concepts that were in the process of challenging the traditional perspective and treatment of the human psyche.

After the expulsion of their Jewish colleagues, which we shall describe in Chapter 4, it should not have surprised those leading psychotherapists who remained in Germany that their philosophical and cultural ideals would bear no fruit in the salt-laced Nazi intellectual soil. But quite apart from helping to explain their motives, the ideals they professed did provide two crucial elements for the development of psychotherapy as a profession during the Third Reich. The first was, to a significant degree, the contribution of a kind of unity among them that proved valuable after 1933 in seizing the opportunity for professional advance as well as in combating the dual threat that arose from Nazi radicals and newly politicized opponents within the medical establishment. The second element was the extent to which these ideals themselves provided a mutually sympathetic link between leading members of the General Medical Society for Psychotherapy and various members and segments of the Nazi movement.

Those we may list as members of a "core group" within the General Medical Society for Psychotherapy after 1928 were not distinguished as such simply because they were the ones (including, of course, no Jews) who stayed on and assumed leadership positions in the society and the institute after 1933; they were, instead, people who had been prominent in the theoretical, practical, and organizational affairs of psychotherapy in Germany before the advent of Hitler. (The only real exceptions to this, and only partial ones at that, were M. H. Göring himself and the fervid ideologue Kurt Gauger, both of whose careers we discuss more fully in Chapter 4.) By 1928, when local branches (*Ortsgruppen*) of the General Medical Society for Psychotherapy were established in Berlin and Munich, Schultz and Künkel were already prominent in Prussia, and Seif, Heyer, and Hattingberg were important voices in Bavaria. These men were also, well before 1933, major representatives of particular philosophical notions—"unpolitical" romanticism and holism—and certain professional concerns—short-term therapy and public mental hygiene, for example—within the psychotherapeutic and psychoanalytic movement as a whole. Because of this, as we shall see, the history of these psychotherapists' association with the Nazis cannot be comprehended purely in terms of crass personal opportunism, unalloyed allegiance to National Socialism, consistently fervid anti-Semitism, or the complete sacrifice of professional ideals and standards.

The second edition of Künkel's *Grundzüge der politischen Charakterkunde,* which appeared in 1934, demonstrates the kind of satisfied optimism that prevailed among some. In his introduction, Künkel referred as follows to a discussion of the community as the fulfillment of individual lives that had appeared in the first edition of 1931: "In some sections it has sufficed to substitute the present tense for the future one, since the formerly impending development has in the meantime been realized."[1] In a 1933 article Hattingberg celebrated "the incorporation of medical psychotherapy in these great events" which "move us in the spirit" of a dynamic and spiritually nourishing *Volksgemeinschaft.* With this formulation, he was able to ignore the massive dangers implicit in such a Nazified appreciation of current events: "Therefore, we as doctors are able to say objectively that we cannot do without the work of that man (Freud), work which a politically aroused youth (from their standpoint, quite correctly) burn."[2] Jung wrote approvingly of the new regime to Hattingberg on 9 and 22 June 1933 in pledging his support for the German psychotherapists. He later ruefully reevaluated this tone:

> Our judgment would certainly be very different if our imagination stopped short at 1933 or 1934. At that time, in Germany as well as in Italy, there were not a few things that appeared plausible and seemed to speak in favor of the regime. . . . And after the stagnation and decay of the post-war years, the refreshing wind that blew through the two countries was a tempting sign of hope.[3]

The figure and image of Hitler himself took on the status of not only a national cultural symbol but even of a professional one. (For doctors, Hitler became the "doctor" of the German people; for psychologists, the "psychologist" of the German people; and so on.) The young physician and psychotherapist Kurt Gauger saw in Hitler the conception of the healthy unconscious united with its asserted national, cultural, racial, and archetypal analogues: "As inheritors of the individualistic epoch, we know much about individual conditions of mental illnesses. What we did not hear so much about, however, before Adolf Hitler, are the general conditions of the health of the soul."[4] Heyer also contemplated Hitler and his effect on the masses with a Jungian eye, exalting the primitive within the individual:

> We understand from Germany's most recent past what it is that the Führer appeals to: to fantasy, the emotions, to the irrational side of the people. And when we read his speeches and listen to them, what convinces, what soars, what carries us along, is not rational argument, but the image.[5]

All in all, the fervent patriotic perspective with which events were viewed by professionals beclouded the critical, rational eye. One physician, later the director of a natural health sanitarium in Berchtesgaden, even went so far as to aver that the new Nazi Ministry of Propaganda was an affirmation of the need for suggestive methods of psychotherapy on a national basis.[6]

Even those who were willing to act on their grave doubts about Hitler and the Nazis lived with laming illusion. Perhaps people who were dedicated by their profession to the treatment of mental illness were even more susceptible to such desperate hope. Georg Groddeck entertained to his death in 1934 the belief that if he could just talk to Hitler, he could effect some change in the Führer.[7]

Beyond the vagaries of their initial reaction to National Socialism, the Göring Institute psychotherapists' idealistic and practical concern for professional identity and development was closely linked, as we have noted, with the cultural and philosophical values of Romanticism, especially its fascination with what had come to be called the unconscious. Matthias Heinrich Göring recalled in 1940 what he believed was the psychotherapeutic perspective that had been adopted and advertised by the new regime in 1933:

> The Reich Health Leader had at that time already expressed the view that the health and thereby the productivity of the individual was dependent on the physician viewing and treating him as a whole. To this whole as well belongs the unconscious in man. Our society sees as one of its principal assignments to call out to doctors, educators, and all fellow-countrymen who are concerned with human guidance, not lastly those in the armed forces and in the economy: Do not forget the unconscious! Do not think that you are grasping the whole man when you close your eyes to the unconscious![8]

It is clear that the psychotherapists' response to National Socialism was not based on any sort of developed political consciousness. Only two of the leading psychotherapists in the society and institute had ever been formally associated with any political group. Industrial psychologist Felix Scherke, who would become the Göring Intitute's comptroller in 1939 (see Chapter 5), served during the summer and fall of 1921 as a lecturer in the province of Brandenburg for the League for the Protection of German Culture (Liga zum Schutz der deutschen Kultur).[9] And neuropathologist Rudolf Bilz joined the Nazi party in August of 1930. We have noted earlier the admission by Werner Kemper, a Freudian who in 1942 was to become director of the Göring Institute's outpatient clinic, that had he been "political," he might have joined the Nazi party in 1933 out of sheer enthusiasm and excitement. The statement illustrates what was a common position for professionals at the time.

The attitude stemmed from the fact that in 1933 for many Germans Nazism was compelling sheerly because of its novelty and energy. Kemper, though he was repeatedly prompted to do so by Göring,[10] never joined the party. Those psychotherapists who did, for the most part, fell into the category of the so-called "fallen of March" (Märzgefallene), who did so in the rush of enthusiasm and opportunism that prevailed in early 1933. A few others joined in 1937, when party membership, after having been closed in 1934 to avoid dilution by opportunists, was reopened to desirable classes of applicants such as bureaucrats and professionals. Membership in the party auxiliary groups (Gliederungen) established for doctors, teachers, students, social workers, and professors, however, was more common.[11]

Who were the psychotherapists who were to function within the protected province of the Göring Institute? How did their pre-1933 values affect their transition into the new regime?

The Adlerians:
Künkel, Göring, and Seif

The Adlerians Fritz Künkel, Matthias Heinrich Göring, and Leonhard Seif were the chief proponents within the General Medical Society for Psychotherapy of what they saw as the therapeutic need for a sense of community. What unified the three was their common belief in what Adler after World War I had described as "community feeling" (Gemeinschaftsgefühl)[12]; it testified not only to the special debt they owed to Adler's psychology but to a peculiar German cultural bias as well.

During the 1920s Fritz Künkel emerged in Germany as a major teacher of the practical system that Adler had labeled individual psychology. Born the son of a Prussian landowner in Stolzenberg, Brandenburg, in 1889, Künkel studied medicine in Munich. He enlisted in August 1914 and gave his left arm for the Iron Cross, first and second class, while serving as a medical assistant with the 48th Infantry Regiment during the war. He became licensed as a physician in 1917. By 1924 he had set up a practice in Berlin-Wilmersdorf as a specialist in nervous disorders and began to gather about him a circle of students and followers who were attracted by his articulation and later modifications of Adler's psychology.[13]

Künkel's response to the Third Reich was both typical and atypical for a man of his background. Although he came from a conservative East Elbian family, Künkel, according to his son, John, had reacted strongly against the greedy acquisitiveness so common to Junker landowners at the turn of the century.[14] This rejection of his familial and social milieu helped turn Künkel away from a familial and social environment dominated by business and government and toward the refuge of a scholarly and unpolitical life, and ultimately to a career in the internal and personal universe of individual psychology. He emerged from World War I without an arm and also without the youthful patriotism that had swept him, like the overwhelming majority of his generation, into uniform in 1914. He turned to psychotherapy when he decided that he could not be a good doctor with only one arm. (His younger brother, Hans, who had lost his right arm in the war, was not so hindered as a novelist and philosopher.)

In 1920 Künkel married a young Jewish woman named Ruth Löwengard. Although she died at the end of the decade, Künkel's response to Nazi rule was complicated by the three children their union had produced. It was this, coupled with his unpolitical nature, which, again according to his son, prompted Künkel to advertise a certain enthusiasm for the ideals of the new regime in articles he wrote between 1933 and 1939. He managed to get the children out of Germany by 1938 and, as we shall see, he himself remained in the United States, where he embarked on a lecture tour in 1939, with the outbreak of war. At the same time, however, Künkel's notion of "community" did represent more than just a defensive or even rhetorical response to National Socialism. As his son put it, "we-psychology was in the air" after World War I as part of a freshly expressed German cultural and historical consciousness. The Nazis appealed to this tradition. Men like Künkel could and did adopt an air of traditional moral and intellectual superiority toward a movement whose very rudeness confirmed the naïve impression and rationalization of such intellectuals that it was their ideas and influence which were coming to fruition and which would dominate crude political arrivistes. Künkel, unlike a number of his colleagues, did not express or reveal any explicitly anti-Semitic sentiments in his writings, his response to Hitler being of a more elevated nature born of fear for his children and some deeply held personal and professional beliefs.

Künkel had long proselytized vigorously the concept of the "we" relationship between individual and community as a sign of cultural maturity. With this perspective, he was particularly susceptible and responsive to the Nazi exhortations about the necessity for a sense of collective and individual mission that would prove both the viability of the racial community and the character of each of its members. As a contemporary jurist put it, "[t]he idea of community, the idea of the 'we' as the totality of a people, comprises the political power of the Führer-state."[15] For Künkel, humanity had evolved from the primitive "we" of feudalism through individualism to the mature *Wir* of Germanic northern Europe. A Führer embodied the will of the people, not in any institutional manner but on an intuitive, organic basis. Therefore, the function of psychotherapy was to ensure the equation of health and loyalty: "We are specialists in the management of transgression, and that means at the same time that we are specialists in the care of hypocrisy, of self-deception and treason against the *Volksgemeinschaft*."[16]

Künkel was moving away from Adler's assertion that *Gemeinschaftsgefühl* was a biological fact and necessity, stemming as it supposedly did from the child's early physical and psychological symbiosis with the mother. For Adler, the "community feeling" was an unconscious element of the personality, accessible only through an understanding of the actual life of an individual as revealed in his disposition; psychotherapy could change and broaden a person's *Gemeinschaftsgefühl* in order to make him more productive. Künkel, in diverging from the Marxist orientation of the Berlin Adlerians, added a Hegelian and a religious orientation to individual psychology. Although his chief concern remained the "dialectic" that existed between subject and object, the "I" and the "we," he drew from Ludwig Klages and Carl Haeberlin the biocentric notion of healthy natural rhythms, and from Jung a reverence before the depths of the soul. His emphasis on the individual's active life and social commitment, the confluence of the deep and indefinable harbored in the soul, and the practical tasks of day-to-day living recalls C. G. Carus's Romantic ideal of the art of living (*Lebenskunst*).[17]

Künkel's concerns also engaged the approach of Hans Prinzhorn. Prinzhorn (1883–1933) was a neuropathologist and professor of psychology from Dresden who was the leading proponent of the "totality approach" (*Ganzheitsbetrachtung*) that was typical of the perspective of most German psychotherapists at the time.[18] Künkel, as did others, would thus criticize Freud for not dealing with the "whole individual," as Adler did.[19]

This conception of the human being as a totality, as articulated by Prinzhorn out of Nietzsche and others, turned a large number of psychotherapists away from Freud. The view of the individual as a whole demanded that a person be regarded as a biological and social entity rather than a disparate and semi-sovereign bundle of drives. Like Adler (and Künkel), Prinzhorn saw the individual as essentially indivisible, a belief that clearly contradicted Freud's conception of man's fundamental ambivalence, vulnerable to internal conflicts.[20] For Prinzhorn there was no external norm to be aspired toward in order to achieve health and happiness; instead, each person laid claim to a private and unique fate (*Schicksal*) that, in the Romantic spirit, had to be fulfilled. But fate was conditioned by a given social and biological heritage. The psychotherapist, therefore, was not to be a passive analyst but an active partner in the healing process, involving himself on a personal level and leading the individual back into a life-affirming communion with himself and, most important, with a suprapersonal entity such as nature, culture, community, or God.[21] This stance rendered the psychotherapist much more of a clergyman—Prinzhorn used the word *Priesterdilettant* ("amateur priest")—than a scientist. The psychoanalytic dyad was replaced by the therapist's engagement in the life of the individual and within a larger whole.

The Romantic concern with totality was linked to another strong German intellectual tradition in the field of psychology and medicine which also found expression in Künkel's work. This was the study of character, a concept that was to be understood as an integral whole composed of an organic disposition and specific psychological characteristics from a given cultural environment. The study of character as perceived in this sense was much more appealing than Freud's conception of personality as an expression of the ego and its compromises with the forces of the id and the superego. In many respects anticipating the psychoanalytic culturalists and the neo-Freudians, the analysis of character was a preoccupation shared by Edmund Husserl's phenomenology, by the existentialism of Martin Heidegger and Karl Jaspers, and by both the "describing" psychology evolved by the historian Wilhelm Dilthey and the "understanding" psychology of Dilthey's student, Eduard Spranger. Rather than seeing individual and environment in primarily causal terms, these philosophers offered a holistic-organic point of view that led to the construction of character typologies.[22]

The importance of characterology lay in its attempt to come to grips with the human organism in all its biological, environmental, and historical complexity. In Germany the Romantic emphasis on the unique and the dynamic—as opposed to the "vulgar democracy" of reason—resulted in a peculiarly German run of thought, culminating in Erich Jaensch's fully Nazified character typology. Künkel's version of character typology based itself on a synthesis of Jung's "continuation" (*Fortsetzung*) of Freudian psychoanalysis with the individual psychology of Adler. The fusion of what Künkel called "internal psychology" (*Innenpsychologie*), or "depth psychology" (*Tiefenpsychologie*), and "external psychology" (*Aussenpsychologie*), or "relations psychology" (*Beziehungspsychologie*), produced a "dialectical science of character" that saw individual human development in terms of an active complementarity between internal character and external environment.[23]

Künkel had ceased to be only an Adlerian when he declared that it was necessary to transcend Adler and reach toward the depths of cultural and religious feeling, experience, and tradition that Jung had explored.[24] In this he was espousing an earlier preoccuption with some new enthusiasm. In 1926, in the first volume of Carl Schweitzer's series on religion and medicine, Künkel had criticized the medical establishment for its materialism and mechanism: "Seventy years ago the asylums were mostly under administration of the church, and that was much less a failing than materialistic medicine would now have us believe."[25]

Künkel clearly drew some encouragement as well as advantage from the advent of National Socialism. He called in 1934 for the "we-ish" [*wirhaften*] reconstruction of the German people,"[26] and in 1936 for the need to strengthen the national character to meet the demands of geography and history: "The German inherits all the heavy burdens that arise from the position of his fatherland in the middle of Europe, the indefensibility of his borders, and the peculiarity of his history."[27] As a former Adlerian, he believed this strengthening of character had to begin with the child's proper environment, created first and foremost by the family and then by the school, with the assistance, if need be, of the psychotherapist or the educational counselor schooled in psychology and psychotherapy.

In 1936, Künkel wrote that neurosis actually thrived in advanced civilizations and among pure races, that it was thus a result of environment and not heredity. The family formed the vital ground on which the continuing mental health and vitality of the nation could be built:

> The great decision as to whether this valuable human material will be rendered viable, valiant, and creative, or broken, cowardly, and sick, at the disposal of the state and the nation, as to whether the *Volk* will be rich in creative spirits or rich in hysterics and obsessive neurotics, this decision lies in the hands of the parents alone.[28]

Künkel anticipated a theoretical union between Adler and Jung that was not so much effected as affected during the Third Reich. M. H. Göring, whose character and career we will examine in Chapter 4, was an Adlerian whose views were fairly similar to those of Künkel, and who enthusiastically adopted Künkel's psychology as a central constituent of a new German psychotherapy.[29] Adler himself, of course, was in the rational socialist tradition, animated by an optimism that was based on an enlightened faith in reason. The Romantic tradition, on the other hand, exalted the irrational and the unconscious, and these differences received great attention in the early years under Hitler's rule. According to M. H. Göring, Adler

> wishes to level men so they can live next to and among one another as free from friction as possible. So it is explicable why [Adler's] individual psychology found strong approval among the Marxists, and why individual-psychological Marxist [professional] societies under Jewish direction were established, while other societies, like that in Munich under Seif, form a front against the Marxist orientation with their Aryan instinct. . . . German psychotherapy does not recognize any leveling; it wishes to force all abilities from a person, not for his own sake, but in service to the *Volksgemeinschaft*.[30]

The Adlerian Göring, devoutly religious and charged to defend psychotherapy against both political and newly politicized medical criticism, embraced the Romantic propensity of Jung even more enthusiastically than the Adlerian Künkel did. Göring coupled Adler's worldly communal teleology with Jung's perspective: "The goal-orientation points to the future. We must also look to the past. A person does not enter the world as a blank page, as Adler believes, but belongs to a family, to a people, to a race."[31]

Künkel's views reveal one dimension of the era's thought, but Künkel himself did not emerge as a major force in the society or in the institute under Göring. He became a member of the Nazi social welfare organization (the NSV), and on at least one occasion, in 1933, eagerly pointed out to the authorities the crucial family affiliation of his official professional mentor, Göring. But given his eventual departure from Nazi Germany, perhaps these were opportunisms that were grasped so that his frequent tours abroad (to Holland, Sweden, and the United States) and foreign publications could continue uninterrupted—rather than to solidify his position at home among German psychotherapists. When he enlisted the support of Karl Haedenkamp, who was in charge of matters abroad for the Reich Physicians Chamber (Reichsärztekammer), and requested continued membership in the Reich Chamber for Literature, it was, Künkel argued (signing off with the customary *"Heil Hitler!"*), to ensure the continuing effectiveness of his "popular" writings and their translation into foreign languages.[32]

Künkel was unhappy with the political situation in Germany and he continued to accept invitations to lecture abroad, a direction he had set for himself before the advent of Hitler and the resultant new course for psychotherapists under Göring. In 1939, he embarked on another lecture tour of the United States, which he had first visited in 1936 and whose "frontier" nature appealed to him. When the war broke out, he elected to stay there.[33] Künkel went on to become a popular speaker and writer in America; he fused the religious impulse with the doctrine of self-improvement à la Norman Vincent Peale, a combination that proved to be appealing to general audiences.[34] He died in Los Angeles in 1956.[35]

Another Adlerian who continued in the mainstream, and one whose personal influence in German psychotherapy between 1933 and 1945 remained great, was Leonhard Seif. He was born in Munich in 1866, the son of a railroad official, and after studying philosophy for a year in the wake of passing his university qualifying examinations (*Abitur*) in Freising, he began the study of medicine at the University of Munich. In May of 1895 Seif set up a Munich practice in neuropathology. He was a co-founder of the International Psycho-Analytic Association in 1910 and became president of its Munich branch the following year. In 1922, under the leitmotif of prevention before cure and a typical Adlerian stress on concrete, practical psychotherapeutic assistance, Seif founded an educational advisory board (*Erziehungsberatungsstelle*) in Munich. He became internationally known, and in 1927 and again in 1929 accepted invitations to lecture and teach at Harvard and Boston University; between 1928 and 1937, he gave a series of lectures at the universities of London, Birmingham, and York. His last summer course in England ended a few days before the outbreak of war in 1939. Later that same year, his organization became an official branch of the German Institute for Psychological Research and Psychotherapy; Seif had made his first governmental affiliation with the Popular Education Chancellery of Bavaria (Volksbildungskanzlei) in 1936.[36]

Seif, like Künkel, placed a heavy emphasis on Adler's *Gemeinschaftsgefühl* and, also like Künkel, added a religious flavor by way of his insistence on the necessity of a spiritual dimension for the complete life. In the German context of heightened national consciousness around 1933, such an emphasis seemed congruent—as Seif himself put it in his 1934 essay, "Volksgemeinschaft und Neurose"—with the Nazi insistence that the interests of the individual be subordinated to those of the community. Citing Nietzsche and Clausewitz, Seif continued on in this vein by declaring that while politics created the institutional framework of a *Volksgemeinschaft,* pedagogy and psychotherapy would work to ensure the education of each child to his or her life tasks within the national community.[37] Seif's essay was one of a number excerpted from the 1934 *Zentralblatt für Psychotherapie* and published separately under Göring's editorship in *Deutsche Seelenheilkunde.* The consistent theme in Seif's work during the Third Reich was, as he put it in 1940, that "[e]ducation or psychotherapy is the task of forming a vital community [*Lebensgemeinschaft*], a 'we' relationship."[38] The close of his 1934 essay cited not Nietzsche, Prinzhorn, or Clausewitz, but rather Kant, on the formation of the true national community as a means toward the ideal world community—an invocation very much in the Enlightenment spirit of Seif's chief mentor, Adler, from whom he had by now drawn away.[39]

Although he conceded a great deal in ideal, word, and deed to the Nazi regime, Seif remained close to his original intellectual roots in the traditions of psychoanalysis and Adlerian individual psychology. In spite of his having remained in Germany while his fellow Adlerian, Künkel, left, it is by no means clear that he was more devoted to the Nazis. Never a party member, he apparently joined the Nazi Physicians League and the NSV as a means of ensuring the effective existence of his Munich operation.[40] As we shall see in Chapter 5, he remained suspect in the eyes of some Nazi offices. And, as we will see in Chapter 6, his work exhibited a continuity of practice and purpose on both sides of the year 1933.

The Jungian: Heyer

Gustav Richard Heyer was born in 1890 in Bad Kreuznach on the Rhine River; his father's family had been foresters from the area surrounding nearby Darmstadt. Heyer grew up in Bad Kreuznach, Cologne, and Neuwied am Rhein until his father, a district judge, became a ministerial director in the Reich Financial Office in Potsdam. The younger Heyer elected to go into forestry and went to Munich to study. There he became interested in medicine and philosophy and, after passing his preliminary exams (the *physikum*), went to Heidelberg. His education, like that of most members of his generation, was interrupted by World War I. Returning to Munich, he continued his work in medicine as an assistant to internist Friedrich von Müller. But Heyer, by his own account, became increasingly estranged from the physical and chemical orientation of his mentor, and it was for this reason, he later claimed, that even after five years as his assistant, Müller refused to recommend him to become a member of the faculty.[41]

Heyer quit his post and, abandoning his experiments on the psychological aspects of stomach and intestinal secretions, established a practice in internal medicine and neurology. In 1918 he married Lucy Grote, the daughter of a noted chemist. She was a gymnastics teacher, and through her Heyer became convinced of the value of using physical therapy in psychotherapeutic practice. Impoverished by the inflation of 1923, Heyer remained exclusively in private practice and in 1926 he began giving lectures on psychotherapy to interested medical students at the University of Munich. Meanwhile, he had become more and more interested and involved in the growing international psychoanalytic movement. He quickly discovered differences with the Freudian school (which, in his 1944 curriculum vitae, he termed "the old system of the Jewish analysts"[42]) and embraced Jungian psychology. In 1928 he founded an informal Jungian discussion group in Munich.

Nevertheless, in spite of the German Romantic bias which was partly responsible for the attraction, Heyer found Jung too ethereal—a reaction common among German doctors interested in psychotherapy who were concerned with the task of the practicing physician rather than that of the researcher or the philosopher. Still, something in Jung's thought tugged at Heyer.

Heyer publicly greeted the advent of Hitler with enthusiasm. With typical personal and professional brashness, he asserted in 1935, "How could health in the Germany of Adolf Hitler be contemplated without psychotherapy?"[43] Although he did not become a party member until 1937, colleagues remember him as a staunch supporter of the regime from the beginning, one of those who joined up out of conviction that the Nazis spoke to some deep sense of identity within the German people and nation. Among others, both Fritz Riemann, a Munich psychoanalyst, and Wolfgang Kranefeldt, a fellow Jungian who worked in Berlin from 1935 to 1942, recall Heyer as an enthusiastic Nazi who proudly wore a party lapel pin. Lucy Heyer-Grote, Heyer's first wife, claims, however, that Heyer became disillusioned with the Nazis and came to wear the pin on the inside of his lapel for use only when absolutely necessary. In general, though, Heyer is recalled by his colleagues at the Göring Institute as a politically dangerous and combative individual, a characteristic that reportedly led to a potentially dangerous conflict in the early 1930s with one of his patients, Rudolf Hess.[44]

In 1942 Heyer appropriated Nazi rhetoric in attempting to analyze for the readers of the *Zeitschrift für Geopolitik* the psychological dimensions and characteristics of Eastern Europe (*Ostraum*). He had volunteered for medical duty in early 1942 to help fill the gaps left by Barbarossa, and pointed in Nazi blood-and-soil fashion to the dangers of what he referred to as "spatial-racial russification."[45] He feared that the German soldiers in the East, far from their roots in the rich and reverberating soil of Germany, might lose those characteristics which made them soulfully dynamic. Like a significant number of German psychotherapists, psychologists, and philosophers at the time, he was concerned—almost obsessed—with the preservation of character. The conviction that German culture was peculiarly blessed with the conditions for creating strong, healthy character fit nicely with the Nazi celebration of aggressive (*kämpferisch*) heroes. Such types had to be cultivated as well as bred, they believed, a concept that provided a natural rhetorical and practical opening for Nazi-era psychotherapists and psychologists.[46]

For all the inheritors of the German Romantic ethos in the field of psychology, the fate of humanity and civilization rested in the diagnosis and treatment of modern ills to free latent creative and assertive energies, a perspective very different from Freud's stoic resignation in the face of what he saw, unromantically, as inherent conflict within and between the individual and civilization.

Although Heyer, as we saw above, greeted Hitler effusively and remained a defender of the regime among the psychotherapists, his primary significance for this study lies in his practical activities on behalf of the evolving profession of psychotherapy during the Third Reich. Although too rebellious to be regarded as a strict Jungian schoolman, he displayed the cast of mind that caused Jungians to be loudly and eagerly hailed by Göring and other like-minded conservative nationalist psychotherapists as the heralds of a new German psychotherapy, all because of the apparently deep Germanic and Romantic soulfulness they exhibited, as against the crass materialism of Jewish psychoanalysis.

But there was to be no "new German psychotherapy" under Hitler, only the considerable and eventually historic task, shared by all the schools of psychotherapeutic thought including the Jungians and the Freudians, of protecting, preserving, and advancing the professional interests of psychotherapy within, without, and against the medical establishment.

The Freudians:
Schultz-Hencke and Rittmeister

Harald Schultz-Hencke was a Berliner by birth. He was born in 1892; his father, a physicist and chemist, had founded a photographic institute in the German capital the year before. The double name came from his grandfather Karl, whose stepfather, Karl-Ludwig Hencke, because of his scientific accomplishments—as an amateur astronomer he had discovered two planetoids—won permission for his devoted stepson to carry the name Schultz-Hencke. Harald's mother was a graphologist, and it was because of her, he later recalled, that he became interested in the "psychological and human sciences."[47] He also early on cultivated a lively interest in biology.

Schultz-Hencke began his medical studies at Freiburg in Breisgau, concentrating on anatomy and pathology, but he also pursued his interest in philosophy by attending seminars given by the neo-Kantian Heinrich Rickert and the phenomenologists Edmund Husserl and Martin Heidegger. His experience in the war, particularly in the winter battles of 1915–16 on the Hartmannweilerskopf, left him sickly and, he claimed, even stunted his growth. He was forced to turn from an active life to one of pure scholarship.

Schultz-Hencke had learned about psychiatry for the first time from

August Hoche at Freiburg. Hoche's sharp skepticism toward psychology only encouraged Schultz-Hencke to devote himself to the medical study of the mind. He was further inspired by Freud's work. In 1921 he joined the psychiatric clinic at Würzburg as a volunteer assistant, and there he witnessed dramatic confirmation of a number of the central theses of psychoanalytic theory. The following year, in the best tradition of the *peregrinatio academica,* found Schultz-Hencke at the neurological clinic of the Charité Hospital of the University of Berlin. In 1922 he also began his own psychoanalysis.

After three years of learning and practicing psychoanalysis, Schultz-Hencke had become critical of a number of its assumptions, and he welcomed what he saw as the necessary expansion of psychoanalytic theory in the work of Jung and Adler. As his own interest turned ever more away from orthodox Freudian doctrine, his views produced friction with his colleagues at the Berlin Psychoanalytic Institute, where by 1927 he was giving lectures and holding seminars. His growing preference for psychotherapy, as opposed to orthodox analysis, was regarded with suspicion, and his criticisms of Freudian sexual theory finally resulted in the loss of his teaching position at the institute. The revolutionary change (*Umbruch*), as he described it, that came in 1933 allowed him to turn toward systematizing his thought in a way he described in 1940 in *Der gehemmte Mensch.*[48] Schultz-Hencke's urge for synthesis, shared by many of his medical colleagues, had been evident as early as 1927, when he had posed the question of how to unite the psychological (psychoanalysis), the organic (internal medicine), and the technical (suggestive [active] therapy).[49] The following year he was criticizing Künkel for not recognizing the indispensability of Freudian theory.[50] What Schultz-Hencke saw as fundamentally wrong with psychoanalysis was its claim to universality, a criticism he shared with his fellow neo-Freudians.

Acknowledged as part of the neo-Freudian movement within psychoanalysis, Schultz-Hencke went on to found his own school of thought in Germany, which he called "neo-psychoanalysis." He was vigorous in his criticism of traditional psychoanalysis, and his eclectic intelligence drew him into regular and rewarding contact with members of other schools of psychotherapeutic thought. His theories were a mixture of Freudian and Adlerian concepts: He described the root of all neuroses and psychoses as "inhibition" (*Hemmung*), discounting the role of the unconscious.[51]

Schultz-Hencke's words and actions between 1933 and 1945, like those of so many of the other psychotherapists in Germany at that time, reveal a complex picture of motive determined, appropriately enough, by the past. He had been a member of the Youth Movement (Wandervogel) and was a proud veteran of World War I. In its wake he had edited a series of impassioned little books on the necessity of a revolution by the young against the stagnation bred by political parties. In 1944, even burdened with the doubts, regrets, and sufferings he had accumulated during the Nazi years, he could still write with pride that in the youth movement he had found "like-minded comrades."[52]

In 1934 Schultz-Hencke wrote an essay for the *Zentralblatt*—it also appeared in *Deutsche Seelenheilkunde*—entitled "Die Tüchtigkeit als psychotherapeutisches Ziel." The goal of psychotherapy, it maintained, was to free the powers of fitness and proficiency within the individual, to allow patients to overcome the various physical and psychological inhibitions that prevented them from leading productive and happy lives. Its emphasis on therapy over analysis was in both the neo-Freudian and German Romantic traditions, but Schultz-Hencke, obviously responding to the ethos and the opportunity of the hour, went further, contending that the achievement of this kind of psychological health was a duty that each individual owed to his community, and that its maintenance was the corresponding duty of the psychotherapist.[53]

For Schultz-Hencke, life goals were determined by ideology, not by science. In the case of psychotherapy, health was defined in terms of blood, strong will, proficiency, discipline (*Zucht und Ordnung*), community, heroic bearing, and physical fitness. He also took the opportunity of this 1934 essay to criticize psychoanalysis for providing an unfortunate tendency toward the exculpation of the criminal. He faulted it, too, for the notion that religion was a product of the Oedipus complex, and that, as a discipline, it presumed to offer its own distinct pedagogy—all criticisms that were particularly well received by one Nazi reviewer of *Deutsche Seelenheilkunde*. Schultz-Hencke also averred that psychoanalysis was the study of the inhibited individual, and consequently should be renamed *Desmologie,* its method that of *Desmolyse*—from the Greek δεσμός, which Schultz-Hencke translated as "chain" (*Fessel*).[54]

A marginal cultural accessory before the fact, like so many others, Schultz-Hencke briefly perceived the new regime as an opportunity to realize ideals that had already been formulated and pursued. In doing so he displayed neither pure opportunism nor conversion and continuing allegiance to Nazi views. In his case, as in Künkel's, perhaps the fact of physical disability or weakness played a role in the evolution of the style and substance of an intellectual position. Schultz-Hencke's rather unique combination of Freud and Adler, his interest in the political persuasion of youth after World War I, his 1934 celebration of fitness (*Tüchtigkeit*), his 1944 characterization of his scholarship as, in part, a substitute for an active life, and the acute intellectual energy he displayed until his early death in 1953 were all important features of a personal commitment to a pre-Nazi constellation of ideas.

While Schultz-Hencke's professional position and philosophical views resulted in a long and important association with the Göring Institute, Freudian John Rittmeister's professional and philosophical background led him to play only a short and tragic role in the affairs of psychotherapy in the Third Reich. Rittmeister joined the newly established German Institute for Psychological Research and Psychotherapy in 1937, became director of the outpatient clinic in 1939, but was arrested by the Gestapo on a charge of high treason in late 1942 and was executed in the spring of 1943.

Rittmeister was born in Hamburg on 21 August 1898, the eldest son of a businessman of Dutch-English-Huguenot extraction. He had served on the Italian and French fronts during the last two years of World War I and went on to study medicine at the universities of Marburg, Göttingen, Kiel, Munich, and Hamburg. It was in Munich that he came into contact with psychotherapy for the first time through the work of Hattingberg. Rittmeister continued his medical education in Paris, London, and at the Burghölzli in Zurich. In 1936, after some clinical work in Holland, he settled in Münsingen, Switzerland, at the cantonal sanitarium there.[55]

In his study of medical psychology Rittmeister had come to adopt the psychoanalytic perspective. In 1936, in fact, he took a critical stance toward Jung that revealed a strong Freudian point of view.[56] Rittmeister was much closer than the great majority of the more provincial German members of the General Medical Society for Psychotherapy, including Schultz-Hencke, to the traditional iconoclastic bent within psychoanalysis that had originated with Freud himself and to the tendency among many European psychoanalysts to adhere to the social and political left.[57] Rittmeister saw in Jung's "ahistorical image-collectivism" the symptoms of the frightened and confused bourgeois response to the great social changes of the twentieth century. In his critique of Jung, Rittmeister was echoing Ernst Bloch's designation of German psychologists Hans Prinzhorn and Ludwig Klages (see below) and Jung as "crypto-fascists."[58]

It was sentiments such as these that led to the threat of a Swiss ban on Rittmeister in 1937 for alleged communist propaganda activities.[59] Rittmeister opted to return to Germany in order, as he put it later in an entry in his prison diary dated 24 January 1943, to seek a wife and a professional position in his homeland.[60] He went to Berlin to work at the Göring Institute and began a training analysis with the Freudian Werner Kemper.[61] By 1939 he had been named to direct the opera-

Eva Hildebrand

John Rittmeister (1898–1943)

tions of the institute's outpatient clinic. He also became involved with a group of young students and professionals who were part of a left-wing resistance and espionage organization, one of whose members, an aspiring actress named Eva Knieper, he married in July 1939.[62] It was this involvement, as we will see in Chapter 5, that was to cost Rittmeister his life.

Rittmeister was led onto the path of resistance to the Nazis by his longing for a "new humanism" to take the place of what he saw as the crass and heartless bourgeois culture of the West. However, instead of turning fully, as had so many of his German colleagues, to a fuzzy

chauvinistic Romanticism, Rittmeister had begun to construct a critique of modern civilization in the Freudian spirit that retained a critical rationalism and thus avoided sliding off into the emotionalism,
mysticism, and relativism he found so disturbing in the thought of
Jung. Inspired by the work of Eduard von Hartmann and Schopenhauer, Rittmeister saw the opposing poles in human relations as sub-
jectivism/egocentrism on the one hand and the sovereign independence
of the individual self on the other. By subjectivism and egocentrism
(what Schopenhauer and Hartmann called egoism), Rittmeister meant
the tendency toward enlargement of one's ego at the expense of others,
a sort of psychological imperialism. This subjective tendency, Rittmeister believed, deprived others of their own essential individuality (*Wesenidentität der Individuen*), what Schopenhauer and Hartmann labeled the experience of the generous and respectful unity
between the self and others. Rittmeister saw this dangerous, grasping
subjectivity as "a consequence or at least a danger of the Jungian world
view."[63] For Rittmeister, Jung taught the virtues of introversion, a
subjective immersion in the self to the exclusion of others, while
Freud instructed humanity in the ecumenical virtues of love. Further,
against the "refined egoism" of Jung's archetypal mysticism, Rittmeister praised the systematic doubt of Descartes, seeing in such doubt a
humble and necessary acknowledgment of man's imperfection.[64]

Rittmeister considered himself to be a pessimist by nature. To save
himself from despair over a world devoid of meaning, he wrote in
prison on 13 January 1943, he had thrown himself into "social eudae-
monism and optimism" and fought "mysticism . . . solipsism and skepticism" for the sake of working for a realistic and realizable social
good.[65] Rittmeister was not the only anti-Nazi or socialist at the
Göring Institute (Dietfried Müller-Hegemann, a student of Schultz-
Hencke's, for one, was a modestly active communist during the Third
Reich), but his philosophical and political convictions made him a
restless critic of the status quo at the institute and in Germany. The
results ranged from the "snub" the Jungian Wolfgang Kranefeldt remembers receiving from Rittmeister to Rittmeister's successful but ultimately tragic search for comrades within the secret salons of opposition in Nazi Berlin.

Rittmeister has become a celebrated figure among psychotherapists
in both East and West Germany—in the East for his socialist struggle
against "German fascism" and in the West for adding a needed luster
to the presence and activities of psychoanalysts at the Göring Institute.[66] He does indeed stand out in word and deed from his colleagues
at the Göring Institute, but he was not completely divorced from
those traditions that animated those psychotherapists in Germany who
continued their professional campaign after 1933 on the basis of a
shared allegiance to a particular German philosophical, cultural, and

national heritage. His study of Hartmann and Schopenhauer has already been mentioned, and he had also been an admirer of the work of Hattingberg and Schultz-Hencke.[67] He was also happy with his work at the Göring Institute, wishing only to ask Göring to relieve him of his responsibility for the outpatient clinic so that he could devote himself more fully to research.[68] Rittmeister even confessed in his prison diary, on 7 February 1943, that after World War I he was "conservative" and had sought a *"Führer"* in the person of Hattingberg.[69] Before the Nazis came to power, however, Rittmeister had embraced a broader, humanistic vision of mankind united in its common humanity rather than divided by the narrow and parochial concerns of a mind set that Rittmeister's guide, the genius Freud, had labeled "the narcissism of small differences."

The Independents:
Hattingberg and Schultz

Many of the psychotherapists who were members of the General Medical Society for Psychotherapy adhered to none of the three major schools of thought or to any of their offshoots. In integrating perspectives on psychotherapy into their medical philosophy and *Weltanschauung,* they drew from a variety of sources. Hans von Hattingberg and I. H. Schultz were the most distinguished representatives of this unaffiliated position, both before and during the Third Reich. While both held strong philosophical and professional convictions, they were also synthesists by nature. Indeed, the broad "interdisciplinary" nature of their German Romantic bent and the practical demands entailed by the task of developing psychotherapy, as a profession, combined to strengthen the catholic view they took of psychotherapy's potential and promise for the practice of German medicine.

Hans von Hattingberg was born in Vienna in 1879, the son of a jurist who had become the director of the lower Austrian State Mortgage Association. Hattingberg at first studied jurisprudence, but an interest in psychology sparked by August Forel at the University of Berne in Switzerland led him to a degree in that subject there in 1906. In addition to studying under Forel, Hattingberg studied zoology in Naples and brain anatomy with Oskar Vogt. He began his medical studies in 1908, passing the *physikum* at Heidelberg and the state licensing examinations (*Staatsexamen*) in Munich in 1912. He became a Bavarian citizen in 1913 and the same year received his doctorate in medicine with a dissertation on multiple sclerosis and muscle atrophy.

From November 1913 to Easter 1914 Hattingberg worked with Bleuler at the university psychiatric clinic in Zurich. By the fall of 1914 Hattingberg had established himself in practice in Munich as a specialist in psychotherapy (*Facharzt für Psychotherapie*). He later recalled how he had wished to join the philosophical faculty at the university there because the presence of Kraepelin on the medical faculty barred work in psychotherapy. During the war he operated a neurological aid station on the Russian front, later claiming to have studied 1,000 cases of war neurosis there. His treatment of these cases was based on "active" therapy, both of the hypnotic-suggestive and psychocathartic (acting out) varieties. His impoverishment after the war forced him, however, to abandon his plans for obtaining a university position; he, like Heyer, devoted himself to earning a living as a doctor for himself and his family.

Even before the war Hattingberg had been enthusiastically involved in the affairs of the International Psycho-Analytic Association as well as in those of Forel's International Association for Medical Psychology and Psychotherapy. From the beginning he was critical of much of the Freudian system. Like Schultz-Hencke, though without such great orchestration and effect, Hattingberg eventually found it necessary to divorce himself from the psychoanalytic movement. In searching for a comprehensive solution to the debates among the various psychoanalytic schools, he worked successively on the subjects of ethology, suggestion, and then graphology and physiognomy. This last turn brought him to Berlin in 1924 with the intention of founding an institute for applied anthropology. Although he found graphology erratic in its findings—occasionally bringing to light a meaningful cultural or personal characteristic, but also often missing the mark completely—he helped the publisher, graphologist, and physiognomist Niels Kampmann to found the *Zeitschrift für Menschenkunde* in 1925.

The institute did not work out, partly because Hattingberg's temperament was not that of an administrator, and he returned to Munich to turn his full attention to psychotherapy. There he wrote a biological critique of psychoanalysis and a study of the importance of religion in psychotherapy. In 1932 he resettled in Berlin in order to pursue the possibility of providing psychological training to candidates for the German diplomatic corps. This hope, ultimately disappointed, was based on the fact that in 1924 the Foreign Office (Auswärtiges Amt) had employed Hattingberg to instruct its trainees in anthropology. In November 1932, however, he did found a psychotherapeutic clinic at St. Gertrude's Hospital in Berlin and, he later wrote, dedicated himself not only to the practice of psychotherapy but to a resolution of those sectarian differences which, in his view, inhibited its acceptance among members of the medical profession. This motive lay behind his desire to gain a teaching position on the medical faculty of the University of Berlin, a post he acquired in 1933.[70]

Hattingberg's career reflected his character and philosophy: He was a man of enthusiasms, filled, as his obituary in the *Zentralblatt* of 1944 would put it, with a "youthful élan" carried over from his days in the Wandervogel before 1914.[71] As we have noted, he responded enthusiastically to the events of 1933; if he had reservations then, or regrets later, we do not know about them. Hattingberg did not join the party, taking only the prudent step—in terms of his desire for a university teaching position—of joining the National Socialist German University Lecturers League (Nationalsozialistischer Deutscher Dozentenbund).

It is clear that Hattingberg shared the "unpolitical" orientation so common at the time among German academicians and professionals. In a lecture at the Academy for Politics (Hochschule für Politik) in Berlin on 13 February 1931, he had confessed with a touch of Romantic pride that he knew little of politics save that it was the duty of psychotherapists to make people its "objects."[72] Hattingberg was quite willing, out of both nationalism and professional opportunism, to place psychotherapy in service to the state. He put this lucidly in 1936 when, in comparing the "individualistic" liberal ethos of psychoanalysis to psychotherapy as it was then regarded in Germany, he claimed that "[t]oday state morality is more important to us than sexual morality."[73] By contrast, Wladimir Eliasberg, who left Germany in 1933, soon warned from Vienna that a profession had a responsibility to impose its standards on state policy, and not vice versa.[74]

What concerned Hattingberg most was the mission to unify the various trends of psychotherapeutic thought, especially to resolve those sectarian tendencies ("private religions") that he saw manifested in the psychoanalytic movement.[75] It was this preoccupation that provided a significant degree of continuity to Hattingberg's thoughts and actions before, during, and after 1933. In proselytizing for psychotherapy in front of medical audiences that were often skeptical, if not openly hostile, he always articulated his belief that unity would be necessary among the often warring psychotherapeutic schools if the widespread use of therapy among doctors was to be effected. For Hattingberg, unity did not mean the triumph of one particular psychotherapeutic or psychoanalytic mode over the others, for that was a prospect that his own failed attempts at theoretical synthesis had already told him was unrealizable. Rather, what he aspired to, and what he believed would be most appealing to doctors in general, was a practice based on an eclectic appreciation and exercise of various therapeutic methods. It was precisely this theme that had run through Hattingberg's early writings on behalf of psychoanalysis, namely, that it deserved the attention of the medical profession as one valuable approach among others.[76]

On 11 January 1933, nineteen days before Hitler became Chancellor of Germany, Hattingberg addressed the Berlin Medical Society on Freud, Adler, and Jung. He began by praising the psychoanalytic movement's brave and fruitful *analysis* of the unconscious human dynamics that had been ignored by rationalistic "school medicine." This was Freud's fundamental contribution, said Hattingberg. Adler, for his part, had contributed a laudatory emphasis on "therapeutic activity." But it was Jung, Hattingberg declared, who had performed the great breakthrough by moving away from seeing mental conflict purely in medical terms and thus gaining an appreciation of the fundamentally religious nature of humanity and its strivings. Jung's failings, according to Hattingberg, included a tendency to ignore therapy in favor of constructing typologies, as well as a tendency toward sectarianism that was aggravated by the great pioneer's religious musings. Indeed, it was Hattingberg's opinion, in January 1933, that the analytic movement had come to a standstill precisely because of an emphasis upon the theoretical, and because of the consequent academic battles over concepts and narrow scientific dogmas.[77]

Like so many of his professional colleagues, Hattingberg's Romantic emphasis on the "religious" depths of the human psyche and his conservative nationalist perspective were stimulated by the advent of National Socialism. Although his early essay "Neue Richtung, Neue Bindung," which appeared in the *Zentralblatt* and in Göring's *Deutsche Seelenheilkunde* in 1934, was a relatively restrained restatement of his remarks to the Berlin Medical Society in January 1933, as time went on Hattingberg became more radical in expressing a philosophy heavily influenced by the Romantic tradition in German psychology. This was, perhaps, a natural outcome of the freedom that he felt after 1933 to turn from criticizing the leaders of what he saw as an increasingly divided psychoanalytic movement to developing his own theory and practice.

As we have already seen, Schultz-Hencke saw 1933 as just such a professional watershed in his own career, and most of the psychotherapists who pursued their careers in Nazi Germany perceived the advent of the new regime in parallel ways. Hattingberg did remain an eclectic, however, another tendency that was manifested by the Nazi-era psychotherapists as a group in their determination to prove the worth of psychotherapy. In line with the trend that was already evident among a number of leading psychoanalysts during the 1920s, and in keeping with the general orientation with which most physicians regarded the cure of disorders, whether physical or mental, the result was a strong emphasis on active, short-term therapy in as many realms of human activity as possible. Hattingberg himself, as we shall see, was to become heavily involved in the application of psychotherapy to marriage counseling, an interest that was particularly appropriate for a man who had been married three times.

In his enthusiasm over the development of psychotherapy under the new regime in Germany, Hattingberg chose to ignore the irrational and violent features of Nazi ideology that should have been anathema to his celebration of man's higher powers, or "spirit" (*Geist*). In his

1933 address, he had set his notion of spirit against what he saw as a
new and disturbing trend toward the elevation of instinct, the irrational, and the "blood."[78] Yet his own future statements, and the subsequent evolution of his thought, employed a rhetoric about will and
spirit that ill served his ostensible championing of the rational.

The other major independent among the German psychotherapists
under the Third Reich was Johannes Heinrich Schultz. Schultz has
rightly been called "the Nestor of German psychotherapy."[79] His interests and capabilities ranged widely, and he was unsurpassed in his
energy and ability to present psychotherapy's case and to represent its
interests. While Hattingberg remained an enthusiastic and capable
eclectic, Schultz emerged from his independent position as nothing
less than an ecumenicist, as we will see in Chapter 5.

Schultz was born in Göttingen in 1884 and received his medical license in 1908. He subsequently studied with the psychiatrist Otto
Binswanger at Jena in 1913. Binswanger was one of the few German
psychiatrists to have taken seriously the study of hysteria.[80] By 1914
Schultz had become a specialist in psychology, an indication of his
early commitment to medical treatment of the mind. After serving as
a medical officer in World War I, he became a professor of neuropathology at Jena in 1919. He also worked with Hans Prinzhorn at
Heinrich Lahmann's natural health sanitarium in Dresden. In 1924 he
moved to Berlin and established there a practice in neuropathology.
Most significantly, after World War I Schultz had emerged as an en-
ergetic propagandist for all modes of psychotherapy, and especially
for those based on hypnosis and suggestion.[81] Beginning in 1924, he
also became involved in the continuing education program of the Berlin Medical Society, apparently regarding it as an effective means of
introducing doctors to the use of psychotherapy in medical practice.[82]
As we have noted, he also rose swiftly in the ranks of the General
Medical Society for Psychotherapy.

Schultz's response to National Socialism was typically measured. He
joined no party organization save for the innocuous Nazi Motor Corps
(see Chapter 5), and continued on as he had before, practicing and
proselytizing for psychotherapy. Yet he was not without conservative
nationalistic cultural convictions that could be excited by the Nazi
mobilization of Germany. In his professional concern with the psychological problems of individuals living in an industrial society, he
tended to wax enthusiastic, in the spirit of National Socialist spokesmen, for the virtues of the natural life of strength and virtue that were
waiting out on the landscape of the fatherland. For Schultz, though,
the issue was not the Romantic business of converting an urban society
into a rural one, but the practical one of mobilizing medical resources

Georg Thieme Verlag

Johannes Heinrich Schultz (1884–1970)

to soothe and strengthen the mental resources of the population. It was as both a physician and a patriot that he wrote of the necessity for cooperation between educators and psychotherapists in strengthening the German youth during the "nervous time" spawned by modern civilization.[83]

Schultz's major distinction was to have displayed throughout his career a balance with respect to his profession that was composed of rationalism and ecumenicism. Like Hattingberg and other German psychotherapists, he had a weakness for Jung, whose religious emphasis seemed to offer a new and comprehensive view of the workings of the human soul.[84] Schultz, too, placed an importance on spiritual guidance (*Seelenführung*) and human religiosity, but he did so without abandoning scientific method. He condemned those Romantically inclined psychotherapists and philosophers who sometimes discarded scientific method as narrow-minded materialism.[85]

Schultz never slipped into the relatively empty philosophizing that characterized some of his colleagues. During the Third Reich, he was first and foremost a proselytizer for psychotherapy and a devoted practitioner of it. As deputy director of the Göring Institute, as original organizer of the institute's outpatient clinic and as the guardian of its continuing medical education department, Schultz remained at the forefront of those German psychotherapists who continued to emphasize the importance of inexpensive, short-term therapy, which he specified could legitimately include advice (*Beratung*), discussion (*Aussprache*), instruction (*Belehrung*), enlightenment (*Aufklärung*), encouragement (*Ermutigung*), reassurance (*Beruhigung*), hardening (*Abhärtung*), exercise (*Übung*), and prohibition (*Verbot*). These, he advised, were all methods of general psychotherapeutic guidance that could be used as rational, conscious therapy by any doctor without intensive psychotherapeutic training. Also included were the more sophisticated suggestive procedures like hypnosis, Schultz's own method of autogenic training (self-hypnosis), and psychocatharsis.[86]

Schultz's interests were in close harmony with the demands of both a society and a profession that had to be ever more concerned with human productivity. During World War II, Fritz Mohr, attached to the Düsseldorf affiliate of the Göring Institute, offered an example of the use of the power of suggestion in the case of a German mother who had lost the ability to lactate after witnessing the death of a number of children in an English bombing raid. Mohr told her to think of secreting on the basis of the unity of body and mind, and thereafter, despite day and night bombing, she was able to function normally. He concluded:

> This case certainly does not reveal anything that is at all new for us psychotherapists, but it does illustrate how a relatively simple mode of psychotherapy that is accessible to every doctor can perform worthwhile *völkisch* work.[87]

Mohr's example was also in full consonance with the Nazis' insistence on breastfeeding, a process whose biological function was linked in the Nazi mind with a crucial psychological dimension, as demonstrated by the slogan *"Stillfähigkeit ist Stillwille"* ("The ability to nurse is the will to nurse.")[88]

For Schultz, the assumption of psychoanalysis that the depths of every neurosis had to be exhaustively plumbed preempted a genuine grasping of the patient's whole personality within the shared value system of the *Volksgemeinschaft*. Analysis was not only too expensive and too long-term to be an effective tool on a popular basis; it was also prejudicial, Schultz believed, to a healing synthesis. The didactic aim of Freudian psychoanalysis favored knowledge over healing, he observed, and *"Neue deutsche Seelenheilkunde,* on whose construction our institute now labors, has broken radically with this bias."[89]

Schultz, like many other psychotherapists at the institute, believed that it should be dedicated to the healing function of medical psychology. In this task, an intuitive understanding of human nature (*Menschenkenntnis*) was also important. The distinction these psychotherapists made between *grosse* and *kleine* psychotherapy, therefore, was accompanied by a discussion of the required balance between training and the proper selection of psychotherapists from among medical and nonmedical candidates who displayed a knack for understanding and resolving psychological problems. Too great an emphasis on the intuitive was dangerous, however, since this invited psychiatric criticism of psychotherapy as unscientific and unsystematic. The psychotherapists were indeed vulnerable on this score, in part because of their association with Nazi medical apologists who substituted claims for an innate empathy and *Gemeinschaftsgefühl* in place of any formal training in psychology or psychotherapy. Schultz himself constantly reminded psychotherapists not to slide off too easily into the realms of empathy while abandoning science. The admonition helped psychotherapists to strike an advantageous balance between the two—a balance which, for example, allowed them to stress a practical point: that doctors could be taught psychotherapy without specializing in psychiatry, and that their innate human empathy would complete the process.[90] Both the viability of instruction and the ideal of *Menschenkenntnis,* therefore, constituted important parts of the profession's response to the preferred ideal of *Volksgesundheit.* While at the same time trying to evolve a consistent vocabulary and theory, psychotherapy strove to retain its *völkisch* attributes both in terms of social and national service and the human rapport between therapist and patient.

Schultz claimed that 50 percent of all neuroses could be handled through the application of various methods of *kleine* psychotherapy, sometimes in groups.[91] He evolved a schema, eventually adopted by the Göring Institute, that outlined four types of neurosis and the requisite therapy for each: exogenous alien neuroses (*exogene Fremdneurosen*), which resulted from a hostile environment and therefore required only advice and the improvement of external conditions; physiogenic border neuroses (*physiogene Randneurosen*), which were the product of "bad habits" suggested by the patient's life context, and which could be eliminated through *kleine* psychotherapy, i.e., concerned consultation with a therapist and perhaps a change in environment; psychogenic layer neuroses (*psychogene Schichtneurosen*), which were disturbances at one or more levels of the patient's instinctual or affective life, composed around half of all neuroses, and had to be dealt with through the use of *kleine* and/or *grosse* psychotherapy; and characterogenic core neuroses (*charakterogene Kernneurosen*), which demanded depth treatment of the whole of the patient's character.[92]

A clever opportunist whose patriotism and ambition for his profession made it natural for him to give lip service to the regime, Schultz

was distinguished among the psychotherapists at the Göring Institute
by the sheer breadth of his knowledge. This synthesis of opportunism,
patriotism, and professional advocacy is demonstrated by the following
quotation from 1942:

> A person's first six years, which usually lie beyond his conscious recall,
> are of decisive importance for his character development, a further con-
> tribution to the axiom which has been militantly assured today in Ger-
> many for the first time: that the family is the irreplaceable nucleus of the
> organic *Volk*.[93]

The *Völkisch* Observers:
Achelis, Bilz, Cimbal, and Haeberlin

Some psychotherapists were even more enthusiastic about National
Socialism. Their greater philosophical receptiveness to the Third Reich
was by and large accompanied by an intellectual aloofness from any of
the major schools of psychotherapeutic thought, and what they contributed during the Third Reich was, generally, rhetorical observation
rather than professional substance. This does not mean that their general theories and values were necessarily at variance with those of their
colleagues who were aligned with the various schools. Indeed, as we
have seen, there were a number of significant common philosophical
threads running through the German psychotherapeutic tradition that
would provide a basis for intellectual fraternization with the Nazis.

The mistake some psychotherapists made by virtue of their sometimes naïve conservative nationalism was to believe without reservation that the Third Reich constituted the healthy environment of a
"natural" community. The four psychotherapists we discuss in this
section fall into this category. Werner Achelis, for one, was in fact a
philosopher by university degree, who, although close to the Jungians,
drew his inspiration for psychology from comparatively marginal German thinkers such as Hans Blüher. The second of this group was Rudolf Bilz, a neuropathologist who busied himself with research into
neurophysiology, ethology, anthropology, and mythology. Walter Cimbal was also a specialist in neuropathology, with particular interests in
childhood neuroses and public mental health care. Carl Haeberlin, the
fourth, was a physician at a sanitarium in Bad Nauheim.

There are a number of reasons that account for their relatively minor impact, individually and professionally, on the field of psychotherapy during the Nazi era. First, as a group, they were not the intellectual peers of such theorist/practitioners as Schultz-Hencke or Schultz,
who had also been more or less closely affiliated with one or more of
the leading schools of thought in medical psychology. Also, they were
unable to draw either conceptual or practical strength from the work
of Freud, Adler, or Jung; for the most part, they remained mired

either in fuzzy Romantic philosophical notions (Achelis) or bogged down in the kind of organizational pedestrian concerns that appealed to the Nazis (Cimbal). Their own doubts about Freud and Adler were reinforced by the Nazis' virulent actions against psychoanalysis and its practitioners, and thus they were further encouraged to pursue their own course. When they did, they found that National Socialism was hardly fertile ground for the cultivation and growth of ideas. Like so many others who cast their lot with the Nazis and were disappointed or disillusioned by them, they were also discredited after the collapse of the Third Reich.

Werner Achelis is perhaps the best example of this particular breed of German psychotherapist. Born in Berlin in 1897, the son of a university professor, he studied philosophy and psychology at Berlin and Marburg, taking his degree in philosophy. He served as a reserve officer in World War I and during the 1920s concerned himself increasingly with psychotherapy, founding an informal Jungian discussion group in Berlin. He undertook medical studies, and was licensed as a general practitioner in 1939, completing his medical dissertation at the University of Berlin in 1940. Achelis joined the NSDAP in 1933 and was also a member of the National Socialist German Students League (Nationalsozialistischer Deutscher Studentenbund) and the NSV.[94] His primary activity during the Third Reich was to propagate his own neoconservative critique of a materialistic Western civilization, and to celebrate the cultural revolution that he saw sweeping the "new" Germany up into an ultimate "world-historical" role.

Achelis saw the ravages of civilization everywhere. He found no use for the panacea of a "back-to-the-land" campaign, rejecting Rousseau as a philosopher of pessimism and resignation. (In the latter, he echoed Hattingberg.) But he saw an alternative in National Socialism: the acceptance of civilization's strengths (expertise, division of labor, organization) along with an accelerated development of the "natural forces" within the individual. For Achelis, the Nazi heroes of 1933, arrayed against the pernicious doctrines of 1789, represented the new ethic of human existence:

> In the contemporary battle cry of blood and soil, there exists . . . the great inspiration that there is only one way to recovery: back to nature, not in the original sense of Romantic flight from the world, or in the pseudo-realistic sense of an artificial reconstruction of relationships one construes to be natural, but in the sense of back to nature in ourselves![95]

Achelis posited a balance of rational and irrational, to be struck within each individual and within the *Volk* as a whole through the unity of its members on a deep, unconscious level. It was this integral, abiding sense of community that would provide the resources for productive lives, which, in turn, would further the interests of the *Volks-*

gemeinschaft. While the demand for productivity and performance was, for Achelis, the cause of individual isolation, ruthless competition, and physical and mental disability in all modern urban society, the same qualities within the Germanic racial community were celebrated as the result of shared cultural strengths. The rootedness of every person in the community would nourish the nation's productive capacity. Only depth psychology could illuminate such processes, through the expert yet empathic application of its therapeutic theory. And at the highest organizational level of the community, such therapeutic suggestion was manifested as propaganda: "That after which propaganda strives is spiritual guidance. Existing natural impulses must be coordinated and blended."[96] For Achelis, obedience and common interest were not to be achieved by coercion, but by applying shared values, values to be articulated by the government and embodied in a leader, whether family doctor or head of state.

Achelis went beyond this chauvinistic and Romantic fusion of hygiene, psychotherapy, and propaganda to a vision of the decline and fall of Western civilization as the result of the blurring of sex roles. The materialistic bourgeois industrial civilization of the West had been built on the male attributes of initiative and rationality. But now the Promethean fire of Western man's factory furnaces had burned over his roots, and, with the burgeoning development and increasing complexity of the modern world, turned on itself in destroying the patriarchal order which had ignited it. Detached from the feminine-irrational ground of earthly being, men found themselves isolated and dispossessed, and women, most systematically under Marxism, began to usurp traditional male roles. What Achelis thought especially disturbing in such a trend was the softening of the distinction between man and woman (*Vermännlichung der Frau*), and the subsequent destruction of the family. The process had begun, he charged, with the declining authority of the husband, and was being completed by the increasing independence of the woman as an economic cipher under both communism and capitalism, and through the rise of feminism and liberal-socialist doctrine. To return to the old patriarchal order, however, was as undesirable as it was impossible. A new, and family-centered, ethic had to be adopted which would strike a balance between the male-rational and the female-irrational polarities within the species.[97]

Before we continue to describe the individual psychotherapists who gathered under the protection of the Göring Institute, we must briefly survey the Nazi perspective on psychotherapy and its utility within the general vision of the new regime. Achelis's prognosis and prescription were based on the mistaken belief that National Socialism was dedicated to, and capable of, the resurrection of a renewed rhythm of human life in time with that of nature as a whole. Among other things, Nazi pictorial representations of the Aryan family, composed of equal parts of male and female physicality and naturalness, comprised a fiction that belied not only the lack of substantive change under Nazism, but also the Nazis' traditional notions about women and their place in a male-dominated society. Such fictions ultimately left naïve systems and sentiments such as Achelis's in a philosophical and practical limbo, far removed from the genuine advances that had been made in the past by psychotherapists active in the field of medicine.

The concern and rhetoric about health and culture did allow the forging of revealing alliances early on with like-minded activists inside and outside the Nazi party. In general, for the Nazis the state existed as an extension of what they regarded as nature, ensuring the well-being of its inhabitants while at the same time cultivating their potential for its use.[98] Psychotherapy would contribute to this cultivation of a healthy spirit (Gesinnung), a term dear to the Nazi heart and for this reason singled out for attention by Achelis at the psychotherapeutic congress at Breslau in 1935.[99] This contribution to the psychological health of the race would be a vital complement to the fashioning of strong bodies within the Hitler Youth (Hitlerjugend), the Reich Labor Service (Reichsarbeitdienst), the SA, and other party and government agencies.[100]

The Nazis regarded the regeneration of the health services—for the purpose of strengthening the whole of the German people—as an absolutely necessary priority. The urgency stemmed from the xenophobic and Social Darwinian nature of the Nazi Weltanschauung. In the words of Reich Physicans Leader (Reichsärzteführer) Gerhard Wagner, "[o]nly a people that is physically, spiritually, and mentally healthy and able to defend its right to existence with all available means will achieve a worthy and respected place in the world."[101] Within this context, the Nazis bestowed on the profession of psychotherapy—or, as it was Germanically renamed in the first years of Nazi rule, neue deutsche Seelenheilkunde—the respectability that the German medical establishment had denied it: The new regime regarded it as not only a broad cultural health medium, but an important medical science. The psychotherapist in this völkisch view of things was not to be simply an analyst but an active agent of the community, performing the vital function of leadership.

The partnership between doctor and patient was to involve the joyful exercise of authority by the former and the willingness toward subordination—what Prinzhorn had called ἔρος παιδαγωγὸς ("pedagogical love")—on the part of the latter. The Nazis placed the emphasis not on the doctor-patient partnership but on the ideal of the service of both to the racial community: "Despite the importance of analysis, spiritual guidance and the active cooperation of the patient represent the best way to overcome individual mental problems and to subordi-

nate them to the requirements of the *Volk* and the *Gemeinschaft*."[102]
Such *Seelenführung* demanded the psychotherapist's personal involvement in the dysfunction of his patient, his concern for him as a whole
person, and a commitment to bring him into harmony with his community: "The personality is not a goal in and of itself; it is by nature
linked to the community and is dependent in its functioning on its
conformity to the demands of the community: profession, love, comradeship."[103]

This new ethos was intended to constitute an obvious break with
the recent past, in which, according to the Nazis, the German ideals of
community under Weimar dissolved into crass and divisive social conflict: "In the Third Reich these limitations [e.g., materialism] of the
medical profession, 'complexes of a bygone era,' must fall away, for
we see in the hysteria of the German people the biological sickness
of a negative bearing of will under the [Weimar] system."[104] In other
words, the doctor could now concentrate on enhancing the physical
and psychological strengths of a basically and racially sound *Volk*
instead of catering to the nervous afflictions created by an artificial
and degenerate civilization imposed on Germany by enemies both
without and within. Johannes Neumann, a young member of the
Göring Institute from Giessen with a degree in philosophy, summed
up the resultant task for the psychotherapist in Nazi Germany:

> The notion of *Volksgemeinschaft* demands a science which serves life.
> . . . The inevitable duty thus presents itself: the cure of neurosis and the
> cure of the times, to join genuine self-sufficiency with genuine community
> and to bring both into a right and true relationship with each other.[105]

In quite another context, many of the psychotherapists also found
themselves in some sympathy with the nature cure (*Naturheilkunde*)
movement, the noisy and impassioned champions of ecology, sunshine,
fresh air, rural splendor, and natural medication that was newly inspired by such leading Nazi personages as Deputy Führer Rudolf Hess,
Walter Darré, the *völkisch* prophet of agriculture, and Reich Physicians Leader Gerhard Wagner. Its leaders urged a return to the land
that would defy the crass and unhealthful industrialized world and
reinvigorate the German body and the German spirit. The natural
health movement discussed the virtues of whole-meal bread (*Vollkornbrot*) and the dangers of Coca-Cola as important ingredients for a
national and racial commitment to a program of *Volksgesundheit*.[106]
Haeberlin, who was a physician at a sanitarium in Bad Nauheim, applauded the ostensible efforts of National Socialism to "win back the
earth" and to reestablish the natural rhythmic tempo and orchestration of the human body and psyche. For him, the role of the physician
was clear: to take an active interest in the patient as a whole individual and to communicate with him or her on the basis of a shared

community loyalty. The doctor would not only act as a healer but as an example of the healthy comrade in a common battle for the common good. The natural forces within each individual would thrive under, and unite with, the natural environment through the mediation of the *Volksarzt* ("people's doctor").[107]

Two basic assumptions spanned the gap that might otherwise have existed between psychotherapy and the natural health movement. The first was the proposition that the external environment powerfully affected a person all his life. It followed that psychosocial engineering was viable not only on a hereditary basis under the new order—by breeding out congenital mental disorders—but that it could also be used for the proper structuring of the environment and the care of its inhabitants. That structuring incorporated certain values which constituted the second assumption, that a purely rational, "mechanistic" approach to the health of the synergy of body and mind was insufficient in dealing with the natural ebb and flow of physical and psychological functions. Gerhard Wagner, the party's guardian of medicine, continually harped on the importance of appreciating the totality of the individual and the relationships between body and mind.[108] The care of a human being was not to be equated with the regulation of a machine, but was to incorporate a responsiveness to physical and psychological needs in a naturally elastic manner.

The ability to maintain the natural order of things, especially in disrupted circumstances—serving meals and adhering to domestic routine in the midst of severe crisis, for example[109]—was widely celebrated as an asset of the German people. Their proclivity for order under stress was attributed to the strength of a people essentially freed from the unnatural, artificial, and chemically poisoned atmosphere of urban life. Modern industrial civilization, according to this view, had left the masses uprooted and mechanized, the effects of which could be traced in the indices of physical and psychological debilitation. Franz Wirz, a member of Wagner's Expert Advisory Council on Health, criticized the city worker's unhealthful breakfast of tea or coffee and pointed with approval to Hitler's ban on smoking in party offices. For dedicated Nazis, of course, Hitler himself served as the model of abstinence from the pollutions of modern life.[110]

Hitler, however, could not turn back the clock to preindustrial times in Germany; methods to deal with the continued stresses and strains of urban and industrial life would be required to ensure the health and well-being of the populace. The method of autogenic training that I. H. Schultz evolved was intended to relax the blood and the muscles through concentration. Schultz was inspired by yoga, but he made a sharp distinction between it and his own system of self-hypnosis. Yoga, after all, required an exacting posture as a prerequisite to the proper level of concentration, an inappropriate means of relaxa-

tion for the harried, burdened man of Western industrial civilization.[111]

To put it kindly, those psychotherapists who were most attracted to
Nazi health campaigns tended, unlike Schultz, to give themselves over
to less than scientific or professional thought and sentiment. Styles of
course varied. The only prominent psychotherapist to join the NSDAP
before 1933, neuropathologist Rudolf Bilz, produced dense, heavily
documented works on the cloudy interface of biology and psychology.
Bilz, born in 1898 in Thalheim, a village south of Chemnitz, became
a party member in 1930, the year after he became a physician.[112] By
1934 he had settled in Berlin as a specialist in neuropathology. Five
years later he became the editor of the *Zentralblatt;* in 1943 it published a supplement composed of a collection of the lectures he gave
at the Göring Institute during the previous year.
    In these talks of 1942, Bilz condemned what he labeled as the cold
and brutal rationality of the urban civilization the liberal ethos born
by the French Revolution had created. He included in his soupy
critique a vigorous defense of the values of "feeling states" connected
to the biological rhythms of birth and orgasm, and the human qualities of love, tenderness, and reverence, all united in an organic and
emotional tie to the *Volk* and the fatherland.[113] Psychoanalysis, he
instructed, was only one example of an intellectual tradition which
reduced the rich biological, cultural, and religious aspects of humanity
to a single explanation—instead of properly understanding the "wholeness" of human experience from the biological to the metaphysical.[114]
Bilz's approach was in fine tune with the Nazis' elevation of German
culture over the crass materialism of the West—as represented most
troublingly, of course, by the Jew.
    Walter Cimbal, secretary of the German General Medical Society for
Psychotherapy from 1933 to 1935 (see Chapter 4), was a more typical
example than Bilz of the type of fervor, ephemeral expression, and
fuzzy thinking that obtained in the Nazified realms of official health.
In contrast to the younger and less flamboyant Bilz, Cimbal was one
of the early boosters of a psychotherapy that would be welcomed in
the spirit of the new regime. In a 1934 essay that outlined the mission
and means of a Germanic psychotherapy, he envisioned the future in
the rapturous tones of familiar Nazi verbiage. He depicted the German people as bound bravely and healthfully to the land, adopting
the language of the dreamy rural idealists who were caught up in the
new Nazi fervor: "All of us as Germans are basically farmers to a
certain degree. When we administer an office we cultivate it like the
field on which our forefathers lived."[115]
    Cimbal, born in Neisse, a small town south of Breslau, in 1877,[116]

was especially excited about what he perceived as the Nazi commitment to public mental health through the reassertion of traditional and healthful communitarian values. In a movement that prided itself on its "organic" link to the life of the *Volk,* the family occupied a prominent place in Nazi ideology as the basic productive and educational unit. But the family was heavily supplemented and, in both an ethical and practical sense, supplanted by the state.[117] Cimbal addressed himself to the question of how the state should cultivate the family and thus the psychological health of its most vital resource, its children.[118]

Cimbal joined the party in 1933, and passed from the professional scene in 1935 because of enemies within the regime. In comparison with those by Heyer, Schultz-Hencke, Schultz, and others, his essay in *Deutsche Seelenheilkunde* is notable for the intensity of its rhetoric and its shallow exhortative style and content. It concludes with a warm recommendation of *Mein Kampf,*[119] a sentiment that was typical of the style and substance of this group of *völkisch* observers among the psychotherapists—but even that, as we see in the next chapter, did not necessarily protect Cimbal and his ilk from the wrath of opponents in the Nazified medical profession.

This brand of admiration for National Socialism on the part of psychotherapists resulted in a contribution to the renewed and especially virulent outbreak of what Fritz Stern has labeled "vulgar idealism" (*Vulgäridealismus*).[120] While their saccharine prose about the individual's confrontation with his or her own "volcanic" inner life was elaborately communicating the Romantic concern with the depths of the human soul, it also served to mask the paranoia and aggression that were inherent in Nazi ideology and practice.

The anti-Semitism of Göring Institute psychotherapists never reached the intensity of those intellectual apologists for the Nazis who saw Jews as racially inferior, but they were certainly guilty of indulging in racism and anti-Semitism, as we see throughout what is to follow.

Along with Cimbal, Carl Haeberlin was another of the early propagandists for a Germanic psychotherapy who faded quickly from prominence in the professional affairs of psychotherapists during the Third Reich. Haeberlin, born in Frankfurt in 1878, became a licensed physician in 1903 with a degree from the University of Munich, and established himself as a general practitioner in 1906. After serving in World War I, Haeberlin became a doctor at a sanitarium in Bad Nauheim. He apparently had strong conservative nationalistic feelings early on,[121] joined the Nazi party and the Nazi Physicians League in 1933,[122] and became an outspoken supporter of medical reform and psychotherapy in "the new spirit."

For Haeberlin, as for so many others, this new spirit reflected what was actually an old spirit. He once asserted that freedom, equality, and brotherhood, the battle cry of the French Revolution, were only the deceptive phrases of charlatans, and that behind them loomed the guillotine,[123] a hyperbolic metaphor that, horribly, would turn out to be prophetic in the case of one anti-Nazi Göring Institute member. John Rittmeister, the institute's only member to die for resistance activities, *was* beheaded by a guillotine at the SS prison at Plötzensee in Berlin.

Like Haeberlin, whom he inspired, Prinzhorn had seen in 1929 political perils for Germany lurking in the "democratic and socialistic" features of Freud's thought.[124] Prinzhorn had gone on to condemn the "revolutionizing" of Western civilization by what he charged were three deceptively utopian ideals: the social and political utopia of "freedom-equality-brotherhood"; the utopia of scientific positivism; and the utopia that was promised by the "doctrine of class conflict."[125] Haeberlin saw the thought of Prinzhorn and that of the philosopher/ graphologist Ludwig Klages[126] as the foundation on which a Germanic psychology and psychotherapy could be built. He used both to support his contention that the Germanic triad—of life (*Leben*), blood, and people—was superior to the Western ideal of freedom, equality, and brotherhood.[127] Like Prinzhorn, Haeberlin believed that Freud had to be transposed into a heroic German tradition: The concept of instinct must be accepted, but Freud's "analysis, destruction, reduction and devaluation of human deeds,"[128] what Haeberlin saw as a "logo-centric" world view, had to be replaced by a "biocentric" ideal that Haeberlin saw in the thought of Klages.[129]

Haeberlin stayed at his sanitarium in Bad Nauheim all during the Third Reich, never becoming significantly involved in the affairs of the society or the institute. He continued to be vitally interested in a holistic approach to medicine, one that, in appreciating the unity of mind and body, could use the biological "rhythms of life"[130] to maintain, restore, and enhance human health. Haeberlin remained one of those enthusiasts for the cause of National Socialism who gave way to more substantial minds and reputations within the psychotherapeutic community during the Third Reich. He died in 1947.

It should be clear from these summaries that there was a significant degree of philosophical harmony between a wide array of German psychotherapists and the ideals celebrated by National Socialism, a phenomenon that forms an important frame for the motives and reactions of individual psychotherapists in Germany beginning in 1933. It was a harmony that was at least partly responsible for the success psychotherapy enjoyed during the Third Reich, and it is therefore an important ingredient in the continuity the Nazi era afforded to valid and fundamental psychotherapeutic ideas, and the development of psychotherapy as a profession.

The thrust of the rising psychodynamic challenge to positivist and physicalist medical psychology and nosological psychiatry gave psychotherapists in Germany, as elsewhere, the weapons they needed for progress: to press even more successfully for the recognition and institutionalization of a more broadly conceived brand of medical psychology. As we will see, among those psychotherapists who stayed on under the Third Reich, the ones who were closely affiliated with the major schools and traditions in the movement had an advantage over those who were hostile to or aloof from them, those ephemeral philosophers (like Achelis) and practitioners (like Cimbal) whose nationalist professional aspirations flared brightly at moments under Hitler. This latter category's impact was ultimately and significantly weaker than that of the psychotherapists like Heyer, Schultz-Hencke, and Seif, among others, who, given varying degrees of sympathy with the Nazis, were all associated with major schools. The eclectic and ecumenical independents like Hattingberg and Schultz, however vitiated they were by individual insufficiencies or quirks of interpretation, and by the depredations occasioned by the Nazis, could also draw theoretical and practical strength from the giants in the field.

As much as groups tend to fracture and divide—and there was considerable evidence that this was happening in the General Medical Society for Psychotherapy before 1933—so do they adhere to certain bases for cooperation, and even for the resolution of differences. Such positive group tendencies among the psychotherapists who remained in Germany were strengthened with the advent of the Nazis, and the threat *and* opportunity they brought with them. The new regime kindled among them the desire to play down differences for the sake of mutual protection, a response that was reinforced by the pariah status suddenly accorded to a psychoanalytic tradition which had traditionally inspired significant criticism among psychotherapists within the General Medical Society for Psychotherapy. These factors played on a general desire for unity in place of the contention that often had prevailed. After all, the very catholic General Medical Society for Psychotherapy had been originally established to introduce effectively and propagate the practice of psychotherapy among physicians. Indeed, even in the year before the society had been formed, Schultz was already making an ardent plea for unity among the competing schools as a phenomenon that would be in the common interest of the aspiring young profession as well as its patients.[131]

The empty slogans of National Socialism and its ignorant, frenzied activities could not fulfill the conservative nationalist aspirations professed by so many of the psychotherapists who lived under it. Nor could the Nazis offer the psychotherapists a victory in the battle they had mounted against their enemies in the medical establishment. But the regime could provide a vehicle that would make it possible to preserve the young profession as well as to maintain its challenge through the Nazi years, and actually propel the Göring Institute psychotherapists in strengthened form into the postwar era. In the next chapter we examine why the psychotherapists were in need of protection, and measure the price they paid for it.

CHAPTER 4

Peril
and Opportunity

Save for the cold flicker of *neue deutsche Seelenheilkunde*, the history of ideas per se in German psychotherapy was suspended in 1933. But between 1933 and 1936, the psychotherapists who remained in Germany managed not only to preserve the General Medical Society for Psychotherapy but to enhance its professional and public standing. Its 1936 amalgamation into the Göring Institute gave the profession even greater status. Yet even with the crucial advantage gained by naming Matthias Heinrich Göring president of the loyally renamed German General Medical Society for Psychotherapy, this was no mean feat.

The Persecution of Psychoanalysts

During the Nazi years, the National Socialist elevation of the "German spirit" seemed to pose a mortal threat to all of psychotherapy. Radical Nazi ideologues storming about within the new Reich tended to associate any form of psychotherapy with psychoanalysis, the despised "Jewish science," and rejected almost all psychology out of hand. The Berlin Psychoanalytic Institute reported not only attacks that were newly enhanced with national and racial vitriol from psychiatrists at the Friedrich Wilhelm University's Charité Hospital but also from Alfred Rosenberg's Battle Group for German Culture (Kampfbund für deutsche Kultur). The most vehement and pathological attacks were the turgid outpourings of the notorious "Jewbaiter of Nuremberg," Julius Streicher, Gauleiter for Franconia. Along with issuing the pornographic *Der Stürmer*, Streicher, in collaboration with Heinrich Will, published *Deutsche Volksgesundheit aus Blut und Boden*. This paper undertook to explain the concept of Nazi natural and racial health policy. The first issue introduced a continuing feature, entitled "The Role of the Jew in Medicine," with an hysterical outburst against psychoanalysis, describing it as a Jewish "poisoning of the soul" (*Seelenvergiftung*) whose aim was to *remove the last ethical support* from the patient's soul in its battle over control of its instinctual life, and cast it down before the Asiatic world view, "Eat, drink and be merry, for tomorrow you die!" And that was Freud's *aim,* or perhaps his *assignment,* for he lined up dutifully with other Jewish endeavors *to strike the Nordic race at its most sensitive spot, its sex life.*[1]

Psychoanalysis was an especially suitable target for Streicher, for it allowed him not only to vent his bloody racist spleen against a prominent Jewish intellectual, but also, as he did with *Der Stürmer,* to exploit the subject of sex. The cartoon by Fips that accompanied the article features a typically caricatured Jew as a psychoanalyst, and a blonde Aryan female patient complaining of headaches. Free associations include the word "knife," whereupon the analyst springs to the couch with his personal solution for the sexual frustrations arising from her marriage.

Although all the criticism was not so extreme, psychoanalysis was commonly labeled a "foreign body within the German nation,"[2] and it attracted the critical attention of the highest levels of Nazi officialdom. The Reich Chamber for Literature, which, under the direction of Propaganda Minister Joseph Goebbels, regulated literary production in the Third Reich, prepared lists of subjects deemed injurious to the *Volksgemeinschaft,* and these included birth control, family planning, and psychoanalysis.[3] Freud himself remained a favorite object of scorn, vilified as a major representative of Jewish nihilism and entrepreneurship, and accused of perverting the work of the Aryan German creators of "depth psychology"—Novalis, Carus, Schopenhauer, Goethe, and Nietzsche—by turning it into a business enterprise which thrived on a clientele of rich hysterics. Like Marx, Shaw, and Darwin, Freud was portrayed as part of the modern trend toward destroying the anthropological and historical reality of heroic, soldierly man. In this view, psychoanalysis belonged to the overrationalized corruptions of late capitalism, and its obsession with sexual drives that plagued primitive peoples, such as Jews, made it a proper therapeutic method only in rare cases under strict psychiatric supervision. This particular critical concatenation from 1938 also singled out Schultz-Hencke and Groddeck as especially distressing examples of "psychological gangsterism."[4]

There was little psychoanalysts could do to counter such attacks save to try and keep a low profile. The many who were Jewish were of course effectively denied the right to speak as prelude to the denial of their right to exist as German citizens, their right to exist as psychoanalysts, and, ultimately, their right to exist at all. A couple of psychoanalysts attempted to illustrate the compatibility of psychoanalytic thought with the ideals of the new regime. Schultz-Hencke, as we have seen, was one. The other, Carl Müller-Braunschweig, likewise in 1933

"Oh, doctor, I'm having such terrible headaches."

"So, please lie down on the couch and say whatever comes into your mind."

"Roast . . . medicinal waters . . . blotter . . . handkerchief . . . knife . . ."

"Stop! Knife! That's it! The thought 'knife' manifests your sexual desires. Your headaches thus arise from the fact that you find no sexual gratification in your marriage. Hence it follows automatically how you can be cured . . ."

A Nazi view of "Jewish" psychoanalysis

published a defense of psychoanalysis, describing it as a technique which in the proper hands transformed weaklings and asocials into heroic and productive members of society. In so doing, however, Müller-Braunschweig indirectly but clearly condemned his Jewish colleagues in terms not dissimilar from those employed by the Nazis themselves.[5]

Three days before Hitler became Chancellor, Max Eitingon, founder and director of the Berlin Psychoanalytic Institute, had visited Freud in Vienna and expressed his concern over the course of events in Germany. Freud advised him to hold out as long as possible, but the political success of the Nazis soon proved that the future of the institute was in grave doubt. By April, a decree had been issued that prohibited the membership of foreigners in the executive of any medical society. Jews were defined as foreigners. By the end of May, Freud's works were being burned in the quadrangles of German universities. By November, the institute's executive consisted of only two members, both "Aryan," Carl Müller-Braunschweig and Felix Boehm. The number of psychoanalysts at the institute had dropped from around 65 to between 12 and 15, the number of candidates from 34 in 1932 to 18 in 1934, and the number of students had fallen from 222 in 1931 to 138 in 1932 and to 34 by 1934.[6]

In a letter to Boehm of 21 November, Eitingon resigned from the DPG and left Germany forever on the last day of 1933. A two-year-long hiatus then ensued, during which time the institute was allowed to function, more or less, without direct interference from the new government. Although a distinct pall hung over its activities, the educational work of the institute went on almost as before. By the end of 1935, however, the repercussions from the proclamation of the Nuremberg Race Laws on 15 September reached the DPG, and an effort to save the society from dissolution was undertaken through the voluntary resignation of its few remaining Jewish members on 1 December. In March 1936 the SD seized the stocks of books at the central warehouse of the Vienna-based International Psychoanalytic Press in Leipzig;[7] the regime's warning of the previous month that no psychoanalytic society would be licensed in the "new" Germany had become all too real. It was after having failed to persuade the C. G. Jung Society under Eva Moritz in Berlin to a union[8] that the DPG decided to accept the invitation of Matthias Heinrich Göring to join with other groups of psychotherapists in a common institute. Göring had made assurances at a July meeting in Basel, Switzerland, with Ernest Jones and A. A. Brill concerning the degree of freedom the psychoanalysts would be able to exercise under such an arrangement.

The Reich Physicians Decree (Reichsärzteordnung) of 13 September 1935, effective as of 1 April 1936, had already declared the medical profession as a whole to be engaged in national service of the highest order; under this decree, the Ministry of the Interior could reject the membership of anyone in the Reich Physicians Chamber on the basis of "national unreliability." The membership was a prerequisite to practice; only those of German blood could now hold administrative positions.[9] The final assaults against medical practice by Jews were launched during 1937 and 1938. Heinrich Lammers, head of the Chancellery, reported how on 14 June 1937 Hitler explained to Bormann the importance of moving against Jewish doctors: "The Führer regards the cleansing of the medical profession as far more important than, for example, of the bureaucracy, since in his opinion the duty of the physician is or should be one of racial leadership [volkführende]."[10]

A subsequent decree sent down from Berchtesgaden on 25 July 1938 elaborated on the Nuremberg Laws: The state medical licensing of Jews would end on 30 September of that year, and Jews would be barred from state medical examinations after 31 December. In response to this Nazi legislation, the German General Medical Society for Psychotherapy promptly banned Jews from membership and a year later the Göring Institute prohibited the training and, save in emergency, treatment of Jews.[11]

In any case, of course, the number of Jewish doctors had been declining steadily.[12] Most of the Jewish psychoanalysts escaped abroad, although fifteen of them, including Karl Landauer, died in concentration camps. Remarkably, Landauer and some others managed to provide psychotherapy inside Bergen-Belsen.[13] By 1939 a Reich Association of Jews in Germany (Reichsvereinigung der Juden in Deutschland) had been founded in Berlin under the direction of Leo Baeck for the care and schooling of Jews. All Jews who had been institutionalized for mental illness were weeded out and required to be lodged at the Berndorf-Sayn sanitarium in Coblenz and then, after that facility was taken over in 1942 by the SS-Lebensborn, at the Jewish Hospital in Berlin, which was under the authority of Baeck's organization. At the Jewish Hospital, according to director of neuropsychiatry Herman Pineas, "selections" were regularly made among these patients by the Nazis for transport to the extermination camps in Poland.[14]

The Anschluss of Austria in March 1938 spelled the end of the Vienna Psychoanalytic Institute. Göring, at the suggestion of the Freudians in the Göring Institute, sent Müller-Braunschweig to Vienna in the hope of incorporating the institute and the publishing house there into his own institute in Berlin. Max Schur, Freud's personal physician, has recalled that the psychoanalysts in Vienna learned (accurately, through Müller-Braunschweig) that there was sharp division among the Nazi leaders as to their fate. The more radical faction around Goebbels and Himmler wanted to "throw the whole group in prison. Göring, under the influence of his psychiatrist cousin, was in

favor of moderation."[15] The moderate view, with the support of a
German Foreign Office that was concerned about the international
protest that would ensue should anything happen to Freud, won out,
but M. H. Göring's own plans for the Vienna institute fell through.

One of the reasons for this was that a letter from Müller-Braunschweig to Anna Freud was intercepted by the Gestapo. In the letter
Müller-Braunschweig had contradicted Göring by expressing the hope
that the institute in Vienna could maintain its own separate existence,
not only in order to ward off National Socialist influence but also to
avoid the consequences of the longstanding rivalry between the analysts in Berlin and Vienna. When Göring was informed of the letter,
he pronounced it a betrayal of his intention to preserve the Vienna
institute from destruction through affiliating it with his Berlin institute. Both Müller-Braunschweig and Anna Freud were interrogated by
the Gestapo, and Göring consequently denied Müller-Braunschweig
the right to teach or to publish. According to Ernst Göring, however,
his father, as director of an officially recognized institution in Germany, managed to persuade the Gestapo to allow Müller-Braunschweig to keep his psychoanalytic practice, including a training
analysis for Ernst himself. Göring also prohibited Boehm, the only
other remaining member of the Berlin Psychoanalytic Institute's executive, from providing training analyses, although he also was permitted to retain his private practice.

In Austria Anton Sauerwald, a surgeon and member of Reich Physicians Leader Wagner's staff, was assigned by the Nazis to supervise
the liquidation of the Vienna institute, press, and clinic. At a meeting
of the directorship of the Vienna institute on 20 March 1938, attended
by Sauerwald, Jones, Anna Freud, Paul Federn, Müller-Braunschweig,
and others, it was decided that the institute would become part of the
DPG with the simultaneous exclusion of all "non-Aryan" members.
After the exclusion and the resignation of some non-Jewish members
in protest, of the thirty-six analysts in Vienna, only two, Wilhelm
Sölms and August Aichhorn, remained. Sauerwald, although a dedicated anti-Semite, had studied chemistry at the University of Vienna
under Professor Herzig, a lifelong Jewish friend of Freud's, and
claimed to hold great respect for the founder of psychoanalysis. It is
reported that Sauerwald consequently concealed the fact of Freud's
foreign bank account until Freud had left Austria and thus was able
to refuse Nazi demands that the money be handed over to them.[16]

August Beranek, since 1935 the technical director of the Vienna
institute's pubishing house, presided over the actual destruction of the
instiute, joined the NSDAP, and moved to Berlin as a bookseller. The
Austrian psychoanalytic society was officially dissolved on 25 August
1938, leaving behind only a Vienna study group (*Arbeitsgemeinschaft*)
that was connected with the Göring Institute. Göring appointed the
psychiatrist and neurologist Heinrich von Kogerer as its leader,

announcing that the "stronghold of Jewish psychotherapy . . . has fallen."[17]

In November 1938 the DPG itself lost its status as a registered association, becoming the Göring Institute's "Arbeitsgruppe A," although its private meetings were allowed to continue. Freud's works, which up until that time could still be purchased publicly even if they were not to be openly displayed, were formally banned. The institute's own copies, presumably inherited from the Berlin Psychoanalytic Institute, were kept under lock and key by Göring, an act that at the outset only most charitably could be called protective custody. Furthermore, according to Dietfried Müller-Hegemann, who trained at the institute, there had ensued for two years a staring contest in the foyer between opposing portraits of Sigmund Freud and Adolf Hitler. This jarring image evokes the confrontation between portraits of Beethoven and Hitler that Günter Grass describes in *The Tin Drum:* "Hitler and the genius, face to face and eye to eye. Neither of them was very happy about it."[18] But in 1938 it was finally adjudged that Freud had lost, and he, though unblinking, was taken down.

The Style and Substance of Loyalty

In light of the destruction of psychoanalysis as an independent entity in Germany and Austria, psychotherapists in general, even when they protested their loyalty and pointed to a properly German intellectual tradition, were as a group suspect. The atmosphere was evident in a 1934 review in the party medical journal *Ziel und Weg*. The review focused on the current volume of essays from the *Zentralblatt*, under Göring's editorship, entitled *Deutsche Seelenheilkunde,* a collection that was designed to present a new German psychotherapy in the spirit of National Socialism. It was obvious from the essays contained in this volume, the reviewer commented, that neither protestations of loyalty nor citations from the works of acceptable German authors on the subject of the unconscious could hide the fact that psychotherapy was still to a great extent dependent on the teachings of the Jews Freud and Adler.[19] Subsequently, Hattingberg's *Über die Liebe* (1936) was criticized in *Ziel und Weg* for "perverse" notions of what love should be.[20] Even Cimbal was the object of a condemnatory article that appeared in the Nazified pages of *Der Öffentliche Gesundheitsdienst* in 1936, criticizing him as one who attempted to paper over his preferences for psychoanalysis with quotations from *Mein Kampf*. The author of the review, a psychiatrist by the name of Gerhard Pfotenhauer, saw as particularly disturbing Cimbal's neglect of heredity for an emphasis on environment. According to Pfotenhauer, the emphasis was contrary to the principles of racial biology established by the new regime, and could not be rendered acceptable even through Cimbal's use of such terminology as "prenatal education" and "nordicization."

The very title of Pfotenhauer's piece, " 'Nordicization' and 'prenatal
education'—'Racial Hygiene' of a Psychoanalyst" (" 'Aufnordnung'
und 'vorgeburtliche Erziehung'—'Rassenhygiene' eines Psychoanalytikers"), not only demonstrates the hostile position academic psychiatrists maintained against psychotherapy during the Third Reich but
also reveals a common strategy the psychotherapists adopted in order
to ward off such criticism. They reached beyond their attacks on Freud
to cosmetize their own works. Cimbal himself echoed the common
Nazi criticism of psychoanalysis as a "dismemberment of the soul"
(Zergliederung der Seele) by asserting: "A ground rule for all of these
[psychotherapeutic] situations is that the psychological drilling machine [seelische Bohrmaschine] which had been formulated in the psychoanalytic method must be avoided."[21] We have seen that they were
often aided in this task of cosmetization not only by the affinity in
substance and style between some of their own conservative/nationalis-
tic ideas and ideals and those of the Nazis, but also by the general
rhetorical excess that was cultivated by National Socialism. This alter-
nately crass and silly appropriation, exploitation, inflation, and, ultimately, trivialization of words like Seele and Charakter[22] permitted
the inspired manipulation of the language by psychotherapists who
were hoping to disguise and cover a host of intellectual and spiritual
sins. Cimbal is a particularly good example, as Pfotenhauer discovered; he managed to impose a racial grid over a discussion of child
neurosis in the second edition of Die Neurosen des Kindes- und
Jugendalters (1935) by stressing heredity and the use of psychotherapy
in the "nordicization" of Jews. Pfotenhauer found this last claim especially objectionable from a National Socialist point of view. Cimbal
even expanded the volume—which had first appeared in 1931 and had
included a subtitle addressed to learning difficulties—by adding to its
beginning a separate book, published the year before, which bore an
advantageous title referring to character, race, and education (Charak-
terentwicklung des gesunden und nervösen Kindes, ihre Beeinflussung
durch Rasse und Erziehung). We will recall, however, that he had
indulged in both a rhetorical and substantive excess in this direction
before Hitler came to power—a fact that was displayed, for example, in
the battle imagery in a title of 1931, Neurosen des Lebenskampfes.
Had it appeared in 1933 or after, it would have fit neatly into the
cosmetic mode.

Clearly, the psychotherapists both felt the need and sensed the opportunity to identify their professional interests with the goals and
methods of the Nazi regime. For his part, I. H. Schultz altered the
title of a handbook on psychotherapy designed for medical specialists
and general practitioners, which already had appeared in four editions
between 1919 and 1930, from Die seelische Krankenbehandlung to
Ziele und Wege der seelischen Krankenbehandlung, to include a vari-
ation of the title of the NSDAP's journal for medicine, Ziel und Weg.

Heyer, who, like Cimbal, was one of the relatively few psychotherapists to join the NSDAP, and who could, emotionally as well as strategically, celebrate the advent of National Socialism through the effective use of specific Nazi terms like *Brauchtum* ("custom") and
Betreuung ("care and control"),[23] is an even better example of the
process by which rewriting could accentuate the positive and down-
play the negative.

In 1930 Heyer had written in an article in the *Münchener medizinische Wochenschrift* that Freud, while decisively influenced by the
individualism of his era, had spearheaded the fight against medicine
without a soul. Two years later, Heyer published the first edition of
what was to become one of his major works, *Der Organismus der
Seele,* and again acknowledged Freud's contribution: "Every confrontation with the venerable master demands a gesture of respect, appreciation, and admiration." The second edition, which appeared in 1937,
displayed quite another stance: "Every confrontation with Sigmund
Freud, each sharp criticism, nonetheless demands the acknowledgment
of his historic contribution." In 1932 Freud was a "master," but by
1937 he had been demoted to "teacher"; the "ingenious pioneer" had
become a "prisoner to his race"; his "sexual democracy" now constituted "psychological Bolshevism." While formerly Heyer had criticized Freud for a tendency to distort (*verzerren*) his intuition by "rational and concrete formulations," he now degraded Freud's intuition
into "comprehension" and underlined the new and negative aspect he
perceived by repeating it: "rationally and concretely indicates, or
rather, distorts" (*"rational und konkretistisch dar- bzw. entstellte"*). He
also simply eliminated a number of references to Freud, Adler, and
other Jewish psychoanalysts and philosophers whose names had appeared in the 1932 edition. Heyer's treatment of Zionism also underwent a marked transformation. From being labeled "romantic-
regressive," Zionism now was relegated to part of a racial critique
which suggested that it could solve the problem of Jewish rootlessness
by establishing a Jewish homeland, a concept which, of course, also reflected the Nazi aim of expelling the Jews from Europe: "The Jew especially suffers from the unconnectedness of his blood—the 'race'—
with the soul of the spiritual world in which he lives. Zionism attempts a solution through the denial and abandonment of the latter,
an experiment whose result is yet to be learned."[24]

Psychiatry versus Psychotherapy:
The Regime's Fickle Needs

Psychotherapists continued to face the traditional opposition they had
always encountered from the psychiatrists and neurologists within the
medical establishment, but now their critics' attacks were dangerously
politicized by their medical claim on National Socialism, a claim that
was based on their racial interpretations of hereditary biology. Even a

staunch anti-Nazi like the psychiatrist Oswald Bumke could exploit the prevailing atmosphere to professional advantage by pointing out the debt of "German psychology" to "Jewish" psychoanalysis.[25] Bumke's observation appeared in the 1938 second edition of a book originally published in 1931, entitled *Psychoanalysis and Her Children (Die Psychoanalyse und ihre Kinder)*; by its very title it effected a dangerous equation for German psychotherapists as "children" of Freud. Bumke's abiding criticism of psychoanalysis and psychotherapy was founded on the old nineteenth-century psychiatric notion of the untouchable psyche, which charged that any attempt "to reduce the psyche to its humble and primitive elements"[26] was, at best, irreverent. This was a view that could be used with great effect in Nazi Germany where Freud was regarded as the quintessential Jewish panderer of a contumelious pansexualism.[27]

Although many psychiatrists were opposed to Nazi aims, or at least to their methods, psychiatry still occupied an important place in the Nazi plans for biological engineering and the exclusion of those who were descended from poor racial stock. The 1933 Nazi promulgation of the Law for the Prevention of Congenitally Diseased New Blood (Gesetz zur Verhütung erbkranken Nachwuchses) was a first step toward euthanasia for all those deemed unfit for inclusion in the *Volksgemeinschaft;* in the words of the party office for such matters, "Those persons are asocial [*gemeinschaftsunfähig*] who on the basis of a hereditarily determined and therefore irremediable mental disposition are not in the position through their personal, social, or national behavior to fulfill the minimum demands of the *Volksgemeinschaft.*"[28]

With its strident emphasis on youth, health, and activity, National Socialism had almost made illness of any sort a crime against the state, and the cause for such transgression in the Nazi scheme of things remained basically racial and biological: Pure blood and healthy sexual relations were to be the guarantors of a master race. In 1937, for example, the *Monatsschrift für Kriminalpsychologie* became the *Monatsschrift für Kriminalbiologie;* heredity and constitution became the biologically tyrannical balance and scale for criminality and law-abiding citizenship.[29] In 1941 the Tobis production of Wolfgang Liebeneiner's *Ich klage an!* appeared. It was a feature film about a doctor's mercy killing of his pianist wife, who is suffering from multiple sclerosis, and was apparently intended as propaganda for the unpopular euthanasia program. Hitler had originally hoped that the German populace would be distracted from their opposition to it by the war, but public outcry compelled him to limit the program severely in September 1941.[30] Official psychiatry, of course, tended to view neuroses as "psychopathic adjustment disturbances," and there was some opinion expressed among psychiatrists that neurotic conditions as well be included under the sterilization law.[31]

There were attempts to bridge the gap between psychiatry and psychotherapy, most of them initiated by the psychotherapists. They were, after all, for the most part physicians themselves, who had received instruction and training in psychiatry, and they were eager to establish themselves as a profession alongside that of psychiatry. The founder of the General Medical Society for Psychotherapy, Robert Sommer, was a psychiatrist, as were Jung and Kretschmer, and Göring had studied with Kraepelin. The Göring Institute itself required courses in psychiatry for all nonmedical candidates and affirmed the traditional division of labor among psychotherapists, psychologists, and psychiatrists. The institute's clinical-diagnostic scheme also stressed the limits of psychotherapy with regard to the treatment of psychoses and various hereditary and organic mental illnesses. Patients in its outpatient clinic were regularly referred to the medical clinic under Friedrich Curtius, or to the neurological and psychiatric clinic under Karl Bonhoeffer, at the Charité, as well as to Ernst Jaensch's University Institute for Constitutional Research (Institut für Konstitutionsforschung der Universität).[32] Perhaps it was this recognition of the limits of psychotherapy, as well as the opportunity effectively to proffer the young profession's allegiance to the regime, accompanied by the ethically and politically laming sense that their aims were being realized by the Nazi regime, that inspired Schultz in 1936 to admire and praise the 1933 sterilization law.[33]

Psychiatrists were not uniformly hostile to the young profession. Ernst Speer, who after World War I had established a psychotherapeutic sanitarium in Germany at Lindau on the Bodensee, was one of the few psychiatrists to be a member of the Göring Institute. In addition, the distinguished psychiatrists Johannes Lange of Breslau and Hans Luxenburger of Munich, as well as Berlin's Bonhoeffer and Curtius, brother of the institute's Otto Curtius, retained an interest and a respect for the work psychotherapists performed. And Otto Pötzl at the psychiatric clinic of the University of Vienna provided facilities for a psychotherapeutic outpatient clinic to the Göring Institute's Austrian branch beginning in 1938. It should also be noted that even such often virulently critical psychiatrist opponents of psychotherapy as Bumke—and even the rabid Nazi Max de Crinis—could act in accord with traditional professional standards. According to Ernst Göring, Bumke helped a group of psychotherapists obtain a lecture hall at the University of Munich after it had suddenly become "unavailable" in 1933. De Crinis supported and worked with his student, the Jungian psychotherapist Wilhelm Bitter and, according to August Vetter, had a collegial relationship with Hattingberg, who on 14 May 1940 was promoted to honorary professor at the Friedrich Wilhelm University in Berlin.

The first two congresses of the German General Medical Society for

Psychotherapy, at Breslau in 1935 and Düsseldorf in 1938, had as their themes the possible areas of fruitful collaboration between psychotherapists and psychiatrists. Both Lange and Sommer gave papers on this subject at Breslau, and three years later Göring declared in his opening address: "We [psychotherapists and psychiatrists] cannot help our *Volk* by fighting, but only by trying to understand and come to friendly terms with one another."[34] Luxenburger gave a paper at the Düsseldorf meeting in which he elaborated on the psychotherapy of neuroses from the standpoint of hereditary biology under his famous dictum, "Heredity is not destiny, only potential destiny."[35] And at the last congress, held by the society in Vienna in 1940, Pötzl spoke on the need for psychiatrists and psychotherapists to cooperate in meeting the country's urgent demand for increased productivity by strengthening both the physiological and psychological elements that compose human will.[36]

It was precisely this emphasis on will and character, and the necessity of maintaining it within the *Volksgemeinschaft*, that provided a potential place for psychotherapy in the official life of the Third Reich. We have already observed how psychotherapy's position as an outsider allowed its proponents to align themselves with Nazi health reformers.

Psychotherapy shared with the proponents of natural health an especial disdain for university psychiatry. Traditional psychiatry stringently separated the individual's biological existence from the mysteries of his or her spiritual life; German psychotherapy exuded the ideal of the unity of body and soul that found God in the individual. Psychotherapy and naturopathy therefore formed somewhat of a natural alliance, based on their mutual conception of the unconscious as both biological and spiritual. In 1934 the new natural health hospital, the Rudolf-Hess-Krankenhaus (May 1941: Gerhard-Wagner-Krankenhaus) in Dresden included plans for a psychotherapeutic section. The division was established under the direction of Alfred Brauchle, who had been a directing physician at Priessnitz Hospital in Berlin-Mahlow, the first natural health hospital in Germany.[37]

The Nazis were also drawn to psychotherapy because it avoided using the distasteful psychiatric diagnosis of hereditary taint within the "master race" (*Herrenvolk*), and offered instead the practical virtues of repair and improvement. At the 1935 psychotherapeutic congress, August Hanse pointedly criticized "official psychiatry with its therapeutic nihilism."[38] And Hattingberg argued before the Kaiser Wilhelm-Gesellschaft in 1943 that in the majority of mental cases, even when viewed from a genetic standpoint, it was not a question of what the Nazis generally termed "life not worthy of being lived" (*lebensunwertes Leben*), or what Justice Minister Franz Gürtner even more ruthlessly called "useless eaters," but of "people who can at least be brought to live normal lives, and sometimes extremely productive lives, once they are freed from their inhibitions."[39] Hattingberg was echoing the assertion by Achelis, among others, that psychotherapy, unlike psychiatry, was not in the business of treating hopeless psychopaths but precisely in treating the healthy, civilized individual[40]—an argument which also distanced psychotherapy from the Nazi charges that psychoanalysts greedily exploited degenerate hysterics and other such undesirables.

There were signs of concern within the psychiatric establishment that its role must be expanded, a belated response to the psychodynamic challenge raised by Freud in 1900. At a 1941 psychiatric congress, Carl Schneider concluded a session on the psychotherapy of psychoses on a note of concern that the political leadership might limit the role of psychiatry to the sterilization and euthanasia of the congenitally diseased. If this were to be the case, once these tasks were completed, psychiatry would become superfluous: "Should not eugenics, racial improvement, and other measures taken by the state be able so to free the *Volk* from the social, moral, and economic burden of the insane that psychiatry will no longer be needed at all?"[41] (Ernst Rüdin, a leading psychiatrist involved in the initial stages of the eugenics program, had warned in 1939 of just such ignorant optimism based on simplistic notions about race and heredity.[42]) Schneider proposed that psychiatrists respond to such a challenge by reaffirming the biological basis of all mental life, and the improbability of the easy and quick solution to the problem of biological engineering. Among other things, Schneider pointed out the continuing influence worked by the environment, even if endogenous and exogenous psychoses should somehow be eliminated. But an assured future awaited psychiatry, he warned, only if it acknowledged the totality of the human organism, addressed itself to psychological disturbances of all kinds, and immersed itself "in the religious, philosophic, and mythic ideas of the whole *Volk*."[43]

This was in line with what another psychiatrist, Johannes Bresler, termed "national psychotherapy." Bresler believed that some psychotherapeutic work was possible with "incurable" psychopaths and on the collective plane postulated the therapeutic value of the "national will" (*Volkswille*) in responding to a "national" psychotherapy.[44] In adopting this position, psychiatrists recognized the importance of the "supply side" of the Nazi demand for racial purity. Even the SS had taken the time and trouble to note that the aid that had, in the past, been given to asocial individuals would, under the new order, go to mother and child in the prophylactic spirit of the therapeutic *Volksgemeinschaft*. It was, according to the SS, the state's duty to foster a healthy sense of "life management" (*Lebensführung*).[45]

This necessity became even more acute during wartime. In October

1944 Martin Bormann, Hitler's secretary, complained in a letter to Reichsführer-SS Heinrich Himmler in the latter's capacity as Minister of the Interior that the ministry's offices of public health (*Gesundheitsämter*) should return to their accustomed duty of "positive" work in promoting the health of the populace, and not be restricted to the "thankless" task of euthanasia and sterilization. To this end, Bormann wrote, the overall control in such matters of the NSV, or National Socialist Welfare Organization (Nationalsozialistische Volkswohlfahrt), should be strengthened in accord with Hitler's decree of 22 August 1944 on the "racial mission" of the NSV, "Die Volksaufgabe der NSV."[46] Once again, as we shall see, psychotherapy would rise to the moment.

Psychotherapy, the Patient, and the State

The status of neurosis as a genuine medical problem—and thus worthy of compensation by medical insurance—is not a unique question for the postwar period and beyond. Pre-Hitler Germany had been engaged in an ongoing debate among doctors, jurists, and insurance administrators over the issue of whether compensation should be provided for neurosis that stemmed from an accident. The debate continued into the Nazi era, and sharpened issues that affected the status of both psychotherapy and psychiatry in the Third Reich.

The Reich Insurance Office (Reichsversicherungsamt) had never recognized neurotic sequelae to an accident (*Unfallneurosen*) as meriting compensation, while the Reich Supreme Court (Reichsgericht) tended to regard neurotic suffering resulting from a trauma, even in the presence of a neurotic predisposition, as a common phenomenon that was worthy of the award of damages. Under National Socialism, the lower courts increasingly regarded neurotic reactions to trauma as a sign of abnormality and deviance, and the plaintiff was often regarded as a slacker of apparently sound body and mind who simply wanted a pension. The attitude displayed the Nazis' steady pressure for productivity in service to the national community. Those physicians who were called on to provide expert testimony in such cases were also usually constrained within the new ethos, with the result that the Supreme Court's more liberal attitude placed it increasingly at variance with the lower courts and with the medical profession on the question of neurotic causation and juridical remedy. This had not been the case when doctors had been more or less united in the opinion that "accident neurosis" was a genuine physical illness.[47]

Psychotherapists, of course, were part of the movement in medical thought and practice which entertained a more comprehensive conception of neurosis. The idea that an individual finds psychological reinforcement in his social environment, and that beyond that he has a responsibility to lend his strengths and talents to the community, was also, as we have seen, an integral part of the pre-Nazi intellectual tradition of German psychotherapists. Under National Socialism this bias elicited some ethically ambiguous features, not only of the German psychotherapy of the time but of the neo-Freudian tradition as a whole.

Although Freud himself remained to the end of his life an old-fashioned liberal who supported authority in public life, moderation in private, and a "formidable rationalist suspicion of enthusiasm,"[48] psychoanalysis carries within itself, as Herbert Marcuse has shown, an ineluctable core of individual resistance to a fundamentally repressive civilization. The neo-Freudian emphasis on progress, conformity, and "adjustive" success "eliminates all the reservations with which Freud hedged the therapeutic objective of adjustment to an inhuman society and thus commits psychoanalysis to this society far more than Freud ever did."[49] By ignoring the instinctual dynamics that form the basis of Freud's theory, the neo-Freudians, Marcuse argues, throw out the critical questioning of the individual's relationship to society in favor of a therapeutic function designed to integrate the neurotic individual into society and to make of him a productive and loving total personality. The resultant emphasis is on the healthy, happy sublimation of Eros in service to the controlled happiness available to the dutiful businessman or administrator, thus, as Paul Roazen has observed in his study of the thought of Erik Erikson, throwing into sharp relief the fact that "one of the attractive features of the earlier psychoanalytic viewpoint was its respect for disability and failure"[50] in contrast to the neo-Freudian concern with distinction and success.

It was a similar respect for the individual that had animated many jurists and physicians in Germany before 1933. But this view was largely eclipsed by the conjunction of the German Romantic tradition in medical psychology with the rule of the National Socialists. Neo-Freudian psychoanalysts in fact retained a faith in reason that facilitated their critique of an oppressive society, and featured a fundamental respect for the individual. These values informed Fromm's 1939 denunciation of Rank's "will therapy." As Fromm put it, "truth as effecting change"[51] and an enthusiasm for the variety and richness of human cultures contrasted sharply with the German Romantic celebration of the irrational, the dynamic, the unique, and the exclusively German. While neo-Freudian psychoanalysts sought progressive rational unity in cultural diversity, these Romantic German psychotherapists participated in a putative display of the German model that paralleled their own push for professional recognition. While classical psychoanalysis probed the individual's lonely struggle against society, the Romantic version of neo-Freudianism stressed the individual's duty to be as one with his community through the artful intercession of the therapist. This outcome would be the predictable result of a therapist's natural alliance with the patient, which would entail rediscovering the patient's psychologically nourishing links to the past, present, and future of his society and his people. Conflict would be resolved in terms of guiding the individual into harmony with his environment.

In the long run, the advertisement of these principles had more to do with the varying degrees of enthusiasm psychotherapists and the Nazi regime displayed for one another than it did with either the actual treatment afforded by the psychotherapists to their patients or with the professionalization of their discipline. Although these were principles that were hardly as deadly as that merciless psychiatric doctrine bent to the purposes of Nazi eugenics which insisted that the unconscious was nothing but a willful evasion of responsibility for one's actions, or an indication of congenital mental illness, such principles said patients were not simply individuals with medical problems, but duty-bound members of a racial community—or racially unfit for treatment.

Both M. H. Göring and Jung asserted that psychoanalysis was a creation of the Jewish mind for the Jewish mind, and that race was a determining factor in any psychotherapeutic situation. For some it followed that a therapeutic alliance could not be formed between an Aryan and a Jew. The only serious attempt to deal with the issue of race and psychotherapy beyond what proved to be primarily sloganeering protestations of allegiance to the new regime, however, was a paper presented to the Austrian section of the International General Medical Society for Psychotherapy on 1 December 1936 by Erwin Stransky. The most unusual thing about it was that Stransky was Jewish, a fact he presented to his audience as assurance that he was meeting the issue squarely. His purpose, he declared, was to deal with the question of race and psychotherapy in a completely objective fashion, and his essay, "Rasse und Psychotherapie," as it appeared in the *Zentralblatt* in 1937, does display a rigorous rationality. But the long and involved formulations and sentences also betray a psychological tension that perhaps supports Wladimir Eliasberg's judgment that Stransky, born a full Jew and then baptized when he was an adult, "became the typical *persecute persecutor.*"[52]

But whatever Stransky's unconscious motives, his paper attempted to deal with the questions of the therapeutic alliance between Aryan and Jew and the "Aryanization" of psychoanalytic theory. He concluded that the documented successes of such racially mixed doctor-patient relationships were due to the "deghettoized" or "ariotropic"[53] nature of the Jewish physician, or to the natural social subordination of the Jewish patient, both of which derived from their experiences in the predominant Aryan racial culture. As for the utility of Freudian and Adlerian doctrine, Stransky cited the work of Jung, Göring, Künkel, and others as proof that in the proper racial hands even Jewish thought could be beneficial to non-Jewish practitioners and patients.

Given the unconditional Nazi stigmatization of Jews, objections to psychotherapy between Jews and non-Jews, if morally damning, remained undeveloped in theory and in practice. (Indeed, among the private patients handled by psychotherapists during this time, there were some Jews.) The major question for psychotherapists in the Third Reich was how to deal with neurosis among their patients. Psychotherapists, of course, rejected the notion of most German psychiatrists that neurosis was a physical illness. In doing so they brought mental illness closer to the Nazi realm of will and responsibility, although they tempered this subordination of the individual to the whole by stressing that mental dysfunction was a result of conflict, not heredity, conscious disobedience, greed, or cowardice. Göring, for example, in an address before the Reich Insurance Office on 2 February 1938, objected that the common policy among insurers not to cover an individual who "knew" he had no physical ailment was based on an insufficient understanding of unconscious mental processes.[54]

Only patients with private insurance funds (*Ersatzkassen*) were covered for psychotherapy and treated regularly in the Göring Institute's outpatient clinic; even so, the limits of insurance coverage impinged on the time and effort a doctor or psychotherapist could devote to the psychological health of a patient. Negotiations between the institute and government insurance officials, moreover, led to no changes in the law.[55] Göring also told the insurance officials that the state could be saved the greater expense of the psychological and physical treatment of adults later on if an appreciation of the dynamic unity of body and mind were exercised through preventive medicine, beginning with the family doctor (*Hausarzt*) and his use of *kleine* psychotherapy on infants and children.[56]

While prevention from an early age would presumably reduce the number of adult neuroses and psychosomatic complaints, the psychotherapists also argued that the psychotherapeutic treatment of individual neurotic complaints would also save financial and human resources—by returning the patient to work, for example, instead of giving him a pension. The issue touches on one of the inherent problems of any social health program, one that had apparently been aggravated in Germany during the Weimar Republic by a government program to aid the sundry casualties of the Great War. One German hygienist declared that the encouragement of productivity under National Socialism would counteract the cultivation of what were called pension neuroses (*Rentenneurosen*) that had grown up under Weimar.[57]

Psychotherapists in the Third Reich claimed that neurosis was an individual experience subject to alleviation and cure. From the Nazi standpoint of productivity, this interpretation was a vast improvement on the financial and therapeutic resignation conveyed by the Supreme Court's standard of "adequate causation in the normal course of events," the term the Court used in recognizing the viability of claims for compensation for accident neuroses. The psychotherapists presented a solution to these troubling issues: The new profession could repair the damage caused by the precipitating or aggravating event by dealing with the individual in the context of his entire life.[58]

In treating work-related neurosis, industrial psychologists of the Göring Institute were naturally disposed to display this emphasis on the ideal of repair: Their position was that work assignments were not to be gratuitously changed or work loads immediately lightened, and pensioning was to be only a last resort. Instead of resorting to such drastic measures, the cause of the difficulty was to be examined through the personal as well as the professional involvement of the psychologists in the individual's problem. According to the psychologists, most accidents were not the result of inadequate workplace safety measures but rather due to an improper inward orientation on the part of the injured worker. Education and testing therefore had to supplement therapy and counseling. This holistic concept of human personality and productivity as employed by German psychotherapists and psychologists, with its emphasis on rehabilitation, not only underlined the responsibility of the individual to the state but also served the aims of industrial management. The Hermann Göring Works were supposed to be particularly advanced in having applied this policy to prevention and rehabilitation.[59]

While the full extent of the perversion of psychotherapy as an active exercise of racial anti-Semitism in medical practice remained unrealized by the Nazis, we have noted that this was not the case with psychiatry. Psychotherapy held out the hope of repair for psychological dysfunction, and, while subordinating the individual to the social order, still offered more flexible, comprehensive, and humane standards of evaluation than those of congenital, organic, and racial degeneracy that were the province of the psychiatrists.[60] The psychiatrists' scientific tendency to objectify the human subject was often lethal in Nazi hands. Under the liberal interpretation of the Supreme Court, sickness meant compensation, but within the National Socialist context, mental illness as defined by the psychiatric establishment meant sterilization and euthanasia for "psychical deviances" (*psychische Abwegigkeiten*). Psychiatry might have entertained a long-range optimism inherited from the Enlightenment about the eventual scientific solution to what it regarded as the chemical or neurological problem of mental illness, but the consequences of its genetic views were deadly in Hitler's Germany. Even in the case of the psychiatric diagnosis of war neurotics, in the absence of some hereditary degeneracy or physical damage such individuals could be branded as "malingerers." The damning prognosis had been presaged by the "disciplinary therapy" and "moral view of neurosis" that had prevailed in military psychiatric clinics during World War I—while psychotherapy and psychoanalysis, on the other hand, in both wars emphasized the war neurotic's tragic conflict between fear and duty, and the empathic and therapeutic treatment that was necessary to rehabilitate him.[61]

M. H. Göring himself taught a course on forensic psychiatry at the institute, but we do not know if any other psychotherapist besides Göring was called upon to render prepared expert opinions for courts in sterilization or euthanasia cases. We do know, aside from the fact that university psychiatrists monopolized this function through their exalted position and training, it was institute policy to prohibit psychotherapists from providing evaluations of private patients for a hereditary health court (*Erbgesundheitsgericht*), where, presumably, the diagnostic deck was stacked against them and they faced the danger of official disapproval. In contrast to the practice among psychiatrists, Göring stressed the necessity for exhaustively filling out that section of an evaluation that called for a psychological diagnosis. This would ensure that the court would not confuse a neurotic with a psychopath, and allow it to render judgment accordingly, Göring believed. For the latter category, Göring hoped, psychotherapy would increasingly be mandated. The same reparative emphasis informed Göring's view of the medical evaluation of accident and pension neuroses. It was obvious, he commented—with what one suspects was a mixture of conviction and resignation, as well as a clear idea of how, in this case, to promote the application of psychotherapy—that at the present time no neurotic could be given a pension. He contradicted the punitive notion that a pension neurosis could be cured through the denial of a pension; obviously, it was psychotherapy that was essential in such cases.[62]

Göring's son claims that his father also acted on behalf of a number of psychiatric patients who were threatened by the Nazi policy on sterilization and euthanasia, allegedly by using his authority and influence to have them placed in the Bodelschwingh asylum at Bethel, near Bielefeld in the Ruhr. Individual psychiatrists, too, opposed the implementation of the Nazi plans. Arthur Gütt of the Interior Ministry resigned after voicing some reservations, while others simply fell away to varying degrees from any participation in or argument for a eugenics policy—a policy which, under different auspices, they might well have supported.

Kretschmer claimed after the war that while Ernst Rüdin publicly supported forced sterilization, he did so only because he was helpless in the face of Nazi insistence; Bumke made the same claim for himself. Bonhoeffer, himself a victim of the regime, pointed out after the war that eugenics had a long history all over the world, that the law under which the Nazis operated had been proposed under Weimar, and that those psychiatrists who took part in the program for the most part did so because they believed that the policy was nonpolitical. Pötzl of Vienna was more active in his opposition to the Nazis. According to the psychoanalyst Viktor Frankl, Pötzl protected him and a number of Jewish patients, as well as other patients who were in danger of sterilization or death.[63]

The Psychiatrists Move to Appropriate the New Profession

The evidence presented so far should make it amply clear that psychotherapy was not thrown purely on the defensive with the advent of National Socialism. Sommer, who until his death in 1937 was honorary president of the society he had founded, demonstrated this at Breslau in 1935 by observing that psychotherapy's concern with character and repair distinguished it from psychiatry in the narrow sense, and thus it was easily accommodated into the National Socialist *Weltanschauung*.[64] And while Göring could note that in 1933 it appeared as if psychotherapy would be overwhelmed by psychiatric "racial hygiene," he was able in the next breath to counter with a quotation from *Mein Kampf* that was more than cosmetic:

> Certainly the essential features of character have already been preformed in some men. . . . But along with fully distinct characters, there are also millions that seem vague and unclear. The born criminal is and will remain a criminal; but numerous people in whom there is only a certain disposition toward the criminal can by sound education still become valuable members of a national community, while, conversely, through bad education, wavering characters can grow into really bad elements.[65]

Given the ferment in medicine over matters of the mind as well as the demands the new regime placed on psychiatry, there was continued movement among physicians from psychiatry to the practice of psychotherapy. Kurt Delius, a Dortmund neurologist and psychiatrist and later a member of the Göring Institute, for example, took the opportunity in June 1933 officially to broaden his practice under German commercial law (and publish rates under the requirements of private insurance coverage). The expanded list of psychotherapeutic services he offered prominently included eleven types of psychotherapy.[66]

Traditional psychiatry, skeptical of a psychotherapy advanced under any aegis but its own,[67] now confronted a challenge organized at the political as well as the professional level. At the end of 1935 the psychotherapists, since 15 September 1933 assembled under the leadership of Göring in the German General Medical Society for Psychotherapy (Deutsche allgemeine ärztliche Gesellschaft für Psychotherapie), rejected a proposal made by the Ministry of the Interior to join the Society of German Neurologists and Psychiatrists (Gesellschaft Deutscher Neurologen und Psychiater), which had been founded in that year, explaining that psychotherapy was related to all disciplines, especially internal medicine. The board of directors of the German General Medical Society for Psychotherapy declared its willingness, however, to have their organization as a whole become part of a new umbrella organization, the Society of German Neuropathologists (Gesellschaft deutscher Nervenärzte). All that came of these proposals was an oral agreement in the summer of 1936 to share knowledge, a process asserted to have begun at the August 1936 Frankfurt Congress for Neurology and Psychiatry.[68]

Another example of the psychiatrists' two-pronged concern about their own capacity for psychotherapy and the Nazis' deadly threat to mental patients was the creation in 1940 of the German Society for Child Psychiatry and Medical Pedagogy (Deutsche Gesellschaft für Kinderpsychiatrie und Heilpädagogik) alongside the older Association for the Care of Juvenile Psychopaths (Verein zur Fürsorge für Jugendliche Psychopathen, e.V.). Paul Schröder of Leipzig noted at the society's first congress that the traditional interest of psychiatrists in the borders shared by medicine with education and therapy had been given an added urgency by the Nazi concern for productivity.[69] Schröder, the founder of the new organization, had been an early proponent of psychoanalysis becoming one of the psychiatrist's tools; under his leadership, these psychiatrists declared their profession's sovereignty over this realm.

The Society of German Neurologists and Psychiatrists, for its part, attempted to gather both groups under its wing so as to reassert the primacy of psychiatry in the field of general mental health and medical therapeutics. In the spring of 1941 the president of the society and head of its psychiatric division, Ernst Rüdin, sought, together with the Interior Ministry's Herbert Linden, to organize a spring meeting in Munich on the subject of psychotherapy. Besides Rüdin, the participants were to include Göring, Kretschmer, Schultz, and the psychiatrist Max de Crinis. It seems certain that this meeting never took place, but the correspondence entailed by its proposal and planning showed that the old-school psychiatrists who ran the Society of German Neurologists and Psychiatrists felt themselves severely threatened by the psychotherapists' monopolistic claim to therapeutic competence. Rüdin, noting his own earlier conversations with Göring, stressed to a Berlin associate that psychiatry must spare no effort to remain in charge of medical psychotherapy. In light of this necessity, Rüdin continued, the society had to tread carefully in the conflict—which we shall soon describe—between Kretschmer and Göring over the direction the professional affairs of psychotherapy should take. Beyond prudence, Rüdin obviously envisioned that his society would grandly incorporate all the professional groups that dealt with psychotherapy. As a first step in such a process, he proposed the holding of joint congresses.

The first of these gatherings of psychotherapists, psychologists, psychiatrists, and neurologists was planned for 1941 in Würzburg. Rüdin allowed in his correspondence that Kretschmer could help reliably introduce psychotherapy into the university curriculum and direct the affairs of psychology and constitutional pathology within the psychiatric society. Rüdin also proposed to Linden that Göring would likewise represent the psychotherapists on the new board of the Society of German Neurologists and Psychiatrists. Both Kretschmer and Göring, Rüdin thought, could separate the wheat from the chaff among those who would follow them into the unified society. Rüdin's colleague, the managing director of the society from 1935 to 1939, responded that the 1941 congress must give witness in questions of psychotherapy to the "unconditional preponderance" of the psychiatric point of view.[70]

The plans for the Würzburg congress, which never took place because of wartime exigencies, specified that the gathering was open only to physicians. The sessions on its basic theme of psychotherapy were structured in such a way as to make it appear that the treatment and cure of mental disorders was indeed a task that was exclusive to the psychiatric profession. Following a first day to be devoted almost nostalgically to military psychiatry and brain injury, Carl Schneider of Heidelberg was to report on the therapy of endogenous psychoses; five psychotherapists from the Göring Institute were to lecture in the context of reports on suggestion and training by Kretschmer and Schultz, amid contributions from twenty-seven psychiatrists and neurologists.[71]

The German Society for Child Psychiatry and Medical Pedagogy was also to hold its own, second, congress in Würzburg in October, on the heels of the psychiatrists' gathering. The timing was the result of an agreement between Rüdin and its founder, Schröder, both of whom were concerned by the growing number of nonmedical members of Schröder's group. In July Rüdin had averred darkly to Linden that Göring was seeking to take over the German Society for Child Psychiatry and Medical Pedagogy in order to leave the psychiatrists without an organizational or professional claim to therapeutic expertise. In Vienna in 1940 Göring had in fact announced that Schröder's group was meeting jointly with the psychotherapists. The precise truth of the matter is difficult to determine, since the Schröder psychiatrists and teachers met on 5 September, the psychotherapists on the sixth and seventh. The official report of the former group made no mention of the psychotherapists' congress,[72] a silence that perhaps revealed the Schröder society's desire to avoid being overshadowed or subsumed by an aggressive organization of practitioners they considered their inferiors. Göring's announcement, on the other hand, may have revealed precisely the motive ascribed him by Rüdin.

Thus it was professional rivalry that inspired Rüdin's loyal May 1941 assertion to Hans Reiter, the president of the Reich Health Office within the Interior Ministry, that the efforts toward a common congress of the three groups had represented an efficient and *völkisch* attempt at unifying group resources for the "care and control of the central nervous system" (*"Betreuung des Zentralnervensystems"*).[73] Certainly, in any case, the numbers were in the psychiatrists' favor, with around 800 members of the Society of German Neurologists and Psychiatrists as against the much smaller memberships of the two other groups. But the psychotherapists were not vulnerable on this particular front: The German General Medical Society for Psychotherapy had met for the last time in 1940, but even before then, with the wartime infusion of money from the German Labor Front, the Luftwaffe, and other agencies, the Göring Institute itself was the locus of the psychotherapists' unprecedented professional capacity.

These newly dynamic professional concerns and conflicts had their genesis in the change in leadership of the old General Medical Society for Psychotherapy during 1933. It was on 6 April of that year that Ernst Kretschmer resigned as president. Kretschmer was not at all sympathetic to National Socialism, nor was he, as a psychiatrist, committed to any sort of independent profession for the practice of psychotherapy—a phenomenon he regarded as professional dilettantism. He was also strongly opposed to state control of a scientific organization. As a result of these feelings, Kretschmer had decided to seek a return to the relative anonymity of the psychiatric clinic at the University of Marburg. His attitude has been attested to by a number of his contemporaries, including Bumke, who recalled Kretschmer's remark to him in 1933: "It's a funny thing with psychopaths. In normal times we render expert opinions on them; in times of political unrest they rule us."[74] The Nazis themselves were fully aware of Kretschmer's views, as reported in one instance by the National Socialist German University Lecturers League:

> Seen from a National Socialist point of view, the National Socialist German University Lecturers League could never approve the hiring of Kretschmer, because, on the basis of positive evidence, we are of the opinion that he has never subscribed to National Socialist ideals.[75]

Kretschmer remained professionally active, and in 1934 Cimbal reported to Jung that there were "difficulties" over the former president's position in regard to the two camps of psychotherapy and psychiatry. Cimbal feared that Kretschmer's theory of the psychology of body types so resembled the Nazi fixation on racial characteristics that the Nazis would tend to ignore psychotherapy's emphasis on psychodynamics and the environment. In a letter to Göring of 7 June 1934, Jung responded to Cimbal's concerns by saying that the subordination of psychotherapy to psychiatry would be a "catastrophe" and that if it were to come about, he would resign as president of the newly formed International General Medical Society for Psychotherapy, having lost "faith in the future of psychotherapy in Germany."[76] It was also in this vein that Jung wrote to Kretschmer himself on 21 December 1938, expressing the hope that the attacks on psychotherapy from Bumke did not represent the attitude of psychiatrists in general, and requesting that Kretschmer write an article for the *Zentralblatt* about the appreciation which psychiatrists had for psychotherapy as a profession. The article never appeared, for Kretschmer, though no apologist for psychiatry's racial hygiene, remained a firm critic of psychotherapy as a profession outside of psychiatry, and so of the new society and the institute. Even while he disparaged the group gathered under Göring as the "remains of a psychotherapeutic society," Kretschmer also, on at least one occasion, reported to his psychiatrist colleagues that there was continuous, if indirect, pressure from Nazi health authorities on psychiatrists to establish closer relations with the psychotherapists.[77] There can be little doubt that the Göring name was the cause of this farrago of warning, threat, and concern so typical of the Nazi "order."

At first it was Jung who formally succeeded Kretschmer on 21 June 1933 as president of the General Medical Society for Psychotherapy, at the invitation of its executive committee. Jung had served under Kretschmer as vice-president since 1930. In a letter to I. H. Schultz on 9 June 1933, Jung had agreed to assume the post and named Heyer as his deputy.[78] The German psychotherapists, with the approval of the regime, chose Göring as their *"Führer"* and his cousin opened doors to consultation with Bavarian Minister of Culture Hans Schemm, Education Minister Rust, and the Interior Ministry's Conti and Gütt, causing the founding on 15 September of the German General Medical Society for Psychotherapy. There were now two new societies: the German one under Göring and the international (Überstaatliche allgemeine ärztliche Gesellschaft für Psychotherapie) under Jung. The latter, formally constituted in 1934, was a continuation of the old society; all the new national groupings, including the new German one, belonged to it. Göring named a provisional governing committee that was composed of Cimbal as managing director, Haeberlin as vice-president, and Hattingberg, Heyer, Künkel, Schultz, Schultz-Hencke, Seif, and Viktor von Weizsäcker.[79]

Paterfamilias, Parvenu,
and Patriarch: Choosing a Leader

Under Göring's leadership, psychotherapists could adopt an aggressive professional posture, assured of protection against their enemies both among the Nazis and the medical profession, as well as of the advantage of financial support for their profession's development. Lacking an established position in the universities or the medical profession, psychotherapy was at least respectable enough to offer the Nazis its expertise without having to rely only on the illusory revolutionary slogans of National Socialism. Within this context, it is misleading to portray Matthias Heinrich Göring merely as "Hitler's appointee."[80]

We do not know for certain who first suggested Göring and what reservations, if any, there were about him among the psychotherapists, but it is unlikely that the initiative originated or resided even over the short run with a Reich Interior Ministry that was otherwise officially oblivious to psychotherapy. That it stemmed from Nazi party organizations, also essentially uninvolved in the internal affairs of the aspiring profession, seems equally unlikely. (See Chapter 5.) In any case, there is no evidence that Hitler had anything to do either with the society or the institute.

For M. H. Göring, Hitler served as a focal point for national allegiance, not as direct inspiration for an aggressive rise to the top of his profession. It seems clear that the leadership of both the German General Medical Society for Psychotherapy and the German Institute for Psychological Research and Psychotherapy was thrust on him by his colleagues. Ernst Göring recalls that his father was especially hesitant about assuming the position of institute director in Berlin in 1936 because of his age (he was 57), his painstakingly established medical practice in Wuppertal-Elberfeld, and the new home he had just built there. But he gave in under the pressure most likely exerted by the majority of all the psychotherapists, who believed out of a composite of willingness and resignation that Göring was their only salvation. These included the psychoanalysts, who had learned in April 1936 from the Interior Ministry that they were not to be permitted an independent institutional existence under the new order. He was also welcomed by those few psychotherapists who were actually committed to some sort of genuinely Nazified psychotherapy, and who saw Göring as their guarantor of success. In 1933 he also served as a compromise candidate satisfactory to rival contenders Hattingberg, Schultz, and Heyer.[81]

Matthias Heinrich Göring was the eldest living member of the Düsseldorf branch of the family, the oldest branch of the Westphalian Görings, from whom his cousin Hermann was descended. As such he held a respected place among his relations in a family that was characterized by close ties and loyalties. Matthias Heinrich's father, Peter, was the author of the family genealogy and, along with his son, organized regular family gatherings between the two wars. During the Third Reich, this general familial sentimentality emerged in Hermann as a "beefy hedonism"[82] that made him an impassioned and effective defender of his relatives as well as his fortune. That Peter Göring had also assisted Hermann financially after World War I presumably did

S. Hirzel Verlag

Matthias Heinrich Göring (1879–1945)

not hurt the relationship between the two cousins; in 1935 Matthias Heinrich sat at the head table at the banquet following Hermann's sumptuous state wedding to actress Emmy Sonnemann.[83]

Born on 5 April 1879, Matthias Heinrich Göring earned a doctorate in law at Freiburg/Breisgau in 1900 and, following travels through Palestine, Ceylon, and India, a doctorate in medicine at Bonn in 1907. During 1909 and 1910 he was a medical assistant at Kraepelin's psychiatric clinic in Munich, where he continued his work in forensic medicine. By 1913 he was a member of the clinical psychiatric staff at Giessen under Robert Sommer, a position to which he returned after the war. It was during this time that he became interested in psychotherapy and hypnosis, and in 1923 he founded a neuropathology practice in Elberfeld. Göring participated in the 1927 congress of the General Medical Society for Psychotherapy and joined the society the following year. In 1928, after undergoing a training analysis with Seif in Munich and attending a course of lectures by Künkel, he set up an educational counseling service (*Erziehungsberatung*) in Elberfeld. In the following year he founded a study group for psychotherapy in Wuppertal.[84]

By all accounts, Matthias Heinrich Göring was a shy, gentle man with a stammer. He was a patriot of the old school, a member of the nationalistic ex-serviceman's organization, the Stahlhelm, and a dedicated Lutheran pietist whose town, Wuppertal-Elberfeld, was a stronghold of pietism. According to Lucy Heyer-Grote and others among the psychotherapists active during the period, Göring always carried a Bible with him, and the concern for the individual, the attention to the needs of the common man, the emphasis on popular education, as well as the enthusiasm and irrationalism which all characterized the pietist outlook decisively influenced his notion of psychotherapy. He once told Werner Kemper, the Freudian director of the outpatient clinic of the Göring Institute from 1942 to 1945, that one of his major objections to psychoanalysis was the physical positioning of the analyst behind the analysand: Eye contact was vital, he believed, in order to allow the pair to face mental problems honestly and manfully in the spirit of Christ. As he put it in a 1933 book on the relationship between Adler's individual psychology and religion, "To love means to be able to merge into another, to understand one's fellow man, and to desire to help him in an effective manner."[85]

Although he was trained as a neuropathologist and a psychiatrist as well as a lawyer, Göring was firmly in the German Romantic tradition, with all its concern and fascination with the individual, the internal, the unconscious, and the irrational. This inward orientation, joined with his beliefs in medical and religious rehabilitation, made it easy for him to accept National Socialism, as many did, on what he thought were his own terms, coupling belief with opportunistic rhetoric, as here in 1935: "External drill does not suffice: the core of man must be grasped, as the Führer has repeatedly emphasized, and treated instinctively so that our subconscious is directed along the right path."[86] Göring affirmed the therapeutic necessity for the individual's integration into the community and, beyond that, the duty of the individual to remain healthy in service to his nation, his people, and his race. Psychotherapy, of course, was the means by which these ends could be attained in an otherwise distressing age when debilitating psychological conflict was more common than tuberculosis or cancer.[87]

Göring obviously saw an opportunity in 1933 to put his ideas into effect. At least part of the reason he accepted the invitation from the General Medical Society for Psychotherapy to become leader of the psychotherapists in the "new" Germany was his desire to unify the various schools of psychotherapeutic thought into some sort of Germanic psychotherapy. According to his son, Göring was a synthesist by nature, a characteristic that would be in harmony with his future role in protecting and promoting psychotherapy through the submersion of Freud and Adler. His criticisms of Freud, for example, were both prelude and accompaniment to his exclusion of the psychoanalysts Boehm and Müller-Braunschweig from any exercise of influence or authority. But his toleration of the Freudians as a group, in line with a *professional* as well as a patriotic desire to unify the ranks of medical psychologists, would gradually grow into interest and some degree of grudging admiration for their work in the Göring Institute. Although he pursued his personal vision, especially in the early years of the Third Reich, the result of the combination of his nature and his assignment was a general toleration for all points of view. Although he was basically a sincere and intelligent individual, Göring had neither the drive nor the intellect to produce a synthesis that had escaped greater minds. And in terms of a combination of his own philosophical and psychotherapeutic views with those of National Socialism, such a synthesis was illusory.

It is difficult to gauge the degree of anti-Semitism in Göring. At the fourth psychotherapeutic congress in 1929, he had indicated his philosophical problems with Freud,[88] and his words and actions between 1933 and 1945 leave no doubt over his condemnatory public stance then toward Jewish influence in the profession. But what of his private attitude toward Jews themselves? Ernst Göring has recalled the many Jewish patients his father had, and what mutual devotion existed between them and the "good doctor." And yet, in 1937 Göring himself could assert that between 1930 and 1933 only eleven Jews came to him, and that he was unable to help any of them because of the "racial" difference.[89] With no real certainty, we can only speculate that such an odious claim might have exacted some sort of psychological toll on a man like Göring, the thrashing about of a conscience within the tangle of ambition, fear, the striving for professional identity, and the philosophical hysteria mobilized by the Nazi regime. Anti-Semitism was an all too common adjunct to the aristocratic German traditions of which men like Göring partook, and the many brilliant Jews in medicine, especially those who dominated the elite and exclusive corridors of the psychoanalytic movement, could only have served to add professional jealousy to common cultural bigotry. But the association of such men as Göring with the Nazis did not derive from an uncomplicated and unconditional acceptance of National Socialism. Göring did not join the Nazi party in order to exercise his anti-Semitism; he joined as part of a process of professional necessity and national-cultural loyalty. It may or may not be true that before 1933 Göring had many Jewish patients with whom he was on excellent terms, but even dedicated anti-Semites were known to cultivate relationships with "good" Jews (*Persiljuden*). In any case, whether or not he was an anti-Semite before the advent of Hitler, a complex of personal and professional motives seemed to compel him to advertise that he was after 1933.

Most of the Jewish psychotherapists had fled the profession by 1933, and all were gone by 1938; the only practical reason for someone like Göring to continue to attack them was as a rhetorical means to a professional end. This motive was evident in a report by Göring on the 1938 psychotherapeutic congress in Düsseldorf, published in the Nazi party daily, the *Völkischer Beobachter*. In it, Göring prominently mentioned the exchange of telegrams with Hitler, quoted approvingly from *Mein Kampf*, and briefly praised hereditary biology. He also decried the former influence of Jews in the field of depth psychology. But even more important, he claimed, was the fact of the disunity that had prevailed among psychotherapists before 1933, and the phenomenon of the professional unity that had been achieved in Germany since that time. None of this justifies bigotry and nonsense about "German" psychotherapy versus "Jewish" psychoanalysis, but Göring's promotion of the activities of his society and institute in this article and in a subsequent interview with the *"VB"* seemed to take precedence over his regulation attack on Freud and Adler.[90] For the Nazi hierarchy, anti-Semitism was to be pursued as an expression of the Führer's will, and thus as active Nazi policy at home and abroad. For Göring, as for most of the German psychotherapists, such racism, while building on a widely held prejudice, was probably more or less an occasionally necessary means of expression to a professional end.

Göring was known to his colleagues as "Papi" or "Father Christmas" by virtue of his long white beard and grandfatherly personality; despite his early enthusiastic support for the Nazi government and his wartime loyalty to Hitler as commander-in-chief, they did not regard him as a dangerous political agent of the regime. In 1933 and 1934, he designated *Mein Kampf* as required reading for every psychotherapist, but few, if any, read it, and there ensued no enforcement or sanction of the assignment.[91] In the fall of 1944 he broached the subject of Hitler's order for the suspension of medical confidentiality, but, according to Gerhard Maetze, took no action when it was overwhelmingly rejected by members of the institute.[92] According to Kemper, Göring also ignored provocative remarks, as when at an institute meeting in 1942, Schultz-Hencke, in response to a threatening challenge to his loyalty toward the Nazi government by one of the psychotherapists who was a member of the party, said that he was no National Socialist and would never be.[93] Göring also provided employment and protection for at least two colleagues, August Vetter and Ludwig Zeise, who were otherwise professionally and personally disadvantaged by having Jewish wives, and apparently ignored the fact that Käthe Bügler, one of Heyer's students, was half-Jewish. On the other hand, Göring's relationship with deputy director Schultz deteriorated to the point of rupture early in 1945 with Göring's insistence that they, as those in charge of a psychotherapeutic institute, serve as psychological advisors to the last German units defending

Berlin against the Russian invaders. When Schultz refused and pointed to the futility of such an action, Göring branded him a defeatist and continued to badger him about it.[94]

It was not untypical of him during the Third Reich to attempt to protect his colleagues, and thus his budding profession, from the regime's assaults. As we have seen, he reportedly intervened with the Gestapo on behalf of Müller-Braunschweig in 1938, and he did the same for a Munich member of the institute who was accused by the Gestapo of child molestation in the treatment of several cases of bed-wetting. According to Franz Jung, Göring protected the Jewish Jungian Gerhard Adler while he was still in Berlin, and facilitated his eventual emigration to Switzerland in April 1936. Adler had been the object of an anti-Semitic attack by Achelis at the congress in Breslau in 1935 and, like all Jewish psychotherapists and psychoanalysts, was prohibited from treating "Aryan" patients. But Adler himself claims that Göring's protection of him is a myth; Jung wrote to Göring on his behalf, Adler recalls, and all Göring did was write "a short and completely meaningless note . . . without any influence on the course of events."[95] One result of this imbroglio was that even Jung's disciples were regarded with suspicion by the German authorities. This was pointed out in a letter from Otto Curtius to Olga Fröbe-Kapteyn, founder of the annual Eranos meetings in Switzerland, which remarked that the *Deutsche Allgemeine Zeitung* had refused to run a story on Curtius's presentation on the Jungian Adolf von Weizsäcker. Göring failed in his role of protecting non-Jewish colleagues only in the case of John Rittmeister, the anti-Nazi therapist at the Göring Institute who was arrested and then executed for espionage during the war (see Chapter 5); his tentative attempt at intercession was rebuffed by the Gestapo, and he did not repeat it.

Göring's obsequious personal and professional prudence was reflected by the society's statutes which permitted Jews to be members but not to hold office or present papers. In accordance with German law, article 1 of these statutes stated that on 15 September 1933 the society had been founded in Berlin, that it was to be registered as an association in Wuppertal-Elberfeld, and that it was a section of the international society which temporarily maintained its executive in Marburg. Article 2 pledged unconditional allegiance to Hitler, while article 3 laid out the activities of the society with respect to the furthering of the aims of the profession. The fourth article and those following epitomized the Nazis' new ethic of governance. The president alone named his advisory council and all other holders of executive office, since he "alone comprises the governing body in the spirit of the civil code." According to article 5, the president also had the right to veto any membership application and to expel any member of the society. Article 6 gave him control over all fees and dues, while article

7 expressed the protective function to be exercised through the application of this "leadership principle" (*Führerprinzip*):

> The chairman has the right to approve all reviews, lectures, and essays made public under the society's name before publication and to prevent variations from the approved text through immediate suspension. He also has the right to interrupt all approved speakers and to prohibit further exposition when, in his opinion, they have said or intend to say something impermissible. Copies of intended lectures and reviews as well as the content of discussion remarks must therefore be submitted to the chairman or to his deputy for approval.

Article 8 allowed for the election of a new chairman/president on the resignation of the previous officeholder, but only from a list of candidates prepared by the outgoing president. This article, along with article 9, stressed the importance of consultation with the proper government offices within the Ministry of the Interior. All these paragraphs witnessed the perceived need for dictatorial control, not only by decreeing an administrative aping of the Reich government but also by ensuring the maintenance of a loyal professional profile.[96]

The December 1933 issue of the *Zentralblatt* appeared under Jung's editorship and contained Göring's hortatory version of the society's statutes:

> This society has the mission to assemble in the spirit of the National Socialist German government all physicians who are motivated by the belief that the doctor in every treatment must consider the whole personality of the patient so that he does not ignore the person's soul; above all, those physicians who are willing to acquire and to practice a psychotherapeutic medicine in the spirit of the National Socialist *Weltanschauung*.[97]

Göring went on to say that the statutes themselves would be published in the special edition of the *Zentralblatt* dedicated to the new German psychotherapy. It is significant that when *Deutsche Seelenheilkunde* appeared in 1934, the statutes were not included. The statutes, like the Göring name, were essentially a protective device composed of rhetoric.

According to former members of the society and the institute, Göring did not exercise the broad censorship powers granted him within the society or, later, the institute—which, in any case, as we will see, operated under its own statutes. In part he did not have to, since the members themselves, out of both caution and conviction, displayed care in their public presentations, especially in the early years of the regime. More important, however, was the nature and identity of Göring himself, which allowed a significant degree of security and independence inside the profession's walls.

Even so, the psychotherapists as a group were required to exercise prudence toward the outside. Perhaps it was this prudence that lay behind Göring's refusal of a request by Oluf Brüel, president of the Danish psychotherapeutic society, that the *Zentralblatt* print an obituary notice for Freud, an act that Göring regarded as needlessly provocative. In a letter of 9 November 1939 to C. A. Meier, the Zurich editor of the *Zentralblatt*, Göring asserted that any such article must be cleared through him, and that in no event would a portrait of Freud be permitted to accompany the notice. It was this same fear of the new order in Germany that animated the society's statutes. In the same spirit, Göring's imprudent misappelation of himself in 1933 as *"Reichsführer"* betrayed an anxious imitation of Nazi rhetorical symbols, as did the slightly less pompous designation of *"Reichsleiter"* that accompanied his foreword to *Deutsche Seelenheilkunde* the following year. It was a sign of a reduced level of fear that in later years Göring was content to be officially and publicly designated as director (*Direktor* or *Leiter*) of the institute and as chairman/president (*Vorsitzender*) of the society.

But what followed the title was vastly more important than the title itself. In one sense, it is true, the name was a burden, since its owner was expected by the Nazis to fulfill certain responsibilities. Membership in the party, for one thing, was all the more imperative for Göring because of his family name, even though membership was the obvious and prudent step for any executive to take in Nazi Germany and one that, in Göring's case as in many others, carried a certain degree of sincerity and conviction. His son claims that Göring told him that since he could not convince or coerce all the psychotherapists under his authority to join the party, he would lift the burden from their shoulders by doing so himself. This specific rationale was in some measure, at least, post hoc, for he was among those who joined the party soon after the Nazi seizure of power on considerably more than such tactical grounds, being enrolled formally along with the rest of the so-called "March opportunists" on 1 May 1933. It was only after he joined the party, during the following summer, that he agreed to assume leadership of the German psychotherapists in the form of a national professional body to be formally established in September.

What does seem the case, however, is that with Göring at the helm, psychotherapists were in general spared the necessity of forging closer "political" ties with the Nazi regime. When Nazi articles and books on race were reviewed in the *Zentralblatt*, it was most often Göring who did the reviewing, again displaying an admixture of conviction, opportunism, and sentiments aimed at protecting the new profession he now led. The complex of motives is typically human, but its measure may be further taken with the observation that Göring's name more often meant that he, and thus the profession, was relieved of the necessity of constantly proving allegiance to the regime. For example, while psychotherapists were often heavily criticized in the party medical press, Göring himself by and large received favorable attention. Such was the case with his 1937 book on psychosomatic disorders,[98] a highly technical work that was devoid of the Nazi rhetoric contained in those of his articles that German medical weeklies, prudently in part, now and again agreed to publish.

It was also unnecessary for Göring to appear before his colleagues in an SA uniform, even though he was a member of the SA; Walter Poppelreuter, the director of the Institute for Clinical Psychology in Bonn, did not enjoy this luxury.[99] Thus, Göring was not compelled to flaunt his name even had it been his nature to do so. According to Ernst Göring, his father was of the opinion that if there were someone from whom he needed assistance, then that person should be approached directly (i.e., not through channels), a tactic born of Göring's generally forthright nature and rendered especially effective by his name in the personalistic Nazi hierarchy. Often as not, the Göring name, along with his distinguished bearing and academic titles, won him at least a hearing, if not always success. It does not seem to have been the case that powerful Nazi individuals and organizations came to Göring in order to exploit his name in the constant process of jockeying for power. This kind of opportunism, however, could very well have been a partial motivation for institute association, if not active engagement, on the part of Reich Physicians Leader Gerhard Wagner, Labor Front boss Robert Ley, and Reich Health Leader Leonardo Conti, whose careers we shall be noting later. On balance, it seems that the psychotherapists' chances for the survival of their profession after 1933 rested less on what the Göring name would effortlessly bring them than on how far it would take them in their active efforts to establish a professional place and identity for themselves in Hitler's Germany.

Göring was not personally close to any of the major power brokers in the Third Reich apart from his cousin Hermann, but he would not hesitate to approach his cousin when he needed his help; and he did so in as direct a manner as he employed with others. Marie Kalau vom Hofe, director of the criminal psychology division of the Göring Institute, remembers accompanying Göring to the Reich Air Ministry on one occasion and hearing him comment on how nice Hermann looked in the huge portrait of him hung in the ministry's entry hall. But, according to his son, apparently Göring did not visit his powerful cousin often; Hermann was there if Matthias needed him, but for the most part the name itself was enough. It seems predictable that the direct personal access to the Reich Marshal that Matthias Heinrich Göring enjoyed added little official documentary debris to the channels of Nazi bureaucracy. Only a single recorded instance of an official

Staatsbibliothek Berlin

Hermann Göring's Wedding, 1935 (Matthias Heinrich Göring marked with arrow at upper left). This photograph of prominent guests leaving the Berlin cathedral after the wedding of Hermann Göring to Emmy Sonnemann not only documents Matthias Heinrich Göring's attendance but also symbolizes the curious yet crucial role of Hermann Göring in the history of psychotherapy in the Third Reich: not directly visible but an obvious and indispensable focus of attention for everyone. The guests are identified by number as the following: (1) Field Marshal von Mackensen; (2) State Secretary Meissner; (3) Count Rosen, brother-in-law of Göring's first wife; (4) Reich Minister Rust; (5) Rudolf Hess; (6) War Minister von Blomberg; (7) Reich Bishop Müller; (8) Foreign Minister von Neurath.

meeting between the Göring cousins has been found, the scheduling of a discussion on 25 September 1942 concerning the German Penal Code statute that defined homosexuality as a crime.[100]

The indirect, or inferential, power of Göring's name, in any case, was most likely enough for Heinrich von Kogerer, who was named by Göring to direct the activities of the Vienna branch of the institute. When Göring, referring to the Vienna Psychoanalytic Institute, announced in 1933 that what he called the "stronghold of Jewish psychotherapy" had fallen, he did not realize that Kogerer's own wife was half Jewish. Although a half-Jew could, under certain conditions, escape being defined as a Jew and be designated a crossbreed (Mischling),[101] Kogerer's party membership of 1 May 1938 was nevertheless suspended on 27 May as a result of this discovery and finally withdrawn in September 1939. On 14 December 1941, however, Kogerer was granted a special dispensation (Gnadenentscheidung) by Hitler to be a party member. Due to some errant shuffling of papers and objections from intermediate officials that Kogerer's induction into the Wehrmacht made him ineligible, he was finally readmitted into the NSDAP on 27 August 1943 with retroactive membership (and past dues payable) to 1 January 1942.[102] It is not farfetched to speculate that Matthias Heinrich Göring may have had a hand in this rather exceptional process, and that his cousin may have spoken to Hitler himself about it. In any case, the affair points to the probable influence of Matthias's fat, illustrious cousin, the ruthless hedonistic pragmatist who proclaimed, "I decide who is Jewish" ("Wer Jude ist, bestimme ich.").

Matthias Heinrich Göring was a man of modest mien and accomplishment. As a psychotherapeutic theorist he was undistinguished; as a medical practitioner he was competent and committed. He owed his meteoric rise to professional prominence in 1933 not to his abilities but to his name. He did serve as an effective protector of his incipient profession, but as a psychotherapist he could not begin to rival those illustrious predecessors of his, many Jewish and some not, whose place he took and whose careers he helped the Nazis destroy and whose reputations he helped them besmirch.

To the negligible degree that psychotherapy during the Third Reich has been discussed in the historical literature, it has been subsumed under the common rubric of Gleichschaltung. George Mosse, in Nazi Culture, his very useful compendium of primary Nazi sources on various social and scientific subjects, includes portions of an essay by a young psychotherapist named Kurt Gauger. The words are fervent claims of allegiance to Hitler and National Socialism, and the implication of Mosse's selection is that these words tell us all we need to know about psychotherapists during the Third Reich. But to understand

Kurt Gauger is to understand the real story of the Nazi "coordination" of medical psychology. Gauger played an early and significant role in the affairs of psychotherapy under Hitler, and he remained connected with the society and the institute up until the end. But his importance diminished rapidly as a result of the nature of Nazi governance, the advantages enjoyed by the psychotherapists under Göring's leadership, and Gauger's own personal limitations. His actual career in the Third Reich stands in meaningful contrast to the confident, ambitious words quoted by Mosse, and thus it merits our scrutiny as a study in the ultimate poverty of the hopes of muddled chauvinists and racists who were so common in Nazi Germany. By placing Gauger's words and actions in their proper perspective, we can gain further insight into the history of psychotherapy in the Third Reich.

Matthias Heinrich Göring had no real rival for the institutional leadership of the profession, but in the tension and trouble of the regime's early years, the psychotherapists certainly might have believed otherwise. At the seventh congress of the General Medical Society for Psychotherapy in Bad Nauheim in 1934, quite a stir had been caused by the appearance of a young physician and psychotherapist in a dark beswastikaed uniform, who had harangued the audience on the National Socialist revolution in medical psychology. The words Kurt Gauger spoke on that day in May 1934 carried malevolent weight, for his listeners believed that the dark blue of Gauger's SA Marine uniform was the dreaded black of the SS. His address, and its subsequent expansion into a book, constituted a wholehearted endorsement of National Socialism and a vitriolic attack on Western materialism. In terms of its theoretical content, it displayed a relatively simplistic approach that was vaguely Jungian in derivation.

Gauger chaired a study group at the congress on the incorporation of psychotherapy into the medical professions. Its proceedings show him expressing all the rhetoric of the Nazism that, in truth, meant a great deal to him: "The Third Reich has not inscribed happiness on its banners, but courage."[103] The next year, 1935, found him giving a lecture on ideals and character, and in 1936 he addressed the inaugural meeting of the NSDAP task force on medical reform, taking as his topic the subject of conscience.

For psychotherapists in the early years of the Third Reich, Gauger loomed like Spenser's Archimago, seeming almost melodramatically dangerous, and all the more threatening for his frequent invisibility. This selective seclusion on Gauger's part was not calculated to inspire notoriety, however, but was rather a symptom of a personal struggle that would remove him from the influence he wielded over psychotherapy in the early period of the Third Reich. Like Göring, he was not a party man who was imposed on the psychotherapists from the outside. Indeed, his friend since boyhood, Kurt Zierold, has recalled that Gauger was not personally acquainted with anyone in the party leadership, a significant handicap in an organization that depended so much on the importance of personal contacts. In actuality, Gauger was typical of the muddled idealist whose gamut ran from the pathological likes of Julius Streicher to scions of German culture like Martin Heidegger and Gerhart Hauptmann, all of whom ran afoul of the limits to revolution and substantive change in the Nazi blur of mobilization. And his preoccupation with the realms of philosophy and conscience was an expression of his problems with self-esteem.

Kurt Emil Otto Gauger was born on 10 March 1899 in Stettin on the Baltic, the fourth of six children of school rector Albert Gauger. He graduated from the Kaiser Wilhelm Gymnasium there in 1917; he was drafted, but did not see combat in World War I. During the early years of the Weimar Republic, he later claimed, he was a member of a Free Corps regiment in Stettin and active within the ranks of the right-wing terror apparatus, Organisation C. Attending the universities of Greifswald, Leipzig, and Rostock, he majored in philosophy, psychology, and pedagogy, taking minors in comparative linguistics and history. He received a doctorate in philosophy in 1922 with a thesis on Eduard von Hartmann. Gauger spent the next three years at sea, traveling to North and South America, Japan, China, and finally Italy, where, like many Germans in fact and fantasy, he lingered to study under the lemon blossoms. In 1925 he returned to Germany, and the following year took up medical studies at Berlin and Rostock. He was licensed as a physician on 10 December 1931.[104]

In 1926 Gauger had come into contact with psychotherapy. He was dissatisfied at the time with his studies, and sought help in Berlin from a Jungian psychotherapist, Mila von Prosch. It was she who inspired him to turn to medicine and become a psychotherapist. His friend Zierold had a contact on the scholarship commission and was able to procure funds for Gauger's medical education. Gauger fell in with the psychotherapy circle that flourished around Werner Achelis and his wife. He and Achelis grew to be close friends, and Gauger later dedicated his *Politische Medizin* to him, "a fellow worker in the construction of a German psychotherapy," to which Achelis was to write a "comprehensive cultural-political supplement" (which never, in fact, appeared). Gauger was also a poet and fiction writer; he had already displayed, in a 1923 volume of poems entitled *Gotische Gedichte,* the Romantic bent that enabled him to establish and maintain a close working rapport with the Romantic philosopher Achelis. His poetry accompanied the text of Achelis's *Principia Mundi* of 1930. Gauger's lowercase romantic inclinations allegedly led him to become Frau Achelis's lover. He subsequently set up a psychotherapy practice in Berlin near the Kurfürstendamm, but he had trouble attracting patients and again sought out Zierold, who was director of the Film

Evaluation Board (Kammer für Filmwertung). In this way he landed the job as director of the Reich Institute for Film and Illustration (Reichsanstalt für Film und Bild) that was to serve as his primary occupation during the Third Reich. Zierold also introduced Gauger to the woman he was to marry in 1935.

Gauger was short of stature and suffered from weak eyesight that caused him to squint continually. These conditions exacerbated a severe inferiority complex, and compensation for it was, in Zierold's view, the primary inspiration for Gauger's attitudes and actions toward Nazism and psychotherapy after 1933. Zierold perceptively maintains that Gauger was always seeking approval, reassurance, and praise, but that, because of his dependency on others, he succeeded only in sowing further doubt within himself. Gauger broke off his friendship with Zierold during the 1950s, most probably, as Zierold surmises, because of the overwhelming sense of indebtedness he felt toward him. It is probable that feeling beholden to his friend threatened the tenuous feelings of superiority which Gauger periodically tried to utilize as a defense against the depression that was linked to his feelings of inferiority.[105]

Gauger's desperate search for affection and admiration found expression in the stories he wrote about the sea. His 1930 novel (published in 1940), *Christoph. Roman einer Seefahrt*, was a release from his landlocked difficulties in dealing with his professional identity in the midst of the Depression. With a characteristically Gaugerian mix of guilt, aggression, egotism, and self-pity, his hero remarks that hard work brings nothing but pain: " 'I know that it is a sin if one has bad luck and stands alone. No one could be more forsaken than I am.' "[106] The year in which Gauger wrote these words saw him publish a work on psychotherapeutic method, *Der richtige Atem*, with Achelis's publisher, Püttmanns. The novel, like a 1943 collection of his short stories, was published by the same firm, Hohenstaufen-Verlag, which published material from Zierold's Office for Educational Films (Reichsstelle für den Unterrichtsfilm). Gauger dedicated the novel to Paul König, a dead sea captain and director for Norddeutsche Lloyd, to whom he declared his indebtedness for having been taught seamanship. The novel's protagonist, Christoph Fählmann, is a young doctor in the small town of Falkenberg. One of his patients comes to him with venereal disease, and Christoph feels it his duty to tell her father, one of the town's leading citizens, despite the fact that the girl, Grete, is of age. Once he does so, he is detained for questioning about his breach of medical confidentiality, and then released. Escaping the "revenge of a small town," full of intimate obligations, guilt, and regrets, Christoph abandons his medical career to go to Hamburg and begin a life at sea. There, in despair, he throws himself into the Elbe. " 'The physician is dead, and therefore Christoph Fählmann must also die.' "[107]

Kurt Gauger (1899–1959)

From the perspective his writings conveniently offer us, Gauger's fleeting feelings of superiority—as a release from his depression and the ambivalent dependence on others he experienced—were aroused by National Socialism. Since 1928 he had belonged to a water sports club, Hochseesportverband Hansa e.V., and he joined the NSDAP on 1 May 1933 after the club had been coordinated under the Nazis, becoming active as a physician with SA Marine Standarte 77 in Berlin. He wore his blue uniform with the gold buttons proudly; a photograph of him at the time shows him in a belligerent pose, hand at his service dagger, but with his eyes betraying the insecurity that is masked by the otherwise blank face.

In addition to the psychic income that was provided by his official 1933 identification with Hitler and National Socialism, Gauger now also saw his chance to establish himself prominently and independently as a psychotherapist. According to Kemper, Gauger claimed to have sought out a prominent Nazi health official, Leonardo Conti (see below, Chapter 5), in order to realize Carl Jung's imputed aim to protect psychotherapy from the Nazis. This involved recruiting M. H. Göring, to whom Gauger was related, but Gauger later asserted that he had been betrayed by Göring's collaboration with the authorities. In fact, he had simply been passed over in the profession's rush for security and advantage. He resigned his post as honorary deputy director of the Göring Institute soon after its founding in 1936 and devoted himself full-time to his film work.

In fact, it was not because of the coordination presided over by Göring that Gauger left, nor did he do so in the year that he specified. The coordination process had, after all, begun in 1933, and in 1937 he still listed his position at the Göring Institute on an SA questionnaire.[108] He continued to be an enthusiastic propagandist for the Nazis, winning promotions and decorations as an SA doctor right through the war.

Gauger was regarded by the psychotherapists at the institute with dislike and fear. When Göring called a meeting at the film institute in 1935 to present *Die Ewige Maske*—the film on which Gauger had collaborated with the director Werner Hochbaum and the writer Leo Lapaire—attendance was sparse. The film, adapted from a novel by Lapaire, concerns a physician suffering from delusions. It celebrates the advance that psychodynamic therapy represented over the old psychiatric search for physical cause, with its concomitant dismissal of the patient's own vital testimony. Produced by a Swiss-Austrian subsidiary of the German Tobis company, it starred Olga Tschechova and Mathias Wiemann, two prominent actors of the era. Gauger claimed after the war that Goebbels banned the film, and that he showed it in defiance at the university in Berlin on 31 May 1935. His old friend Zierold does not remember its being banned, however, and there is no record of it among the blacklisted films of the Nazi period. In fact, it is listed as having passed censure on 12 October 1935, premiering in Dresden on 8 January 1936 and in Berlin on 3 March. The film even won a medal as the best psychological study at the biennial Vienna film festival.[109] In light of all of this, it is unlikely that the psychotherapists stayed away on the basis of either the film's subject matter or its lack of quality.

As we shall see, even after he had left the institute, Gauger continued to serve as somewhat of a talisman or bellwether for the psychotherapists' fears of official disapproval or sanction. I. H. Schultz reportedly maintained contact with him, and as late as 1942 Göring approvingly noted the ever-close professional relations between the institute and Gauger's Reich Institute for Film and Illustration, mentioning the production of a film on hypnosis by the Heidelberg neuropathologist Ludwig Mayer. Göring also took the trouble to label Gauger's novel "psychotherapeutic," and he was most likely the moving force behind a favorable review of it in the *Zentralblatt* in 1942.[110]

Although he later asserted that he had maintained a medical and a psychotherapeutic practice along with increasingly heavy duties at the film institute, Gauger never really became an active member of the Göring Institute. According to Zierold, Kemper, and Alexander Mitscherlich, Gauger suffered from an hysterical blindness after the war as a depressive reaction to his unwillingness to acknowledge the collapse of his world in 1945. His constitutionally weak eyes already had suffered damage in a fire at the film institute in 1943, and his collection of sea stories published the same year were all in the first person and contained elements of suicidal urges; one character in "The Beautiful Adventure" pretends to be a doctor in order to visit a dying friend, a striking *Doppelgänger* image. Gauger again was seeking an outlet to the sea to refurbish his self-image, positive in terms of a modestly creative sublimation but also replete with many of the doubts that continued to plague him.[111] Zierold loyally contends that Gauger was never a rabid Nazi, and that he did seek to shield psychotherapy from the Nazis by using Göring as a protector.

Gauger's literary sensitivity and personal charm, characteristics which Zierold cities in defense of his friend, were only the most positive elements of the kind of troubled personality that not uncommonly sought help for a time within a specific sphere of the Third Reich. What we have in Gauger is the apparent rather than the real, the noisy ideologue who tried to jump on the National Socialist bandwagon but whose own personal deficiencies allowed him only the most transitory of roles. Gauger most likely did intervene for the psychotherapists within certain provinces of the new regime, but it was Göring and the nature of psychotherapy itself that provided for, first, the survival and, ultimately, the institutionalization of the profession.

While Gauger imposed himself on the psychotherapists, Carl Jung was drafted to preside over them for the protection and prestige they hoped his name would bring to their profession in the Third Reich. Like Gauger, however, Jung and his reputation were rendered superfluous to them over time by the presence of Göring. It seems unlikely that, had Göring not existed, Jung's fame, ideas, or practical efforts could have provided them much genuine protection, much less advantage. What Jung hoped was to make the old society formally international in nature and thus to protect psychotherapy in Germany from extinction. In a letter of 23 November 1933 to Rudolf Allers of Vienna, Jung concluded that "Göring is a very amiable and reasonable man, so I have the best hopes for our cooperation."[112]

The international society was headquartered in Zurich, and Jung held a three-year term as president of the international body as well as heading the Swiss contingent. The international society's statutes, adopted at the seventh congress of the old General Medical Society for Psychotherapy at Bad Nauheim on 15 May 1934, showed its concern about the possible Nazi co-option of the large German society by prohibiting any single national member group from contributing more than 40 percent of the voting members at any electoral meeting. On 22 January 1934 Jung had written to Poul Bjerre—who in 1936 formed a Swedish group under the International General Medical Society for Psychotherapy—expressing just such a concern.[113] When Max Guggenheim of Lausanne objected to Jung's role in working with the psychotherapists in Germany, Jung claimed that, among other things, he had enabled Allers, a Jew, to stay on as editor of the review section of the *Zentralblatt*. Further, in an attempt to provide professional protection for Jewish colleagues in the international society, Jung inserted a circular letter in the December 1934 number of the *Zentralblatt* which declared that the "international society is neutral as to politics and creed"; the statement was based on both Jung's and the German psychotherapists' efforts to emphasize that the international and German bodies were completely separate and independent of each other while still continuing to work together. This policy allowed German Jewish doctors to join the international society on an individual basis.[114]

In a letter to Alphonse Maeder of Zurich, on 22 January 1934, Jung wrote that Kretschmer had stepped down because matters had become too complicated, and that he, Jung, would not have accepted the presidency had it not been that the Germans had insisted that no German could effectively assume a post in an international organization under the then prevailing conditions. There is no evidence that Jung forced Kretschmer's resignation in order to further imputed designs to build a Nazified psychotherapy, and in his autobiography Kretschmer himself expresses no hostility toward Jung.[115] The German psychotherapists' preference was determined not only by their desire for the protection they believed Jung's worldwide reputation would provide, but also by Jung's great popularity and respect among proponents of a new German psychotherapy that was ferociously opposed to Freudian theories.

Both motives were almost painfully evident when Jung was interviewed by one of his disciples, Adolf von Weizsäcker, on Radio Berlin on 26 June 1933, when Jung was in the German capital to give a seminar at the C. G. Jung Society there. Weizsäcker's first question concerned his mentor's perceptions of the differences between the German and Western European souls. Jung's response was that the primary distinction was the "youthfulness" of the German soul. He went on to stress the importance of appreciating the totality of the human organism, casting the greatest doubt on any psychology that, as he said, reduced the individual to the sum of his sexual drives or his lust for power. It was this particular aspect of Jung's psychology, Weizsäcker agreed, that made it one of "vision," as opposed to being steeped in the "intellectual basis" of Freudian and Adlerian psychology. In addition to his obvious awe of the master, Weizsäcker pursued his questions in the service of psychotherapy's place in the new Reich along the distinct lines established in his reverential introduction to the interview. There, among other things, he celebrated the fact that "Dr. Jung does not tear to pieces and destroy the immediacy of our psychic life, the creative element which has always played the decisive role in the history of the German mind. . . ."[116]

Another student of Jung's, Wolfgang Kranefeldt, has recalled that when he went to Berlin in 1935 to give a series of lectures on archetypes, he was received with great joy and admiration, especially by Göring, specifically because of his affiliation with Jung. The second issue of the *Zentralblatt* was devoted to Jung's analytical psychology, and many articles from Jungians appeared in the journal between 1934 and 1936. As a result of this kind of official approval, German psychotherapists did almost all they could to link Jung's name with their own activities. According to Jung's close friend, Barbara Hannah, while Jung was in Berlin in 1933, Otto Curtius, whose brother Julius was a former Chancellor and Foreign Minister, persuaded Jung that Propaganda Minister Joseph Goebbels wanted to see him. On being shown into the minister's office, it became apparent that Goebbels had extended no such invitation to Jung, and that, on the contrary, he had been told that Jung wished to see him.[117] Curtius (and Göring) clearly had seen that the meeting would be another potential plus for the profession they represented. The same motive of identifying German psychotherapy with Jung most likely accounted at least in part for Göring's proposal to Himmler in 1939 that the SS-Ahnenerbe fund a Göring Institute research project on trees and forests as mythological symbols in dreams, based on Jung's psychological theories. (See Chapter 6.)

More than one German racial theoretician saw Jung's work as indispensable in providing rich material for the history and culture of a race:

> By means of this unconscious, one seeks to unlock an ancient spiritual heirloom, and the famous practitioner of depth psychology, C. G. Jung, goes so far as to maintain that within the unconscious lie deep spiritual strata whose disclosure even makes possible a "reconstruction of the prehistory" of cultures.[118]

But this did not mean that the German psychotherapists received ideological carte blanche from the Nazis as a result of their highly publicized claim on so acceptable a representative. The editor of the journal in which this 1939 article on depth psychology and race appeared felt compelled to add a note to the effect that, while the essay was a welcome addition to an "as yet open area of research," the author's assertion that heredity may be equated with the unconscious could not be endorsed without reservation. Nonetheless, the article was listed in the official Nazi bibliography.[119] The German General Medical Society for Psychotherapy continued to do all it could to involve Jung in its efforts to survive and develop. In 1935 the editors of the *Zentralblatt* praised Jung for his actions on behalf of psychotherapy in Germany in no uncertain terms:

> In 1933 he assumed the presidency of the "International General Medical Society for Psychotherapy," taking on the difficult assignment of supporting a gravely threatened psychotherapy in its struggle for existence and at the same time preserving as far as possible international scientific relations.[120]

Because of the fissured reality of the Nazi regime and the luck of the professional draw with Göring, there was still a budding profession of psychotherapy in Germany, and it required protection from the more dangerous individuals and organizations that were storming about during the early years of the Reich. Jung's motives for his actions at that time have been widely questioned and attacked. It is true that most of his protests about the course of events in Germany went exclusively into the ears and eyes of non-Germans, but perhaps this was only prudent given the German environment. And even though Jung corresponded with Gauger concerning the protection that the eager professional parvenu and party man might be able to provide for psychotherapy, he professed to be aghast at Gauger's book on "political medicine,"[121] and in a letter to Heyer on 20 May 1935 declared himself against naming Gauger as managing director of the society. Furthermore, aside from sending his suggestions for a training curriculum to Göring in 1935,[122] Jung never became directly involved in the operation of the German General Medical Society for Psychotherapy or the Göring Institute. But even his role in the protection of psychotherapy was ambiguous in terms of effect. His claim to have succeeded in "tucking away Psychotherapy in a remote department where the medical Nazi boss could not reach it"[123] is most probably an exaggeration. Apart from the fact that state institutions were successfully fighting off party challenges, the equation of party with threat and state with opportunity (or at least protection) is a far too simple, and ultimately erroneous, formulation. The Nazi preference for mobilization over reform, coupled with the conservative nationalism and the Romantic medical orientation shared by party health ideologues and so many of the psychotherapists, as well as the presence of Göring, made the party far less of a threat than it might have appeared at the time.

To understand fully Jung's motives for his involvement with psychotherapy in Germany in the 1930s would require a psychological analysis of his life and work, a complex and problematical undertaking. To view his actions within the context of the history of German psychotherapy, however, is to see that, whatever weaknesses and prejudices Jung might himself have had, he was drawn into the situation by both the threat and the opportunity that confronted psychotherapists during the Third Reich. The starting point for criticism of Jung was the introduction he contributed to the resuscitated *Zentralblatt* of December 1933. There he wrote that, in his capacity as editor, he saw his purpose as the clarification of various teachings, theories, and practices within a political context even though psychotherapy itself had nothing to do with politics. Jung's ambiguous embracing of forces, symbols, races, and elites led to the same sort of relativism that had paralyzed German intellectuals of the nineteenth and twentieth centuries. Beyond this, his statements of the Nazi era exhibited a fairly distinct disdain for what he saw as a shallow and mechanical democracy in its denial and denigration of the awesome depths of the human soul and the soul's unique and dynamic cultural and racial manifestations.

Jung had observed in his interview with Weizsäcker that "every movement culminates organically in a leader."[124] Europe could not, he said, understand Germany because it was not in the same situation and did not share the same historical and psychological experiences. He endorsed Hitler's constant assertion that the individual must have the courage to go his own way. In the same manner, in his introduction to the *Zentralblatt,* Jung found a formulation that fit both his own anthropological tendency toward national and racial characterization as well as the practical demands of the moment: "Genuinely independent and perceptive people have for a long time recognized that the difference between Germanic and Jewish psychology should no longer be effaced, something that can only be beneficial to the science."[125]

Jung's words, and the fact they were published alongside Göring's call to the Nazi colors, raised an international furor. Jung later claimed that Göring's essay was to have been published only in a special German supplement to the *Zentralblatt,* and that it was only by accident that it had appeared in the "international" journal.[126] Perhaps Jung was thinking of what was to become "Die nationalsozialistische Idee in der Psychotherapie," Göring's introductory essay to *Deutsche Seelenheilkunde,* and did not anticipate the strident pro-Nazi rhetoric of Göring's little communication, but surely he should have been—and probably was—aware that his remarks would be placed within a framework of loyalty to the cause in a journal that, while under Jung's nominal editorship, was published and printed in Germany as the main public vehicle for the German psychotherapists. This was especially so in light of his German colleagues' efforts to associate his name, person, and theory with themselves.

Regardless of their context, Jung's observations were objectionable in and of themselves to many, as they seemed to support the official anti-Semitism of the Nazi government. In February 1934 the Swiss psychiatrist Gustav Bally attacked Jung's future credibility as editor of a coordinated periodical and pointed to what he considered to be the damning emphasis Jung had placed on the supposed distinctions between Jewish and Germanic science, a common theme among Nazi intellectual apologists. At best, Bally concluded, Jung was, even if unwittingly, abetting National Socialism.[127] Jung replied to Bally by citing his "disappointment" at the publication of the Göring pledge of allegiance to Hitler in the *Zentralblatt,* and by asserting that he was president not of the German society but of the international society. "As conditions then were, a single stroke of the pen in high places would have sufficed to sweep all psychotherapy under the table. That had to be prevented at all costs for the sake of suffering humanity, doctors and . . . science and civilization."[128] Jung's use of the past tense in 1934 is indicative of how his perception of the danger to psychotherapy in the previous year had changed. This could evidence rueful reappraisal on the basis of a guilty conscience and/or an honest sense of having accomplished something positive in terms of the protection of psychotherapy. At the same time, Jung continued a somewhat anxious correspondence with Gauger and others in Germany through 1936.

In response to Bally's objection to his distinction between German and Jew, Jung denied that he was thereby making any value judgments, and rejected the assertion that he had only recently and strategically begun emphasizing racial and cultural differences among peoples. It is clear in this instance, however, that he was attempting to use his own particular psychological view, with its criticism of the materialism of Freud's perspective and the rootlessness of modern Jewish culture, to protect psychotherapists in Germany. In an essay in the *Zentralblatt* in 1934, Jung again sought to distinguish between the Jewish and the "Aryan" unconscious, claiming that Freud "did not know the German soul, and neither do any of his blind adherents. Has not the shattering advent of National Socialism, upon which the world gazes with astonished eyes, taught them better?"[129]

The basis for the profession's concern, of course, was the association in Nazi minds of all psychotherapy with psychoanalysis. In 1936, when the DPG anxiously approached the C. G. Jung Society in Berlin with a proposal for merger, Jung advised against it on these grounds. In a letter of 14 May 1936 to Gauger Jung noted,

You know that I am no absolute Freudian zealot [*Freudfresser*], rather I acknowledge the correctness of a number of Freudian statements with respect to the special structure of neuroses and most especially their sexual aspect. However, these things must be taught in a positive philosophical context so that they cause no public harm.

It does seem fair to conclude that the primary emphasis in this still disturbingly ambiguous statement was on Jung's concern that the official Nazi prohibition of the continued existence of an independent psychoanalysis in Germany might prejudice the existence of all the schools of psychotherapy there rather than that he attributed "harm" to the substance of psychoanalytic theory itself. Whatever the depth of Jung's early naïve enthusiasm for the dynamism of National Socialism, and no matter how strongly he may have worked to promote his own theories at the expense of those of Freud, it seems that these did not translate themselves into concrete activity on behalf of National Socialism.

By 1936 Jung was contemplating National Socialism with a more critical eye: "The impressive thing about the German phenomenon is that one man, who is obviously 'possessed,' has infected a whole nation to such an extent that everything is set in motion and has started rolling on its course to perdition."[130] The words are from Jung's essay, "Wotan," which the Göring Institute Jungian Lucy Heyer-Grote claimed to have used psychotherapeutically with comforting effect on patients who were opponents of the Nazi regime. It was a work that anticipated Jung's September 1939 judgment that "Hitler is reaching his climax and with him the German psychosis."[131]

In the realm of psychotherapy, Jung was appalled in 1937 to learn from C. A. Meier, a managing editor of the *Zentralblatt,* that Göring had written for publication there a short review of Nazi philosopher Alfred Rosenberg's *Der Mythus des 20. Jahrhunderts* (1930). In a letter to Göring of 16 November, Jung suggested that the book be passed over in silence, and in fact the review did not appear, perhaps a sign that Jung and Meier could exercise some influence over what appeared in the journal's pages.[132] Two years later, Jung himself turned down a request from the editor of the *Zeitschrift für Rassenkunde,* Egon Freiherr von Eickstedt of Breslau, to write an article on contemporary racial problems.[133]

Our conclusion must be that Jung acted primarily out of his concern with the survival of the profession in Germany when he involved himself in its affairs there and in Europe after the advent of Hitler. Given a *Weltanschauung* that, even as late as 1936, with "Wotan," embodied, if not a reverence, an awe as well as a certain degree of resignation before the depth and power of the unconscious in all its collective manifestations, he had a clear predisposition to behave in the way he did. The critical rationality of the Freudian tradition, by contrast, stressed the common and universal individual human pathology in such phenomena as Nazism, and was therefore much more disposed to an immediate and forceful rejection of National Socialism. All in all, Jung seems to have acted far less extremely than either his defenders or his detractors have claimed. It is by no means clear that the personal philosophical beliefs and attitudes behind Jung's dubious, naïve, and often objectionable statements during the Nazi era about "Aryans" and Jews motivated his actions with regard to psychotherapists in Germany. The statements themselves reveal a destructive ambivalence and prejudice that may have served Nazi persecution of the Jews. But Jung conceded much more to the Nazis by his words than by his actions. A study of Jung's actions, then, is important because it illuminates from another angle the struggle of psychotherapists in Germany for survival and advancement.

In 1940 Jung ended his participation in the affairs of the International General Medical Society for Psychotherapy. Following a meeting of delegates from Germany, Italy, Sweden, Switzerland, and Hungary, and the refusal of Poul Bjerre to succeed Jung as president, the society was placed for the duration of the war under German direction, and its headquarters were moved from Zurich to Berlin. The *Zentralblatt* officially remained the journal of the international society, but, in Göring's words, in order to ensure a "strict execution" of its "care and control," Rudolf Bilz, the Berlin psychotherapist and Nazi party member, took over as editor from Otto Curtius of Duisburg and C. A. Meier of Zurich.[134] Jung had attempted to resign in July 1939 when Göring announced the formation of groups from Italy, Hungary, and Japan, but he was induced to stay on until these groups actually had been accepted into the international society. Negotiations dragged on into the following year, and since the additions represented a strengthening of German influence through the procurement of two Axis partners and a revisionist Balkan state, Jung saw no reason to continue purely as a figurehead president.

Whether the Nazis instigated Göring's actions is not known, but it was a strategy that was similar in intent to the regime's reversal in 1936 of its earlier command to the DPG to withdraw from the International Psycho-Analytic Association. The purpose of that strategy, according to Kemper, was not so much to cultivate a certain degree of international goodwill in an Olympic year as it was to provide an opening for German influence in the international professional affairs of the future. In 1937, Göring, in touting psychotherapy to the German medical establishment, boasted that one-third of the participants at the international psychotherapeutic congress in Copenhagen that year were "Reich Germans" (*Reichsdeutsche*), and that half of all the papers had been given by Germans.[135] After the tenth and last International Medical Congress for Psychotherapy held at Oxford, England, from 29 July to 2 August 1938, however, the German General Medical Society for Psychotherapy fell away from genuinely international scientific dialogue. No congress was held in 1939; the Vienna congress of 1940 was a German-Italian affair dedicated to the war effort; and the society, with its 291 members, was eclipsed by the Göring Institute and disappeared from the public record in 1941. By 2 September 1939, in a letter to Hugh Crichton-Miller, since 1938 vice-president of the international society, Jung was complaining of Göring's "simple psychology" and "general inability."[136]

By 1940, when Hitler ruled the Continent, Germany had become the center, the undisputed locus, of organized European psychotherapy. How the profession managed to reach this point is the subject of the next chapter. It takes us into the often warring realms of the Third Reich's party and state apparatus, and shows how the embattled profession, devoid of its best minds and officially pledged to serve National Socialism, was able to steer a middle course between them. We will also note some of the surprising benefits that accrued from the psychotherapists' enforced cooperation with one another.

CHAPTER 5

Between Party and State

The first three years of Nazi rule gave way to a feudal amalgam of bureaucratic retrenchment, satrapy building, and, with the Four-Year Plan of 1936 under Hermann Göring, preparations for war. Within the ensuing confusion, psychotherapy under the Göring family banner was able to forge a successful institutional existence, but not without continuing buffeting and frequent assaults from its enemies.

How did the Göring Institute manage to make its way between the demands and rivalries of party and state? The answer to this question takes us into the convoluted corridors of Nazi administration and governance. In the Third Reich party and state, offices and agencies were strewn about and piled onto one another. The Nazis had not swept away the bureaucratic structures they had inherited from the Empire and the Republic; they had taken them over, using, exploiting, and duplicating them. As a result, there never was a visible, direct struggle between the established organs of the German government as it stood in 1933 and the Nazi party. What emerged instead was a tangle of accommodation, conflict, and infiltration. The first losers were those within the party who hoped for swift and radical change in the institutional and social order.

The failure of early party zealots and reformers was particularly marked in the health field. In this chapter we examine how Julius Streicher and Gerhard Wagner, two high-ranking Nazis with special interests in reforming the field of medicine, were forced to pull in their horns in the face of opposition from the medical establishment and the Reich Interior Ministry. We also see how the successor to their efforts at change, Leonardo Conti, worked from within the Reich Interior Ministry to establish control over matters of health in the Third Reich.

Such early Nazi health ideologues posed a double threat to the psychotherapists. On the one hand, a rabid anti-Semite like the primitive

Streicher, co-publisher of *Deutsche Volksgesundheit aus Blut und Boden,* saw all of established medicine as a Jewish conspiracy and condemned all psychotherapists as followers of Freud; his brief reign imperiled the very existence of any sort of responsible or sophisticated medical psychology in Germany. Wagner, head of the party Physicians League, though far more restrained in these matters than Streicher, endangered psychotherapy by attempts to impose Nazi party control on medicine while many Nazi physicians opposed psychotherapy. This bureaucratic threat, which, like Streicher's poisonous blatherings, remained unrealized, took the form of systematic interference in the provinces of psychotherapy by Nazi mediocrities and incompetents.

At the same time, as we have seen, the very fact of the Nazi challenge to German medical orthodoxy, as well as some of the ambitions of party reformers like Wagner, also constituted an opportunity for the psychotherapists, giving rise to an interplay of personal power and influence that occupied the vacuum left by the Nazi failure even to propose, much less to effect, any comprehensive institutional or programmatic reforms.

With the exception of their exclusionary racial and political policies, the Nazis offered no ideological criteria by which ideas, positions, or disciplines could be accepted or rejected. Indeed, once represented by someone with the ability to command attention, a discipline, group, or cause was invariably judged by both its inherent usefulness to the regime and any advantage it offered to a respective Nazi patron or ally. This hardly means the Nazi ideals played no role in the functioning of the Nazi state. In fact, Nazi racism was both a cause of, and a complement to, the venal utilitarianism that was apparent within the bureaucracy of the Third Reich. As we have already observed, gross racial distinctions took the place of thought in the Nazi universe. But the racism of the Nazis also imputed internal qualities to the master race, the cultivation of which was seen to be the task of German psychotherapists, among others. We have seen how such cultivation directly and substantively contributed to the success of psychotherapists in the Third Reich.

The Nazi belief in racial superiority based on inherent physical and psychological characteristics tended to disparage any sort of mere institutional reform as superficial and unnecessary. Nazi pragmatism was not a purely rational process of *Realpolitik* in the *absence* of ideology, but was in part *a function of* incoherent and irrational racial fantasies. What had passed away after the first three or four years of Nazi rule was not the awful racism of Hitler and his cronies—which, as we noted in Chapter 1, inevitably found expression in war and extermination under the aegis of the SS. Rather the casualties in the Nazi takeover of the institutions of German government and society were the party activists, whose enthusiasms, feuds, and ambitions generated a blizzard of rhetoric, plans, and organizations in the first years of the Third Reich. The resulting environment allowed not only the persistence of traditional professional concerns but also the emergence of challenges to the established order in Germany as it had stood before 1933. The Health Practitioners Law of 1939 (see below) is an excellent example of the balance that was struck between Nazi reformers and their governmental and professional opponents. It was in this dynamic environment that psychotherapists found a way, under Matthias Heinrich Göring, to advance their professional claims within the field of health and medicine during the Third Reich.

It is the purpose of this chapter to show how the struggles for power over administering the medical affairs of the Third Reich, with all the institutional, judicial, and ideological baggage that accompanied it, enhanced Göring's efforts to further the interests of psychotherapy as a profession in National Socialist Germany. The personalistic nature of the Nazi state and hierarchy was made to order for M. H. Göring. His name permitted him to indulge his forthright nature by going here and there among the Nazi elite, seeking support and leverage for the budding profession whose official representative he had now become. Göring was also immune to the dangerous residue of the intense rivalries within the Nazi leadership. His early association with Gerhard Wagner, for example, caused him no problems in his working relationship with Leonardo Conti, Wagner's rival and successor. Indeed, as we will soon see, Conti himself had special reason to cultivate a good relationship with Göring.

Nazi Health Organizations

Nazi health propagandists and activists had carried on a spirited battle with their adversaries within the medical establishment and the state bureaucracy as well as having continued to fight among themselves. The extreme radicals within the NSDAP—who wished to abolish a "materialistic" and "un-German" health profession and bureaucracy—had met defeat by 1935, and the more moderate party reformers would do so two years later, but the insistence on National Socialist *Volksgesundheit* continued to produce a veritable barrage of organizations.

Gerhard Wagner, since 1932 leader of the National Socialist German Physicians League (Nationalsozialistischer Deutscher Ärztebund) founded in 1929, the party's Main Office for National Health (Hauptamt für Volksgesundheit der NSDAP), and the Expert Advisory Council for National Health (Sachverständigenbeirat für Volksgesundheit der NSDAP), was also General Plenipotentiary for the Health System (Generalbevollmächtigte der NSDAP für das Gesundheitswesen) and Deputy for all University Affairs (Der Beauftragte für alle Hochschulangelegenheiten).[1] As a result, Wagner was involved almost immedi-

Gerhard Wagner (1888–1939)

ately after Hitler became Chancellor in a competition with the health departments of the Ministry of the Interior (Reichsministerium des Innern/Reichsinnenministerium) for control over the administration of the country's health services.

The form the rivalry took was almost comical. During the spring of 1933, Wagner had established a Reich Study Group of Professions in Social and Medical Service (Reichsarbeitsgemeinschaft der Berufe im sozialen und ärztlichen Dienste). The Interior Ministry countered on 20 November by setting up a Reich Commission for National Health (Reichsausschuss für Volksgesundheit), chaired by departmental head Arthur Gütt and deputy director Gustav Frey. Frey and Gütt also ran the State Medical Academy (Staatsmedizinische Akademie) in Berlin, while Hans Reiter was director of the research activities of the Reich

Health Office (Reichsgesundheitsamt), and Edward Schütt presided
over the Scientific Society of German Doctors in the Public Health
Service (Wissenschaftliche Gesellschaft der deutschen Ärzte des öffent-
lichen Gesundheitsdienstes). In 1934 Gütt became a ministerial director and head of the Interior Ministry's Division for National Health
(Abteilung für Volksgesundheit).[2]

Even when, during the early months of 1934, some rationalization of
this confused and competing mass of sovereignties was attempted, the
little accommodation that was achieved was tentative and cosmetic; it
produced only agglutination and the persistence of party-state rivalry.
On 15 December 1933 Wagner had announced that the Reich Study
Group for Professions in Social and Medical Service operated under
the jurisdiction of the Interior Ministry and its minister, Wilhelm
Frick, and was to be headed by a party man named August Fleck. As
if the names of the participants were not confusing enough, Fleck, in
addition to being subordinate to Frick, was also a member of the
party's Expert Advisory Council for Health, and thus under Wagner's
authority as well.[3] Fleck's agency was located within the Reich Central
Office of Health Leadership (Reichszentrale der Gesundheitsführung)
run by Fritz Bartels, an Interior Ministry department head who was
Wagner's deputy in the Reich Physicians Chamber. The Reich Central Office was strongly oriented toward the NSDAP, with Bartels,
Wagner, and Erich Hilgenfeldt, director of the NSV, holding the key
positions. Reiter was deputy director of the Reich Study Group for
Public Hygiene (Reicharbeitsgemeinschaft für öffentliche Hygiene)
under Bartels. According to *Der Öffentliche Gesundheitsdienst* in 1935,
the Reich Central Office composed section 2 of the Reich Commission
for National Health Service (Reichsausschuss für Volksgesundheitsdienst) and included groups charged with combating various specific
threats to the national health (drug addiction, tuberculosis, cancer,
etc.), section 1 concerning itself with the tasks of national and racial
prophylaxis (*Volkspflege*). However, in a schema published by Reiter
in 1933 and reprinted by Fleck early in 1934, the Reich Central Office
buried the Reich Commission in an avalanche of organizations and
capacities.[4]

With the promulgation of the law concerning the unification of
health service on 30 March 1935, the state medical bureaucracy
launched an effective counteroffensive in service to its own prerogatives, and in September 1937 Frick happily confided in a letter to
Heinrich Lammers at the Chancellery that in the party city of Munich
Wagner was complaining of being shut out. Frick, with his own in-
clination for the bureaucratic and the statist, naturally felt that the
duties of the state health administration had to be preserved against
disruption from any source.[5] This was also the position the Reich
Chancellery adopted in the documentation it appended to the health

services proclamation. In 1938 Wagner, in desperation, pressed for a policy that would have the party assume all new assignments in the field of medicine and health care, but the Chancellery's response was firmly negative.[6]

The first major casualty in the Nazi process of tempering its early rhetoric and blunting its ideologists' more extreme efforts at change had been Julius Streicher, the gross corruptions of whose functions were by 1940 to deprive him of his party offices and power altogether. Streicher's *Deutsche Volksgesundheit aus Blut und Boden* propagandized stridently during the two years (1933–1935) of its existence for the virtues of the simple, clean life of the countryside, rejecting the "poisons" of modern civilization. Inoculation was a favorite target, labeled, like so many other phenomena, a Jewish plot to sap the strength and vitality of the Aryan race. The German medical community responded to Streicher's views with unanimous distress, particularly with respect to his attack on inoculation. In 1934 the Interior Ministry prohibited the dissemination of anti-inoculation propaganda, and the following year Wagner declared that neither the party Physicians League nor the Main Office for National Health had any connection with *Deutsche Volksgesundheit aus Blut und Boden*.[7] Streicher and Wagner had already clashed over the question of "cure freedom" (see below) and Streicher's contention that moves to terminate it constituted a Jewish conspiracy to destroy the German natural health movement.[8]

The last issue of *Deutsche Volksgesundheit aus Blut and Boden* appeared on 15 September 1935 and included an upbeat capitulation in the form of announcing that the publication was ending its life and would henceforth be subsumed into the Reich Study Group of Organizations for Life and Health Reform (Reichsarbeitsgemeinschaft der Verbände für Lebens- und Heilreform) under another of Wagner's deputies, Georg Gustav Wegener. This group had been formed on 24 May 1935 in Nuremberg along with the Reich Study Group for a New German Medicine (Reichsarbeitsgemeinschaft für eine neue deutsche Heilkunde) under the direction of Karl Kötschau, succeeding the Reich Study Group of Biological and Natural Health Doctors (Reichsarbeitsgemeinschaft der biologischen and Naturheilärzte), which had been founded on 24 November 1933.[9] These organizations represented a mustering of Wagner's forces, gathered to foment fundamental change in the health sciences and their administration. As Wagner proclaimed, "National Socialism is a renewing movement: It has never intended to be satisfied with a formal transformation of inner political relationships and the conquest of indefensible methods of governmental control."[10] Although Wagner's statement itself reflected the vague subjectivity of Nazi "renewing," the basis for his attack on the retrenched medical bureaucracy was his advocacy of natural health in a highly national, racial, and anti-Semitic context. He mobilized the reform-minded medical journal *Hippokrates,* which had been co-founded in 1928 by Erwin Liek, by making it the organ for Kötschau's Reich Study Group, supplementing *Ziel und Weg,* the organ of the Nazi Physicians League, and *Volksgesundheitswacht,* mouthpiece for the party's Expert Advisory Council on Health and edited by Bernard Hörmann, director (*Reichsamtsleiter*) of the German Society for the Control of Abuses in the Health System (Deutsche Gesellschaft zur Bekämpfung von Misstände im Gesundheitswesen).

The Reich Study Group for a New German Medicine embraced those disciplines on the margins of established medicine: the Reich League of Nature Healers (Reichsverband der Naturärzte), the Society for Spas and Climatic Science (Gesellschaft für Bäder und Klimakunde), the Central Association of Homeopathic Physicians (Zentralverein homöopathischer Ärzte), the League of Hydropathists (Kneippärzte-bund), the Reich League of Private Health Institutions (Reichsverband deutscher Privatkrankenanstalten), the Association of Anthroposophic Physicians (Vereinigung anthroposophischer Ärzte), and the German General Medical Society for Psychotherapy. The medical ethic that bound them all together was their belief in the necessity of preventive medicine, based on an appreciation of the totality of the human organism. The first and last congress of the Reich Study Group was held on 18–20 April 1936 in Wiesbaden, a month before the Göring Institute's official founding, and included addresses by Göring on the theory of neurosis, Heyer on the dynamic unity of mind and body, and Gauger on conscience. These meetings were held in conjunction with those of the German Society for Internal Medicine (Deutsche Gesellschaft für innere Medizin).[11]

By January 1937, however, Wagner's party front had collapsed, and the psychotherapists, along with the League of Nature Healers, became affiliated with the Reich Health Office under Reiter and loosely joined with the German Society for Internal Medicine.[12] Reiter was more sympathetic toward National Socialist health reform than some other medical bureaucrats within the Interior Ministry, but it was evident by this and other arrangements that channeled Nazi tasks through the established offices of the Interior Ministry that Frick had emerged victorious in his battles with Wagner. Moreover, the Reich Physicians Leader also faced the jealous claims made on health operations by Reich Labor Leader Konstantin Hierl, Reich Labor Minister Franz Seldte, who supervised national health insurance, and the ambitious Labor Front boss Robert Ley, who had acquired a wide range of offices in his visionary scheme to extend National Socialist care and control into every corner of German life. As a result, Ley clashed with Deputy Führer Rudolf Hess, who also was devoted to natural health; Wagner remained, as one contemporary foreign observer of the Nazi scene noted, a "ubiquitous old fighter"[13] in Hess's employ.

On 15 May 1934, Hess had ordered Wagner to assume leadership of the NSDAP's entire health organization, a province which had until then been claimed by Ley. By December Wagner had created the Main Office for National Health, technically incorporating the health agencies of all party organizations save those of the SA and the SS.[14] With the failure of Wagner's institutional offensive of 1935–36, and given Hess's limited abilities and powers, Ley regained some of the initiative in the sphere of health policy and administration. This was the dizzying context, of factional feuding amid the Nazi turn from reform to mobilization, for the fact that when the Göring Institute was created in 1936, it was affiliated with the Labor Front's Office for Vocational Training and Works Management (Amt für Berufserziehung und Betriebsführung).

The German Institute for Psychological Research and Psychotherapy: Founding and Funding

On 18 February 1936 Felix Boehm met with a representative of the Medical Division (Medizinalabteilung) of the Ministry of the Interior, possibly Herbert Linden or his deputy. It will be recalled that Boehm was one of the only two remaining members of the Berlin Psychoanalytic Institute's executive, and he was representing the DPG's request for continued licensure. The Medical Division was of the opinion that psychoanalysis would not be forbidden, since it was a useful therapy, but that under no circumstances would the official existence of an organization dedicated to the teachings of Freud be allowed. There was a solution to the problem, however, the ministry believed, since Matthias Heinrich Göring, the director of the German General Medical Society for Psychotherapy, was just then attempting to establish a psychotherapeutic outpatient clinic in Berlin.

Gauger was to assert after the war that Göring had intended from the beginning to establish a complete institute, financed by party organizations. But funding was a problem for the institute from the beginning—as it would continue to be until 1939. By the time of Boehm's meeting with the Interior Ministry's Medical Division, Göring apparently had solicited the Jungians about cooperation in the venture, but the president of the C. G. Jung Society in Berlin, Eva Moritz, wrote to Jung in the spring of that year saying that the project had failed, presumably for lack of funds. (In his letter to Gauger of 14 May 1936, Jung cited this information in stressing that something must be done to unite the various orientations in psychotherapy for their own protection.) The authorities suggested to Boehm that the psychoanalysts combine with the other psychotherapy groups in Berlin in a common institute; in this respect, as we observed earlier, the government seemed less frightened of the psychoanalysts than were the other psychotherapists. The Medical Division reasoned that by such a merger the psychoanalysts would acquire the necessary sanction to continue their work, and Göring and the other psychotherapists would gain the use of the Berlin Psychoanalytic Institute's offices and clinic, located at Wichmannstrasse 10.

Boehm reported back to the Medical Division on 18 March that the DPG was willing to accept this arrangement, whereupon the division's representative wrote to Göring in Wuppertal with the proposal for a common institute that would include the DPG, the C. G. Jung Society, and Künkel's Study Circle for Applied Characterology (Arbeitskreis für angewandte Charakterkunde). Details were worked out at a meeting on 26 April with Wagner's deputy, Franz Wirz, and Göring was formally requested to assume leadership of the new institute. The actual founding of the institute, in May–June 1936, followed in the wake of discussions among Wirz, M. H. Göring, an Interior Ministry representative, and two university psychiatrists. Göring was named director and Boehm was designated to serve as secretary. In November Göring moved from Wuppertal to Berlin to take control, addressing the first meeting of the membership on the subject of "Weltanschauung und Psychotherapie." His inaugural remarks on the therapeutic and political importance of the proper world view to be held by German psychotherapists reflected his own recent failed pursuit of an alternative that would realize his vision of a German psychotherapy on a non-Freudian, pro-Nazi, and anti-Semitic basis. This was the reason, combined with general trepidation and disagreement, for his hesistancy, as later reported by Müller-Braunschweig and Boehm, in admitting the psychoanalysts and his subsequent early attempts to limit their role.[15]

When the German Institute for Psychological Research and Psychotherapy (Deutsches Institut für Psychologische Forschung und Psychotherapie e.V.) began functioning with the winter semester of 1936–37, it did so as a registered association (*eingetragener Verein*) as of 1 October 1936, including the suffix "e.V." in its name. This last detail might well have been an indication of the psychotherapists' newly close formal affiliation with the Ministry of the Interior, along with a growing sense of establishment and respectability, since the inclusion of "e.V." in the name of a registered association was not required by law. The title had not appeared in the German General Medical Society's name, either before or after 1933, as it did, for example, in the case of the DPG.

The Göring Institute's statutes were administered by Herbert Linden, a senior civil servant (*Ministerialrat*) in the ministry's Medical Division, who became a member of the administrative board (*Ver-*

waltungsrat) of the institute. Linden was also a psychiatrist by training (and involved in the Nazi euthanasia program), and during the winter semester of 1939–40 gave a course on racial and biological hygiene at the institute. Although he was a member of the body responsible for assessing and promoting the progress toward unifying the various theories of the three schools of psychotherapy that prevailed in the institute, by all accounts this function was actually controlled and exercised by Göring and the other psychotherapists on the board.[16] In all of its manifestations, this goal of unification remained a professional, and not a governmental, responsibility.

Aside from the routine details required by its formal supervision of the Göring Institute and some continuing negotiations over questions of professional certification and licensure, the Interior Ministry did not figure prominently in the affairs of psychotherapy during the Third Reich. The ministry's major involvement seems to have ended, in fact, with the establishment of the institute, the solution to the problem of the remaining psychoanalysts, and the securing of Göring. Indeed, as the government's representative of established medicine, the various medical departments of the Interior Ministry continued to entertain no official notion of medical psychology apart from traditional university and clinical psychiatry.

The Göring Institute was funded by various means and to varying degrees in the course of its existence. From 1933 to 1936, German psychotherapists had supported the German General Medical Society for Psychotherapy out of their own pockets. This was no easy task given the poor financial condition in which many of the psychotherapists found themselves, a situation that ultimately spurred unsuccessful efforts on the part of the society to resolve with the government the questions of the professional status of psychotherapy in the medical profession and the inclusion of psychotherapy in the state health insurance program.[17] The maintenance of an institute, even with the ostensible loan of the teaching and treatment facilities and the accommodations of the Berlin Psychoanalytic Institute, was an even more demanding proposition. Although the Göring Institute received some money from the Labor Front (the Nazi organization that had taken the place of the trade unions) from its founding in 1936, until the outbreak of war it was primarily self-supporting. Ernst Göring claims that his father spent a great deal of his own money during the first years in order to help keep the institute going.

That things were difficult for the first three years was rather pathetically underlined in the institute's report for 1937 that a committee to oversee the library had not yet been named since there was no money with which to buy books. Appreciation was expressed to those who had donated books, including Hattingberg, Heyer, Schultz, Schultz-Hencke, and "to our joy also C. G. Jung."[18] Furthermore, during

1937–38 only one volume of six issues of the *Zentralblatt* appeared. Although C. A. Meier has asserted that this was a result of his editorial policy of quashing "Nazi nonsense" before publication, it is more likely that the journal's difficulties stemmed from a lack of funding, aggravated by the disruptions occasioned by Nazi rule. Franz Jung has recalled that the International General Medical Society for Psychotherapy, whose organ the *Zentralblatt* officially was, experienced problems with the publisher, S. Hirzel of Leipzig, over the small subscribership to the journal. It was precisely this scarcity of money, according to Ernst Göring, which prompted the psychotherapists to seek closer ties with the Labor Front. The affiliation was effected primarily through those psychotherapists who had connections in German industry, and the complementary imperialistic interest of Ley in extending DAF control over all aspects of the productive sectors of German society.

Industrial psychologists like Felix Scherke, August Vetter, Hans Meyer-Mark, Erika Hantel, and Gustav Schmaltz were already professionally active within industrial circles, and with the help of the Göring name they established working relationships with various large firms. Scherke, who came to the Göring Institute by way of the Institute for Consumption Research (Institut für Konsumforschung) in Nuremberg, had especially extensive contacts within German industry, including the huge dye trust I. G. Farben. Vetter, who headed the Göring Institute's psychological testing division in the outpatient clinic from 1939 to 1945, became a consultant for I. G. Farben in 1940 through an arrangement made by his eminent teacher and friend, Gustav Kafka. The firm even sent Vetter to Sweden in 1942 to give a series of lectures on German diagnostic testing. Meyer-Mark, like Scherke a somewhat shadowy figure, cultivated, according to Erika Hantel, a number of important relationships with industrial leaders, especially in the textile industry. Hantel herself—who had studied under Heyer in Munich, Viktor von Weizsäcker at Heidelberg, and Ernst Jaensch at Marburg— was a consultant, along with Wilhelm Bitter, with Robert Bosch in Stuttgart during 1939, and from 1942 until the end of the war she was the chief psychologist at the Arado aircraft works in Brandenburg-Neuendorf, just west of Berlin. Schmaltz, a member of the Düsseldorf affiliate of the Göring Institute, was himself the owner of a machine tool factory; he was prominent within a modest segment of the industrial leadership of the Ruhr, and also director of the Technical Group for Woodworking Machines of the Economic Group for Mechanical Engineering (Fachgruppe Holzbearbeitungsmaschinen der Wirtschaftsgruppe Maschinenbau) in Berlin.[19]

While German industry contributed employment opportunities for a number of psychotherapists at the Göring Institute, it was the German Labor Front that contributed the major portion of its financing from 1939 to 1942. On 30 September 1939, as a result of negotiations based on mutual interests and needs as well as the now accelerated national girding for war—that was to bring the institute additional financial support, from the Luftwaffe—the Labor Front assumed formal supervision over the Göring Institute. (Göring reported that the e.V. would continue to carry out small administrative duties under the direction of secretary Boehm and treasurer Müller-Braunschweig through the secretarial and bookkeeping offices, respectively, of the new "DAF-Institute."[20])

Friction would eventually develop between the Göring Institute and the Labor Front, but the search for adequate funding was over. Ernst Göring recollects that his father, parsimonious by nature, was even compelled to halve the salaries proposed by the DAF, and that he rejected the proposal for automobiles to be provided for the official use of the institute's leaders. Even so, in 1940 the institute was able to take on fourteen new employees, including two domestics, as compared to a total of two the year before; in 1941 the number of employees climbed to nineteen. By the summer of 1941 the institute had also completed a move from its expanded offices at Budapester Strasse 29, which it had occupied since 1 April 1937, to still larger offices at nearby Keithstrasse 41.

Göring credited the work of reorganization that was necessary as a result of the important new financial support provided by the DAF to Scherke and Meyer-Mark, and in 1941 Scherke became managing director of the institute, succeeding Hilde Strecker, who from 1936 to 1939 had watched over the comparatively modest funds of the original institute. As a result of all this, at the 1940 congress Göring expressed a justified appreciation to the Labor Front, an organization that in 1939 took in RM 539 million, or around $135 million, more than three times the income of the NSDAP itself: "Herr Dr. Ley has recognized how important depth psychology is, not only in medicine but for all segments of life, especially the economy. He has made it possible for our institute to be well financed, for which we thank him most heartily."[21]

Party and State Submerged: The Rise and Reign of Leonardo Conti, SS

On the eve of the war for racial supremacy that was the Darwinian raison d'être of Hitler's Reich, Gerhard Wagner died. He had been seriously ill since 1938, and his death, on 25 March 1939—a month after the promulgation of the Health Practitioners Law (Heilpraktikergesetz)—marked the end of Nazi attempts at health reform, however compromised. The state and the established medical profession had already begun a successful defense of its prerogatives and policies against the attacks of party activists. As early as 1933, both Hess and Wagner were asserting that their statements and program proposals were not intended to bypass or prejudice traditional university medicine, but only to expand the borders of medicine to include natural health theory and method. Later, Wagner was constrained, as a result of protest in the press and from the medical profession, to "clarify" remarks he had made regarding his apparent intention to provide qualifying examinations for nonmedical healers in his own medical schools. His "clarification" emphasized the indispensability of a university education.[22] But expanding the state supervision and promotion of medical practice and shortening the course of study in medicine, which constituted the reforms that were effected, were designed to accelerate the efficient production and utilization of health care personnel in national service. So while Wagner had to compromise on his support for natural health and to abandon his hopes for some fundamental organizational and conceptual reform, he was able to embody his own aims in legislation enacted by the Interior Ministry: national service for the medical profession through centralized control, the ideal of prevention, and the promotion of a racial consciousness. The problem for him was that he and his party agencies were pushed aside by the state and the SS in the struggle for power and the mobilization of the health services for war. This exhortative ethos of control over genuine institutional reform found dramatic expression in the so-called Health Practitioners Law of 1939. This law, which in modified form is still on the books in the Federal Republic of Germany, ended the freedom to cure that had existed in Germany since 1870. According to the Nazi health leadership, such a "liberal-democratic" policy had merely served as a license for Jews to swindle gullible German citizens through the sale of patent medicines, the use of occult cures, and general medical and pharmaceutical malfeasance. Under the new law, the government would closely supervise the training of all medical personnel, including officially approved health practitioners. This represented a compromise between the proponents of natural health and traditional medicine, but one which gave professional preference to regular physicians and organizational power to the Interior Ministry.[23]

But this compromise was part of the eclipse of the early party activists' power and influence. The halcyon days of 1933 had passed very quickly, and Wagner had become one of those "old fighters" (*Alte Kämpfer*) overshadowed and left behind by his Führer, who was courting new supporters in the anterooms, boardrooms, and barracks of German society. The somewhat apologetic and disclaiming words written by Martin Bormann in a 1944 introduction to a volume of Wagner's speeches underlined the outdatedness of such noisy attempts at overturn and change: "The speeches are characteristic of the stormy period of development after the revolution."[24] The book was edited by Wagner's successor, Leonardo Conti. Conti had become director of the party's Main Office for National Health on 22 April 1939, and im-

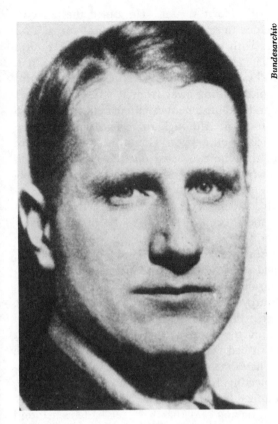

Bundesarchiv

Leonardo Conti (1900–1945)

mediately festooned himself with the brand new Nazi neologism of Reich Health Leader (Reichsgesundheitsführer). On recommendation by Frick, Conti was also named by Hitler to replace Wagner as Reich Physicians Leader; at the same time he became a state secretary in the Ministry of the Interior, an occasion on which *Der Öffentliche Gesundheitsdienst* editorialized with a sincerity born of a certain degree of institutional loyalty: "We welcome with joy the news that our professional associate, party comrade Dr. Conti, has been entrusted with the united direction of party and state health organizations."[25]

Conti had impeccable credentials as far as the party was concerned. Born Leonardo Ambrosis Georges Giovanni Conti in Lugano, Switzerland, he claimed to have debated communist leader Karl Liebknecht in 1919. He had participated in the Kapp putsch against the Weimar government in 1920, and from 1921 to 1923 he was a member of the rightist student Wikingbund. In 1923, while studying at Erlangen in northern Bavaria, he joined the SA and later in Berlin became chief

physician for SA Standarte V "Horst Wessel." He joined the party in
1927 and the same year helped to establish the SA medical corps. Two
years later he was involved with Bormann and Wagner in the reform
of SA insurance, and in 1930, as Wagner's overseer (*Gauobmann*), had
become head of the Nazi Physicians League in Berlin.[26] By the critical
year of 1934 Conti was rapidly falling away from Wagner and the SA
and into the more elite and establishment-oriented realms of the SS
and the Ministry of the Interior. Although there exists no evidence
of a major personal or official feud between Conti and Wagner, there
are significant indications that the two acted out the traditional ani-
mosity that played between SA and SS, between party and state, between Munich and Berlin.[27]

When, as Reich Health Leader, Conti was charged with preparing
the edition of Wagner's speeches in 1944, it was Bormann, a party
patron of both Wagner and Conti, who produced the regulation praise
that was in order for the dead Reich Physicians Leader. Much earlier,
in 1930, Conti had warned of the ultimately abortive Stennes putsch
that was then bubbling up out of the SA, and four years later he was
reaping the vengeful rewards of the aftermath of the Röhm putsch.
Conti was charged by Reich Physician of the SA (Reichsarzt der SA)
Emil Ketterer with alluding to, or even originating, the rumor that
Ketterer had been found in bed with Röhm on the night of 30 June
1934. Conti also allegedly had drawn Wagner into the affair, by claiming that Wagner was protecting Ketterer—a friend of Erwin Villain,
whom Wagner had recommended for a post over Conti's objections.
For his part, Conti denied having said that Ketterer had been found
in bed with Röhm; what he had said, he maintained, was only that
Ketterer had been in the same house as Röhm on 30 June and was
therefore unfit.[28]

It was in fact Conti's skirmish with Villain before the putsch that
showed more clearly and violently where the lines of sovereignty and
loyalty were being drawn in the struggle for power over the administration of the medical affairs of the Reich. Villain was the Nazi chief
of the Greater Berlin Physicians Association (Gross-Berliner Ärztebund) and Wagner's agent (*Vertrauensmann*) in Berlin. Wagner had
demanded the naming of Villain to the presidency of both the physicians chamber and court of honor (*Ehrengericht*) for Berlin. Conti, as
the responsible official in the Prussian Interior Ministry, had recommended to the Minister-President of Prussia, Hermann Göring, that
this appointment not be made, citing what Conti regarded as Villain's
personal deficiencies. Göring accepted Conti's recommendation and
informed Wagner of his decision and the rationale behind it. On hearing a report on all of this from Wagner, Villain wrote Conti, challenging him to a duel with sabers. Göring forbade Conti to accept the challenge, but the affair did not end there.

Villain's desire to extract what he regarded as satisfaction from Conti for this affront took the form of a physical assault by Villain on Conti in Munich on the night of 4 March 1934. Villain was arrested, and what ensued was an almost farcical exercise of opposing interests and influences. Ketterer managed to have Villain freed in his custody, but Göring had Villain arrested again in order to bring him back to Berlin. The Bavarian Minister of the Interior, Adolf Wagner, then had Villain released. Ketterer hid the fugitive in Partenkirchen where, under the official protection of the SA, he resisted all attempts at arrest and transport to Berlin after he was found by a public prosecutor who had been sent to Munich from Berlin. At this point, Reich Interior Minister Frick and Reich Justice Minister Gürtner involved themselves in the case, and Villain finally agreed to return to Berlin under the care of Berlin SA leader Karl Ernst and stand trial. All the while Villain remained on active duty with the SA and was even awarded its dagger of honor. Despite attempts by the SA to have the trial aborted, and a clumsy attempt by Ketterer to influence the court while it was in session, Villain was convicted of assault and sentenced to eight months in prison. He filed an appeal, and an SA court of honor convened by Röhm found Conti in contempt of the SA.[29] Any effects of such prosaic and petty proceedings were eclipsed, however, by the 30 June purge of the SA by Hitler at the urging of Göring and Himmler. Villain was one of the victims.[30]

Although in 1935 Wagner himself declared his belief that Conti was innocent of wrongdoing in the Ketterer and Villain affairs,[31] this declaration must be viewed as an expression of resignation rather than rapprochement. The tide had already turned from brown to black, and after Wagner's death in 1939 Conti set about assembling all capacities and prerogatives concerning health and medicine within his offices at the Interior Ministry.

Conti was a teetotaler and a nonsmoker, but his relatively moderate views on the need for natural health practices aided and abetted by the achievements of the German drug industry made him a more attractive ally for the medical establishment than the radical Wagner and his noisy cronies had been.[32] In 1942 Conti clashed with the arch-dabbler Himmler over state regulation of "people's doctors,"[33] insisting that the Interior Ministry must have control over their activities.

Conti's first task on being named Reich Health Leader was to install men loyal to him at key positions in the state medical bureaucracy. Conti himself replaced Arthur Gütt as state secretary while Kurt Blome supplanted Wagner's deputy, Fritz Bartels. These appointments were made by Hitler on Frick's recommendation. On 30 March 1940 Conti announced the dissolution of the Reich Central Office of Health Leadership, which under Bartels had been a bastion of party health activities within the Interior Ministry. The surviving Reich Commission for National Health Service was to be bound closer than ever to the Interior Ministry, and on 12 April Reiter's Reich Health Office was also placed more firmly under ministry control. Interior Ministry bureaucrats Robert Cropp and Herbert Linden were named to direct the activities of the Reich Commission, and close cooperation was proclaimed between it and the party's Race Political Office (Rassenpolitisches Amt der NSDAP).[34]

These moves gutted what was left of the party's health apparatus, leaving it with only the broad but insubstantial direction of the racial consciousness of the nation as part of overall healthfulness. Conti also moved against the Labor Front, first by becoming a state secretary in the Labor Ministry and thereby assuming authority over the management of national health insurance. Ley protested to Hess that this made Conti his own superior, because as state secretary in the Interior Ministry he already controlled the Panel Doctors Association of Germany (Kassenärztliche Vereinigung Deutschlands), which represented doctors participating in state medical insurance programs, and the Reich Physicians Chamber, and such a monopoly prejudiced DAF efforts in the sphere of what Ley called social politics: "[a] personal union of Reich Physicians Leader–Reich Health Leader–state secretary for social insurance in the Reich Labor Ministry and the exclusion of the party contains great dangers."[35] Previously, Ley had separated the Labor Front's Office for National Health (Amt für Volksgesundheit) from the party's Main Office for National Health in an attempt to retain some sovereignty in the medical field, but Conti in the meantime had acquired formal control over DAF health activities through the creation of a new DAF office (Fachamt Gesundheit) under his direction. He also installed his choice, Werner Bockhacker, as director of another Labor Front organization, the Office for Health and Popular Protection (Amt für Gesundheit and Volksschutz), and moved Bockhacker's offices from the party city of Munich to the seat of the Reich government in Berlin.[36]

Although he eventually fell prey to hierarchial intrigue,[37] Conti, in contrast to the coarser brutes carrying SA knives, had the lean and hungry look of the smooth, intelligent, ambitious SS man. As such, his activities on behalf of the Interior Ministry at the expense of party organizations delighted Frick, who was "at heart a civil servant who abhorred wild and uncontrollable actions by undisciplined party members."[38] Frick's campaign for control of the Reich's internal affairs had met with early success since he possessed in the Interior Ministry a sophisticated base of operations from the beginning in 1933. By the time party forces began to organize effectively in 1934, Frick, in the interest of the "seizure of society's strengths,"[39] was able over the next five years to check and repel them.

Most disturbing, of course, had been the threat of the brownshirts under Röhm who had pressed for a soldier's state, not so much in the spirit of a genuine "second revolution" but in a chaotic demand for state aid, for the spoils of victory in monthly checks; in the words of Joachim Fest, they were "desperados in search of a pension."[40] By contrast, Conti was to Frick a shining example of the process begun in 1933: to subordinate the party to the state by way of ordained party-state unity. The key element for the state's victory was the channeling of party influence through the state ministries and their bureaucracies. In the field of health, the legal basis for this was the legislation of 1934 that decreed the unification of Germany's health system.

What Conti actually represented, however, was the creation of an SS "collateral state" which "gradually penetrated existing institutions, undermined them, and finally began to dissolve them."[41] Frick himself fell prey to Reichsführer-SS Himmler in large bites: Himmler's assumption of control over all police forces in 1936 and his acquisition of the post of Interior Minister in 1943. These were, however, only major instances in a constant process whereby the Third Reich lost the characteristics of a state as it degenerated into a jumbled agglomeration of action centers, plenipotentiaries, and various and sundry deputations of the only thing that consistently counted in Nazi Germany: loyalty to Hitler. Conti's collection of offices and capacities inside the Interior Ministry therefore constituted not a unification of the health system, but rather the construction of a personal realm of power and authority that perversely capitalized on the state's earlier efforts to centralize and rationalize the health bureaucracy. In this way the nature of Nazi rule prefigured and paralleled the physical destruction that justly and inevitably followed from its existence and its excesses. Berlin under the Allied blitz took on the bureaucratic features of the regime that had brought the bombers over and the occupiers in:

> The straight-ruled boulevards built to be marched along are now winding pathways through the wastepiles, their shapes organic now, responding, like goat trails, to laws of least discomfort. . . . Smooth facets of buildings have given way to cobbly insides of concrete blasted apart, all the endless-pebbled rococo just behind the shuttering. Inside is outside. Ceilingless rooms open to the sky, wall-less rooms pitched out over the sea of ruins in prows, in crow's-nests. . . . Advertisements for shelter, clothing, the lost, the taken, once classified, folded bürgerlich inside newspapers to be read at one's ease in the lacquered and graceful parlors are now stuck with Hitler-head stamps of blue, orange, and yellow, out in the wind, when the wind comes, stuck to trees, door-frames, planking, pieces of wall—white and fading scraps, writing spidery, trembling, smudged, thousands unseen, thousands unread or blown away.[42]

Both the party and the state were gradually submerged in a "series of undulating layers of influence, operating simultaneously above, below and parallel"[43] that constituted Hitler's law and governance of a besieged fortress. This organizational jungle was a signal element in the opportunity for psychotherapists in the Third Reich to organize themselves and operate professionally. It was a result of the superficial nature of the Nazi transformation of Germany that initially gave the appearance of efficiency, unanimous popular and institutional acquiescence, and coherent and aggressive plans for reform. The Nazi concerns with mobilizing expertise and avoiding disruptive reform—along with the pervasiveness of personal loyalties and feuds—filled the vacuum that constituted Nazi ideas.[44] There was, all things considered, just enough upheaval to allow the psychotherapists through the door, and the right amount of conformity to preserve them from inflamed Nazi ideologues.

In the midst of this swirl of chaos and conformity, and consistent with the *sauve qui peut* symptomatic of the Nazi state, Reich Health Leader Conti himself had ample reason to appreciate the Göring name. As we have already seen, Conti had benefited from the support of Hermann Göring, his boss as head of the Prussian Ministry of the Interior, in his struggle with the SA in 1934. But Conti's ties with the Göring bastion in Prussia had a longer history. In December 1930 Conti had been a member of SS-Gruppenführer Kurt Daluege's staff in Berlin when Daluege was assigned to Hermann Göring, in Göring's capacity as Reich Commissar for the Prussian Interior Ministry, to rid the Prussian police administration of all politically unreliable officials, and Daluege was to become one of Göring's chief operatives in the short struggle with Himmler for control of the police and the Gestapo.[45] And on 13 February 1933, Göring delegated Conti to rid the medical profession of Jews and Marxists; on 12 January 1934 he named him a Prussian state councilor for life.

Conti's success under Hermann Göring's aegis, a success which was to continue under Frick after the Prussian and Reich Interior ministries were fused during 1934 and 1935,[46] reached its peak in 1939. That year it was Göring who resolved the tug-of-war between Munich and Berlin over the succession to Wagner's post by naming Conti as Reich Health Leader.[47] Göring's liking for him would certainly not have been diminished by an earlier decision Conti allegedly made. According to Matthias Heinrich Göring, in 1933 Conti "was consulted by the Prussian Minister-President for his opinion on whether our society should continue on in existence."[48] Although elder cousin Göring's reconstruction of the events of 1933 understandably implied that this consequent decision was based on the proper consideration of scientific merit and *völkisch* value, it would be fatuous to ignore Conti's political motivation for having rendered a positive evaluation of the General Medical Society for Psychotherapy. Ernst Göring has recalled that his father often mentioned Conti's name, although he feels that Conti was at best ambivalent about psychotherapy, a fact which would hardly be surprising given the strong dimensions of self-interest in Conti's assistance and/or lack of obstruction. And, in any case, in 1940 M. H. Göring may have exaggerated Conti's 1933 mission given his advanced status by then as Health Leader.

It is possible, of course, that Conti was either directed by Hermann Göring to see to the preservation of the psychotherapists' society, or that he acted on his own initiative after having approved Gauger's offer to help organize the psychotherapists—on learning from him of the existence and identity of Matthias Heinrich Göring. Conti seems to have figured very little in the affairs of the society and the institute after 1933, although Kemper remembers at least one Conti visit to the institute. And it is recorded that in 1944 it was Conti who awarded Göring the Badge of Honor for German Racial Cultivation (Ehrenzeichen für Deutsche Volkspflege), second class.[49]

Enforced Cooperation: The Assets

All this indirection left the psychotherapists somewhere between party and state, and worked at all levels to create room for the practical and professional exercise of their expertise. The following episodes supply some sense of the prevailing atmosphere, in which to be banned from one arena was to be welcomed or ignored in another. In 1939 Kurt Seelmann, a young teacher and member of Seif's Adlerian circle in Munich, was being considered for promotion to the rank of senior master (Hauptlehrer), a rank he achieved in 1940. In the course of deliberations in the government and the party, the regional party education office produced an evaluation on 19 May 1939 that virtually gushed approval.[50] Two years later, however, Seelmann was the subject of a more critical evaluation by an agency of the NSDAP. The German Popular Education Service (Deutsches Volkbildungswerk), a semi-independent part of the Labor Front's "Strength through Joy" program that competed in modest fashion with Goebbels's propaganda empire, was planning a series of nationwide lectures on the preservation of mental health (seelische Gesunderhaltung), and Seelmann was to be one of the participants. In 1935 Ernst Göring had given lectures on psychotherapy for the same agency, but the NSDAP office for the overseeing of "cultural-political" activities, under Alfred Rosenberg, on 28 July 1941 requested the party leadership in Bavaria to supply an evaluation of Seelmann's suitability for such a role.[51] The response from Munich has not survived, but we might well assume that, as in the case of Seelmann's promotion, Bavaria, with traditional independence (or, from the Prussian point of view, a peculiarly particularistic and uniquely boorish and beery Bavarian cussedness), protested that there were no subversives active within its borders. In any case, the final recommendation of the Rosenberg office on 15 August 1941 to those in charge of the lecture series was that Seelmann should not be invited to participate. Although, in the opinion of the office, there were no obvious political liabilities apparent in Seelmann's background, his professional associations were suspect:

> he however was already working during the Weimar period with Leonhardt Seiff [sic], the Munich representative of Freudian-Alderian psychoanalysis. He directed an educational counseling clinic that was abolished after the taking of power, since operations were conducted by the rule of individual psychology and psychoanalysis. Today the aforementioned Dr. Seiff has switched to "Gemeinschaftspsychologie." It is to be assumed, however, that Seelmann is still as before a prisoner to the former way of thinking.[52]

This example shows the practical persistence of Rosenberg's Nazi ideological fervor long after it had ceased even to appear to mean anything to the Nazi leadership. And Seelmann recalls that even though he had to be careful in delivering lectures that were occasionally monitored by Nazi informants, up to 1943 he regularly spoke in Munich and elsewhere in Germany for the German Popular Education Service and other groups. Furthermore, the assertion that the "Freudian-Adlerian" educational counseling clinic had been abolished after the Nazi seizure of power in 1933 was inaccurate. In actuality, the only genuine change in its status was the affiliation of Seif's Munich group with the Göring Institute in 1936, and its formal incorporation together with Heyer's circle in Munich three years later, whereupon work went on as before. Seif himself had been cleared in like manner to Seelmann by the Nazi Teachers League (Nationalsozialistischer Lehrerbund) and by the party's Main Office for National Health; in addition, a book of which Seif was the senior author and which described the operations of his educational counseling clinic, was included in the Nazi bibliography edited by the Chancellery's Philip Bouhler. All of this happened in January 1941, the same year in which he was being written off as an agent of Jewish thought by Rosenberg's organization.[53]

In 1942 Seelmann published his first book, *Kind, Sexualität und Erziehung*, and it also was included in the Nazi bibliography of that year. Seelmann's book was essentially a popular guide to the prevention of psychological disorders through proper parental, medical, and educational guidance of children and through an understanding of their sexual development. The tiny abstract which accompanied its listing in the bibliography expressed the common utilitarian approach that had replaced ideological passion among the Nazis:

> This work stems from the experiences of the medical-psychological counseling office of the Munich neuropathologist Dr. L. Seif and his associates

and therefore champions the theoretical principles of that school. Without giving credence to the content in all its details, the book may be recommended as a practical aid for parents and educators.[54]

Like Seelmann's *Kind, Sexualität und Erziehung*, the two books by I. H. Schultz which were included in the Nazi bibliography were also practical works, one for the layman and the other for the general practitioner. *Geschlecht, Liebe, Ehe* (1941) was similar to Seelmann's work in content as well as form, and the bibliography praised it for its "cautious introduction" to human sexual life and the development of a sexual ethic united with the new Germany's conception of natural ties to the race (*Erbgebundenheit*). *Die seelische Gesunderhaltung* (1942), based on a Schultz address to the press in January 1941, was recommended as a sound set of principles and guidelines for the practicing physician.[55]

Since National Socialist virtues rested within the nimbus of subjectivity and shared experience, the tendency toward controlled manipulation, utilitarianism, and mobilization spared practical and technical disciplines whose devaluation required much more than the generally short-lived, half-hearted, and intellectually inadequate attempts at "Aryanization." Hitler's Germany demanded obedient productivity and judged a discipline in the end by its usefulness within the context of vague notions of inherent German racial superiority. As Alan Beyerchen has shown in the case of physicists in the Third Reich, what ultimately concerned the Nazis was political opposition, not professional debate: The failure of "Aryan physics" was based on the inability of its proponents to show the Nazi leaders that their aims had practical benefits and that professional opposition to their theories and programs was a threat to the development of physics as a practical profession. Indeed, what became clear was that the opposite was the case. The Nazis contented themselves with tirades against "Jewish physics" and, as elsewhere, forcing Jews from their posts.[56]

Among psychotherapists it was therefore anything but inappropriate for Matthias Heinrich Göring to refer to the published text of a speech given at the University of Cologne on 16 November 1934 by Hitler's press chief, Otto Dietrich. The thrust of Dietrich's remarks was an extended, indeed overblown, paraphrase of Goethe's aphorism *"was fruchtbar ist, allein ist wahr"* ("only that which is fruitful is true").[57] Dietrich's emphasis, like Göring's in his citation of him in the context of his own inaugural address at the institute, was that, given the proper inward orientation as guaranteed by race and upbringing, standards of productivity and excellence must obtain in Nazi Germany. This practical, racially deterministic orientation undercut the attempt by Göring and others to construct an exclusively and genuinely Germanic psychotherapy, the most absurd notion of which had been Göring's anxiously enthusiastic, though transitory, assignment of *Mein Kampf* as a basic text. No substantively new psychotherapy was required, only a properly loyal and effective one.

A significant result of this atmosphere was that psychoanalysis remained as important in the history of psychotherapy in the Third Reich as did the amalgam of Adlerian and Jungian precepts that seemed to be such an obvious part of the new value system. The viability of psychoanalysis and the expertise and energy of its remaining practitioners allowed not only its survival in Germany but the growth of its influence within the Göring Institute. Rhetoric counted for something, especially in the earlier years of the regime, but the value, and hence the continued existence and development, of psychotherapy under Nazism was gauged by its effectiveness. Like all other therapeutic means in the field, where Freud worked, Freud was used, an exercise of what had been the party's attitude from the regime's start. Ernst Kris, a psychoanalyst who managed to flee Austria, observed during the war that the army and the Ministry of Propaganda incorporated a psychoanalytic perspective in their psychological work, unconcerned that Freud's writing had been publicly burned in 1933. To be sure, Kris was making the general and partisan point that no psychology in the twentieth century could dispense with Freud. But the army did, as we will see, refer to Freud. And although there is no evidence for any enthusiasm on the part of Goebbels for Freud, we do know that in 1940 Göring announced the existence of contacts with the Propaganda Ministry (Reichsministerium für Volksaufklärung und Propaganda). In addition, Johanna Herzog-Dürck recalled one institute meeting with representatives of Goebbels's ministry.[58]

Heinrich Himmler was also a prime example of this kind of practical convenience, even though he had expressed his distrust of medical psychologists in general to his masseur, Felix Kersten, in no uncertain terms: "They're a trade union for pulling people's souls to pieces, headed by Freud, their Jewish honorary president—though they may quietly disown or supersede him for their own ends."[59] Himmler did not hesitate in his ignorance to affirm portions of the psychoanalytic point of view in erecting the SS-Lebensborn for the procreation and cultivation of a master race:

> Ignoring the obvious contribution which a Jew, Sigmund Freud, had made to his analysis, Himmler asserted that sex was natural and that in establishing artificial restrictions on sexual relations society created the unhealthy conditions which currently threatened Germany.[60]

And beyond typical Nazi conceptual fuzziness, Himmler's rejection of Freud as a Jew would not prevent him from working, at least indirectly, with the Göring Institute on the regime's problems with homosexuality and psychogenic sterility, or from directly engaging the institute to treat the psychological crisis in the life of one member of an SS officer's family. (See Chapter 6.)

In light of the accelerating demand for performance over purity of doctrine, what precisely was the fate of the new German psychotherapy within the Göring Institute? Article 2 of the statutes administered by the Interior Ministry for the Göring Institute declared that the purpose of the institute was the creation of a German psychology and psychotherapy through scientific meetings, research, and publications. Article 9 called for monthly meetings of all members of the institute, during which papers would be presented and discussions held on the question of the unification of the three major schools of thought in psychotherapy as well as the cultivation of relationships with neighboring disciplines, such as psychiatry and psychology. Article 9 also required occasional meetings of each study group, the Adlerian, the Jungian, and the Freudian, to which members of the other groups would be invited to hear presentations on that group's work. During 1936 the psychoanalytic group held three such meetings, at which, in turn, a Frau Mitscherlich, Karen Horney, and Felix Schottländer spoke. The Jungians presented a series of public lectures, two of which were given by Jung himself.

The monthly meetings were labeled "tri-seminars," since they were conducted by three instructors, one from each group; they were intended to vitiate and then eliminate the differences among the separate schools of psychotherapeutic thought. This was to be done in the rhetorical and substantive context of state service and individual and professional duty to the community. As Fritz Mohr put it at the Düsseldorf congress in 1938,

> In order that we may, as nearly as possible, attain this goal, to lead the many inherently valuable people back into our *Volksgemeinschaft* as active and sound members, to protect the healthy from illness and thus on the whole to contribute to *Volksgesundheit,* requires basic cooperation and not theoretical conflict.[61]

In 1938 a common training program was established to replace the separate curricula formerly maintained by the Freudians, Adlerians, and Jungians; it was designed to produce a new generation of psychotherapists who would be unencumbered by the prejudices and narrow views of the past. Although almost every survivor of the Göring Institute acknowledges that some good came from the enforced cooperation among the various directions in psychotherapy, no genuine unification ever came close to being realized. Göring, for all his nativist and parochial enthusiasm for a German psychotherapeutic consensus, had neither the vision nor the character to carry through such an ambitious, indeed illusory, plan. Although the crippling loss of practitioners that the Freudians had suffered gave an advantage to the other groups, the loyalty to a school of thought that was cultivated by intense personal involvement in the training and the natural competition among the groups made the curriculum remain somewhat of a psychotherapeutic smorgasbord, and the continued requirement of a training analysis for each candidate tended to reinforce a personal and professional commitment to a specific orientation.

All of this was imposed on top of the notorious individuality of psychotherapists and their often vicious conflicts and feuds over doctrine and method. Käthe Dräger, who received her training in psychoanalysis at the Göring Institute, has recalled the pervasive feeling among the students that the tri-seminars often were windy wastes of time, and that it was far preferable to pursue one's professional training instead of tilting at theoretical windmills. Even Göring observed obliquely that in the tri-seminars the trend was not toward genuine unification of competing theories but rather toward a continuing process of communication that bore only the rudiments of true synthesis:

> Special value is placed during these evenings on simple formulations and the avoidance of technical terms such as Oedipus complex, Künkel's psychological notion of a "vicious circle" [*Teufelskreis*] and anima. I believe that—apart from our lectures—we have these seminars to thank for the fact that our young members and candidates can grow beyond the orthodox schools and can recognize the good as well as the partiality of these orientations.[62]

On another level, the effort to construct a new theoretical and practical framework for a German psychotherapy culminated in a tentative and abbreviated exposition on the nature of neurosis and its cure: a forty-one-page manuscript—the content of which we shall describe in a moment—prepared by the research division of the Göring Institute entitled "Thesen zur Neurosenlehre." Written chiefly by Hattingberg, the division's director, it surfaced in draft during late 1939 or early 1940. Hattingberg complained, however, in the division's report for 1940 that the response to his questionnaire concerning the progress made by the members of the institute in developing a common language and in resolving the differences in theory and method had been disappointingly small.[63] Although Werner Kemper has professed amazement at how professionally neutral the document now appears, these theses were not simply a nonprovocative theory of neurosis or, as Kemper has maintained, intended simply as a defense against the Nazis.[64] Hattingberg, of course, believed that psychotherapy had to respond to the *völkisch* assignment set it by the state by actually achieving the unification of theory and practice within the walls of the Göring Institute. Not surprisingly, therefore, the unpublished manuscript also bore the distinct stamp of Hattingberg's own ideas. By itself, therefore, it is further evidence of the sort of offhand synthesis that occurred under Göring's leadership during the Third Reich. This synthesis derived from Göring's outlook and character as well as from the eclecticism that prevailed within the general and specific intellectual traditions the German psychotherapists and psychoanalysts shared.

According to the document, neurosis was a disruption of the natural rhythm of the human organism and its active relationship with the whole. The family unit was to remain the basic expression of a natural balance and psychological well-being while the role of the psychotherapist was to be not that of a passive analyst, but a spiritual guide. Any member of the community who did not actively share in the collective *Weltanschauung* would eventually become unworthy and superfluous. The healthy, self-sufficient individual would exercise virtues and ideals determined by his race, his community, and his own character acting in harmonious concert: "The healthy perceptive person sees his honor in remaining true to his *Volk* and to himself."[65]

Like the tri-seminars, the Göring Institute's theses toward a theory of neurosis floundered amid its members' more immediate professional interests and obligations, responsibilities that were given an even greater urgency with the onset of war. Added to this was a perceptible dimming of the bright enthusiasm that had emanated from the early proponents of a specifically German psychotherapy.

When psychoanalytic terminology was officially banned at the Göring Institute in 1938, the ban was occasioned, of course, not only by the drive for theoretical and practical synthesis but also by a sense of considerable trepidation about the possibility that all psychotherapy would be condemned as viciously as psychoanalysis was. The "Oedipus complex" became the "family complex," "psychoanalysis" became "developmental psychology," and the Freudian group was officially designated "Arbeitsgruppe A," with the Adlerian and Jungian groups becoming—out of a sense of proportion as well as some wishful thinking about transcending old labels, rather than out of necessity—"B" and "C," respectively. In 1942, under the additional shadow of institute member John Rittmeister's arrest for espionage, the psychoanalysts' meetings were renamed "lecture evenings for casuistry and theory." As with the rhetorical flourishes of 1933, however, these Aesopian terms of camouflage never achieved full sovereignty of usage, and the original terms crept increasingly back into use, even in public forums.

The titles of the review categories in the *Zentralblatt* had been altered along similar lines in 1935. "Psychotherapie" became "Seelenheilkunde"; "Psychologie" was changed to "Seelenkunde"; and "Physiologie" turned into "Körper-Seelenhaushalt." At the end of 1936 the *Zentralblatt* became the official organ of the Göring Institute, with Göring as co-editor. As a result, the category of "Psychoanalyse" disappeared, and psychoanalytic works, when they were reviewed at all, appeared under "Tiefenpsychologie." In the same year "Erbbiologie and Rassenkunde" was added, but in 1939 the titles introduced in 1935 reverted to the originals, and the only change after that came in 1941 with an expansion of the review categories that honestly reflected the institute's activities and the interests of psychotherapists dating back to the inception of the journal.

Gerhart Scheunert recalls that he did not receive his subscription to the *Internationale Zeitschrift für Psychoanalyse* during 1934 and 1935, but began receiving it again in 1936 after the DPG had been assimilated by the Göring Institute. This bagatelle reflects how heavily Freudians were forced to depend on the Göring Institute, whose official and oft-expressed attitude toward psychoanalysis was such a critical one. But like Scheunert's subscription, psychonanalytic works were received, if not always welcomed, by reviewers in the *Zentralblatt*. Most were only briefly reviewed, though generally given greater consideration than Schultz devoted in his brusque 1943 dismissal of Sandor Lorand's article, "Hypnotic Suggestion" (1941): "Orthodox psychoanalytic gossip."[66] Immediately preceding this smug critical eructation, in fact, is Schultz's admiring assessment of the Freudian Kemper's study of sexual dysfunction in women.

The *Zentralblatt*'s reviews as a whole displayed an essentially professional posture that was only partially bowed by a genuflection toward Nazi ideals. Even after the *Zentralblatt* came completely under German control, there was, in 1941, a long and positive review of Karen Horney's *New Ways in Psychoanalysis* (1939). During the 1930s, more or less fair and sober reviews of works by Freud, Richard Sterba, Theodor Reik, Anna Freud, and Ernest Jones appeared, but again it was a work of Horney's, *The Neurotic Personality of Our Time* (1937), which attracted the longest and most positive review, by Edgar Herzog. This was because Horney's critique of Freud stood closest to the eclectic orientation of the psychotherapists in Germany at the time, including, for example, a common interest in Eastern religions and in the Japanese "Morita system" of rest, encouragement, and work. Müller-Braunschweig, who was still officially *persona non grata*, in 1941 published a long review of Josef Meinertz's *Psychotherapie. Eine Wissenschaft!* (1939); and C. A. Meier, who had been ousted from his position as a managing editor of the *Zentralblatt* in 1940, published a review of Henry V. Dicks's *Clinical Studies in Psychopathology* (1939) the following year.

The unexpected bonus of a new pride in their profession that grew out of the psychotherapists' forced association with one another produced an increasing distance between them and the proponents of natural health. While bases for agreement and cooperation still existed, the psychotherapists in the Göring Institute no longer felt constrained to associate their professional tenets and identity with the somewhat tenuous and sentimental nostrums prescribed by natural medicine. Alfred Brauchle was the object of a typically critical assessment by Heyer in the *Zentralblatt* in 1942. Brauchle's use of mass hypnosis and suggestion, as described in his *Seelische Beeinflussung in der Gemeinschaft* (1940) as a type of communal therapy (*seelische Gemeinschaftsbehandlung*), seemed to Heyer too casual and inflexible a psychotherapeutic device to be relied on so exclusively.[67] Psychotherapy's own struggle for professional independence could too easily be prejudiced through association with the indiscriminate application of a vague and commonplace "community feeling" possessed by everyone. Furthermore, such an association could be pointed to by critics of psychotherapy as another indication of its unscientific approach. This was all the more intolerable now, when the Göring Institute was able to provide the forum for the practice and development of a more sophisticated medical psychology.

What was true of psychotherapy's professional profile toward the outside was even more the case within the Göring Institute itself. The Freudians, although subject to official discrimination and excluded from their fair share in the institute's leadership—and, in any case, crippled by the loss of their experienced and effective standard-bearers who had fled the Nazis—gradually asserted themselves. The process was made possible by the fact that, increasingly, the institute was concerned above all with the development of psychotherapy as a discipline, and with its ever more urgent applications in wartime. The Freudians had been forced to sacrifice a great deal in order to have been allowed the protection of the institute; it was, after all, the DPG that had originally provided the newly merged profession with the building, the equipment, the library, the clinic, and the expertise necessary to utilize them in an efficient and productive manner. But representatives of the psychoanalytic school assumed important roles in the institute. The large number of courses given at the institute by the Freudians Schultz-Hencke and Kemper stood in revealing contrast to the fewer and fewer courses offered by such early fervent ideologues as Achelis, Bilz, Hattingberg, Heyer, and other, lesser, lights. Of course, these men were active in the running of the institute, the handling of private and clinical patients, and the business of research and publication. But this was true as well of leading Freudians like Schultz-Hencke and Kemper.

As the years passed, Julius Schirren, Heyer, and Hattingberg, among others, continued to entertain various versions of the earlier and enthusiastically promoted Jungian tradition, and continued to wield an influence on the course of study, but their importance bore no resemblance to that previously envisioned in terms of the value of Jung's "anthropological" depth psychology for a truly German psychotherapy. The teachings of Jung, while continuing to serve as a guide for many of the institute's members, were relegated by virtue of their philosophical and religious orientation to reside in the cultural realm, which held less immediate significance for the practical aims of Nazi policy and the psychotherapists' own professional goals. Göring himself, who had been one of those most bitterly opposed to "Jewish psychoanalysis," gradually came around to tolerating and even accepting psychoanalysis as he witnessed the valuable theoretical and practical contributions the Freudians made in seminars and practice. According to Kemper, even Göring's wife, Erna, who had been a strong and dangerous defender of some sort of Nazified psychotherapy, came to appreciate and even to admire psychoanalysis. A housewife who was a member of the Nazi party, the Nazi Women's League (NS-Frauenschaft), the Red Cross (Rotes Kreuz), and the NSV, Erna was analyzed by Kemper, during which sessions she would reportedly pass on information obtained from her husband regarding colleagues who were in proximate or immediate danger for one reason or another.[68] The outpatient clinic, under the direction of John Rittmeister from 1939 to 1942 and Kemper from 1942 to 1945, became the prime arena for the display of Freudian expertise, as we will see in the next chapter.

But perhaps the single most dramatic individual example of the professional orientation of the Göring Institute, and the position it occupied between party and state, was the person of deputy director Johannes Heinrich Schultz. Around the institute Schultz was known as *"der kluge Hans"* ("clever Hans") because of his administrative abilities, his cool ambition, his formidable intellect, and his expertise at political and professional survival. He had suffered some harassment in 1933 because his first wife had been Jewish; to deflect such attacks he joined the Nazi Motor Corps (Nationalsozialistisches Kraftfahrerkorps), and stayed a member until it was taken over in 1935 by the SA. According to his Reich Physicians Chamber file, he never joined the party, remaining only a candidate (*Anwärter*). He was a strongly patriotic German with a sure feel for professional survival and success. The two Schultz books that were included in the Nazi bibliography were issued by firms—Reinhardt and Mittler—whose lists consistently toed the Nazi party line. Moreover, the Schultz books were printed in Gothic, or Germanic, script (*Bruchschrift*), another sign during the Nazi era of the devotion to the "German spirit" in books that were designed more or less for popular consumption by the *Volk*. But both books also took the opportunity to advertise the Göring Institute and its work in the style of Schultz's longstanding commitment to an ecumenical balance between medicine and psychology. Whatever advantage he sought for his person was always connected to advantage for his profession.

While Göring provided the protection of his name, Schultz, as before 1933, applied himself exhaustively to the task of presenting psychotherapy's case in as many forums as possible. (See, for example, his article in Goebbels's prestige paper, *Das Reich,* in 1943.[69]) He lectured and wrote widely and was director of the Göring Institute's division for continuing medical education. This institutional capacity was especially appropriate, for Schultz had been active in the affairs of the Berlin Academy for Continuing Medical Education (Berliner Akademie für ärztliche Fortbildung) since 1924 and was an editor of an international journal for continuing medical education. In 1944 the Berlin Academy, where Schultz and other psychotherapists, including Göring, Schultz-Hencke, and Hattingberg had given lectures on a number of occasions, listed a workshop on psychotherapy to be conducted by Schultz.[70] He was the prototype of the in-house pragmatist who regularly snapped *"Heil Hitler"* over the telephone but who, in actuality, had no real party or government affiliation. Of the psychotherapists at the Göring Institute, Schultz was by far the most highly regarded by the members of the German psychiatric establishment. Thus his value to the aspiring profession in the Third Reich, though not as great, of course, as Göring's, was multifaceted and considerable. In his commitment to his profession and his effectiveness as a representative of it, Schultz stood in marked contrast to Gauger, the noisy and impassioned ideologue whose place he took as deputy director of the institute.

The Rittmeister Affair

Even Göring's influence, however, had limits, both external and self-imposed. This became evident during 1942 in the course of the unhappy affair of John Rittmeister, director of the institute's outpatient clinic. On 26 September 1942 Rittmeister and his wife, Eva, were arrested by the Gestapo and charged with being members of the so-called "Red Orchestra" (*Rote Kapelle*), an espionage network that supplied information to the Soviets. The group was headed by Harro Schulze-Boysen, an officer in the Air Ministry's intelligence branch. Schulze-Boysen himself had been arrested on 30 August when the Gestapo began a sweep of the group's hideouts in Berlin.

Rittmeister had returned to his native Germany against the advice of his friends to work at the Göring Institute. In Berlin he subsequently gathered about him a circle of idealistic young leftist students who were convinced that reading and discussion would lay the basis for a campaign to convince the German people to change their form of government.[71] This group came into contact with Schulze-Boysen in 1942 and became part of his apparatus. Rittmeister and his associates, however, apparently did not share the activist politics of Schulze-Boysen's operatives and knew little or nothing of their espionage activities, although Rittmeister himself did help Schulze-Boysen compose anti-Nazi newssheets.[72] When Rittmeister and his wife, an actress he married in 1939, came to trial, they, like the others, were charged with high treason. They denied the charges, but Rittmeister was condemned to death in January 1943 and was executed at Plötzensee Prison on 13 May 1943.[73] His wife was sentenced to a term of imprisonment.

Rittmeister's arrest, trial, and execution naturally aroused the anxiety of his colleagues at the Göring Institute. Fear of the Gestapo was part of everyday consciousness in the Third Reich even before the strain of war on the Nazis intensified the search for traitors, malingerers, and scapegoats. Would Rittmeister's predicament draw censure and reprisal down on the institute and its members? This fear must have tempered the members' collegial and personal concern for Rittmeister and his wife. Added to this was the conviction on the part of a number of psychotherapists that the issue in the Rittmeister case was not Nazi oppression but treason in wartime; the result of such a formulation was that they regarded Rittmeister with a mixture of patriotic indignation, anxious and angry resentment, and some pity. It was certainly out of some such combination of motives that Schultz, according to Kemper, approached Gauger to ask what might be done.

Rittmeister's arrest did not necessarily mean that the psychotherapists as a group would suffer at the hands of the Gestapo, although, as we will see, at least one professional antagonist tried to use his own Nazi credentials to discredit the Göring Institute over the Rittmeister affair. At the time the level of anxiety, naturally enough, was quite high, and postwar accounts may further have exaggerated the degree of danger as a means of expressing sympathy, whether genuine or retroactively feigned, for a victim of the Nazis as well as identifying with him as an endangered opponent of the regime. Whatever their sympathy for their colleague, the psychotherapists were also concerned, of course, for their own personal safety and for the survival and integrity of their institute and profession.

Göring must have been the focus of the psychotherapists' hopes during this dangerous affair, as a number of them have since affirmed. The feeling among them after the war was that Göring had saved the institute from destruction simply by virtue of who he was. This is probably an exaggeration. It is clear, however, that the degree of Göring's concern about the matter led him to take steps to practice damage control.

Göring ostensibly met with his cousin on 25 September 1942. (See Chapter 4.) The subject, according to the official record of the meeting, was homosexuality and the law. Whether or not the listed topic was in fact a camouflage for a discussion of the Rittmeister matter, and what, in any case, might have been said about the subject, is impossible to determine. But given the fact that Rittmeister's arrest was to occur the very next day, we might at least assume that the issue came up, and we can postulate that Matthias might have been making a last-minute plea for Hermann's intercession, or, at the least, that he might have been discussing the implications of Rittmeister's impending arrest for the institute. All this is possible, even probable, since the Gestapo had been arresting members of Schulze-Boysen's group for almost a month.

Göring's family concern over the matter went even deeper, however. Schulze-Boysen himself had been able to obtain his position at the Luftwaffe Research Office, in spite of his left-wing activities and arrests by the authorities, because his wife was the daughter of an aristocratic friend of Hermann Göring's. It is thus certain that the affair sent shock waves through the Göring family as a whole. Perhaps it is even possible that Matthias Heinrich Göring had had some inkling of Rittmeister's sympathies and associations, and that August and September of 1942 at the Göring Institute were months of shared anxiety, or warnings and appeals. Although Kemper would not say, his psychoanalytic sessions with Erna Göring and her alleged confidences may well have concerned Rittmeister before and during this period of crisis.

In any case, we have Kemper's testimony and Ernst Göring's assertion that Matthias did seek out his cousin to discuss the possibility of doing something for Rittmeister and the institute. The record of the meeting on 25 September might therefore be confirmation of testimony to discussion on the subject. No matter what the accuracy of this scenario might be, however, it is likely that the Göring cousins would have met at some point or other for no other reason than the coordination of damage control. Indeed, we should probably assume that, given the repugnant and dangerous charge of high treason, Matthias Heinrich Göring was from the beginning more concerned about the institute than he was about Rittmeister. On the basis of Ernst Göring's recollections, it seems that Rittmeister and his wife were compromised to the degree of arousing the patriotic wrath of the institute's director.[74]

We have already noted that many of the members of the institute apparently saw things in much the same light, particularly in view of the threat to themselves, their institute, and their work. In addition, it is possible, though not likely, that Matthias was called on the carpet—not likely because Hermann, of course, was even more vulnerable to criticism and embarrassment than he, since the spy ring had thrived within a Luftwaffe that had long since begun to lose its luster for Hitler, as well as for those avaricious and vengeful rivals of the Reich Marshal within the Nazi hierarchy. Whatever the actual situation, Göring's stock with Hitler sank lower and lower, for on the heels of this scandal came the Luftwaffe's failure to supply the German garrison at Stalingrad, and the growth of the Allied bombing campaign against the Reich.

Hermann Göring could hardly have been either in the mood or in the position to do something for Rittmeister, even if his cousin had solicited his help. It is true that Rittmeister was granted the dubious respect of being guillotined instead of hanged, and that his wife was imprisoned instead of sentenced to death. Hitler, foreshadowing the punishment he would ordain for the conspirators of 20 July 1944, had insisted on strangulation by a rope and death sentences for the wives of those condemned in the first set of Red Orchestra trials in December 1942. It is probable, however, that the Rittmeisters' fate as two comparatively minor figures in the case was the result not of any Göring family influence but of the waning of the intensity of Hitler's desire for revenge and the less vengeful, if hardly indulgent, attitude of the presiding Luftwaffe judge on the Reich Court Martial (Reichskriegsgericht), Manfred Roeder.[75]

We have no evidence of any investigation or action launched against the Göring Institute by the authorities—or squelched by the Reich Marshal—as a result of the affair. What we do know is that the Göring family was seriously concerned, and that institute members believed then and believe now that it was the Göring name that protected them so that the institute could survive and prosper.

The Göring Way:
Psychotherapy Ascends to State Status

Aside from such crises, there were professional reasons as to why, in the twilight of the Third Reich, the psychotherapists at the Göring Institute turned to a fuller reliance on the Göring family name. There was a general desire among institute members to free themselves from the influence of the Labor Front, and the potentially dangerous consequences of its control, as it became an increasingly chaotic organization whose finances and bureaucracy were bogged down in wartime eclipse. Ley himself "spent most of his days in an alcoholic stupor,"[76] and even before the war Hermann Göring had correctly, if perhaps jealously, pointed to the fat accumulating around the Labor Front and suggested to his Wehrmacht audience that the DAF "should produce more strength and less joy."[77] In 1942, therefore, Matthias Heinrich Göring sought to have his institute affiliated with the Kaiser Wilhelm-Gesellschaft—a request that apparently was turned down, although it may have resulted in some funding.[78]

The Kaiser Wilhelm-Gesellschaft had been founded in 1911 to support scientific research free from the obligations of a university position. After World War I, an Emergency Association of German Science (Notgemeinschaft der deutschen Wissenschaft) was set up to fund and coordinate research that was endangered by the nation's financial and political crises. Later renamed the German Research Association (Deutsche Forschungsgemeinschaft), it embraced universities, academies, and societies, including the Kaiser Wilhelm-Gesellschaft, and was funded through government and private industry. On 16 March 1937 Bernhard Rust, chief of the Ministry of Science and Education (Reichsministerium für Wissenschaft, Erziehung und Volksbildung/ Reichserziehungsministerium), established the Reich Research Council (Reichsforschungsrat) in cooperation with Hermann Göring's Four-Year Plan. Its task was to sponsor research and development in technology and natural sciences. The Reich Research Council became in effect the natural science branch of the DFG, since the latter had been established by law and the former only by administrative decree.[79]

Army General Karl Becker was appointed president of the RFR and served in that capacity until his death by suicide in 1940, whereupon Rust himself assumed the post for the next two years. By 1942, however, Albert Speer had become convinced that the war could be won only if a new and devastating weapon were developed. Albert Vögler, president of the Kaiser Wilhelm-Gesellschaft, called Speer's attention to the neglected field of nuclear fission, complaining that the Education Ministry and the RFR lacked the requisite energy—under the alcoholic Rust—to encourage and fund vital research. Speer recommended to Hitler that Hermann Göring be appointed head of the RFR, "thus emphasizing its importance."[80] For his deputy, Göring chose Rudolf Mentzel, an SS officer and since 1936 president of the DFG. Werner Osenberg, head of Mentzel's planning office, along with Göring's own technical advisor, Fritz Görnnert, was given the task of revitalizing the war-related work of the Reich Research Council. Its resources grew to gargantuan proportions. Funds out of Göring's vast holdings flowed into the RFR from the Reich Office for Economic Construction (Reichsamt für Wirtschaftsbau) to the tune of thirty to forty million Reichsmarks ($7–10 million) a year, and in 1943 a special *"Kriegsetat"* was established to provide another fifty million ($12.5 million) Reichsmarks annually.[81]

As director (*Fachspartenleiter*) of the Medical Division of the RFR Göring appointed the eminent surgeon Ferdinand Sauerbruch, who had headed the same division in the "old" Reich Research Council. Sauerbruch had earlier been appointed a state secretary by Göring in appreciation for his treatment of the ailing President Hindenburg; he had a particular interest in the psychological dimension of aviation medicine.[82] Sauerbruch and the Reich Marshal were hardly close, but the confluence of interests and acquaintanceships in this particular corner of Hitler's Reich made Sauerbruch an appropriate administrative link between the RFR and the Göring Institute, a capacity confirmed by the institute's former managing director, Felix Scherke. The formal association of the Göring Institute with the Reich Research Council dated from Hermann Göring's assumption of the RFR's presidency.

According to Scherke, from 1942 to 1945 the institute received financial support from the compensation fund (*Verrechnungsfond*) of the

Labor Front, from the city of Berlin, from the Reich Air Ministry (Reichsluftfahrtministerium), and from the RFR.[83] Funding during these years was more than adequate. Müller-Hegemann has recalled the contrast between the Göring Institute, where nothing was lacking, and the common privations elsewhere due to the war; Dräger reports that during these years the institute's outpatient clinic was enlarged.[84] On 20 January 1943 Göring requested RM 136,400 (the equivalent of $34,160) from the DFG, which handled RFR finances, for work in the realm of mental hygiene (seelische Gesundheitspflege). Throughout the year he was in correspondence with various officials of the DFG, including Mentzel, Kurt Blome, and Sergius Breuer, chief of the DFG's medical section from 1938 to 1945. On 16 December the DFG granted the Göring Institute RM 318,000 ($79,500) for 1943–44 and RM 818,000 ($204,500) for 1944–45.[85]

This generous degree of financial support allowed the institute to continue to maintain itself in good professional fashion. According to institute records from the first quarter of 1944, Göring received a monthly salary of RM 1500 ($375) while the four main department heads received RM 1000 ($250). The directors of the eight subdivisions were paid RM 500 ($125) a month. Full-time staff also received RM 500 and participation in special research projects (e.g., Müller-Braunschweig on basic research, Schultz-Hencke on homosexuality) brought an additional RM 500 monthly. All this was in addition to whatever income resulted from the members' private practice, which, according to Ernst Göring, was a source of considerable income for individual psychotherapists until the end of the Nazi regime.[86]

Hermann Göring's stock with Hitler had been falling ever since Dunkirk, and he increasingly contented himself with the luxuries that ill-gotten power and wealth had brought him, generally sacrificing his influence and initiative for the assembling of personally ostentatious titles and prerogatives. Goebbels's Total War program, announced after the defeat at Stalingrad, posed a potentially grave threat to Göring's possessions. In February 1943, for instance, SA cadres at Goebbels's urging smashed in the windows of one of the Reich Marshal's favorite haunts, the gourmet restaurant Horcher on the Lutherstrasse in Berlin.[87] Although a concerned Göring prevented the closing of the restaurant, more serious inroads could be anticipated, and during late 1943 and all through 1944 Göring made some effort to shore up his bastions of strength, wealth, and influence. By October 1944 all institutes and groups that were members of the RFR had had the prefix "Reichs-" added to their official titles. According to Kurt Zierold, the redesignation was intended to draw public limits for the purveyors of total war in their fervent rallying of the Germans for the final desperate battle against their many enemies.[88]

As a result, on 1 January 1944 the Reich Institute for Psychological

Research and Psychotherapy in the Reich Research Council (Reichs-institut für Psychologische Forschung und Psychotherapie im Reichs-forschungsrat) came into being.[89] Although the German Institute for Psychological Research and Psychotherapy remained in official exis-tence until the end of the Third Reich, the psychotherapists under Gö-ring were no longer simply members of a registered association but of a state institute entitled to legal status. This status was in the process of being formalized amidst the chaos of the collapsing Reich, and thus was never legally confirmed. Göring's widow discovered this in 1956, when she was denied a widow's pension by the West German govern-ment on the grounds that the RFR had itself never been fully incor-porated, and thus had not been included under the requisite public assistance regulations.[90]

The incipient status of the Reich Institute in 1944, however, was why Göring lost no time in seeking in February of that year to have bestowed on both Heyer and Schultz-Hencke the title of full professor. In the case of Heyer, Göring asserted to Karl Brandt, Hitler's personal physician and General Commissar for Public Health Services (General-kommissar des Führers für das Sanitäts- und Gesundheitswesen), that aside from a record of longstanding scholarly achievement and service as a university lecturer, Heyer merited the title of professor as director of a major division of the Reich Institute. Göring perceived this honor as one that was obviously overdue, for both he and Schultz had achieved the rank of professor from university teaching, and Hattingberg had in 1940 won the comparable rank of honorary professor.[91] It is clear that Göring, with apparent justification, regarded the Reich Institute as an official state institution, to be staffed, like a university, by full and associate professors who were salaried civil servants under the aus-pices of the Reich Interior Ministry. As a further step in the direction anticipated and charted by Göring, the RFR in July 1944 granted the institute a formal research commission in psychology,[92] anchoring the psychotherapists securely to leeward of Hermann Göring's still bulky isle of power and influence.

Other, explosive, events of July 1944 testified that as the burdens of war grew heavier and the military tide turned ever more disastrously against the Nazis, Nazi threats to vulnerable individuals and groups inside Germany would proliferate. The threatening environment ren-dered the critical assaults made on psychotherapy by its omnipresent professional enemies all the more dangerous. Chief among these was Max de Crinis, the most outspoken and influential Nazi within the German psychiatric establishment. In 1944 he took the occasion of his opposition to Heyer's proposed promotion to attempt to discredit the Göring Institute as a whole.

Berlin Document Center

Max de Crinis (1899–1945)

De Crinis had been a psychiatrist at the University of Graz in Austria, and fled his homeland in 1934 after the failure of the local Nazi putsch against the Dollfuss government. He eventually became director of the psychiatric clinic at the University of Cologne. It was rumored within the Göring Institute that de Crinis in fact had been forced to flee Austria because he had been involved in the coup attempt. A party member since 1931, de Crinis joined the SS in 1936 and in 1939 replaced the politically discredited Bonhoeffer as psychiatric director at the Charité in Berlin. Shortly after this, in a revealing act, de Crinis had the bust of the great nineteenth-century Jewish neurologist and psychiatric director of the Charité, Carl Westphal, removed from its position at the entrance to the psychiatric wing of the hospital; the daughter of the nineteenth-century Viennese psychiatrist Theodor Meynert was engaged to find a bust of her father to replace Westphal's. It was also in 1939 that de Crinis became active in the operations of the SS Race and Settlement Main Office (Rasse- und Siedlungs-hauptamt); by 1941 he had also taken over the post of medical director in the scientific office (Amt W) of the Ministry of Science and Education.[93]

Along with colleagues like Bumke and August Hoche, de Crinis was strident in his criticism of psychotherapy. Like Freud, he had studied psychiatry in Austria under Meynert's influence, but, unlike Freud, he had retained a resistance to any attempts to instill what he considered to be "speculative philosophy" into a medical discipline. He saw the whole "crisis in medicine" movement as a Jewish conspiracy to destroy the sound biological and scientific bases of modern medical psychology. For de Crinis, psychotherapy was to be only an adjunct method to a nosological and physiological science.[94]

Heyer was a representative of exactly the type of thinking de Crinis abhorred. As an internist, Heyer was based in a solid biological foundation, but, as a Jungian, he saw a necessity for the psychotherapist to act as a spiritual guide. Working before World War I as an assistant at the University of Munich to the noted psychiatrist Friedrich von Müller, Heyer became increasingly estranged from the physical and chemical orientation of university medicine and psychiatry. Back in Munich after the war he began to interest himself in the synergy of mind and body. Most notably, he performed experiments on stomach secretions, which, he asserted, displayed evidence of psychosomatism. As demonstrated in his 1935 work, *Praktische Seelenheilkunde*, Heyer was highly critical of "materialistic" medicine—its dead facts, machines, apparatus, and commercial nature—that contradicted the idea of the physician as bound closely to patient, *Volk*, and God; "the new Germany" would, he noted confidently, hasten the end of such a materialistic outlook.[95]

De Crinis, in a 1944 letter to Paulus Rostock of Brandt's medical staff at Hitler's headquarters, insisted that Heyer, whose name Göring had put forward for the title of full professor, should not be named a full professor but only an unsalaried titular professor. (Heyer had become a university lecturer in internal medicine at Berlin on 1 December 1939.) De Crinis placed his negative judgment in the context of a threatening observation about the Göring Institute as a whole:

> The activity of the Institute for Psychological Research and Psychotherapy has satisfied me neither scientifically nor politically. Confidentially, I should like to note that a year ago one of their most zealous collaborators was executed on account of espionage. . . . Herr Heyer is not so scientifically important as he is depicted to be by Professor Göring, and in a review of Heyer's last book (*Praktische Seelenheilkunde*) I pointed to his inconsequential and unscientific approach to the question of body and mind.[96]

Furthermore, de Crinis went on, the Göring Institute had not abandoned the "speculative and philosophical dogma" of Jewish Freudian-
ism, which lacked a sound scientific and racial basis:

> The Reich Institute for Psychological Research and Psychotherapy has
> unfortunately not given up the Jewish orientation of Freudian psycho-
> analysis, and German psychiatry will in the near future find it necessary
> to move against this degenerate phenomenon that continues to wear a
> puny national cloak.[97]

De Crinis's critique of psychotherapy did not confine itself to associating all the activities of the Göring Institute with psychoanalysis. He
also professed wrath at the emphasis placed by German psychotherapists of the period on active modes of psychotherapy that could be applied not only by physicians but by lay psychologists as well. One of
these modes was the training of nonmedical "attending psychologists,"
who worked under a doctor's supervision; Heyer had headed the Göring Institute's program for this training since 1939. In a classic period
double entendre, he maintained that, with the proper supervision, being a *Heiler* (literally, "healer") often outweighed a physician's technical training and expertise in meeting the demands for ensuring the
health of the German *Volk*.[98] De Crinis, asserting that the Wehrmacht
had had bad experiences with psychologists, and that the Luftwaffe
had stopped using them altogether, charged that such training efforts
were scientifically and medically unsound.[99]

De Crinis won out in the battle over Heyer's promotion to full professor,[100] but it is interesting to find, in the midst of his vigorous criticism of Heyer, of the institute, and of the profession of psychotherapy,
the following assertion about the Rittmeister affair: "Of course Professor Göring cannot be held responsible for this, and I emphasize ex-
pressly that I have the greatest confidence in Professor Göring in every
respect."[101] De Crinis's unqualified assurance of his confidence in Matthias Heinrich Göring could not have been based on agreement with
Göring's professional views, but rather confirmed the accuracy of the
observation of an anonymous functionary (perhaps de Crinis himself)
in the Ministry of Science and Education in 1942 that the German Institute for Psychological Research and Psychotherapy was assured of
existence only for so long as Göring remained its director.[102] The pas-
sage of time allows a broader perspective. Given the nature of the organizational confusion, and the primacy the Nazis after 1936 accorded
to the mobilization, however compromised, of existing resources in
Nazi Germany, the German General Medical Society for Psychotherapy probably would have survived in one form or another, as did
those other groups that were fleetingly allied under Wagner's Reich
Study Group for a New German Medicine. Those physicians and laymen who cared to would have continued to practice psychotherapy

and to argue for it as a valuable and respectable profession. But it is unlikely that an institute exclusively devoted to its practice and development would have been created, and certainly not one that approached the scale of the one constructed under Göring. The presence of the Göring family name among the psychotherapists spared them the risks of throwing in their lot with one side or another in the dangerous and many-sided struggles between party and state which characterized Nazi rule.[103] Göring was immune to the necessity of having to win or preserve political influence among various state and party factions; his name and nature alone produced a powerful personal influence which could be wielded in both arenas, as well as sufficing in the bastions of academic medicine. It was this unique aspect to the history of psychotherapy in the Third Reich that proved to be the young profession's most valuable asset in avoiding its personal, political, and institutional enemies and seizing the ample opportunities that were prescribed to it: Göring was able to cruise safely between the Charybdis of swirling party factionalism and the Scylla of stony state resistance.

CHAPTER 6

The Institute at Work

While the 1933 statutes of the German General Medical Society for Psychotherapy comprised a document composed of anxious rhetoric, the 1936 statutes of the German Institute for Psychological Research and Psychotherapy reflected a calmer and more professional outlook. Articles 4, 5, and 6 called for a director, a secretary, a treasurer, and an administrative board. Besides Göring and Linden, the administrative board consisted of representatives of the three groups gathered within the institute: Künkel and Edgar Herzog for the Künkel (Adler) group; Moritz, Kranefeldt, and Adolf von Weizsäcker for the Jungians; and the psychoanalysts Boehm, Müller-Braunschweig, treasurer of the institute, and Schultz-Hencke. Also serving on the board at its inception were three members who were close to the Jung faction, Achelis, Otto Curtius, secretary of the German General Medical Society for Psychotherapy, and Gauger, as deputy director. Schultz and Hattingberg sat for the independents among the psychotherapists. Members who served on the board subsequently were Bilz, Herzog-Dürck, Kalau vom Hofe, Kemper, Rittmeister, Schirren, and Vetter.

In addition to its major work in treatment, training, and advisory functions, the Göring Institute also operated as a parent organization for affiliated groups of psychotherapists in other cities in Germany. By 1937 there were four of these: one in Düsseldorf under Mohr, Seif's Munich Work Group for Community Psychology (Münchener Arbeitsgruppe für Gemeinschaftspsychologie), a group in Stuttgart, and another in Wuppertal. In 1939 the four groups became official branches of the Göring Institute in Berlin as a result of the expansion and reorganization that was made possible by the advent of DAF supervision and funding. The groups in Düsseldorf and Wuppertal were combined into the Rhineland branch ("Zweigstelle Rheinland"), although they remained organizationally separate. The Stuttgart branch under Georg Roemer, a board member of the Society of German Neurologists and Psychiatrists, became known as "Zweigstelle Würrtemberg und Baden," and in 1940 the Seif and Heyer groups in Munich combined under Seif's direction into a formal and united Bavarian branch that was by far the most active center for psychotherapy outside the German capital. The "Ostmark" branch in Vienna under Kogerer, however, became merely vestigial and, like the Düsseldorf and Wuppertal groups, was barely active after the outbreak of war. In May 1941 Göring himself assumed leadership of the Stuttgart branch through designating "commissars" Paul Beetz and Gustav Graber, and in 1942 Curtius was put in overall charge of the Munich group, with Seif remaining as head of educational counseling, the primary activity of that branch. In 1943 a group under Josef Meinertz in Frankfurt a.M. became an official branch of the Göring Institute. By 1944 only it and the Munich and Stuttgart groups were still functioning.

In 1937 the Göring Institute and its branches claimed 128 members. Among these were 60 doctors, 25 academics (those with a university degree), 43 nonacademics, and 3 patrons. Ten of the doctors were women, as were 9 of the 25 academics and 39 of the 43 nonacademics. In 1938 the membership increased to 154 members, of whom 78 were doctors, 28 were academics, and 48 were nonacademics. By 30 September 1939 the Göring Institute had 188 members: 87 doctors (16 women), 33 academics (10 women), and 58 nonacademics (49 women). The number of patrons had increased to 10, and of the total membership, exactly half, 94, were in Berlin. Membership in 1940 stood at 88 doctors (17 women), 39 (12) academics, 61 (52) nonacademics, and 16 (4) patrons, for a total of 204 (85), 97 of whom were gathered in Berlin. The last published statistics show that in 1941 membership totaled 240, of whom 100 (22 women) were doctors, 42 (29) were academics, and 80 (64) nonacademics. There were now 18 supporting members, or patrons, and 118 of the members were in Berlin. Subscriptions to the *Zentralblatt* had increased during the year from 303 to 380, including 10 new foreign subscribers to bring their total to 51. This was noted as being remarkable for wartime. Less remarkable and more distressing, however, was the loss of members to military service: 26 in 1940 and 43 by the following year.[1]

The growth of the institute's membership compared favorably with society membership before 1933, which had reached a peak of 479 in 1931, especially when we consider the much greater professional commitment and capacity allowed by institutional affiliation, and if we make the legitimate assumption that splits and secessions might well have reduced the membership of the old General Medical Society for Psychotherapy. The latter would have been particularly likely in terms of disagreements between relatively medical establishment types, like Kretschmer, and the less doctrinaire and more professionally adventurous physicians who found their place in the German General Medical

Society for Psychotherapy and the Göring Institute. Further, a comparison with the higher postwar figures for the various German psychotherapeutic and psychoanalytic societies confirms what a vital role psychotherapy's survival and development as a profession during the Third Reich played in the overall progress these disciplines achieved in the twentieth century. Given the intervening disruptions of economic crisis, political turmoil and oppression, and finally war, these numbers are even more impressive.

The growth of the institute's membership during these years was accompanied by a factor of more dynamic importance, the parallel broadening of the range of the institute's activities. By 1939, in fact, Göring had declared that the statutes as originally composed in 1936 were insufficient to meet the new tasks thrown to the institute, and that they would have to be redrawn. Because he wanted to shape the institute's leadership to his own design as well as to tackle the professional assignments piling up before him, Göring himself went ahead with a reshuffling of personnel and posts. He summoned Heyer from Munich to direct the program for attending psychologists, and chose another party member, Achelis, to head up the literature section. Künkel, through his deputy Herzog, was placed in charge of the consulting psychologists, while Schultz ran the division for continuing medical education. Hattingberg and Schultz-Hencke were responsible for science and research. The outpatient clinic, which until that time had been run by a triumvirate made up of Göring, Boehm, and Schultz, was given over to Gerhart Scheunert, a psychoanalyst from Erfurt. Scheunert was in the army, however, and Schultz was appointed his deputy, leaving the direct supervision of the clinic in the hands of Rittmeister.

By 1940 the institute had expanded to ten divisions: administration (Göring), management (Scherke), literature (Bilz/Achelis), *Weltanschauung* (Achelis), training (Heyer), criminal psychology (Kalau vom Hofe), educational counseling (König-Fachsenfeld), expert opinion and catamnesis—clinical cases—(Boehm), outpatient clinic (Schultz); under advisement of Hans Meyer-Mark, plans were also going forward for a section dealing with industrial psychology. In 1944, with the creation of the Reich Institute, the institute's activities were divided into twelve sections. The four major divisions of these were training (Heyer), clinic (Kemper), educational counseling (Kühnel), and research (Schultz), with subdivisions for literature (Bilz), statistics and evaluation (Boehm), marriage counseling (Hattingberg), archive (Heyer), forensic psychiatry (Kalau vom Hofe), educational aids and curricula (Müller-Braunschweig), industrial psychology (Scherke), and testing (Vetter).[2]

The original statutes of 1936 had outlined four aims for the new institute, and these remained as the foundation for its subsequent activities. The first, which we have already discussed, was the creation of a

"German" psychotherapy and psychology through the unification of the existing schools of thought. The second aim was the maintenance of an outpatient clinic, the third the establishment of advisory boards, especially in the field of education, and the fourth aim was the training of medical and nonmedical psychotherapists.[3]

The Outpatient Clinic: Theory and Practice

The outpatient clinic had originated with the old DPG under Eitingon and Simmel in 1920. When the Göring Institute took it over in 1936, its stated purpose was fourfold. It was to serve as a people's clinic (*"Anstalt für mittellose Volksgenossen"*), hence its name, *"Poliklinik,"* from the Greek πόλις ("city"). It was also to be a methodological laboratory for psychotherapists and students, thereby serving an educational function within the institute as well as constituting a scientific establishment.[4] It began operating on 15 October 1936, and in the first year of its operation—as reported by Boehm, who was in charge of statistics and the recording of the histories of clinical cases (catamnesis)— 412 patients were seen. Of these, 136 were under continuing care; 38 more were being continued in treatment as former patients from the old psychoanalytic institute, bringing the total number to 174. Of these, 31 patients were taken into private treatment, the small honoraria that would result being apportioned to younger colleagues. Patient complaints ranged from psychoses, epilepsy, and idiocy (49 of which cases were determined from the outset to be unsuited for psychotherapeutic treatment) to alcoholism, depression (the largest single category), "organ neuroses," sexual disorders and perversions, character disorders, anxiety neuroses, compulsion neuroses, hysteria, and what in contemporary psychotherapeutic practice is termed "problems in living," mostly difficulties at school or at work.[5]

The next year, 1937, saw 259 patients come to the clinic for the initial consultation for purposes of *triage* (13 were diagnosed as homosexuals) held jointly by Boehm, Göring, and Schultz. Of these, 110 were either unsuited for therapy, did not return for treatment, were cured or substantially improved in one session, or broke off treatment prematurely, while 58 were continuing treatment at the clinic. Forty-three cases were being handled privately, and 52 cases had been continued from the previous year in the clinic, 10 in private treatment. (The clinic's staff was composed of 52 institute members and 15 candidates, under the control of an instructor. Appropriate patients continued to be referred to the Charité clinic under Curtius, the psychiatric clinic under Bonhoeffer, and to Jaensch's university institute.)[6] No statistics for 1938–39 were published, but the following year the clinic handled 144 cases. In 1941, out of 464 people who visited the clinic, 260 were referred for treatment and, of these, 181 continued with it.

Boehm also offered in his report for that year a cumulative evaluation of the work of the clinic from 1936 through 1941. Of the 641 cases handled, 17 for various reasons (death, departure, military service) were without result, 60 were designated as untreatable, 118 remained unchanged, 136 were somewhat improved, 140 improved, 137 substantially improved, and 33 "cured."[7]

According to Kemper, approximately 80 percent of the patients were from the middle classes, 10 percent were workers, and 10 percent were from the upper class. Every full member of the institute was required to have at least one clinical patient under continuing treatment, and every candidate had to carry at least two clinical cases to conclusion during his or her training under the control of the training therapist. Since each candidate was required to have a patient continuously under treatment for the duration of training, one or more additional cases could be handled under the control of someone other than the candidate's training therapist. This proved to be an important source of income for the candidates, since each psychotherapist was guaranteed RM 6 (about $1.50) per hour, any difference between the required honorarium paid by the patient being made up by the institute. The honorarium was, of course, a necessary part of the treatment, not only in terms of giving the patient a stake in getting better, a crucial consideration for both psychotherapist and insurance carrier, but also for the patient's coming to terms with the role of money in psychic life. Candidates were allowed to keep their honoraria while institute members retained only the minimum fee for clinical patients. Therefore, the predominance of bourgeois patients was significant in terms of the institute's finances, since honoraria were based on the ability to pay, beyond the psychotherapeutic maxim of the necessity of sacrifice. Boehm pointed out that the institute's providing funds for the often financially strapped candidates was also necessary in order not to prejudice the candidates' conscious and unconscious attitudes in favor of clinical patients of comparatively substantial means.[8]

Kemper has estimated that around 50 percent of all the cases treated in the outpatient clinic were handled by various modes of short-term therapy. This corresponded to the traditional advocacy of a large number of psychotherapists in Germany at the time for those methods that would best address the widespread incidence of neurosis in modern society. The short-term orientation, as we have seen, was also congenial with the Nazi emphasis on *Volksgesundheit*. Indeed, Göring had more than one reason for selecting the psychoanalyst Scheunert, a student of Therese Benedek's, to direct the operations of the clinic. Scheunert's interest and expertise was in short-term therapies and their efficacy, not only in treating patients efficiently and effectively but in solving some of the worrisome problems of time and expense that prevented psychotherapy's inclusion in the state health insurance system. One of the purposes of the initial consultation between prospective patient and the directors of the clinic was to determine which method, applied by which psychotherapist, would be most effective for the case at hand.[9] Furthermore, the guidelines for the outpatient clinic stipulated the means by which auxiliary methods of treatment, such as breathing exercises, music, and movement therapies, or autogenic training, could supplement a continuing treatment. Reports on the progress of treatment were to be submitted after six weeks, six months, and one year, and they were to avoid terms that were peculiar to a particular psychotherapeutic orientation.[10] This requirement greatly facilitated the filing of insurance claims.

Despite the ordained avoidance of parochial terminology, which was in part a remnant of the early impulse toward a "German" psychotherapy, the work of the clinic was directed toward the dual goal of serving impecunious patients and validating psychotherapy's claim to medical and professional status. The guidelines for the clinic did mention the need for the proper *Weltanschauung* on the part of both patient and therapist, excluding those who did not measure up to the requirements of the Nuremberg laws. This, of course, meant Jews, though, according to one former member of the institute, the institute did allow a Jungian psychotherapist, Gerda Walter, to treat Jews.

The evaluation form (*Auswertungsbogen zum Krankenblatt*) devised by Kemper in 1943 also incorporated a rather large concession to the regime with the inclusion of Jaensch's officially approved typological schema, and a question as to the patient's racial background. An addendum to the clinic's guidelines, consisting of a clinical-diagnostic schema, stressed the incurable nature of congenital mental illness, and the nonefficacy in this regard of the methods taught and practiced at the Göring Institute. This last, however, rather than simply constituting a moral capitulation to the Nazis, was an acknowledgment of the limits of psychotherapeutic treatment as well as a professional concession to the psychiatric establishment, a step to minimize conflict and promote cooperation.

The schema came out of a committee consisting of Göring, Achelis, Boehm, Hattingberg, Herzog, Heyer, Kemper, Kranefeldt, Müller-Braunschweig, Rittmeister, Schultz, and Schultz-Hencke, and therefore represented theoretical consensus and compromise on the nature of neurosis and its treatment. In his report of 1940 Schultz noted the controversies regarding these issues that had marked the work of the committee, and which affected the work of the outpatient clinic in both positive and negative ways. But he characteristically concluded that the intellectual fermentation taking place was a sign of professional growth and necessary for the productive development of the clinic as a weapon in psychotherapy's fight for survival and recognition:

The outpatient clinic is our weapons forge. That sometimes there are metal fragments and sometimes hammers clash may be somewhat disturbing to you . . . but it is necessary. We desperately need that. You are perhaps not entirely clear about how threatened even today your whole existence as psychotherapists is.[11]

Apart from serving its patients, then, the goal of the clinic was also to be living proof of the medical credibility of psychotherapy.

Although various modes of psychotherapy were used in private practice by German psychotherapists and by physicians and laymen throughout Germany, the work of the approximately fifty psychotherapists of the Göring Institute's outpatient clinic alone provides us with a significant sample of the variety of psychotherapeutic methods in use during the Third Reich. Most, but not all, of these methods were short-term therapies, varying in type and scope depending on the school of thought to which the particular psychotherapist belonged, but reflecting the basic neo-Freudian therapeutic turn as well as the common professional and governmental emphasis on what was construed as effective social service.

Once a prospective patient had been diagnosed (often in collaboration with psychiatric and internal experts from the Charité) by means of an interview, a physical examination, and appropriate psychological tests, the form of therapy would be chosen. This depended on the severity of the neurotic symptoms, a measure that was usually taken by means of Schultz's four categories of neurosis: alien (resulting from external trauma); border (arising from bad learned physical habits); layer (from daily stresses affecting various levels of the psyche); and core (deep disorders stemming from constitutional defect and early childhood experiences). According to Rittmeister, the methods in general included "depth psychological treatment," such as, according to Kemper, classical terminable psychoanalysis, with the analysand free-associating in a supine position and the analyst seated behind or alongside the patient's head. Less rigorous and time-consuming was consultation with a "depth psychologist," wherein both patient and therapist would assume a more "active" posture (seated facing each other) in seeking to eliminate debilitating neurotic symptoms. This more active, egalitarian, and present-centered orientation also animated group therapy sessions, educational counseling in which children and their parents were counseled, and the application of hypnosis, autogenic training (autohypnosis), along with nerve end massage (for writer's cramp), gymnastics, breathing exercises, and voice therapy.[12]

Scheunert, as a psychoanalyst specializing in short-term therapy, also advocated the use of hypnosis and autogenic training, the latter, he found, being especially helpful for insomniacs. He also approved of the so-called Happich method of light hypnosis and autogenic training, which used a meditation exercise in which the patient could divest the self of rational/intellectual defenses. In this mode of psycho-therapy, childhood imagoes would be recreated by "walking," first to a stream bank in an open field, from the meadow to a mountain, and then through a forest to a chapel. Scheunert was most interested, not surprisingly, in the short-term applications of the "passive-contempla-tive" approach of psychoanalytic free association. He described a num-ber of cases in which only three or four hour-long sessions were suffi-cient to reveal the outlines of the primary psychological conflict. One of these cases concerned a young man who wished to become engaged but felt he could not because of a longstanding impotence discovered through a number of unsuccessful liaisons with prostitutes. Therapy revealed a tremendous guilt over onanism that stemmed primarily from a tyrannical pietistic father. This revelation, according to Scheunert, resulted in the cure of the patient's impotence.[13]

Klaus Wegscheider, practicing in Berlin-Schöneberg and, like Scheu-nert, motivated in great measure by a desire to shorten the duration and expense of psychotherapy in order to integrate it into the state medical insurance scheme, placed a practical emphasis on suggestion, hypnosis, and autogenic training. But, also like Scheunert, Weg-scheider went beyond these methods to advocate psychocatharsis (a releasing of pent-up emotions) and, most importantly, "functional" psychotherapy. This last approach involved the scheduling of short periods of psychotherapy alternating with periods of no treatment. The advantage of this system was that it met the requirements of lim-ited insurance coverage, eased the patient load on the physician, and (a rationalization from practical necessity?) forced the patient to come to grips with life problems in the interims.[14]

Schultz himself was more concerned with active modes of psycho-therapy that stressed the therapist's expertise and guidance in mo-bilizing the patient's reason against the psychological/physiological dysfunctions of the nervous system. Wegscheider, as a student of Kretsch-mer—who stressed the relative nervous predisposition of physical types and consequently saw neurosis not simply as a psychological prob-lem, but one of a complex interaction of mind and body—expressed this more medical orientation as "the patient performs, the doctor directs."[15] Schultz's autogenic training, even though it was a method to be used by the patient, was designed to address psychomotor and vegetative symptomatology. This reflected a view of neurosis which tended to stress stimuli rather than motives. Kretschmer had insisted that no neurosis could be approached merely from the experiental side by an analytic "working through," but that it had to be grasped from the affective manifestations of physical tone and type. It was this dual appreciation that made it imperative for Kretschmer that every psy-chotherapist be a physician trained to understand the subtle and com-plex interrelationships between body and mind.[16]

Schultz's own emphasis on active modes of psychotherapy drew from the work of the nineteenth-century internist Ottomar Rosenbach and even more from that of Rosenbach's contemporary, the neuropathologist Paul DuBois. Rosenbach and DuBois believed that most mental disorders have psychological roots, but that "psychological functions have a physiological substratum" which nevertheless could be "influenced by psychotherapy."[17] Schultz reserved his greatest praise, however, for the neurologist Oskar Vogt, who pioneered the use of suggestion, hypnosis, narcohypnosis (the use of hypnotic drugs), and autohypnosis.[18] In championing what he called rational waking therapy (rationale Wachtherapie), Schultz was again displaying the rationalistic open-mindedness that was central to his professional life.

Schultz was convinced that the rational ego could understand the reality of its strengths and virtues; he rejected the psychoanalytic view that all human beings (and civilization) were riven with internal antinomies. Neurosis, according to Schultz, in drawing on the Gestalt viewpoint of Viktor von Weizsäcker, was a function of particular social faults, and it was the task of psychotherapy to understand the individual as a subject in all his or her individual physical, psychological, and social complexity. Both psychoanalysis and psychiatry failed to do this, he argued, while individual practitioners such as Klages and Haeberlin, in their holistic emphasis on the rhythm of life (Lebensrhythmus), expressed a valuable appreciation of the "bionomic" reality of living organisms in dynamic relationship with their environment as opposed to the simplistic notion of immutable instinct. To the extent that psychoanalysis was worthwhile for Schultz, it was in its emphasis on the laborious process of rationally overcoming conflicts; from this perspective, Schultz regarded it as a valuable tool in the cure of some layer and core neuroses.[19] Even disorders attributed to heredity, which comprised a portion of these core neuroses, were curable through psychotherapy, Schultz believed, for they were not matters of incurable physical decay, as with genuine psychopaths, but of difficulties buried deep within the physiological/psychological character structure of an individual.[20]

Schultz's approach to neurosis and its cure was marked by its comprehensiveness: a reasoned consideration of various theories about the complexity of the interactions of mind and body. As we have noted earlier, in both intellect and temperament he was a good choice for a leadership role in an all-embracing institute such as Göring's, and an especially valuable asset within the realm of catholic practice as incorporated in the outpatient clinic. Schultz was fully in accord with the institute's policy of training lay psychologists while insisting that their work be conducted under the supervision of physicians. He also pointed to the danger of neighboring disciplines like pedagogy, sociology, hygiene, religion, etc., appropriating at least part of what he saw as fundamentally a medical discipline. To meet this challenge Schultz strove to incorporate the methods of *kleine* psychotherapy into general medical practice. But typically, unlike many doctors and most psychiatrists, he admitted that an organic and mechanical view was insufficient, and (pure Schultz) that the greatest danger in this or any question was a dogmatic attitude that shut out critical, scientific insight.[21]

The third aim of the Göring Institute as delineated in its statutes was the establishment of advisory boards for the active application of psychotherapeutic expertise to problems facing society. On 1 November 1939 the educational counseling service (*Erziehungshilfe*) that had been functioning under Fritz Künkel and his wife, Elisabeth, since 1938 as an undifferentiated operation of the outpatient clinic was expanded into a formal subdivision of the clinic under the direction of Olga von König-Fachsenfeld, a student of Heyer's from Munich. Its function was to bring psychotherapeutic assistance to young people who were having difficulty in school, or whose difficulties at home became apparent in educational problems. König-Fachsenfeld was replaced in 1942 by Gottfried Kühnel, a student of Kretschmer's who ran a home for psychopathic patients in Berlin. König-Fachsenfeld went to Stuttgart to become managing director of the Württemberg-Baden affiliate of the institute and run the educational assistance program there with Jutta von Graevenitz and Wilhelm Laiblin. The educational counseling clinic in Berlin treated and advised children of fifteen years of age and under, along with their parents. Between 1 November 1939 and 1 February 1941, 116 cases were handled; and from 1 January 1941 to 31 December 1941, 129. Diagnoses ranged from idiocy and brain damage to various types of neurotic behavior, but the single greatest number, according to König-Fachsenfeld, suffered from school problems stemming from a disrupted family environment. Therapies included play therapy for children and toddlers (with the child acting out conflicts through drawing, puppetry, pretend-school, toy selection, etc.), family therapy, and auxiliary modes, such as gymnastics and music, as well as group therapy and individual treatment and counseling. The average duration of treatment, according to figures drawn up by Julie Aichele of Beuren, was six months for children under ten years of age and a year for those over ten.[22]

Elisabeth Künkel estimated that about 50 percent of the children who came to the Göring Institute were incapable of integrating themselves into the community, but that only approximately 6 percent were hereditarily disordered and therefore untreatable through psychotherapy.[23] It was the disposition of these latter cases, König-Fachsenfeld has recalled, that brought the shadow of National Socialism into the children's clinic (*Kinderpoliklinik*). The children could be sent to "safe" homes or asylums; in milder cases the institute would advise bringing the child in for treatment so as to protect him or her from harm from the Nazis. In addition, again according to König-Fachsenfeld, the clinic treated a number of cases of children whom the state had asked to spy on their parents and who were torn between conflicting allegiances.

The educational counseling clinic's contact with state authority, however, usually came in the benign form of cooperation with various agencies involved with educational and family matters. All educational counseling services were under the direction of the municipal youth office (städtisches Jugendamt). In many if not most cases, the psychologists and psychotherapists at the Göring Institute were dealing with the same civil servants and social workers with whom they had worked before the Nazis took power. Between October 1939 and May 1940, for example, of the children being treated at the Berlin clinic 23 percent had been referred to the Göring Institute by city, state, or party organizations (e.g., NSV), 28 percent by physicians, 10 percent by teachers, and 39 percent by parents and others.[24]

The institute also sought to publicize the work of other agencies in this field: In Berlin the Transport Works (Berliner Verkehrsbetriebe) operated two convalescent homes for children, as had the local Public Youth Authority (Landesjugendamt der Stadt Berlin), with its Center for Special Psychological Care (Pflegestelle für psychologische Sonderbetreuung).[25] The Göring Institute was also in contact with the Nazi youth organizations, the Hitler Youth (Hitlerjugend) and League of German Girls (Bund Deutscher Mädel), with Josephine Bilz, wife of Rudolf Bilz, active as a physician with the Hitler Youth. The subdivision for educational counseling also published a series of pamphlets on various topics related to child psychotherapy and educational psychology, written by its members. By 1941 three members of the Göring Institute had been put in charge of private homes for disturbed children (Heilerziehungsheime). These were: in Berlin the home directed by Adelheid Fuchs-Kamp; the home run by Karoline Schmidt and Modesta Thimme in Schwallenberg, southeast of Bielefeld; and one at Beuren bei Nürtingen in Württemberg, under the direction of Julie Aichele. Cooperation between these institutions and the Göring Institute was overseen by Adolf von Weizsäcker.[26]

A similar Göring Institute-affiliated program in Vienna reported a significant degree of participation from the local NSV: 53 kindergartens with 1546 children; 84 day nurseries (NSV-Horten) with 3024 children; a juvenile justice assistance program run by the NSV, handling 2422 cases; and 11 counseling offices which reportedly, between November 1939 and April 1940, had conducted 839 consultations in 459 hours. These facilities, however impressive in terms of numbers, were more custodial than psychotherapeutic, and only supplemented the municipal programs begun after World War I. Three psychologists and 19 social workers were active within the Vienna programs. From 1 January 1939 to 31 March 1940, 2302 children, 75 percent of whom were of school age, were attended to. The counselors registered their concern about the fact that only 41 percent of the children were living with their natural parents. The greatest number of children (31.5 percent) were brought for help by their parents; the police referred 20.5 percent, the schools 18 percent, the courts 6 percent, and the NSV only 2 percent. Potential delinquency (34 percent) and school problems (23 percent) headed the list of complaints, a further breakdown in terms of psychological dynamics not being given. In the realm of prevention through supplemental education outside of the home, it was pointed out that by the end of March 1940 Vienna was running 301 kindergartens and 159 day-care centers for 5590 preschoolers and 3274 schoolchildren.[27]

A significant adjunct to the Göring Institute's interest in and support of educational counseling in Vienna was the presence there of psychoanalyst August Aichhorn. According to Ernst Göring, König-Fachsenfeld, and Kemper, Aichhorn was highly regarded by Göring, lectured in Berlin, and was protected by him. Göring, of course, had studied with Seif and Künkel and was very interested in child psychotherapy and delinquency; and Alice Lüps, a relative of his, was also active in the field. Aichhorn himself had been a schoolmaster and worked with delinquent children at reformatories outside Vienna at Ober-Hollabrunn and St. Andrä. Anna Freud had been impressed with Aichhorn's work and suggested he undertake psychoanalytic training. After completing his training in Vienna, he had published his most famous work, *Verwahrloste Jugend,* in 1925. Its perspective was that if a child had an unsatisfactory relationship with a parent, that child would have later difficulties in establishing relationships with other people; Freud himself had contributed a foreword. In 1932 Aichhorn retired to private practice and established a Child Guidance Service for the Vienna Psychoanalytic Society. One reason he stayed in Vienna after the Nazis took over was his son's internment in Dachau.

Aichhorn, although being cold-shouldered by the nominal leader of the Vienna branch of the Göring Institute, Heinrich von Kogerer, supervised, officially as an "attending psychologist," the psychoanalytic training of over a score of medical and nonmedical candidates between May 1938 and June 1944. Some of these candidates were referred by Göring. Kogerer himself was not sympathetic toward psychoanalysis, but his service in the military limited his involvement in the affairs of the Vienna section of the Göring Institute.

In spite of the fact that Aichhorn remained an outspoken representative of the Freudian perspective, criticizing on one occasion Hattingberg's "Thesen zur Neurosenlehre" for being vaguely impressionistic instead of rigorously rational, in 1944 he was named an extraordinary member of the new Reich Institute. In March 1944, however, the Berlin psychiatrist Viktor Emil Freiherr von Gebsattel came to Vienna to discuss the establishment of an outpatient clinic. Apparently by mutual agreement, Gebsattel replaced Aichhorn as acting director of Vienna operations. Gebsattel had been a member of Freud's circle in Vienna before World War I and had been analyzed by Seif in Munich. He had turned away from orthodox psychoanalysis, however, and adopted an "anthropological" point of view that tended toward an existential orientation based on his Roman Catholic background. Gebsattel allegedly had been sent to Vienna by Göring because of the danger to the institute in Berlin posed by his contacts with the German resistance movement.[28] Thus Aichhorn's work in an official capacity under the Nazis came to an end, work that was, however, to be resumed after the war. (See Chapter 7.)

It was at the Göring Institute affiliate in Munich, near Dachau, that what had come to be known as "psychagogy" was most enthusiastically pursued, under the grandfatherly aegis of Leonhard Seif. In all, between 1922 and 1939 Seif's center had held 1221 counseling sessions with 470 families, 2.6 sessions per family. The only other figures available were published for the year 1941, when the number of counselings had numbered 93 for 66 families.[29] It is impossible to say what may have played a larger role in the diminishing number of counselings per family: an increasing efficiency on the part of the psychotherapists and psychologists, the Nazi emphasis on speed over depth, or various environmental influences on families. In any case, with the formal link to the Göring Institute, the work of Seif's groups with various party and governmental agencies increased, and included: the NSV, the Assistance Service for Mother and Child (Hilfswerk Mutter und Kind), Youth Assistance Program (Jugendhilfe), the DAF Women's Office (Frauenamt), the Reich Mothers Service in the German Women's Welfare Organization (Reichsmutterdienst im deutschen Frauenwerk), the party's organizations for teachers, the Hitler Youth, and the League of German Girls.[30] The emphasis throughout remained on short-term suggestive methods, family therapy, play therapy, various auxiliary methods, and the general encouragement of social prevention of child neuroses and difficulties by the maintenance of sound educational practices and environmental standards in the family and at school. Seif's institute also sponsored work on hereditary disorders under psychiatrist Lene Credner, paralleling the work done by Hans Luxenburger in his own practice in Munich.[31]

In 1940, following discussions between Göring and the Reich Criminal Police Office (Reichskriminalpolizeiamt), a second subdivision of the outpatient clinic was established. It would deal with matters of criminal psychology, under the direction of Marie Kalau vom Hofe, a psychoanalyst. Kalau vom Hofe had done her training analyses with

Sandor Rado in 1925 and later under Müller-Braunschweig. She came to the institute in Berlin in 1937 to do work in another one of Göring's fields of particular interest, forensic psychiatry. Since 1926 Kalau vom Hofe had been pursuing work in this field at the Charité and at Berlin Police Headquarters on the Alexanderplatz. She saw her new assignment as twofold: to further the participation of the psychotherapeutic and psychoanalytic point of view in the criminal justice system for the benefit of those before the bench who were suffering from treatable mental illnesses, and to promote psychotherapy as a profession. She cautioned, however, that in both instances the opposite of what was desired by psychotherapists would occur if extravagant claims were made about the healing power of psychotherapeutic methods. During 1940 the criminal psychology division handled fifty-three cases, described as primarily involving compulsive thieves, as well as a broad range of sexual offenders: one case of bestiality, two pedophiles, three exhibitionists, two sadists, and eleven homosexuals (nine male, two female). Children were also treated: one fifteen-year-old boy for cruelty to an animal, and a six-year-old girl for repeated thefts of baby carriages. Kalau vom Hofe reported that in one particular case that involved an exhibitionist, the court of appeals had followed the advice of the institute's expert opinion on the case in recommending psychotherapy. The institute's success in treating these offenders, however, was far less than satisfactory. Of the seventy-three cases investigated in 1941, only six underwent therapy.[32] There is no record of the fate of the others.

Training

The fourth of the institute's aims as specified in the statutes of 1936 was the training of psychotherapists. Article 11 called for the creation of a training committee, which came to be made up of Göring, Schultz, Künkel, Müller-Braunschweig, and Adolf von Weizsäcker. From the beginning the committee insisted that each candidate's own analysis or therapy (*Lehranalyse, Lehrbehandlung*) was an indispensable part of his or her training. This was the aspect of psychotherapeutic practice that traditional psychiatrists found most objectionable.[33] By requiring training therapy, the aspiring profession clearly indicated the specific direction it was taking in its institutionalization under Göring's leadership and protection. The requirement of training therapy was to resurface after 1945 as a major issue between psychiatrists in the reestablished (under Kretschmer) General Medical Society for Psychotherapy, which always had required a degree in medicine, and the various psychodynamic groups emerging out of the Göring Institute.

In addition to the training analysis, the institute stipulated a theoretical course of study and practical experience that would extend over a minimum of two years. Medical candidates were required to take courses in psychology, philosophy, and ethnology, while nonmedical candidates had to take instruction in anatomy, physiology, biology, and psychiatry. The training analysis could be undertaken at any branch of the Göring Institute on the approval of Göring and the local director, but at least one year of the theoretical course work and the entire practical segment for full training as a psychotherapist had to take place in Berlin; one semester, or, under special circumstances, two semesters of the theoretical portion could take place at one of the branches of the Göring Institute. The cost of a two-year course of study ran between RM 3000 and RM 4000 (c. $750–$1000), and subsequent membership in the institute required that the applicant be at least thirty years old and have five years of professional experience. The institute also required continuing education, which included practical orientation to the various modes of theory and treatment, the continuous treatment of at least one clinical patient, participation in seminars, attendance at institute or university lectures, participation in scientific meetings and, where possible, further work in the outpatient clinic, including educational counseling.

The institute also reserved the right to "steer" the choice of location for its candidates' practice in the interest of the profession's equal distribution throughout Germany. Although the curriculum was claimed to lay "special weight . . . upon a fundamental and thorough knowledge of heredity and racial research,"[34] the total of all the hours of instruction actually offered in these subjects between 1936 and 1945 reached only thirty-one.

According to article 7 of the statutes, the institute offered only two categories of membership, ordinary (ordentliche) and supporting (fördernde). While membership in the German General Medical Society for Psychotherapy required a degree in medicine, at the Göring Institute any fully trained psychotherapist could become a member, whether or not he or she was a physician.[35] Beginning in 1940, however, a third category, that of extraordinary (ausserordentliche) membership, was added. The necessity for such a change arose from what was claimed to be the large number of nonacademic candidates at the institute who sought training to supplement their professional work. For the most part, these were teachers and those practicing orthopedic gymnastics, and the great majority were women. In response to this demand, and in an attempt to increase it, the psychotherapists in 1939 instituted a program under the direction of Künkel, through his deputy Herzog, for "consulting psychologists" (beratende Psychologen), stressing the importance of such training for professionals in large organizations but in general for those whose work "involves intercourse with people, the psychological widening and deepening of which seems desirable (e.g., doctors, jurists, clergymen, teachers, plant foremen, social workers, youth counselors, etc.)."[36]

Although the name "consulting psychologist" was dropped in 1941 in favor of the more general designation "extraordinary membership," the aim of the program remained the same: to provide at minimum a year-long course of study in psychotherapy for those who wished to incorporate a psychotherapeutic perspective into their own professions, including a training analysis, but excluding the practical aspect of "control analyses." The original title of "consulting psychologist" probably was considered too presumptuous, especially in light of the rather modest number of candidates the program attracted, and was probably the product of an early and perhaps too provocative proselytizing zeal. In 1938 there were sixteen candidates, and in 1939 fifteen, all seeking training to supplement their primary professions. In 1940 there were nine candidates and twenty-seven in 1941; by then there were also twelve extraordinary *members* of the institute. Women continued to outnumber men in this category. Extraordinary membership did not carry with it the right to practice psychotherapy or to advertise with the title "extraordinary member of the German Institute for Psychological Research and Psychotherapy."[37]

As with membership, the number of candidates steadily increased over the years of the institute's operation. In 1937 there were 42, including 26 candidates for regular membership: 16 doctors and 10 academics from nonmedical fields, exactly half of them women. The next year there were 47 candidates, including 17 doctors and 13 academics; in 1939, a total of 49 (19 doctors, 15 academics). By 1939 the number included 18 candidates (*Praktikanten*) who had begun their control cases in the clinic under the supervision of their training therapist. In 1940 the candidate total had risen to 59, including 24 *Praktikanten*: 25 doctors (20 men, 5 women) and 25 candidates for the title of "attending psychologist" (*behandelnde Psychologe*), composed of 14 academics (9 men, 5 women) and 11 nonacademics (1 man, 10 women). The last year for which we have statistics, 1941, showed a significant increase in the number of training candidates—from 59 in December 1940 to 110 in December 1941. Candidates for ordinary membership numbered 83 (38 doctors and 45 attending psychologists). Twenty-seven of the doctors and 19 of the attending psychologists were men. Seven candidates that year had been called up into the army, and one had died in the fighting.

The training of attending psychologists at the Göring Institute was based on the psychotherapists' conviction that the professional practice of psychotherapy and medical psychology should not be restricted to physicians. The name itself was first used in 1938, but questions pertaining to the attending psychologists' legal and professional status had emerged with the founding of the institute in 1936. Numerous extended discussions were held with the party's Bernhard Hörmann on whether nonmedical psychotherapists should be regarded as health practitioners, but it was finally decided that they would be organized as an independent branch of the Labor Front's Office for National Health. The Interior Ministry had also taken part in these deliberations and had determined that the psychologists should be included under the law governing medical assistants. This solution was satisfactory to the psychotherapists, since in general they regarded the official recognition, control, and practice of lay psychotherapy as necessary to the growth of the profession within medicine and to society's maintenance of mental health, and did not wish to see the psychologists shunted off into the still suspect realm of natural medicine.[38]

Because the psychotherapists at the Göring Institute also insisted that the work of the attending psychologists be supervised by physicians, the application by the Interior Ministry of the law governing medical assistants was acceptable on this basis as well. This particular issue of supervision was to be, as we will see, another postwar point of controversy between the psychiatrists around Kretschmer and the psychotherapists. In any case, because of the war no official guidelines for attending psychologists were issued by the Interior Ministry; in the interim the psychologists were to follow the general guidelines for physicians laid down in the law in 1937. Although by 1941 attending psychologists belonged to the Labor Front's Special Office for Free Professions (Fachamt Freie Berufe), any genuine professional status in the form of the establishment of a set of professional regulations (Berufsordnung) was not regarded by the Interior Ministry as important to the war effort.[39] This whole process revealed not only the conservative medical bias of the ministry's perspective but a general ministerial concern with arrangement and order rather than reform or the wrestling with substantive issues.

Greater progress was made on the question of state-approved training for academically trained, as opposed to "attending," psychologists. On 16 June 1941 the Education Ministry issued instructional guidelines and ordinances for the training and state examination for a diploma in psychology leading to the practical application of psychology in the life of society. This introduction of certification for psychologists followed from the efforts of academic psychologists to promote the field, as well as from the demand for psychologists by industry and the armed forces. As the psychotherapists sought control of all practitioners in the realm of medical psychology, a number of leading academic psychologists now complemented the effort and sought to exploit the prestige of the Göring Institute. Both Göring, who in 1941 became an editor of the Zeitschrift für angewandte Psychologie, and Heyer participated in a series of discussions about developing the standards for certification. These discussions were hosted by the institute, and included prominent university psychologists such as Oswald Kroh of Munich, editor of the *Zeitschrift für Psychologie,* Phillip Lersch of Cottbus, and Friedrich Sander of Jena. General Hans von Voss and army psychologist Max Simoneit were also involved, along with DAF representatives Albert Bremhorst and Carl Alexander Roos, Walter Stets from the Labor Ministry, and educational psychologist Arthur Hoffmann of Cottbus.[40]

The new regulations, retroactively in force from 1 April 1941, required students seeking certification as psychologists to be examined in the general psychology of the conscious and unconscious life of the individual and the community; in developmental psychology; in characterology and hereditary psychology; in the psychology of expression (*Ausdruckspsychologie*); in biological-medical auxiliary sciences; and in philosophy and ideology.[41] The applicant was further required to complete an internship at one of a number of types of approved institutions. Included in the list were homes and educational advisory boards run by the NSV, primary and secondary schools, advisory boards connected with the state labor exchange, training and apprenticeship facilities in industry and trade, psychological installations of the Labor Front, reformatories, psychotherapeutic advisory boards, psychiatric and related clinics, racial hygiene advisory boards, and geopolitical institutes.[42]

The fact that a capacity for medicine was included in the examination of an aspiring certified psychologist reflected the ignorance and the all-encompassing rhetoric that characterized the Nazi attempt at the mobilization of Germany's resources. Awed by experts and guided as well by their own designs for Germany, the Nazis thought and acted in a broad manner that was, in this case, agreeable to both the academic psychologists and to the psychotherapists gathered at the Göring Institute. But the arrogation of a medical function on the part of psychologists elicited a storm of protest from psychiatrists, who were apparently taken by surprise at the breadth of professional capacity spelled out in the new regulations. Max de Crinis, with the urging of colleagues including Ernst Rüdin, Otto Wuth, and Oswald Bumke, launched a counterattack from inside the Education Ministry itself. Through de Crinis, psychiatrists and neurologists protested that they could not be expected, as the regulations envisioned, to teach, examine, and present patients to mere laypersons. More important, the psychiatrists asserted, they could not countenance the official creation of a group of half-educated medical dilettantes.[43] It was as a result of this campaign that in 1942 Education Minister Rust, in an unpublished directive, quietly deleted from the regulations the adjective "medical" in the phrase "medical-biological auxiliary sciences," struck out the provision for practical experience on psychotherapeutic advisory boards and in psychiatric clinics, and removed the words "psychiatrist" and "neurologist" from the composition of the examination committees.[44]

With the exception of medicine, it is difficult to determine exactly what "biological auxiliary sciences" might have meant, but it is clear that the psychiatrists triumphed in formally divesting the certified psychologist of any claim to the practice of the discipline they so fiercely guarded. The requirement for medical capacity could be quietly dropped from the law because the law contained no specific provisions concerning the *practice* of medical psychology. Neither the bureaucrats nor the academic psychologists were ready for the licensing of full clinical psychologists because, from the beginning, both were more concerned with the application of psychological methods and expertise in education, industry, and the military than with the more daunting task of confronting the medical profession in a battle over the pedagogical and professional standards for the practice of medical psychology. As a result, on 22 March 1943 the Education Ministry announced the recognition of four areas of specialization for certified psychologists: educational psychology (*Erziehungspsychologie*), vocational psychology (*Psychologie der Berufslenkung*), industrial psychology (*Industriepsychologie*), and business psychology (*Wirtschaftspsychologie*).[45]

But whatever the formal legal victory the psychiatrists enjoyed, they were still faced with the fact of those (few) certified psychologists who chose to seek postgraduate specialization in medical psychology at the Göring Institute.[46] The institute did not require the degree for its nonmedical candidates, but did claim to prefer it over other university degrees. In addition, state-approved teachers without a full university degree could, on the basis of their professional experience, be admitted to this training as ordinary candidates.

The Interior Ministry had also stipulated that attending psychologists must have a university degree, but that in cases where exceptional professional performance and experience were in evidence, applicants without degrees could receive ministerial permission for admission to the training program.[47] All nonmedical ordinary candidates received special training in medical subjects and also undertook a training analysis of at least 150 hours; extraordinary candidates had only to complete at least 100 hours of their own psychotherapy or psychoanalysis. On completion of training, the title of "attending psychologist" was conferred on the basis of temporary guidelines set down by the Interior Ministry. In addition to having to work with a physician in practicing as a psychotherapist, the attending psychologist was not permitted to prepare expert opinions or to appear in court as an expert witness. The institute, however, declared its readiness to supply experts for these purposes in cases in which attending psychologists were involved. The psychologists were permitted to place their title on their doorplates and stationery and, in appropriate instances, to place there as well the legend "Member of the German Institute for Psychological Research and Psychotherapy." Like physicians, attending psychologists were prohibited from advertising and were sworn to maintain professional confidentiality.[48]

Even though the Göring Institute insisted on medical supervision of nonmedical psychotherapists as ordained under the 1939 decision by the Interior Ministry governing medical assistants, psychiatrists like de Crinis saw this as a wide breach in the walls surrounding the practice of medicine, a break through which poured the great unwashed of ill-trained medical personnel. As if there had not been ample reason to do so before, the academic psychiatrists now regarded the operations of the Göring Institute, in combination with the aggressive efforts of the university psychologists toward their own profession's development, as a dangerous precedent that boded ill for the future direction of medical psychology. As a result of this professionally threatening situation, de Crinis apparently saw the need for positive action to retain control of the entire field of medical psychology in the hands of psychiatrists. By 1944, instead of insisting, as he and others had in 1941, that psychiatrists and neurologists be relieved of the duty of helping train psychologists, de Crinis proposed providing them with courses in psychiatry and psychopathology. In other words, when faced with the *fait accompli* of a significant degree of official recognition for psychologists, psychiatrists like de Crinis were forced to launch a professional counteroffensive rather than continue to rely purely on the defensive advantage of an established position.

In recommending this course to his medical opposite number in the Interior Ministry, Gustav Frey, de Crinis was also worried about apparently renewed efforts by the Education Ministry to give psychologists some measure of legally recognized competence in psychotherapy: "No dilettantism can be tolerated in this field. This would be the case if—as intended—a share of psychotherapy (depth psychology) were to be handed over to the psychologist."[49] By no means, de Crinis continued, should certified psychologists have anything to do with medicine—that is, with the practice of psychotherapy. Furthermore, it was his firm opinion that expert testimony from psychologists should not be introduced in court cases alongside the extant testimonal capacity of psychiatrists. With an eye to exploiting the wartime decline in interest in applied psychology on the part of the military, he also pointed out that the actual need for certified psychologists was so small that all the fuss over professional recognition on the part of "these so-called practical psychologists" was groundless.[50]

De Crinis's concerns testify to the flux within the realms of medical psychology endemic to the era, and particularly to the power and influence of the Göring Institute. Although in the long run, as we shall see in Chapter 7, the 1941 regulations would help lead to a professional advantage for university psychologists, at the time the Göring Institute represented the most significant challenge to psychiatry's claim to sovereignty over medical psychology. This was dangerously clear to de Crinis and his colleagues, and the collaboration on pragmatic grounds of university psychologists like Kroh with the institute underscores this fact. Whatever the guidelines for medical assistants and for the certification of psychologists did or did not say with regard to the practice of medicine, established psychologists at the Göring Institute like Seelmann, Hantel, and Heyer-Grote, among others, exercised a largely independent competence in psychotherapy that made them and others anything but medical assistants. In addition, as we have seen, the role of psychology in education was also intimately related to the psychotherapeutic care of children, as the 1943 specialization guidelines in fact stressed by the inclusion of therapeutic pedagogy (*Heilpädagogik*).[51]

Psychotherapy and Productivity: The Institute and the German Labor Front

The kind of broad professonal competence that the Göring Institute developed and maintained throughout the entire field of psychological research, training, and practice was a crucial element in its subsequent growth and reorganization in the years just before the outbreak of war. This was so because it was exactly this competence that attracted the interest of the gigantic and wealthy German Labor Front. Negotiations during 1938 and 1939 led to a formal relationship between the Göring Institute and the Labor Front; and although the institute continued to cultivate relations with various psychologists and psychological groups—welcoming, for example, the news of the medical-psychological institute founded in 1941 by Hans Bender at the University of Strassburg (Strasbourg) which embraced both the faculties of medicine and philosophy[52]—it was the DAF which to one degree or another supported the institute's work financially and organizationally from 1936 until 1945. The financial support did not mean that the Göring Institute or its professional aims were subordinated to those of the Labor Front. During its Labor Front years, the institute was able to exist and operate essentially on its own professional terms. Indeed, when, during the war, association with the DAF no longer seemed to be so advantageous for the psychotherapists, they were able rather easily to seize the opportunity to move into the Reich Research Council, and henceforth to rely on it and other sources of financial support. The reorganization of the Göring Institute in 1939, however, was directly related to its close ties to the Labor Front, and to its newly concomitant commitment to German productivity in wartime.

The Labor Front's influence was immediately apparent. It was DAF funding that allowed the institute to create the divisions for the training of attending and consulting psychologists in 1939, and to amalgamate them with the training for physicians into the "Hauptabteilung Ausbildung" under Heyer in 1940; all attending psychologists were required to be members of the Labor Front.[53] In 1939 the psychotherapists also published a special issue of the *Zentralblatt*, containing essays selected from that year's volume. Each of the four articles included had in common a concern with the application of psychotherapy to social and industrial problems: Scheunert on short-term therapy, Göring on psychotherapy and social insurance, Hans Kellner on the factory physician and psychotherapy, and Meyer-Mark on neurosis and the economy. And the third, and last, congress of the German General Medical Society for Psychotherapy in Vienna in 1940 adopted the very DAFish theme of "Psyche and Productivity."

The relationship of the Göring Institute to the Labor Front arose from more than a joint technical interest in industrial psychology and the Nazi bias toward harnessing expertise to expedite Hitler's policies. The Labor Front, like the Nazi movement and regime as a whole, placed an inordinate emphasis on the power of political conviction, the national will, and the consequent mission of party organizations to educate the people toward heroic sacrifice for the state. Where education failed, of course, terror, or the pervasive threat of terror, would be used. This was particularly the case with the German working class, which Hitler and the Nazis regarded as a major contributor to Germany's downfall in the twentieth century. As we have already observed, the collapse of the home front in World War I was a phenomenon that obsessed Hitler; he wanted at all costs to avoid a repeat of it in the course of his war for world domination. The Nazis tried to preempt any wartime rebelliousness on the part of the workers over wages, working hours, or trade union autonomy by using a fusion of terror, racial rhetoric, and the sop of plenty of consumer goods, even far into the war. In the later stages of the war, the Nazis opted increasingly for terror, but in 1939 and 1940, at least, there was a real attempt to reproduce the utopia of 1914 by both material and psychological means. Beyond the social anodyne of Strength through Joy (Kraft durch Freude)—modeled on fascist Italy's Dopo Lavóro—and its cruises, vacations, and unfulfilled promises of Volkswagens that had marked DAF labor policy in the 1930s, there would be no leveling with the masses of the working classes, only the cynical rhetoric and false assurances which papered over Hitler's designs for aggression.[54] The Labor Front itself, a far cry under Ley from even the "National Socialism" of the departed Strasser brothers, emphasized "adjustment" (*Ausgleich*) over "struggle"

(*Kampf*), reflecting the typical fascist striving after a superficial and hierarchic harmony of classes in place of the sharp, issue-oriented uncertainties of genuine social change.[55]

Between 1936 and 1939 Ley and the DAF plumped for industrial productivity as part of a campaign against Minister of Economics Hjalmar Schacht, a sharp critic of Ley. Schacht rightly saw that Ley's offensive was based on the political considerations of personal power and the mobilization of labor, not on economic ones. Ley was in a rather strong position since the unemployment that had plagued Germany in the early 1930s had given way to a shortage of labor, especially of skilled workers. Ley could thus use his appropriate demand for higher wages and better working conditions as a means to solidify DAF control over the labor force.

Ley moved quickly to extend his realm and his power. He sought to ally with Hermann Göring, Plenipotentiary for the Four-Year Plan, who was emerging as the overseer of the war economy Schacht so strenuously opposed. The DAF chief saw Göring's incipient ascendancy in the economic realm a wedge by which that sector of German life could be pried loose from its traditional moorings and brought under the care and control of National Socialism as administered through the Labor Front. And the increased demand for skilled industrial labor occasioned by Germany's remilitarization prompted the Labor Front to attempt to gain control over the training of young workers. The attempt intruded directly into one of the spheres of competence exercised by Schacht's ministry. Schacht went straight to Göring to complain, and then to Hitler, whom Ley had temporarily swayed in his direction. The upshot was that although Schacht prevented the DAF from taking complete control of vocational training, he was unable to force the closure of the Labor Front office for these matters in general.

Göring was unwilling to accommodate Schacht in this regard because the director of the Labor Front's so-called Office for Vocational Training and Works Management, Karl Arnhold, had convinced him that his program would accelerate the training of apprentices and alleviate the worrisome scarcity of skilled labor in 1937.[56] At the end of 1936 Arnhold's office by its own count supervised over 400 training workshops, with an additional 150 under construction. These were staffed by about 25,000 instructors and had been visited by approximately 2.5 million workers.[57] The Labor Front also introduced occupational preference guides (*Berufsfindungsmethode*) into schools and youth groups to steer individuals toward appropriate jobs, thus ostensibly avoiding later problems of maladjustment and supplementing the professional education programs built into the factories themselves. Arnhold claimed that by 1940 four million men and women had voluntarily taken part in these programs.[58]

The Göring Institute would come to work closely with Arnhold's office as an indirect consequence of Hermann Göring's admiration for his work. Arnhold was an engineer by training and a professor at a technical college in Dresden. In 1926 he founded the German Institute for Industrial Training (Deutsches Institut für Arbeitsschulung). The creation of DINTA, as it became known, had been sponsored by German heavy industry under the leadership of Albert Vögler, chairman of the board of the newly created German steel cartel, Vereinigte Stahlwerke. The Nazis coordinated DINTA, renaming it the German Institute for National Socialist Technical Industrial Research and Training (Deutsches Institut für nationalsozialistische technische Arbeitsforschung und Schulung), and in 1936 Arnhold became head of the Labor Front's vocational training office. By 1940 he was also ministerial director of the division for Vocational Training and Productivity (Berufserziehung und Leistungssteigerung) in the Economic Ministry (Reichswirtschaftsministerium), an office established under the authority of Reich Marshal Göring's Four-Year Plan. In these capacities Arnhold was able to continue with the work he had begun before 1933. In establishing DINTA, he had given organizational expression to his concern over the shrinking profits of German industry in spite of all the reorganization, rationalization, and beckoning internal and external markets of the 1920s. The reason for this lag, according to Arnhold, was twofold: materialism on the part of the workers encouraged by a socialist government and the trade unions, along with employers more concerned with technology and finance than with leadership. What was needed in the factory was a sense of community, of joy in one's creative and productive labor, as well as discipline and a sense of duty. Education, recreation, and martial order at work and play were the things that would restore German productivity, Arnhold thought.[59]

These ideas were in line with Vögler's emphasis on the "human factor" (what he called *"Faktor Mensch"*) as a challenge to nineteenth-century materialism, liberalism, and Marxism. Such an outlook, especially when Arnhold placed it in the context of 1919, "as we confronted the task of overcoming the material advantage of other nations through the quality of German men,"[60] was very attractive to those within the Nazi party and the Labor Front who thought in terms of racial and national character and comradeship (*Kameradschaft*). In sponsoring DINTA's program of vocational training, which by 1933 was operating in over 350 industries in Germany, Arnhold, who was not a party member, called for an end to the patriarchal factory system in his vision of an industrial brotherhood of management and labor. Rationalization, whether in the Western capitalist form of Frederick Jackson Taylor's motion studies or in the Soviet style of Stakhanovism, could never, he believed, achieve the productivity lying dormant within the collective blood of the "soldierly" German *Volk*.[61]

Robert Ley was alluding to Arnhold's work when he maintained that health was 90 percent of the social question, that productivity was the sign of health, and that war was the test as well as he assurance of Germany's struggle for existence.[62] His widely purveyed contention put an enormous emphasis not only on the physical resources of the German working population, but on its putative psychological strengths as well. The proper combination of worker and machine, for one thing, rested on an understanding of the human psyche, an accurate assessment rendered more attractive to the Nazis through its trust in the qualitative powers of the German will over and above the harder and more tangible coordinates of technology and numbers. Beyond its general lulling of the issues of social conflict and class interest, it was this apparent solution to some of the labor problems facing Germany's rearmament program and plans for military conquest which prompted Hermann Göring to praise Arnhold's activities at the inaugural meeting of the Reich Defense Council (Reichsverteidigungsrat) on 18 November 1938.[63] And it was therefore Arnhold who served as the chief link between the DAF and the Göring Institute.

Apart from conferences with the DAF Office for Health and Popular Protection, the Göring Institute worked closely with Arnhold's Office for Vocational Training and Works Management. For example, the institute's program for consulting psychologists reportedly was established in consultation with the Labor Front office.[64] During 1939 and early 1940 there were also a number of lectures given at the institute by industrial psychologists, including one by Albert Bremhorst, who headed the DAF office for vocational training from 1940 to 1942 while Arnhold was serving in the military.[65] Heyer could thus accurately boast that the "DAF has recognized that the economy as well is constituted by men with souls," while Meyer-Mark proclaimed the necessity of psychotherapy taking the place of religion in maintaining the spiritual strength of the populace in order to guarantee a healthy economy.[66]

Arnhold himself was typically more prosaic in an address to the third congress of the German General Medical Society for Psychotherapy in Vienna in 1940. He outlined three necessary components of industrial psychology in the Third Reich: the political environment, psychotherapy, and psychological hygiene and psychotechnology.[67] The congress also marked an effort at cooperation between German psychotherapists and Italian pedagogical psychologists with an address by Ferruccio Banissoni of the University of Rome. Banissoni's appearance at Vienna paved the way for the formal meeting between Italian and German psychologists and psychotherapists in Rome and Milan on 12–16 June 1941. The eighteen-member German delegation was led by Oswald Kroh and included Göring and Hattingberg. The meetings were presided over by Agostino Gemelli, president of the Commissione permanente per le Aplicazioni della Psicologia within the Consiglio Nationale delle Ricerche. Subjects included industrial and vocational psychology, psychotherapy, and military psychology.[68]

In 1941 the DAF Office for Vocational Training and Works Management founded its own Institute for Work Psychology and Work Pedagogy (Institut für Arbeitspsychologie und Arbeitspädagogik) to deal with the psychological casualties of the increased tempo in Germany's industrial sector which had deleteriously affected the health of the workers. The DAF institute projected a 7 to 8 percent increase (with a maximum of 20 percent in exceptional cases) in productive capacity in the cases handled, but its efforts could not begin to compensate for the acute physical and psychological strain on German labor that composed the objective reality underneath the Labor Front's programs and promises. While general morale among workers during the war remained relatively high due to a combination of circumstances, the ephemeral and cynical nature of the attitude of the Nazi leadership toward the masses was evident here as elsewhere.[69] This reality also undermined the preventive efforts of three Reich Schools for Work Guidance (Reichsschulen für Arbeitsführung) at Windlingen outside Vienna, at Augustusburg near Chemnitz, and in Berlin, which, according to DAF figures, had trained a total of 1725 persons by 1938.[70]

Yet work in this realm went on. The Göring Institute's own division for industrial psychology planned to establish a study group to develop characterological tests for the DAF institute and actually collaborated in the practical application of such testing in three large industrial concerns near Berlin. In addition, with the help of Meyer-Mark, Arnhold had set up a model textile factory which employed an industrial psychologist from the Göring Institute.[71] And drawing on their own industrial contacts, as late as 1944 the psychotherapists had planned a conference on industrial psychology at an I. G. Farben "leisure hostel" (Freizeitheim) near Heidelberg.[72] In light of all this activity in the field of industrial psychology and psychotherapy, it is no wonder that the Labor Front's official in-house journal, Der Hoheitsträger, could run an article—listed in the Nationalsozialistische Bibliographie—that spoke in glowing terms of the Göring Institute in the context of urging the cultivation of psychological health:

The "German Institute for Psychological Research and Psychotherapy" in Berlin, which, under the direction of Professor M. H. Göring, a relative of the Reich Marshal, operates in continued close touch with official agencies, has for years endeavored with success to train capable, practical psychologists and to place the fruits of recent depth psychological research and characterology at the service of a farseeing spiritual *Volks-*

hygiene. Since this important institute also operates an outpatient clinic, every fellow German, including those of modest means, is urged to take advantage personally of the blessed achievements of contemporary psychotherapy and characterology.[73]

Homosexuality, Infertility, and Other Problems: The Institute and the SS

In the unique combination of constraint and chaos that constituted Nazi Germany, Göring Institute contacts with the political masters extended beyond simply the public and official realms of the Labor Front, the Interior Ministry, and the other agencies and institutions with which it had more or less formal relationships. To the extent that this history should include a degree of moral judgment, it must be said that these activities involved a higher order of culpability in their contributions to Nazi projects.

M. H. Göring, whose eldest son, Peter, had joined the SS in 1935 and was active within it as a physician, claimed that Reichsführer-SS Himmler—with whom, it seems, Göring had met at least twice[74]—and SS Chief Physician (Reichsarzt-SS) Ernst Grawitz had expressed personal interest in the work of the institute.[75] It was in fact the case, according to König-Fachsenfeld, that Werner Achelis was on the staff as a psychotherapist at Hohenlychen, Karl Gebhardt's Waffen-SS orthopedic hospital near the Ravensbrück concentration camp north of Berlin, where Himmler himself was treated for nervous stomach disorders and SS General Erich von dem Bach-Zelewski for a nervous breakdown. Achelis's position there is not surprising given the importance that Hohenlychen attributed to the necessity of psychological adjustment for those who had lost limbs and suffered other severe medical problems.[76] Göring himself, according to his son, prepared expert opinions on cases at Hohenlychen, and there is documentary evidence of Göring's physical presence at Hohenlychen on at least one occasion.[77] And Göring Institute psychologist August Vetter recalls that Göring and Hattingberg once asked him to prepare some lectures on any subject he chose to give to a group of SS men. Such an inspirational series of conclaves never took place, but that the Göring Institute and Hitler's elite had association with one another is clear from these bits and pieces of evidence.

In 1939, after having received some copies of the SS journal *Germanien* from editor Otto Huth, Göring wrote directly to Himmler, suggesting a research topic for the SS-Ahnenerbe (project for Ancestral Research), under whose specific auspices the journal was published. The topic Göring proposed was for the project on "Forest and Tree in Aryan-Germanic Spiritual and Cultural History" ("Wald und Baum in der arisch-germanischen Geistes- und Kulturgeschichte"); his proposal was entitled "Forest and Tree in Dreams" ("Wald und Baum im Traum"), and included Göring's note that "in dreams from the collective unconscious (C. G. Jung), forest and tree often play a large role."[78] It is interesting and perhaps noteworthy that this particular Ahnenerbe project was in part funded by the Reich Forestry Office (Reichsforstamt), which was formally under the direction of Hermann Göring. In any case, M. H. Göring proposed Gustav Schmaltz as the author of such a study. Himmler passed Göring's letter along to Walter Wust, curator of the Ahnenerbe, but the forest and tree project was never completed. In the meantime, however, two of the officials involved in an appraisal of Göring's proposal had recommended acceptance, three had advised against undertaking it on financial grounds, two had abstained, and the director of the project had concluded that there were other, more important themes to be taken up with the limited funds available.[79]

Eckart von Sydow, an ethnologist who was a member of the Freudian group at the Göring Institute, and a friend of Felix Boehm, also sought to enlist the financial support of the Ahnenerbe—in 1939, for funding a trip to Africa to study native plastic arts in southern Nigeria. A professor of philosophy at the University of Berlin, Sydow had previously undertaken two trips to the area, one in 1936 on a grant from British sources and another during 1937–38 under the sponsorship of the DFG. He was also a party member, the only Freudian at the institute to become one. (Not surprisingly, one of his early books on primitive art was on the Nazi index of prohibited books.) The Ahnenerbe turned Sydow down, and he applied once again to the DFG, which, in May 1941, granted him further funds for research into the native sculpture of southern Nigeria.[80] From these studies, Sydow published an article of which the SS Security Service, the SD, spoke approvingly; it noted to the Ahnenerbe that Sydow's conclusion—that the continuation of paganism in southern Nigeria would preserve these arts—corresponded to the SD's notion of a successful German colonial policy there. It was decided that more information on Sydow would be gathered to see if he might be suitable for research on the plan.[81]

The Göring Institute was more successful in directly proving its worth to Heinrich Himmler in the practical realm of psychotherapy. Since incurable hereditary degeneracy could not be openly entertained as a possible cause of personal psychological difficulties within the Nazi racial elite, Göring was charged with secretly expediting a case that was troubling the Himmler command. All during 1942 Göring was involved in the clandestine case of the seventeen-year-old daughter of an SS regimental commander who had been killed on the Western front. In February General of the Waffen-SS and chief of Himmler's personal staff Karl Wolff wrote to Göring with the request that he examine the girl, then lodged in a Bodelschwingh house, in order to determine the cause of her disturbed behavior, most notably her compulsive lying. Wolff also mentioned that the paternal grandparents wished to deprive the girl's stepmother of the guardianship stipulated by her husband in his will. Himmler, with indulgent organizational loyalty and typical petit bourgeois sentimentality, was said by Wolff to desire the fulfillment of the fallen man's wishes.[82] Himmler reportedly felt that a psychotherapeutic examination would establish the basis for a legal dismissal of the grandfather's complaint against the stepmother. The Berlin district court agreed with the plan to have the girl examined by Göring and opined that following the receipt of Göring's report, the grandfather's complaint would be voided.[83] The girl was duly examined by Göring, beginning in early March and continuing into the summer, and the results of the investigation were sent to Himmler on 30 July. Interviews had also been held with the girl's stepmother, grandfather, and grandmother.

The actual analysis of her family and personal history was carried out by Kalau vom Hofe in her capacity as a criminal psychologist, and the findings did indeed tend to prejudice the grandparents' case. The girl came from a broken home; her parents had divorced when she was only four. Kalau vom Hofe took pains to point out the tensions within the family that would have affected the infant's development from birth. According to the stepmother, the original mother was to blame for the breakup of the first marriage, and had taken the child to live with her grandmother but then placed her in a home, where the child remained for the next eight years. The girl recalled that during this time she saw less and less of both her mother and her maternal grandmother. She was apparently a difficult ward from the beginning, and was ten years old by the time her paternal grandparents took any interest in her. At twelve she joined her father and his new wife, but difficulties persisted and she was in and out of homes while the conflict within the family over what to do with her steadily became more intensive.

The child's father had always shown great affection for her, but professional obligations and the fact that he was living with his sister prevented him from taking care of her before he remarried. Kalau vom Hofe expressed the opinion that the conflict over custody of the child stemmed from the father's early childhood, which was dominated by an exaggerated fixation on his mother and also on his unmarried sister, with whom he was later to live. Neither woman wanted to let him go; and for the girl's paternal grandmother, it was intolerable that the stepmother should take possession of her son's only child. The effect of this familial struggle on the girl was to reduce her to a mere legacy of her now-dead father, and to increase her isolation from love and affection. Small of stature, shy, and suffering from a partial hearing loss in her right ear, the girl resorted to asocial behavior toward those figures of authority with whom she came into contact. Kalau vom Hofe was quick to maintain, however, that there was no evidence of hereditary illness; the child's lack of genuine personality development and of relationships with other children and adults was the result of her infantile and childhood experiences.

Kalau vom Hofe advised that the girl be placed in a home where she could receive psychotherapeutic care over an extended period of time.[84] Göring subsequently recommended that the girl should live with a family in Munich and undergo psychotherapeutic treatment there. Since the girl's problems were curable rather than hereditary, the cost of her accommodation and schooling were to be covered by the SS orphan pension fund, and the Reichsführer's office assured Göring that Himmler would contribute an additional amount (around RM 50—$12.50—per month) toward the cost of psychotherapy.[85] Wolff reported to Göring that he was quite in agreement with the institute's determination that the girl's mental distress originated from environmental influences and not from hereditary taint.[86] Such relief as Wolff may have felt over this diagnosis is hardly surprising, though there is no indication that Göring and Kalau vom Hofe tailored their opinion in this respect or with regard to the question of guardianship to please the SS.

By mid-September, in any case, it was necessary for Göring to change the location of the patient's residence and treatment. The girl was now to live with pedagogue Wilhelm Laiblin in Stuttgart and to be treated by the Jungian Jutta von Graevenitz. Göring also suggested that the grandparents not be informed of the girl's destination until she had settled in.[87] But the girl did not go to Stuttgart, but ended up in a psychotherapeutic home near Tübingen under the supervision of a Frau Marzinowski. Apparently there was difficulty all along the line in finding a place for her, but Himmler was willing to double his contribution to the girl's psychotherapeutic treatment.[88] It is possible that fear of the SS prompted hesitation and even perhaps refusal on the part of some members of the Göring Institute to assume responsibility for her therapy.

Apart from such singular involvements with the Nazi hierarchy, however, two research commissions (Forschungsaufträge) established within the Göring Institute were significant: one on the subject of homosexuality and the other dealing with psychogenic sterility. According to Werner Kemper and others, both research commissions were initiated either directly or indirectly by the Nazi authorities. If this was indeed the case, we still do not know whether either project was inaugurated and supported through the office of the Interior Ministry, the Labor Front, or, the most likely, was the result of a suggestion made or exploited by Göring himself through the less systematic channels of party and family. Because we have no evidence of when these projects began, it is also impossible to determine whether the Reich Research Council had anything to do with their inception or their funding.

Kemper has claimed (see below) that the Luftwaffe was the first to suggest special psychotherapeutic devotion to the matter of homosexuality, a claim perhaps strengthened by the ostensible meeting between the Göring cousins on the subject in 1942, as noted in Chapter 4. Then it was in 1943 that the Göring Institute first began receiving sizable subsidies from the Reich Research Council; institute records from the first quarter of 1944, after the institute had been fully and formally taken into the RFR, show funding for a work group (*Arbeitsgruppe*) under Schultz-Hencke on the subject of homosexuality. (See Chapter 5.) Although it is not clear who assumed direction of this group, its two most prominent members were Hattingberg and Schultz-Hencke.

Homosexuality was a crime in the Third Reich above and beyond the traditional prohibition of its practice under Section 175 of the German Penal Code. Such transgressions also invited application of Sections 42 and 51 on the institutionalization and medical care of the mentally ill, which were used by the Nazis to proscribe degenerates for the protection of the German racial community. Homosexual activity was held by the Nazis to be inconsistent with the manly attributes of the soldierly German *Volk,* and a deadly peril to the survival of the race. It was regarded as a matter of not just national but biological treason. The SS typically regarded homosexuality as a major element in the cultural decline that resulted from an egotism implanted by the Jew and the Bolshevik. The true artist, according to one SS analysis, was not a "self-impaled" homosexual but one who transcended his homosexuality to touch the pulse of the male-female ethos in service to his race. A mere degenerate homosexual was a "homunculus and therefore excluded from the laws of life."[89]

But homosexuality was as much a problem within the NSDAP as a perceived threat from without, as the unconscious emphasis in the SS resurrection of the artist "transcending his homosexuality" clearly shows. Ernst Röhm certainly was only the most prominent homosexual in the Nazi ranks. Baumeyer goes so far as to say that he believes many high-ranking Nazis sought help from the Göring Institute for problems linked to homosexuality, and his assertion echoes Müller-Hegemann's view that the institute generally and continually served a desperately neurotic Nazi leadership. But, although Seelmann recalls attending a society meeting in Berlin on homosexuality just after the Röhm affair in 1934, there is no evidence that high-ranking Nazis frequented the institute or any of the psychotherapists on a private basis for treatment of homosexuality. The Göring Institute's work on homosexuality seems to have fallen mainly into two areas: adolescent

and forensic psychology. As was usual with the Nazis, biological dog-
matism broke down in the face of short-term practical aims, their
competing emphasis on direction and instruction as well as, in this
particular case, acute embarrassment and sensitivity.

As early as 1930 many, if not most, German psychiatrists supported
the abolition or amendment of Sections 175 and 51.[90] They did so out
of a pragmatic concern that lawyers and judges were increasingly—and
destructively—interfering in a matter properly under medical jurisdiction. But in Germany the medical profession, like the bourgeoisie as
a whole, by and large also saw homosexuality as a widespread disorder
threatening the social order. Despite a vigorous movement at the turn
of the century pressing for the liberalization of views and laws concerning "private" sexual matters such as sexual preference and abortion, in Germany as elsewhere an established nineteenth-century conservative tradition declared, eventually in racist terms, the abnormality
and degeneracy of such attitudes and practices. This anxious bourgeois
concern with order and respectability linked up with a nationalism
that stressed the subordination of private interests to those of the
state. In Germany this trend led to a strengthening of a cultural preference for a hierarchical and authoritarian ideal of *Gemeinschaft* rooted
in the immutable biological laws of nature as opposed to the liberal,
individualistic, and materialistic urban civilization spawned by the Industrial Revolution. The attitude of German physicians toward homosexuality was of course also conditioned by their scientific conviction
that it was an analyzable and treatable disorder. This conviction, a
consensus everywhere among physicians during the era, prompted
them to favor treatment over punishment while at the same time it
bolstered a prevailing cultural bias that saw homosexuals as a "problem" to be solved. Psychotherapists shared in this cultural bias and
their push for professional recognition only exacerbated the general
medical propensity to offer solutions to such "problems."[91]

The Nazi regime of course added its own ideological and practical
imperatives along these same lines. Thus homosexuals sent to the
Göring Institute were to be treated, cured, and sent back into the community as normal and productive members of society. The Nazi government was not averse to a psychotherapeutic view that emphasized
psychological repair. Although the Nazis did not strike the laws against
homosexuality from the books, and indeed expanded and applied
them barbarically in countless instances, their concern about homosexuality did lead to the engagement of psychotherapists to work in this
area. Kalau vom Hofe, as director of the Göring Institute's division for
criminal psychology, treated a number of youths whom the Hitler
Youth and the League of German Girls had referred for homosexuality, including many who had gotten into trouble with the police for
being discovered in homosexual activity. In many cases, she has

claimed, long-term psychoanalysis was used in treating them. Ernst Göring has confirmed that the Nazi youth organizations made use of the institute, and that cases of homosexual behavior were regularly referred to it.

While there is no evidence of excessive homosexuality in the Hitler Youth and the League of German Girls, the leadership of the Nazi youth organizations was indeed concerned about homosexuality among its charges. And while the Nazis strove to avoid publicity, especially to quiet parents' fears, and to blame the incidence of homosexuality on homosexual leaders and youth assimilated from the now defunct Weimar youth groups, they also stressed the need for prevention and, if necessary, "education" through counseling and medical attention. As was usual with the Nazis, simplistic, brutal rhetoric and action were accompanied by pragmatic attempts to ensure the "purity" of German youth in service to the Reich. The Nazis were forced to distinguish between homosexuals per se, whom they declared to be biologically degenerate, and the susceptibility of Aryan adolescents of good stock and breeding to "blunders" (Pubertätsentgleisungen),[92] and to enlist the aid of a number of agencies, including the Göring Institute, to deal with the problem. On a conceptual level, of course, the psychotherapists retained a much more sophisticated view of the origin and nature of homosexuality, though, as we have noted, psychotherapists by and large were one with the Nazis in seeing homosexuality as an urgent problem to be solved through the active intervention of the therapist.

Concern with homosexuality was not confined to the Hitler Youth, however. In 1940 Himmler's masseur was recommending to the Reichsführer-SS special treatment for those young boys who manifested homosexual tendencies, and Himmler reportedly replied, "That's splendid, Herr Kersten. I will nominate you as my advisor on homosexual matters. The Hitler Youth has already taken up something like that, but nothing has yet been done for a fundamental solution to the problem."[93] Despite the evident sarcasm in his "appointment" of Kersten, we know that Himmler did take a strong interest in matters of homosexuality in Germany in general and in the SS in particular. This concern ranged from musings on the possible correlation of left-handedness and homosexuality to his thoughts that it was a perversion related to espionage, sabotage, and evasion of military service. Himmler also acknowledged the desirability of attempts at the cure of homosexuality, even though he was dubious about the outcome. The turn of the war's tide, in any case, dissolved what little commitment he may have had to a medical approach to the problem. On 15 November 1941 Hitler decreed the death penalty for homosexual members of the SS, and it was in this militant and manly spirit that in 1943 Himmler brusquely rejected the proposal of Martin Brustmann, a consulting physician to the SS Race and Settlement Main Office, for such a therapeutic program in wartime. According to Himmler, every human resource had to be committed to the struggle for survival, not wasted on unproductive and degenerate homosexuals. The Reichsführer's animus, expressed in a letter to SS security chief Ernst Kaltenbrunner, also fell on I. H. Schultz, who, in collaboration with the now discredited Brustmann, had rendered at least one expert opinion on a case of homosexuality about which Himmler was concerned.[94]

The SS itself had restricted its own reparative and curative efforts to sadistic and futile biological experimentation. The Danish physician Carl Vaernet, for one, was retained by the SS with a stipend of RM 10,000 ($2,500) per annum to test his method of curing homosexuality through the implantation of artificial sex glands. Vaernet, working in Prague with prisoners from the Buchenwald concentration camp, claimed success for his efforts. One patient, a fifty-five-year-old theologian, had since the age of twenty-two been unable to have heterosexual relations because of what Vaernet reported as "anxiety," and had forthwith become a homosexual. After the operation, Vaernet asserted, the patient began to have dreams, accompanied by erections, of sexual intercourse with women. He was sleeping better and his bouts of depression had disappeared. There was one problem, however. The patient's religious convictions prevented him from visiting a brothel in order to test his new capacity.[95]

Yet even the SS, like other Nazi organizations such as the NSV, apparently cooperated with the Göring Institute by allowing incarcerated homosexuals to undergo psychotherapy. Late in the war, Kalau vom Hofe has recalled, she handled four homosexuals who, in keeping with an SS practice concerning those convicted of "habitual crimes,"[96] had been released from concentration camps and were being held at the Berlin-Charlottenburg jail. Almost all the prisoners referred to the Göring Institute were sex offenders, a fact that, according to Kalau vom Hofe, intimated not only the continuing caricature of psychotherapy in the minds of many Nazis, but also an appreciation of the value of its work that grew as they recognized that strident rhetoric could not solve such problems. And since racial purity seemed to be no guarantee against the incidence of homosexual urges, especially among young men and women, the Nazis were compelled by their own racial ideals to seek psychological correction for such cases rather than resort to biological exclusion.

For their part, the psychotherapists were only too eager to prove their professional competence in this particular area. According to an institute survey conducted by Boehm in early 1938, since 1923 some 60 psychotherapists now at the Göring Institute had treated or extensively counseled 510 homosexual patients. Of these, it was reported that 341 were cured, that is, had undergone a lasting change in their sexual preference. In 1944 Schultz asserted that by 1939 the Göring Institute could report the private and clinical cure of 500 homosexuals. Boehm presented the 1938 figures in the context of a critical review in 1940 of a book by psychiatrist Rudolf Lemke, in which the author argued that the root cause of homosexuality was a congenital disposition, making it a disorder whose effects could be alleviated by psychotherapy but which itself could never be cured by psychological means. In 1944 Schultz was arguing in opposition to a similar point of view in the military.[97]

Under Hitler the problem of homosexuality was linked to another priority: that of combating the declining birth rate. Heterosexual activity, like health, had become a duty. Masturbation was said to result in the loss of valuable *völkisch* sperm, and to lead to weakness and even homosexuality, paths to be avoided by entrance into the Hitler Youth, where the body could be hardened and the character strengthened.[98] A vigorous population policy had always been an integral part of the National Socialist program: For Germany to be reborn, it had to cultivate its most valuable resource, its people. Germany, along with the rest of Europe, had suffered a decline in the birth rate during the twentieth century. The Nazis, as the beneficiaries of Germany's prosperity after the passing of the Depression, did achieve an increase in the marriage and birth rates, but hardly one of staggering proportions. The war naturally arrested any continued improvement, although the rates did not fall as drastically as they had during World War I under the impact of the Allied blockade. The Nazis encouraged large families, emphasized the celebrated and traditional roles of women as wives and mothers, and criticized the "Jewish-inspired" feminist movement, which they characterized as destructive of the home for its opposition to the bearing of large numbers of children.[99] The Nazis also opposed abortion, Gerhard Wagner representatively declaring it to be a remnant of decadent "liberal-Marxist" notions of the individual's exclusive right to his or her own body. Predictably, the onset of war brought more compulsion to the fore: In 1941 the Interior Ministry prohibited the manufacture and/or sale of contraceptives and abortion paraphernalia.[100]

But the Nazis looked as well to the medical profession to abolish physical and psychological hindrances to procreation. As early as 1936 the Labor and Interior ministries declared that social health insurance would cover the cost of curing both physiogenic and psychogenic infertility, as it was in the interest of preserving the new *Volksgemeinschaft*.[101] According to Kemper, there was a "rudimentary" research project established at the Göring Institute on the question of psychogenic infertility, but it remained primarily a matter of the professional interests of a number of members of the institute coming together to meet a declared need. Schultz and Hattingberg, for example, saw the preservation of the natural family unit and the proper social milieu as the guarantors of productive male and female sexuality. Health and fertility could be assured, however, only if the mistake of lumping all the unproductive sexual perversions into the category of psychopathy could be avoided. Two-thirds of all such problems, Schultz maintained, were psychogenic in nature. Thus it was development and therapy, and not racial and biological exclusion, that would provide the *Volksgemeinschaft* with the highest possible percentage of useful members.[102]

The Göring Institute's activity in this realm increased during the war in response to Reich Health Leader Conti's new task force on "Assistance by Childlessness in Marriage" ("Hilfe bei Kinderlosigkeit in der Ehe"). Werner Kemper was the psychotherapist most involved with the issue, as psychogenic frigidity and the psychobiology of sexual dysfunction had long been a pet theme of his. He has claimed that his book on the subject, *Die Störungen der Liebesfähigkeit beim Weibe* (1942), was requested for perusal by Hans Karl von Hasselbach, one of Hitler's physicians at the Führer's headquarters, and there is documentary evidence that Hasselbach had at least been sent the book.[103] Indeed, between 1942 and 1944 there was a great deal of discussion and debate among physicians and psychotherapists over the cause of infertility as well as sterility in men. The medical literature it produced almost uniformly stressed the importance of psychological factors in sexual matters, from deep childhood traumas to the adverse effect that the incessant propaganda for more children could have on the psychological disposition to sexual performance and procreation.[104]

There is evidence that the SS was also involving itself in the question of a cure for infertility. An SS study group charged with the evolution of a "positive population policy" was formed; it included Prof. Carl Clausberg of the Institute for Reproductive Biology (Institut für Fortpflanzungsbiologie) in Königshütte, Prof. Dr. Günther von Wolff of Berlin, and Prof. Dr. Günther K. F. Schultze of Greifswald. Schultze participated in a conference on sterility at the Berlin Medical Society, and Wolff produced a manuscript on infertility in women for an SS study group, which Himmler thought quite good. Himmler recommended, however, that its publication be put off until after the war, when it could be, he wrote, "psychologically still much better constructed" ("*psychologisch noch viel besser aufgebaut werden*").[105] It is not clear whether Himmler was referring to the form or the content of the piece, though the membership of this SS study group reflected the common Nazi preoccupation with matters of racial biology. There also seemed to be what constituted a characteristic tendency among the Nazi leadership on this matter to emphasize female rather than male dysfunction.

The problem of human procreation also naturally concerned that peculiar organization called the SS-Lebensborn (Spring of Life), and its response to these problems engaged an approach that recognized the utility of psychotherapeutic concepts. The Lebensborn was designed to secure the coming Aryan generations through the careful mating of racially desirable women with SS men, as well as the appropriation of "Aryan" children from throughout Europe for placement with German families. The first Lebensborn home for these mothers and children was established at Steinhöring near Munich in 1936. Eventually there were to be ten such homes in Germany and ten scattered over the rest of Europe. Charged by Himmler with the procreation and cultivation of healthy Aryan stock, the Lebensborn was thus vitally concerned with matters of sexual dysfunction.

In a letter to the administrative director of the Lebensborn, Max Sollman, medical director Gregor Ebner maintained that the medical efforts to restore organic capacity for sexual performance through surgery and hormonal therapy had failed, and that to cure sterility "a conversion of the whole organism must be accomplished."[106] Ebner enclosed a report from an SS doctor who served with the Lebensborn in The Hague, professing the effectiveness of solar-heated mudbaths in creating the sense of well-being necessary for fertility and sexual activity. The doctor, named Meyer, pointed out in his report that primitive peoples had a higher birth rate, as did asocials and the feeble-minded. It seemed to him that the higher the mental development, the more likely a disturbance in procreative ability and in conception. Like Himmler, Meyer was interested in natural medicine; he decried the evils of modern civilization which disrupted the natural rhythm of the human organism. But unlike the dilettante Reichsführer-SS, he went beyond condemning the evils of industrial society to observe that such disruptions among more mentally developed individuals were often psychologically determined, and only exacerbated by the perils of contemporary life. Mudbaths alone, then, were not enough:

> At the same time *seelische Beeinflussung* must be utilized. . . . I have experienced cases in which the frigidity of a woman under such treatment, namely healthful nutrition, open-air gymnastics, a regulated daily schedule in combination with a *seelische Suggestivbehandlung* [hypnosis], in a short time was . . . much improved.[107]

Meyer's rejection of a physical and mechanistic approach reminds us that both the natural medicine movement and German psychotherapy could trace roots to the Romantic tradition.

At least one member of the Göring Institute had a direct, if brief, association with the Lebensborn. In 1942 the psychologist Erika Hantel published an article in the national edition of the *Frankfurter Zeitung* on the lessons to be learned by wartime Germany from the homes for women founded by the medieval priest Lambert le Buégne. The first of these was established in Liege in 1148 for the protection of women widowed by the Crusades, unmarried mothers, and older single women and other widows. Hantel saw instructive parallels to Germany in 1942 that were not restricted simply to the care of women whose husbands had died at the front. The medieval homes stressed the preservation of "motherly" qualities, something which Hantel—in line with the thinking of her colleagues Achelis, Hattingberg, and Schultz on the proper balance of male and female within individuals, the family, and society—thought compelling in a wartime society that required women to replace men at the workbench and on the assembly line. Although the Nazis never effectively mobilized women for such work, Hantel believed that before women should be mobilized to exercise masculine qualities, a solid basis of womanhood had to be cultivated and made conscious, not rashly sacrificed to production schedules and wartime alarums. In this, she wrote, lay the future of the nation and the race.[108]

According to Hantel, Himmler, who was dissatisfied with the coverage in the *Völkischer Beobachter,* read the article. Knowing through Göring that Hantel was a psychologist, he decided that she should write an article about the Lebensborn. It was probably not the general subject of the original article or the professional manner of its analysis that appealed to Himmler, but Hantel's positive references to the traditional role of women. In any case, Hantel was contacted by Himmler's press chief, Hans Johst, and ordered in November 1942 to see Sollmann at Lebensborn headquarters in Munich. Heyer accompanied her and she was accommodated at the sumptuous Hotel Vierjahreszeiten. Sollman offered her RM 10,000 ($2,500) to undertake the assignment, but she expressed reservations, saying that she was not a party member and that her husband was regarded as politically untrustworthy by the party. In addition, although she did not mention this to Sollmann, Hantel had visited one of the Lebensborn homes and found it to be a "psychological horror," with too much work and too little medical attention. Eventually, Hantel was rescued by events; the battle for Stalingrad and the subsequent military disaster precluded any further interest in the project on the part of the SS.

During the interview, however, Sollmann confessed to being under pressure from Himmler to engage Hantel because of his failure to carry out another assignment—the impregnation of a Bavarian girl. Beyond the irony of such a situation, Sollmann's alleged admission to Hantel of personal procreative failure suggests another, and less official, capacity filled by members of the Göring Institute: service to an increasingly overburdened elite. Although again there is no hard evidence that the institute was besieged by high-ranking neurotic Nazis, the burdens of high office, war, and, finally, looming disaster, produced a predictable share of mental casualties. Among the Göring Institute patients Lucy Heyer-Grote recalled were a Norwegian SS man torn between his desire to provide his parents with extra rations and his guilt over the atrocities he witnessed in the East; secretaries from the Brown House (Nazi party headquarters) in Munich; and individuals from all walks of life and stations in society who suffered from enforced silence in the face of monstrosities, as well as from personal and familial loss.

But institute psychotherapists also came in contact with some of the psychological difficulties suffered by the Nazi leadership, a phenomenon whose only consistent theme is the historical obscurity in which it is clouded. For example, it was rumored within the institute that Göring was involved in the treatment of his cousin's morphine addiction. And simple professional connections could bring involvement in intrigue within the Nazi hierarchy, as in the case of one psychotherapist who became involved in secret wartime diplomacy that resulted from concern within the Nazi hierarchy over the mental soundness of Adolf Hitler. The concern was nothing new. Earlier, in 1938, Karl Bonhoeffer was involved in a plan to declare Hitler insane, a scheme abandoned after the Munich conference on Czechoslovakia gave Hitler European sanction for his actions. Then, in the autumn of 1939, Carl Jung received a telephone call from Munich from one of Hitler's doctors, requesting Jung to come to Berchtesgaden to render a psychiatric evaluation of the Führer.[109]

But by 1943 the reversal of Nazi fortunes at war also prompted a certain amount of scuttling about in the upper reaches of the Nazi hierarchy itself, in search of a way out of the closing trap. Himmler and his SD foreign intelligence chief, Walter Schellenberg, came up with a plan to abandon western Europe in return for an armistice on that front which would allow Germany to prevent the Russian tide from engulfing the Continent, a major concern of Churchill's. The Jungian Wilhelm Bitter, a former student of Max de Crinis, became a party to the plot, since in Geneva he had some contacts within the British government. De Crinis was a close friend of Schellenberg, and had shared in some of Schellenberg's espionage adventures. After Foreign Minister Joachim von Ribbentrop had suffered from disturbed behavior following a kidney disorder, de Crinis had rendered a psychiatric evaluation at Schellenberg's behest. In Schellenberg's latest scheme, involving Hitler, de Crinis provided a diagnosis of the Führer as unbalanced, perhaps, he speculated, from Parkinson's disease. It was hoped that the psychologically disabled Hitler would be "paralyzed" by the plotters' proposal of an armistice in the West. Himmler even had Conti attend a meeting on the subject, and Conti left behind at his death a medical opinion on Hitler's condition. In any case, the plan fell apart when Hitler, at its mention, did not. Bitter came under suspicion as a defeatist and was forced to emigrate to Geneva in the summer of 1943.[110]

Erika Hantel's professional contact with members of the Nazi elite was more direct. Expressing her fascination with the psychological dynamics of the Nazis, she sought a position as a psychotherapist at a so-called "biological sanitarium" in Berchtesgaden. This institution was run by Werner Zabel, a cancer specialist and a former senior staff physician at the Rudolf-Hess-Krankenhaus, who held great admiration for C. G. Jung. Heyer had recommended Hantel, and she served at the sanitarium during 1940 and 1941. Zabel's sanitarium was run according to the tenets of natural medicine. The cook there, a Hungarian woman named Konstanze Manzialy who specialized in vegetarian dishes, subsequently was taken on by Hitler, and the Führer himself once saw Zabel for treatment of a gastrointestinal disorder.[111] Hantel, in the terminology in vogue at the sanitarium, provided "heart massage" (autogenic training and *kleine* psychotherapy) and other psychotherapeutic methods for a number of inhabitants and functionaries from the Berghof, who would often trail down exhausted after Hitler's late-night and early-morning monologues. These sessions were sporadic and generally only atmospheric adjuncts to rest and relaxation, but among those with whom Hantel had professional contact in this manner were Martin Bormann and Albert Speer.

Bormann, Hantel recalls, was extremely nervous and anxious. Air rattling in the pipes in Hantel's office reportedly irritated him to the point that she had to have them fixed. Given Bormann's position, such a disposition was not surprising. Whatever his own character deficiencies, his job could only burden him further. As Dietrich Orlow has noted in his history of the Nazi party,

> Hitler's authority in the Third Reich rested upon his undisputed claim to omnipotence and omniscience. Bormann did not challenge the first, but sought to control the second. The feat alone required immense energy and perseverance. Daily life with Adolf Hitler even in the years of military success was mentally and physically taxing. Hitler had already settled into his routine of turning night into day.[112]

While Hantel found Bormann extremely primitive and skittish, she perceived Speer as lost in planning architectural monumentalities. Speer has denied ever being under the care of a psychotherapist, recalling only that Zabel was an old school friend of his and that he was treated for a kidney ailment at the sanitarium.[113] Whatever the actual truth of the matter, it is certainly true that the benign nature of this kind of occasional psychotherapy could indeed allow it to pass from memory. Even Hantel's own account of her contact with Speer leaves room for doubt about its frequency and intensity. Hantel, in any case, saw fewer and fewer patients after the German invasion of

Russia in June 1941, when pressing military business kept the Führer and his entourage in Berlin and at his military headquarters in East Prussia.

In the autumn of 1944, when Nazi Germany was reaping the grim harvest of that invasion, Göring, a former member of the institute has recalled, learned that Roland Freisler's wife, Marion, wished to be treated for severe depression. No one at the institute was willing to have anything to do with the infamous inquisitor of the People's Court (Volksgerichtshof), it is reported, and Freisler himself was killed in a bombing raid on Berlin on 3 February 1945,[114] apparently before any possible difficulties stemming from the institute's reluctance could manifest themselves.

The Institute, the Military, and War

With the coming of war, the Göring Institute played an increasingly important role in the military affairs of the Third Reich. Hitler and the Nazis were accomplished amateur psychologists, and although a whole range of more tangible economic, political, and military conditions contributed to Germany's military wartime successes, it is clear that the more formal psychology that was also applied at least paralleled and strengthened these factors in both aim and effect. The expertise of the Göring Institute was an important ingredient.

In 1940 the French historian Marc Bloch sadly observed that the swift German victory over France was "a triumph of intellect," and contrasted the dynamism of the Nazi blitzkrieg to the impotent collapse of his own nation's military efforts. Although Bloch was concerned with composing an historical and cultural critique of France, he accurately perceived among the Germans a quality which lay behind the efficiency, speed, and camaraderie of the Wehrmacht:

> The static order of office routine is, in many respects, the very antithesis of the active and perpetually inventive "order" which movement demands. One is a matter of discipline and training, the other of imaginative realism, adaptable intelligence, and, above all, of character.[115]

On the German side, Karl Pintschovious of the Reich War Ministry (Reichskriegsministerium) observed before the war that courage was impulsive action, while mental endurance, embedded within a strong character structure, so necessary in involved and prolonged modern wars, was a matter of complex inner operations against the anxiety that invariably accompanied participation in battle.[116] In 1940 the German soldier embodied to a certain degree the qualities described by Bloch and Pintschovious.

There was surely a strong element of psychological assault in the terror sown among the Allied troops of Holland, Belgium, France, and Great Britain by the scream of Stukas, enhanced by the Nazi idea of placing whistles on their wings. The relentless advance of the panzer divisions reflected the Nazis' application of psychology to military operations, a quality that was touted by Hitler himself through his preoccupation with will, power, and surprise. The German appreciation of the value of psychological warfare was only one element of a more broadly conceived psychological preparation for war: the psychotechniques of finding the right man for the right job, sustaining morale, acclimating troops to the stresses and strains of mechanized warfare, heightening efficiency, improving the relationship between officer and enlisted man, and preventing war neuroses. Combined with Nazi propaganda about the comradeship that was so important a part of the new Germany, and the concomitant weeding out of disruptive influences in society, these psychological techniques produced an army that at least convinced Allied observers that the Germans, "despite a certain aura of mysticism in their concepts, properly recognize the central significance of 'character'—that is, social, emotional and temperamental qualities that are not adequately determined by the usual paper-and-pencil testing."[117]

In April 1929, eleven years before Hitler's invasion of western Europe, Hans von Voss and Max Simoneit established a department of psychology in the German War Ministry. Despite early and continuing skepticism on the part of a significant segment of the military high command, this reorganization of the various military offices that dealt with matters of psychology represented a significant commitment to the field; by 1942 the Central Psychological Laboratory in Berlin comprised twenty divisions and supervised the operations of seventeen army and two naval testing stations throughout the Reich. The organization employed around 200 psychologists and drew on the work and resources of institutes and universities all over Germany. After 1940 Voss and Simoneit were provided with partial use of Strassburg University in order to study the psychological problems brought about by war. The Luftwaffe, too, mobilized psychologists.[118]

Although military psychology had been given an organizational form by Hitler's military mobilization, and moral sanction by the Nazi obsession with cultivating the inner resources of the German spirit and will, the work of psychologists and psychotherapists came under heavy fire from their old enemies in the psychiatric establishment, this time from within the field of military medicine. When an army psychiatrist criticized psychotherapists like Heyer for attempting to draw psychotherapy and medical psychology in general away from a biologically based psychiatry, Simoneit himself argued the case for the value of a more humanistic approach. Simoneit defended the psychotherapists by maintaining that matters of the complete human organism were the province of the soul, a truth that an artist and philosopher like Goethe and a physician and artist like Carus had recognized in their contemplations on the human condition. The natural spirit of life, the will, and its powers and potential, could not be grasped by a mechanistic, biological approach, Simoneit argued. Psychological insight and psychotherapeutic assistance could never, for example, be effective within the "exaggerated psychiatric setting" of Freudian psychoanalysis that accentuated "the degenerate and the pathological." The military psychiatrist's response was that when all the "finery" had been stripped away, the psychiatrist alone experienced the individual fully.[119]

In the face of this kind of persistent criticism, the Göring Institute became involved with military psychology on three levels: psychological warfare, the treatment of war neuroses, and the training of military psychologists. According to Kemper, the institute assisted the army psychologists at the War Ministry in preparing national psychological profiles (*Völkerpsychologische Untersuchungen*), which would be used to exploit an enemy's weak points. Foreign countries subjected to such analysis included the Soviet Union, the United States, Great Britain, France, and Czechoslovakia. The study on France, by way of illustration, stressed the French heritage of racial prejudice (!) as represented by the works of Gobineau and de la Rocque, and suggested that this prejudice might be exploited to produce friction between French soldiers of different color.[120] Such studies came under the heading of "psychological warfare" (*geistige Kriegsführung*) and thus involved psychotherapists as a matter of course.

Psychological warfare was perceived in the broadest possible terms. In the words of Luftwaffe officer Friedrich von Cochenhausen, director of the German Society of Military Politics and Military Sciences (Deutsche Gesellschaft für Wehrpolitik und Wehrwissenschaften), in an introduction to a bibliography on psychological warfare compiled by Felix Scherke, "spiritual conduct of war is, seen psychologically, the art of collective *Seelenführung*."[121] Psychological warfare was therefore to encompass not only an exploitable understanding of one's opponent but the psychologically sophisticated military and medical leadership of one's own troops as well. This bibliography, though fragmentary, illustrated the broad scope of German work in this field. Included were works by Harold Lasswell (*Propaganda Technique in the World War*), José Ortega y Gasset (*The Revolt of the Masses*), Gustave Le Bon's *Psychology of the Crowd*, Hitler's *Mein Kampf*, and even Freud's *Group Psychology and the Analysis of the Ego*.

The major sphere of military psychology in which the German psychotherapists were most active was the study, diagnosis, and treatment of war neuroses. The purpose of the psychological research carried on by Voss and Simoneit, and of the reforms made in the selection, training, and care of the soldier and officer—reforms inspired by the necessarily careful cultivation of the 100,000-man Reichswehr "nucleus" left Germany by the Treaty of Versailles—was not only to increase effectiveness but to decrease the propensity for mental breakdown under the alternate terror and boredom of warfare. There is no doubt that the incidence of maladaption and neurosis was reduced by this kind of professional concern with the stresses of leadership, the psychological selection and testing of personnel, the general psychology of military life, and the pressures of combat. While old-line officers often saw a disparity between the new psychology and the old discipline, such concern generally augmented the German army's traditional expertise in welding human beings into an effective military instrument.

The context in which these efforts took place was a military era that was very different from that of World War I. Although fighter pilots awaiting scrambles and long-range reconnaissance personnel were both susceptible to the earlier types of hysterical reactions that were generated by long periods of unpredictable waiting, World War II was a war of movement, unconfined by the static trench warfare that had characterized the Great War. According to Gustav Störring, an army psychiatrist associated with the Göring Institute's I. H. Schultz, only during the "Sitzkrieg" of 1939–40 did the strain peculiar to life in the trenches manifest itself to any significant degree.[122]

The German military psychologists hoped that unity, purpose, and community feeling would provide an effective basis for the prevention of neurosis among soldiers.[123] Still, the very fact of its existence demanded that they acknowledge the necessity for psychotherapeutic treatment as well as prevention. Pintschovious had somewhat daringly declared in 1936 that National Socialism was in close touch with psychoanalytic thought through the figures of Nietzsche and Richard Wagner. The strengthening of will and the curing of anxiety, he concluded, were matters of education in peacetime and, through the work of Adler and Künkel, the responsibility of the psychotherapeutic profession.[124] When it became clear that, contrary to the pictorial representations ground out by the propaganda mills of Nazi Germany, outward physical strength and conscious self-assurance were no guarantees against mental imbalance—and, indeed, that neurosis was more common among more highly developed individuals—those psychiatrists who confined themselves to the absolute distinction between normal and abnormal began to lose their credibility.

To be sure, psychopaths per se did represent a problem for the Wehrmacht, and one that was aggravated by the reintroduction of universal military service in 1935, though assertedly alleviated to some extent by the hereditary disease law of 1933. The highest total percentage of such extreme cases among mental disorders, however, was never more than 10 percent in the army and the population as a whole.[125] Schultz, among others, thought it of paramount importance that men suffering from neuroses were not simply dismissed as congenitally and characterologically malformed.[126] Even in its severest forms, echoed one military psychologist, neurosis was a product of human interaction with the environment and demanded treatment, which could lead to substantial improvement or full recovery.[127]

Shortly after the war broke out in 1939, the Göring Institute developed an especially close working relationship with the Luftwaffe. The origins of their affiliation are not recorded. The official link ran through the office of Major Otto Brosius of the Reich Air Ministry, with whom Schultz, himself a reserve air force officer, worked. The Reich Air Ministry even financed the setting up of an institute office for Luftwaffe matters on the Knesebeckstrasse.[128] Matthias Heinrich Göring was also a reserve air force medical officer and so highly regarded in that capacity, according to his son, that he alone among reserve medical officers in the entire German armed forces achieved the rank of a chief medical officer equivalent to the rank of major (Oberstabsarzt), and was the only man serving in the military who was allowed to wear a beard. Whatever the accuracy and significance of these details, it is logical to assume that it was, once again, the family name that opened the doors within the Luftwaffe. Again according to Ernst Göring, it was his father who suggested the institutionalization of psychotherapy in the service. Psychotherapy in fact never achieved major status in the Luftwaffe medical service,[129] but the Luftwaffe, as a new, relatively independent and Nazified branch of the armed forces did not have as strong a psychiatric tradition in its medical service as did the army and even the navy, so there was a comparative willingness to work with the institute.

The Luftwaffe affiliation ranged over a variety of institute functions. Hattingberg's son, Immo, a psychosomaticist and psychotherapist, did psychological research with the Luftwaffe, and Kemper has recalled that it was in fact the Luftwaffe which first requested the institute to perform research into the problem of homosexuality.[130] Furthermore, a number of high-ranking Luftwaffe officers attended seminars and practica on short-term therapy at the Göring Institute designed to improve the handling of their men; according to Ernst Göring, an air force officer could receive up to two years' leave to undertake course work in psychotherapy. In addition, according to institute members Fritz Riemann and Eva Hildebrand (Rittmeister), Luftwaffe personnel frequented the outpatient clinic. One Air Ministry officer even suggested that since Luftwaffe personnel were on the average younger and better educated than their comrades in the army and navy, neurosis could represent a greater problem for the air force.[131] The chief of the Luftwaffe medical services, Erich Hippke, cautioned against confusing pubertal difficulties among young Luftwaffe auxiliaries with psychopathy.[132]

Beyond cooperation in the work of the Göring Institute and discussions within its medical leadership about the problem of neurosis, the Luftwaffe, at the urging of M. H. Göring, also established a number of official psychotherapeutic aid stations in the field, a measure which the army never took. Psychological strain, Luftwaffe doctors believed, was particularly prevalent and particularly dangerous among flying personnel. Psychologically astute selection and training could not guarantee fliers against the psychic consequences of wartime air duty, and the experiences of World War I had shown the desirability of early detection and treatment of "psychic morbidity." Therefore, not only did the flight surgeon have to be especially alert for signs of neurosis or "fatigue," but trained to deal with such problems. To aid in this task, the Luftwaffe did indeed establish a number of medical observation stations where both psychological and physiological investigations could be conducted.

The first such stations were set up in 1940 at Luftwaffe hospitals in Cologne, Brussels, and Paris. (Ernst Göring recalls his father making at least one trip to Paris on Luftwaffe medical business.) These hospitals were all near advanced units which were readily accessible by rail. Each station was staffed by an internist, a physician with psychotherapeutic training in addition to a background in neurology and psychiatry, and "a medical assistant with special training." After five days of observation, the sick fliers were either returned to their units or referred to a hospital for treatment or to a hostel for recuperation under a regimen of psychotherapy, autogenic training, hypnosis, physical therapy, exercise, hydrotherapy, and relaxation. In 1940 as well, special sections for such cases were established at the Luftwaffe hospital in Halle-Dölau and at a convalescent home in Oberschreiberhau. By 1943 so-called medical observation centers were in place at Luftwaffe hospitals in Brunswick, Frankfurt am Main, Munich, Vienna, and at Halle-Dölau, with smaller medical observation stations in Paris-Clichy, Brussels, Athens, Minsk, Cracow, Pleskau, and Oslo. Between 50 and 180 fliers from front-line fighter, bomber, reconnaissance, and transport units and from training schools and rear areas were examined monthly at the larger medical observation centers, and between 20 and 40 at the observation stations.

According to Immo von Hattingberg, there were few purely psychogenic disturbances among the patients seen by Luftwaffe doctors. This was due, he asserts, to the improved selection procedures used by the military, better training and organization of medical personnel, and diagnoses of overfatigue that otherwise would have been more cursorily defined as psychogenic. Genuinely serious psychogenic cases were referred as outpatients to the Göring Institute, although such a recourse was rare since, again according to Hattingberg, those cases requiring extended psychotherapeutic treatment were written off for reassignment in the Luftwaffe. For the same reason, Hattingberg notes in his postwar description of Luftwaffe medical care, psychoanalysis was abandoned by the Luftwaffe after an early trial, since such an intensive and extensive treatment, to be successful, demanded a freedom for readjustment in the patient's external life that was impossible given the tension that came with combat flying duty.[133]

An example of the kind of work done in this realm of medical care in the Luftwaffe comes right out of the Göring family itself. In the *Zentralblatt* of 1938, there appeared one of those rather unique reviews for a scientific journal. These often begin self-consciously with a disarming statement such as "Many will ask why this book is being reviewed here." The book in question on this occasion was . . . *reitet für Deutschland* (1936), a biography by Eberhard Koebsell of Carl-Friedrich Freiherr von Langen, describing his exploits in international equestrian competition. The reviewer was Göring himself, who described the book as a marvelous exemplification of will and a fine expression of the feeling that existed between man and horse.[134] There is little doubt as to how he came across this particular book or why he evaluated it positively in terms of its psychotherapeutic interest and value. The reason had to do with an unusual, but at the same time illustrative, phase in the Luftwaffe career of his son Ernst.

Ernst had taken his medical examinations in 1938 and was to begin training as a psychotherapist at his father's institute in 1939 while serving at the Charité clinic for internal medicine under Friedrich Curtius. He received his degree in 1939 from the University of Munich with a thesis on the psychology of childhood enuresis. But he was also an enthusiastic horseman who, like Langen, had ended up in the SA Riding Corps (SA-Reitersturm). Because he had found that riding relieved him of the tremendous stress and anxiety that had accompanied his exams, he decided that horseback riding could be used as a means of psychotherapy. Göring *fils*, like Göring *père*, had studied with Leonhard Seif, but his early interest and training in gymnastics, combined with his work in medicine and psychotherapy, coalesced with his love for horses into a unique method he came to call "riding therapy" (*Reittherapie*). The junior Göring served a year in the Luftwaffe, and then, in 1940, was given charge over the psychotherapy ward of the Luftwaffe hospital in Brunswick. His assignment was to rehabilitate pilots who were "flown-out" (*abgeflogen*). Göring recognized that the pilot of an airplane is especially susceptible to stress primarily because he is always alone, even in a multi-place aircraft. Göring worked at Brunswick during 1940 and into 1941, but then was transferred to the 1st Nightfighter Group at Venlo in Holland. The stress on the nightfighter pilots was particularly severe, and it was here that he was able to put his idea of riding therapy into practice. He procured horses from local residents—including the woman who was to become his wife—and soon those pilots who could no longer get up in their Messerschmitt Bf 110s were getting up on horses as a major part of a program of rehabilitation.[135] The demands of the Nazi war machine were such, however, that this and other kinds of psychotherapy became a luxury the hard-pressed Nazis could no longer afford; in late 1942 Göring was relegated to work as a regular doctor, and transferred to a Luftwaffe field division on the Russian front.

German psychotherapists also functioned in another sphere of Luftwaffe concern: the impact of air attacks on the morale of the German people. In a speech in Berlin in 1937, Hermann Göring had declared that defense against air attack (*Luftschutz*) was not just a matter of mounting fighter aircraft, flak batteries, detection devices, and early-warning systems, but of preparing the populace for the psychological challenges of the air raids.[136] Schultz was the primary moving force behind the Göring Institute's role in attempting to maintain general mental health and productivity under the strain and disruption caused by enemy raids. In a lecture to the Berlin Medical Society on 1 January 1940, and to the German General Medical Society for Psychotherapy on 7 February, he discussed the psychological effects of blackouts. Schultz explained that darkness was the perfect atmosphere for what he termed "distortion neurosis" (*Entstellungsneurose*), the conviction that within a threatening environment "something could happen." Such mental process was a threat in itself to others, and it could be eliminated or minimized only by psychotherapeutic intervention. Blackouts could also be turned to advantage, Schultz volunteered, by allowing the city dweller to achieve harmony with natural phenomena and to commune in the darkness with the inner self and the community, whence issued the true strength of the nation. Under Schultz's direction, the institute subsequently issued a pamphlet on the "do's" and "don't's" of blackout conduct that engaged the collaboration of Achelis, Hattingberg, Kemper, Meyer-Mark, and others.[137] Schultz also translated the Reich Marshal's imperative into the psychotherapeutic conception of the "air-raid shelter community" (*Luftschutzraumgemeinschaft*), where the mettle of the German *Volk* would be tested and, given the proper psychotherapeutic advice and assistance, hardened. The experience of the common danger would draw the bonds of community tighter and provide a therapeutic environment in and of itself for those whose will was flagging.[138]

For all its participation in the military life of the Third Reich, psychotherapy was still confronted with two major pressures: the opposition of the psychiatric establishment in the Wehrmacht, perenially imbued at the top with unbending Prussian notions of discipline and obedience; and the Nazi regime's increasingly hysterical demands for manpower and production. Except to the extent that they could practice some degree of informal psychotherapy in the course of their medical duties in the military, those psychotherapists who were conscripted for varying periods of time were lost to the developing profession. Heyer, for one, served as an internist and, never hesitant to speak his mind, protested to Hitler's headquarters that the menial and mundane routine of his assignment was an insult to his professional standing and military rank as well as a disservice to the state; and Göring managed to use his influence to get Kemper released from his military obligation after a short "guest appearance" in order that he might continue as director of the outpatient clinic.[139]

Although staff psychiatrists in the army did employ psychotherapeutic methods,[140] many officially continued to deny that war neuroses were a problem in the Wehrmacht. A quarterly report from a psychiatrist attached to Army Group D in France in 1944 claimed that "the so-called war-neurotic question up until now has not been a problem." Conceding that the possible demoralization following the then recent Normandy invasion was not reflected in the accompanying figures, he nonetheless declared that his experience warranted no expectation of an appreciable jump in cases of neurosis.[141] Even though World War II did not produce the same waves of war neurotics as had swept over the ranks and into the medical profession in World War I, the question of definition and interpretation remained no less significant.

The largest classification contained in the Army Group D report from 1944, that of "constitutionally abnormal," would certainly have been open in any number of cases to psychotherapeutic reinterpretation, especially since 78.85 percent of these patients were ambulatory. Those with primarily mental deficiencies also included "asocials," "mental failures," and those suffering from "hysterical superimpositions." Even among army psychiatrists opinions varied. A quarterly report from the eastern front for the same period emphasized the importance of *"seelische Führung"* to provide for the "healthy maintenance of the powers of mental resistance."[142] This psychiatrist, attached to the Fourth Panzer Army, complained that haphazard replacements reduced psychic will by disrupting the organic unity of the formations, and that with continuing Russian breakthroughs, instances of panic among the troops were on the rise. While there was no mention of neurosis in this report either, the language and orientation reflected a point of view about mental processes and dysfunctions distinctly different from that held in the report out of France.

But the very existence of the Göring Institute, along with the then recent aggressiveness of academic psychologists in Germany, also constrained even Wehrmacht psychiatrists to cooperate grudgingly with, and worry about, the newly organized psychotherapists and psychologists in the Reich. Otto Wuth, consulting psychiatrist with the Academy for Military Medicine (Militärärztliche Akademie) in Berlin, and Oswald Bumke, the consulting psychiatrist for the Wehrmacht's Seventh Military District (Wehrkreis VII) in Munich, agreed in an exchange of letters in 1942 that, unless the war lasted a very long time, those suffering from war neuroses or battle fatigue (*Kriegszitterer*) would not be a problem for the military. Should this happen, however, both Wuth and Bumke thought it professionally prudent to have such cases referred to psychiatric colleagues who were practiced in the use of hypnosis and other auxiliary and "active" modes of psychotherapy. In being specific about such an eventuality, Wuth and Bumke were clearly attempting to head off a possible further expansion of the psychotherapists' competence in the now professionally competitive field of medical psychology. Wuth allowed as how three cases in Berlin had been sent for hypnotic therapy to the psychotherapeutic group around I. H. Schultz, but both psychiatrists agreed firmly that if any of these cases were handled "analytically," it would be a "catastrophe."[143] By this time, with the reality of an independent and influential institute for psychotherapy, the use of the adverb "analytically" in the correspondence went beyond the tactical condemnation of psychoanalysis traditionally rendered in the Third Reich and pejoratively referred to all modes of *grosse* psychotherapy. Apart from the standard psychiatric denunciation of the whole psychodynamic school, the general tone of the remarks and observations by Wuth and Bumke was one of frustration and anxiety over the deployment of psychologists and the institutional development of psychotherapy.

It was the turning of the war's tide in 1942 from blitzkrieg to attrition that arrested the momentum that psychology and psychotherapy had achieved in the military. However much the Nazis might have owed to both for the effectiveness of the Germany army, the reversal of fortunes in 1942 led to the jettisoning of the army's Psychological Selection Service and the demise of its journal, *Soldatentum*. The same thing apparently occurred in the Luftwaffe, where psychological research and the use of applied psychology were phased out by 30 June 1942.[144] That the navy did not follow suit may be attributed, perhaps, to the memory of the port-bound boredom, frustration, and mutiny during World War I.

Aside from the increasingly desperate need for doctors to deal with the ever growing number of casualties, the Nazi preoccupation with quality and character became quantified under the pressure of Germany's struggle against her ever more numerous and powerful foes. The determination and improvement of character became a luxury of time, expense, and manpower in a society which declared that every German was the product of a soldierly race. At this point of crisis, the Nazi ethos merged with a military tradition that had remained skeptical of the fancy theories of psychologists and the soft indulgence of psychotherapists. Total war, as announced by Goebbels in February 1943, created a climate in which incapacity would be interpreted as a

lack of will—a failing subject not to the intervention of a psychotherapist but to that of a firing squad or a hanging party. Any psychological
complaint that could not be defined by a psychiatrist as justified
through a finding of organic dysfunction was regarded as a sign of
willful malingering.

In the feverish attempts at mobilizing Germany's dwindling human
resources between 1943 and 1945, the practice of sending "difficult"
soldiers to the front in order to make or break them was accelerated.
According to Müller-Hegemann, when incorrigibles were not subsequently dispatched to concentration camps, they were relegated to
mine-clearing duties or assigned to a penal unit. This was the case in
the Luftwaffe as well.[145] Homosexuality, for its part, had always been
a matter for forensic psychiatrists and the courts-martial. This con-
currence with civil law, that homosexuality was a crime, and with
the psychiatric and general Nazi conception of it as an incurable
hereditary disorder was reaffirmed in the scurry of total war by the
Supreme Military Command (Oberkommando der Wehrmacht) on
19 May 1943. A year later, a Luftwaffe directive concurred.[146] Schultz's
response in turn to the latter was prepared under the authority of the
Luftwaffe medical service but, as far as can be determined, was never
issued as an official directive. On 13 November 1944, psychiatrists
attached to the Berlin military district met with other forensic physicians, jurists, and psychotherapists on the question of the cause and
cure of homosexuality, but little agreement was reached on the matter,
although a study group was formed in order to explore the issue in
greater depth.[147]

Pursuant to the perceived need for increased political vigilance, on
28 November 1943 Wehrgeistige Führung, the organization within the
Wehrmacht assigned the task of furthering the effective mobilization
of the fighting spirit, had become Nationalsozialistische Führung, and
its personnel renamed "N.S. Führungsoffiziere" (NSFO). This system
for the spiritual care of military personnel had been set up after
World War I in response to the collapse of morale in 1918, and had
always manifested an interest in using academic and medical psychology in its work. In early 1943 Karl Arnhold gave a series of lectures
to the organization on the practical relationship between industrial
and military psychology.[148] More significantly, a number of the NSFO's
officers had received training at the Göring Institute after 1936, adding
a psychotherapeutic dimension to their required knowledge of psychology. One, a psychiatrist, produced a manual on the subject that was
dedicated to Matthias Heinrich Göring as the "spiritual father of this
work."[149] Although the manual was heavily influenced by a psychotherapeutic perspective, the word "neurosis" appears in its second
edition of 1944 only a few times, and always in quotation marks.

Like the change in the organization's name and nature, the quotation marks demonstrate yet another aspect of the Nazis' desperate attempt to return to what they regarded as the basics in their struggle for survival. On 30 June 1944 the OKW issued a directive that discouraged the official use of the word "neurosis." The term to be used instead was "abnormal mental reaction" (*abnorme seelische Reaktion*). Purely psychological disorders were to be labeled "abnormal experiential reactions" (*abnorme Erlebnisreaktionen*), and those mental disturbances which gave rise to physical symptoms were to be tagged "psychogenic (experience-conditioned) functional disruptions" (*psychogene (erlebnisbedingte) Funktionsstörungen*): "The word 'neurosis' as a diagnosis is therefore to be avoided in medical documents and correspondence. Expressions such as 'war neurotic,' 'war trembler,' and 'war hysteric,' etc., are forbidden."[150] Clearly, the Nazis feared that a further decline in morale would accompany what was probably an increasing incidence of these cases; they also wished to cosmetize the results of the brutal actions of the SS against soldiers labeled malingerers and deserters.

The Nazis' ruthless quantification of the imputed qualities of the German man also gave new and vigorous life to the old World War I medical perspective of psychotherapy as discipline. One confidential medical officer complained about the "softness" of psychologists and psychotherapists, not only in terms of what he disdained as their medical dilettantism but also for what he perceived as their indulgence of degenerates and malingerers, an old argument by traditional psychiatrists that was given deadly force by the ethics of total war: "In every case the doctor awakens in the patient the conviction that the demand for relief from an assignment is justified, and is driven into neuroses which, as with the pension neurotic of peacetime, never release their hold."[151]

Not surprisingly, the Nazis' repressive new directive only contributed to a noticeable upswing in psychological stress and breakdown in the military. As the cultivated ideal of organic comradeship among officers and men confident of success was replaced by the actuality of political commissars in the midst of retreat and devastation, the morale and mental health of the soldiers could only suffer. As early as 1942 the psychiatrist Gustav Störring noted that the suicide rate in the armed services was up over that of World War I because of the fear of harsh punishment on being branded a "parasite on the nation" (*Volksschädling*).[152]

Although opposition to psychotherapy in the Wehrmacht remained strong and constant, between 1943 and 1945 the Göring Institute was increasingly called on to treat and evaluate members of the military.[153] Heyer, according to Hantel, in August 1944 was treating a general who had lost his voice; he eventually committed suicide. Growing Nazi intervention knocked the last psychological supports out from under the German fighting man. The ethic of "to the front" could have therapeutic shock value in isolated cases, but as a last-ditch panacea in combination with deadly sanctions for weakness and failure, it was ultimately destructive of morale and psychological well-being; according to a postwar American analysis,

> the unity of the German Army was in fact sustained only to a very slight extent by the National Socialist convictions of its members and . . . more important in the motivation of the determined resistance of the German soldier was the steady satisfaction of certain primary personality demands afforded by the social organization of the army.[154]

As these conditions, formed from propaganda, a psychologically informed leadership, and the pride of military victory, fell away, they were replaced by the mental casualties of catastrophe.

Beyond its service to the Wehrmacht in terms of the treatment and evaluation of patients, the members of the Göring Institute now found themselves involved in attempting to save many of these patients from punishment. The reparative ethos of their profession prepared them to do this, and, indeed, found its validation in their conviction that many of the cases regarded by the government, the military, and their psychiatrists as incurable or feigned, and thereby subject to the severest forms of discipline, should instead be treated.

The unsettled conditions often made treatment difficult. Müller-Braunschweig, for example, was eventually able to carry through an analysis with a patient who had at first refused to speak freely in fear of divulging military secrets, but Scheunert had the opposite experience with a similar case, which resulted in the stagnation and eventual breaking off of the analysis[155] There could also have been some concern within the institute because of fears that its few party members, people whom Kemper labeled "firebrands" (Scharfmacher), would conceivably betray "disloyal" or "malingering" patients to the authorities.

There is, however, no evidence that anyone at the Göring Institute ever violated professional ethics in this way. Given the general environment in Germany, the mere presence of party members at an institute that was, after all, run by a relative of Hermann Göring may well have dissuaded people, Jew and non-Jew alike, from seeking help, or adversely affected the therapist/patient relationship in any number of cases that were referred there. Yet the surviving evidence seems to indicate that professional standards were nonetheless maintained, both before and during the war. It is also possible that the familial imprimatur provided by the Göring name might have convinced at least some prospective patients that psychotherapy had the stamp of official approval, and hence even prompted their seeking of treatment. From the other side, there is no evidence of any *agents provocateurs* among the patients introduced by the Nazis into the institute—although Graber in Stuttgart was told by his secretary, who worked at the state Ministry of Education (Kultusministerium), that the Gestapo kept an eye on him simply because he was a psychoanalyst.

Adolf Martin Däumling, a physician and educational psychologist who served at the Göring Institute from 21 August 1944 to 31 January 1945, was given the assignment of evaluating Luftwaffe officers who found themselves in trouble with the military authorities over charges of cowardice before the enemy and high treason. According to him, the institute provided expert psychotherapeutic testimony regarding the officer's state of mind.[156] The assignment was typical of the type of work the institute was increasingly called on to do in the last years of the war, in that it involved a mixture of both personal and professional concerns for the mediation of judgment in such cases. Kalau vom Hofe confirms the heavier wartime caseloads that descended on the psychotherapists in Berlin, and recalls that a great deal of her own work was with Boehm, who was in charge of the Göring Institute's subdivision of evaluations. Boehm has even been given personal credit by Eva Hildebrand, Rittmeister's widow, for saving the life of her second husband. In 1944 Heinz Hildebrand was on trial for making remarks injurious to the fighting spirit of the people, and Boehm was assigned by the court to prepare an expert opinion on him. He determined that Hildebrand was suffering from a mental disturbance and thus was not responsible for his actions; as a result, according to his wife, Hildebrand, a soldier, was sent to prison instead of being executed.

Most cases, it seems, involved only the military, and the psychotherapists at the Göring Institute, according to Kemper, soon became involved in what was called a "back-and-forth game" (hin-und-her Spiel). A number of the directors of military clinics in the Greater Berlin area were former students of members of the institute, and it often happened that a patient in danger of being punished as a malingerer or traitor, or simply of being sent back to the front, would instead be shuffled back and forth between hospital and institute for evaluations, tests, and treatment; diagnoses would conflict or were delayed until the military and the government, still more or less impressed by medical expertise but exasperated by medical bureaucracy, lost track of, and interest in, the case. Those who were protected in this way—in these cases, in a military reserve hospital—included a demoted major and an infantry general.[157] Gerhard Maetze recalls that Müller-Hegemann, as a communist active in the underground, was particularly adept at holding men out of combat for as long as possible. In 1944 the Nazi physician Nitzsche, without mentioning the Göring Institute or any other organization by name, was complaining especially loudly about such treasonable activity.[158]

Since neither the Göring name nor the activities of the psychotherapists could do anything about the course of the war itself, the Reich Institute had to carry on its operations under increasingly difficult circumstances. The ranks of members and candidates were thinned by call-ups for military service, casualties from the bombing, and emigration from a city that had become the major military target for the approaching enemy. The number of courses offered at the Göring Institute declined significantly as a result. Kemper and others have recalled how treatment was also disrupted by the accelerating breakdown of transportation and communication in the city.

But the aims and scope of the institute's activities remained as before; both of the last two curricula distributed by the Reich Institute (summer semester, 24 April to 1 July 1944, and winter semester, 11 September to 18 November 1944 and 22 January to 29 March 1945), contained an impressive listing of courses to be taken during the four semesters of the theoretical course of study for ordinary candidates. The institute's journal, however, was another matter. Although the continued publication of the *Zentralblatt* had been approved by Karl Brandt, Hitler's Plenipotentiary for Sanitation and Health Services (Der Bevollmächtige für das Sanitäts- und Gesundheitswesen),[159] the first thin number of volume 16 for 1944 was its last issue. This demise, according to Graber, stemmed from the economic difficulties that had always dogged the publication, as well as Leipzig's vulnerability to air attack and the resultant disruption of S. Hirzel's publishing business. This vulnerability had been demonstrated to the psychotherapists as early as 1942, when the entire stock of the second edition of Kemper's book on female infertility was destroyed in an air raid that left the warehouse of the Georg Thieme Verlag a smoking ruin.[160] The branch affiliates of the Göring Institute fared as poorly. By 1944 only three branches of the institute—in Munich, Stuttgart, and Frankfurt a.M.— were still in existence, although it was noted that some training was available in Vienna and Düsseldorf as well. But by the winter of 1944, following the destruction of the Munich institute's Akademiestrasse offices on 13 July, Seif had retired to the position of honorary president, and the Frankfurt branch had been reduced to occasional sessions by invitation only.[161] In the last months of the war, the city of Berlin itself edged closer and closer to complete chaos, and during the battle for the German capital in the waning days of April 1945, the four-story building at Keithstrasse 41 that housed the Göring Institute was completely destroyed.[162]

CHAPTER 7

Psychotherapy in the Postwar Germanies

The survival of psychotherapy during the Third Reich is in itself noteworthy, but the more significant historical issue is its growth as a profession during that era and its positive legacy to the postwar development of the discipline in the German successor states. When the Reich Institute for Psychological Research and Psychotherapy was burned to the ground in 1945, a period of difficult yet tangible development was brought to an abrupt end. But the damage was essentially confined to the physical manifestations of the growth of psychotherapy in Germany.[1] The destruction of the Göring Institute did not mean the end of psychotherapy in Germany, for it had provided enough exposure, organization, training, and practice for the nascent profession to propel it into autonomy. Psychotherapy in the Third Reich had achieved de facto recognition as a profession from the state and unprecedented financial support. Though the institute's ideological goal of attaining full conceptual, theoretical, methodological, and practical unity on the basis of a common national and racial orientation never came close to being realized, the involuntary association of all psychotherapists in a single institute produced a surprising reward: the basis for the profession's cooperation and development after 1945.[2] The abrasion worked by the Nazi years and their passing ultimately stripped psychotherapeutic thought in Germany of its abstract Romantic and *völkisch* communitarian tendencies while burnishing psychotherapists' practical medical commitment to the individual patient and to society at large. This kind of experience and commitment, besides being immediately useful, as we shall see, in helping to repair the psychological damage done to the people of Germany by tyranny and war, was advantageously in harmony with the social service ethos called "demostrategy" pervading European governments in the wake of World War II.[3]

But the institute and its clinic were gone. Göring himself—either after having served with the bottom-of-the-barrel popular militia (*Volks-sturm*) against the invading Russians or involved in a clash between the SS and the Soviets at the institute itself—was taken prisoner by the Russians and died of typhus in a detention camp on 24 or 25 July 1945,[4] while his wife Erna, according to Kemper, sought refuge with former Reich Youth Leader (Reichsjugendführer) Baldur von Schirach and his wife in Bavaria. As psychotherapists throughout Germany were faced with the task of reconstructing their personal and professional lives, those psychotherapists who remained in Berlin confronted not only the challenge of living in the shattered city but of doing something for the patients under care at the former institute's outpatient clinic.

Schultz-Hencke found a partially bombed-out school near his apartment in the vicinity of the Fehrbelliner Platz, and it was there that he, Kemper, and a few other psychotherapists and psychoanalysts resurrected in modest fashion the outpatient clinic which had originated with the old DPG under Eitingon and Simmel in 1920, and which had been taken over by the Göring Institute in 1936. Permission to function in this capacity was given by Ferdinand Sauerbruch, who had been placed in charge of Berlin's health administration by the Russians. Discussions with social insurance authorities in Berlin (Versicherungsanstalt Berlin) led on 29 April 1946 to an agreement whereby the social insurance scheme would underwrite the work of the new clinic under the name Central Institute for Psychogenic Illness (Zentralinstitut für psychogene Erkrankung). This marked the first time in history in Germany that neurosis in general was acknowledged by the public authorities as an illness covered by national health insurance. In the midst of the Berlin population's physical and psychological misery, the psychotherapists and psychoanalysts had successfully argued that psychotherapeutic intervention at an early stage might well preclude long and expensive visits to various medical specialists for the diagnosis and treatment of physical ailments induced or aggravated by psychological conditions.

Kemper assumed the post of director of the Central Institute while Schultz-Hencke supervised the programs for research and mental hygiene. The institute was housed in a wing of a former barracks on the Papestrasse, and soon it was staffed by former members of the Göring Institute and the DPG. The guidelines for the institute declared that only fully trained psychoanalysts could serve as directors of the various divisions, but the Central Institute nonetheless became a collecting point for all medical and nonmedical psychotherapists in Berlin. With the support of the Berlin Insurance Institute, the clinic was expanded to include a special division for child therapy, and clinical work as a whole grew to substantial proportions by means of the growing financial support for longer psychotherapeutic and psychoanalytic treatment.[5]

Similar arrangements were established in Stuttgart and Munich, among other cities, with the psychotherapists there drawing on the organizational model and the trained products of the Göring Institute and its branches. On 2 April 1948 Wilhelm Bitter founded the Institute for Psychotherapy in Stuttgart; it was subsidized by both the state and city governments. In October 1967 a psychotherapeutic clinic in Stuttgart, funded by the same public bodies, began its operations. These facilities employed the resources of all psychotherapeutic disciplines, until the Jungians established their own institute in Stuttgart at the end of 1971. The same principle of unity that had been enforced under the Nazis now persisted on a voluntary basis in Munich as well, where, in September 1945, a group of refugee psychotherapists from Berlin, including Fritz Riemann, Johanna Herzog-Dürck, and Felix Scherke established a training institute in cooperation with psychagogues (educational psychologists) from Seif's old institute.

Back in Berlin, Kemper presided over a 1946 gathering of psychotherapists, which came to be called the Berlin University Lecturers Committee (Berliner Dozentenausschuss) and evolved on 9 May 1947 into the Institute for Psychotherapy (Institut für Psychotherapie e.V.). At the end of September of that same year, Gottfried Kühnel organized a meeting at Bad Pyrmont of representatives of all disciplines having to do with psychological care; out of this meeting came the Study Society for Practical Psychology (Studiengesellschaft für praktische Psychologie) under Gustav Störring.[6] This organizational activity among psychotherapists also embraced two other efforts: the founding in 1948 by Bitter of the Stuttgart Association "Arzt und Seelsorger" ("Physician and Clergyman"), and the annual meetings, beginning in 1950 under the direction of Ernst Speer, known as the "Lindauer Psychotherapiewoche."

The Battle Joined Again:
The Federal Republic of Germany

The culmination of these early efforts to rebuild the professional community of psychotherapists constructed during the Third Reich came with the establishment, in September 1949 in the new Federal Republic of Germany, of the German Society for Psychotherapy and Depth Psychology (Deutsche Gesellschaft für Psychotherapie und Tiefenpsychologie) in Brunswick. This society was intended to serve as an umbrella organization for the various psychotherapeutic schools of thought. It arose out of a meeting called by Bitter in March 1949, which included Müller-Braunschweig representing the Freudians, Schultz-Hencke for the "neo-analysts," Schmaltz for the Jungians, Seif for the individual psychologists, Ernst Michel for followers of Künkel, and Alexander Mitscherlich representing the situational therapy of Viktor von Weizsäcker. The society's first task was to assemble a list of psychotherapists who had trained at the Göring Institute. It turned out that less than a hundred of their total number of around 300 still lived in West Germany; but starting with this nucleus, the DGPT by 1972 numbered over 700 members. The organization's first congress was held in Brunswick in 1950 and included papers and discussion from and among representatives of all psychoanalytic and psychotherapeutic orientations. By 1964 the DGPT consisted of the reestablished DPG, the German Psychoanalytic Union (Deutsche Psychoanalytische Vereinigung), and the German Society for Analytical Psychology (Deutsche Gesellschaft für analytische Psychologie).[7]

No full cooperation, much less unification, was achieved by the psychotherapists. As before 1933, conflict and division prevailed. The DPG had been refounded under the leadership of Carl Müller-Braunschweig in 1946, but since it did not have the wherewithal to support an institute, its candidates received their training at Kemper's Institute for Psychotherapy, where various psychoanalytic and psychotherapeutic points of view were represented. Especially influential at the institute was the now established *enfant terrible* of German psychoanalysis, Harald Schultz-Hencke, who was assembling a following for his "neo-analysis" in opposition to the orthodox outlook of Müller-Braunschweig and his small psychoanalytic group. Kemper's departure for Brazil in 1948 strengthened Schultz-Hencke at the expense of Müller-Braunschweig, and in 1949, at the International Psycho-Analytic Congress in Zurich, the differences between the two men came out into the open. Because of the congress's distress about the two factions battling within the DPG, it was admitted to the international association only on a provisional basis. Müller-Braunschweig subsequently redoubled his efforts to steer the DPG in an orthodox direction, and this led to a split in the DPG, with Müller-Braunschweig, Scheunert, and a few others seceding to form the German Psychoanalytic Union—which, in 1951, was officially recognized by the International Psycho-Analytic Association. Although the new group was very small, it managed to found its own institute in Berlin and in the mid-1950s was joined by other groups of psychoanalysts in West Germany, including Alexander Mitscherlich of Heidelberg. Mitscherlich had founded *Psyche. Zeitschrift für Psychoanalyse und ihre Anwendungen* in 1947, which would strive to advance a socially critical "psychoanalytic humanism" against the German bourgeois establishment. With the departure of the Müller-Braunschweig faction, the DPG, under the leadership of Schultz-Hencke, Boehm, Riemann, Baumeyer, and others, retained a cast of thought that reflected its emphasis on therapy and the social environment, the perspective that had been common to the neo-Freudians within psychoanalysis in Germany and elsewhere in the 1920s and 1930s, and which had been a significant tendency among the assemblage of psychotherapists and psychoanalysts at the Göring Institute. In 1954 Boehm and others founded the *Zeitschrift für psychosomatische Medizin* as the DPG's official journal.[8]

The onus of association with the Nazis that periodically surfaced in the professional controversy surrounding Schultz-Hencke also prompted conflict among psychotherapists in general in the postwar period. Established professionals like Schultz and Heyer were affected by their pasts and suffered a certain degree of exclusion. As a result, in 1956 Heyer and Schultz brought out their own journal, *Psychotherapie. Vierteljahreszeitschrift für aktiv klinische Psychotherapie,* in cooperation with some old members of the Göring Institute, including Fritz Mohr of Düsseldorf, August Vetter of Munich, and Klaus Wegscheider of Kassel, as well as Schultz's psychiatric associate Gustav Störring of Kiel and the naturopath Louis Grote. Schultz remained in professional association with Ernst Kretschmer because of the latter's interest in hypnosis as an auxiliary psychotherapeutic method, and founded the German Society for Medical Hypnosis (Deutsche Gesellschaft für ärztliche Hypnose) on 22 June 1959 in Berlin as the West German section of the International Society for Clinical and Experimental Hypnosis.[9] Accusations of collaboration with the Nazis also came hurtling across disciplinary lines. In 1949 Bitter and the managing director of the German Society for Psychology (Deutsche Gesellschaft für Psychologie), Albert Wellek, clashed sharply at a meeting in Würzburg over a widely disseminated pamphlet prepared by university psychologists that sought to discredit analytical psychology. Later, Wellek responded to criticism of German psychology for its collaboration with the Nazis as personified by the racial characterologists of that era, Friedrich Clauss, Hans F. K. Günther, and Erich Jaensch, by insisting that psychologists came nowhere near the degree of collaboration exhibited by Jung and the psychotherapists.[10]

Psychotherapists themselves attempted to put some distance between themselves and those within their own ranks who were particularly closely associated with the Third Reich. In this vein Fritz Riemann recalls that in 1946 or 1947 Erna Göring tried to become a member of the young institute in Munich, but was turned down. (Peter Göring was a pediatrician until his death in 1979, while Ernst went his own way as a psychotherapist, devoting himself since 1969 primarily to the practice of his early affinity, riding therapy.) Kurt Gauger was uniformly shunned.

The older psychotherapists who had been prominent under National Socialism had by and large passed their professional peaks after 1945, and their descents into relative obscurity were only hastened in some cases by the thoroughly noxious nature of Nazism that made heroes only of its victims.

But the crucial issues for psychotherapy in Germany after World War

II cannot be adequately explored through surveying the fates of individual psychotherapists from the Nazi era; they must be examined instead in terms of the institutional, professional, and political contexts of the time. In 1951 Walter Seitz, head of the outpatient clinic at the University of Munich and director of the Institute for Psychological Research and Psychotherapy there, observed that there were four groups of psychotherapists in West Germany in the early postwar period. The first, to which he himself belonged, espoused what he called "classical depth psychology," finding its chief organizational expression in the DGPT under the honorary chairmanship of Viktor von Weizsäcker. Training in psychotherapy and depth psychology for this group rested on two fundamental prerequisites: a specific talent and self-understanding gleaned through a training analysis. Seitz argued that in spite of all the disagreements among psychotherapists and psychoanalysts, there was unity on these two points and a resultant commitment to cooperate in the interest of the profession's development. It is clear that the Göring Institute had contributed no small measure to this postwar orientation, for it had been vigorously and effectively affirmed in the face of the powerful professional opposition it encountered from the medical establishment during the Third Reich. These psychotherapists, Seitz observed, also affirmed the training of nonmedical candidates and required, as had the curriculum of the Göring Institute, that such candidates have completed a university education in the human sciences. Nonmedical psychotherapists were to be supervised by physicians; a full physical examination was to be conducted by the physician before a patient was turned over to a lay therapist.

Seitz went on to contend, in his 1951 assessment, that the current need for both medical and nonmedical psychotherapists was especially acute. He estimated that around one million neurotics, as well as those who were suffering from psychosomatic illnesses, were in need of care in West Germany at the time, and there were only about 200 practitioners of *grosse* psychotherapy in the whole country. He remarked that any potential danger that lay therapists, supervised by a physician, might overlook an organic illness or incipient psychosis was far outweighed by what he saw as the reality of the medical profession's continued underevaluation of the effects of the unconscious mind on the genesis and persistence of physical ailments.

The other group Seitz described as challenging the medical establishment in the realm of medical psychology consisted of attending psychologists. Since 1941 this category of lay psychotherapists had been identified by the formally approved designation of Dipl. Psych., awarded to graduates of German universities with a degree in academic psychology who had gone on to receive training in psychotherapy and clinical psychology. Seitz rightly perceived that the medical profession would eventually face a far greater challenge to its asserted, but then tattered, sovereignty in the field of medical psychology from this group than from any of the various psychotherapeutic groups. This was so, he thought, because of the greater number of university psychologists, and their greater influence for being part of the powerful educational establishment—as well as the fact, unmentioned by Seitz, that the psychotherapists no longer enjoyed the power and influence of the Göring Institute. As we shall see, psychologists have indeed become a powerful professional interest group in West Germany over the intervening years.

Paradoxically powerful in an age of enlightenment and the social demand for expertise, according to Seitz, however, was a third group, the so-called "wild" psychotherapists who had been included under the 1939 Health Practitioners Law. Both the medical profession as a whole as well as all serious psychotherapists, Seitz believed, had to be on guard against this menace to the health of the people and to the status of the medical and psychotherapeutic professions. Quackery threatened the prestige of medicine in the eyes of the populace and that of psychotherapy in the eyes of more traditional physicians. Given these contending groups, Seitz emphasized what he saw to be the fact that the practice of psychotherapy was indeed a profession in and of itself, comprising a comparatively small group of around 200 psychotherapists and lying between the large body of physicians on the one hand and the large group of psychologists on the other. It was, however, a health profession, he maintained, and as such it belonged in the realm of medicine rather than in the humanities or social sciences, in the clinic rather than in the classroom.[11]

The fourth group of postwar German psychotherapists that Seitz identified was made up of the psychiatrists gathered under the leadership of Ernst Kretschmer of Tübingen in the General Medical Society for Psychotherapy, which had been refounded on 11 September 1948 at a congress of neurologists and psychiatrists in Marburg/Lahn.[12] Kretschmer's position was, as always, that psychotherapy should be practiced only by physicians who have been trained in psychiatry and neurology, and that a training analysis was an unnecessary part of such study.[13]

Kretschmer wished to restrict the training of psychotherapists to the university medical faculties, a realm into which few psychotherapists had found entry. Among those who had done so in the immediate postwar era, Fritz Mohr had become an honorary professor at the medical academy in Düsseldorf, and Viktor von Gebsattel taught psychotherapy as a neurologist and as a university lecturer at the University of Freiburg. Immo von Hattingberg was a lecturer and assistant at the medical clinic at Freiburg, while his stepsister Marlies worked at the medical clinic at the University of Munich.

Universities in West Germany have been gradually and perhaps grudgingly opening up to psychotherapy in the postwar period. Annemarie Dührssen, who trained in psychoanalysis at the Göring Institute, is presently a professor for psychotherapy and psychoanalysis at the Free University of Berlin, while Alexander Mitscherlich of the Frankfurt Psychoanalytic Institute is a lecturer at Heidelberg. Many university psychiatrists, however, are still skeptical of any psychotherapy that is conceptualized, taught, and practiced under any competence but their own. And while military psychology is an established part of the West German armed forces, psychotherapy is seldom used within their medical services and psychologists work only under the supervision of a psychiatrist.[14]

The General Medical Society for Psychotherapy under the leadership of Kretschmer was at the forefront of the early postwar psychiatric resistance to the type of psychotherapy proposed by various depth psychologists and psychoanalysts who emerged out of the Göring Institute and the pre-1933 psychotherapeutic movement. By 1964, the year Kretschmer died, the society counted 445 members. But even Walter Theodor Winkler, since 1941 a student and colleague of Kretschmer's at Marburg and Tübingen, and his successor as president of the General Medical Society for Psychotherapy, had inadvertently to acknowledge that the Nazi era had provided a certain advantage for the profession. In a report on German psychotherapy for an international audience in 1956, Winkler stressed the professional vitality of psychotherapy in the Federal Republic as reflected in the organizational, practical, and theoretical work of a number of individuals and groups. Significantly, 21 of the 71 authors listed in his bibliography were prominent members of the Göring Institute, and at least 11 others had been active in the field during the Third Reich.[15]

The same general features obtained in Austria: Even though the Nazis succeeded in destroying Vienna as the world capital of psychoanalysis, taking most of the other schools of psychotherapeutic thought along in the process, the same spirit of cooperation was reported to be active among psychotherapists there. Under the Nazis, with no Göring to directly protect and organize them, the psychotherapists in Vienna felt a special need to band together for sheer professional survival, in addition to the urgency they felt about treating those who so desperately needed their services. Reorganization of the profession began slowly in Austria after the war. Chief among the activitists was August Aichhorn, who in 1946 reestablished the Austrian Psychoanalytic Union. Aichhorn died in 1949, but by that time there were other signs of growth with the subsequent founding of the Vienna Work Group for Depth Psychology (Wiener Arbeitskreis für Tiefenpsychologie), the increased use of short-term methods of psychotherapy at the University of Vienna's psychiatric clinic, and the continuation there of Aichhorn's work in psychopedagogy.[16]

At the same time that Winkler advertised, in 1956, psychotherapy in all of its manifestations, he also proposed that activity in the field in the postwar period constituted a "rebirth of psychotherapy in Germany."[17] This was so, he argued, not only because of the reconstruction of the international dialogue and exchange of ideas that the Nazi years had severed, but (and here Winkler used the emphasis of implication) because of the resurrection of the General Medical Society for Psychotherapy in West Germany and Austria under the leadership of Ernst Kretschmer. What was only implicitly stated in 1956 before an international audience became quite explicit twenty years later, in the context of a Winkler address to the membership of the General Medical Society for Psychotherapy in celebration of the fiftieth anniversary of the founding of the organization. Winkler's 1976 remarks made it all too clear that the General Medical Society for Psychotherapy saw itself as the body that had carried the burden of professionalizing psychotherapy within the medical profession, under the direction of psychiatrists and neurologists. Winkler observed that Kretschmer had been the obvious choice for leadership of the newly constituted group, whose existence had been interrupted in 1934 when the International General Medical Society for Psychotherapy under Jung had assumed formal supervision over the German General Medical Society for Psychotherapy under Göring.[18] Winkler was correct in distinguishing between the two organizations, but the distinction rested on far more than the change in name that the Nazis had occasioned.

The differences in perspective inherent in the two organizations were revealed in the course of the campaign Kretschmer had waged for control over the direction of psychotherapy's development in the first years after the founding of the Federal Republic of Germany. Aside from his formidable professional reputation in Germany and throughout the world, Kretschmer was the beneficiary after 1945 of his silent yet strong opposition to National Socialism. His editorship of a review of German psychiatry for the American occupation authorities was one proof of a status which allowed him to emerge as a powerful proponent of psychiatric sovereignty over psychotherapy.[19] As president of the General Medical Society for Psychotherapy and editor of *Zeitschrift für Psychotherapie und medizinische Psychologie,* the journal founded in 1951 as its voice, Kretschmer joined issue early with professional opponents on vital matters of organization, legal recognition, and training of psychotherapists. It was Kretschmer's view that between 1933 and 1945 the General Medical Society for Psychotherapy suffered only adverse effects from the Nazi era, and that not only was nothing constructive accomplished during that time but the relationship between psychotherapists and the medical establishment had grown even more distant than it had been in the past.

It is certainly true that the German General Medical Society for Psychotherapy and the Göring Institute did not succeeded in resolving the question of the formal medical and legal status of psychotherapy, but Kretschmer's entire argument rested on the traditional notion that psychotherapy must be subordinated to university psychiatry. From this perspective, he refused to recognize the practical gains in terms of professional experience, exposure, and education scored by psychotherapists in the Third Reich, and it was against precisely these gains that Kretschmer fought. He argued that since psychotherapy concerned itself with the complex matter of the interaction of mind and body, medical training for psychotherapists was an absolute necessity.

In the summer of 1948 Kretschmer was called on by the several West German state physicians chambers to serve as an expert witness on the question of the regulation of psychotherapy. Kretschmer was highly critical of the recommendations of the chambers under their president Carl Oelemann, recommendations that had been worked out with the cooperation of psychotherapists Bitter, Weizsäcker, and others. He declared himself against the establishment of special psychotherapeutic training institutes, against the training analysis, and against the training of attending psychologists. Between 1948 and 1950 Kretschmer succeeded in fending off the demands of the independent psychotherapists, for he enjoyed the powerful support of the majority of the neurologists and psychiatrists in West Germany. Bitter, as his opposite number in this dispute, was forced to agree to the stipulation that the Stuttgart institute would receive funding from the government only if it agreed to train no nonmedical candidates in the future. Even a letter from C. G. Jung to Finance Minister Edmund Kaufmann in Stuttgart was to no avail in the face of the powerful opposition that Kretschmer had assembled on the part of neurologists and psychiatrists. Since the financial situation of psychotherapists was extremely precarious, they were forced to agree.[20]

Kretschmer and Bitter also came into conflict over the legal status of those attending psychologists who were already practicing. Kretschmer was opposed to the 1939 decision of the old Reich Interior Ministry that had placed them under the 1938 law governing medical assistants; he felt that even in consultation with a physician, the attending psychologist exercised an ungoverned independent therapeutic capacity that went beyond the far more restricted and closely supervised activities of nurses and other auxiliary medical personnel. These psychotherapists should be placed under the authority of an expanded Health Practitioners Law, he believed, and all further practice of psychotherapy should be reserved for approbated doctors. Bitter and other psychotherapists saw the suggestion as a step toward the prohibition of lay psychotherapy and psychoanalysis, and in 1949 they fought successfully against it. Current law in both German states mandates that nonmedical practitioners be assigned to cases by physicians, and only by those doctors trained in "depth psychology."[21]

In postwar Germany, the process toward making nonmedical psychotherapists almost equal members of the newly respectable profession was a slow one, but the foundation had been laid during the Göring Institute years. For all his influence and success, Kretschmer finally was not able to confine the modern growth of psychotherapy to the narrow boundaries of classical medicine, and the trend toward expansion has been challenged only recently by a resurgence of biological and biochemical research into mental illness and the functioning of the brain. The following sequence of events shows the steady erosion of the taboo that he and his colleagues in traditional medicine had attempted for so long to impose on nonmedical psychotherapists.

The revived General Medical Society for Psychotherapy had held its first congresses after the war in combination with those of the old Society of German Neurologists and Psychiatrists, the succeeding General League of Neurologists (Gesamtverband Deutscher Nervenärzte), and the German Society for Psychiatry and Neurological Medicine (Deutsche Gesellschaft für Psychiatrie und Nervenheilkunde), but by 1955 Kretschmer's organization and the DGPT, under Mitscherlich, had agreed to a common program for introducing a supplementary specification in psychotherapy for medical doctors. This certification of expertise in psychotherapy or psychoanalysis on the basis of further special training was adopted by the executive board of the Federal Physicians Chamber (Bundesärztekammer) in 1956, and the following year at Baden-Baden the General Medical Society for Psychotherapy, the DGPT, and the German Society for Psychiatry and Neurological Medicine settled on a course of training in psychotherapy and psychoanalysis for physicians. By the mid-1960s, despite objections from a number of psychiatrists and neurologists who wished stricter university clinic control over the teaching and use of psychotherapeutic methods, an approved list of clinics and institutes for such training was worked out by a committee composed of representatives of all three societies. And by 1962 the Federal Physicians Chamber recognized the official status of psychotherapy by approving a fee schedule for psychotherapeutic services. More important, by 1967 the West German government had agreed to include psychotherapy in the national health insurance program, and in 1971 private insurance companies also adopted this policy. In the process, relations between the General Medical Society for Psychotherapy and the DGPT grew closer: In 1965 at Bad Nauheim, in 1969 at Heidelberg, in 1973 at Berlin, and in 1975 at Düsseldorf the two organizations held their congresses in common.[22]

In its desire to promote psychotherapy against intransigent opponents among psychiatrists and neurologists in the medical profession, the General Medical Society for Psychotherapy was finally forced to abandon its early stands against nonmedical psychotherapists and the training analysis. In 1970 the West German government explicitly included nonmedical psychotherapists and psychoanalysts in the national health insurance program, and the training analysis has remained a required part of training in officially approved psychotherapeutic and psychoanalytic institutes in the Federal Republic.[23] The society also sought to strengthen its ties to general practitioners by forming, in 1969, a study group for "general psychotherapy." This led to the founding in 1973 of the German Balint Society (Deutsche Balint-Gesellschaft), which was dedicated to the development of Michael Balint's "patient-centered" therapy.

Along with the Medical Society for Autogenic Training and Hypnosis and the Association for Continuing Psychotherapeutic Education (Vereinigung für psychotherapeutische Weiterbildung), the Balint Society became a corporate member of the General Medical Society for Psychotherapy. A change in the statutes of the society in 1975 even provided for the extraordinary membership of nonmedical psychotherapists and psychoanalysts. The official reason given for these changes was the necessity of maintaining the society's voice in the growing status of professional psychotherapy.[24]

Although it is clear that psychotherapy and psychoanalysis have achieved significant gains in professional status since World War II, the structuring of this status in terms of the intersection of the disciplines of psychology and medicine has transcended the disputed but rather straightforward question of the acceptance or rejection of medical and nonmedical psychotherapy. As early as 1951, Munich psychotherapist Seitz had warned that medical psychotherapists should worry professionally far more about university-trained psychologists than about traditional depth psychologists per se. This was so because of the formidable power base that the university represented, the same bastion on which established medicine had built so much of its power. In 1976 the regulations governing national health insurance were changed to declare that only those nonmedical psychotherapists with a degree in psychology (numbering in 1977 ca. 5800) would be recognized by law—a signal advance for university-trained psychologists, since until that time other academic professions such as sociologists, teachers, and ministers could qualify for certification as psychotherapists given postgraduate training in psychotherapy.[25] Medical psychotherapists increasingly found themselves in conflict with psychologists over their sovereignty over the development and application of psychotherapy.

It is instructive to recall at this juncture that the Göring Institute only *recommended* the degree of Dipl. Psych. for nonmedical candidates in psychotherapy. The failure to require the degree arose from some appreciation of the eventual competition in the field that would come from university psychologists, in addition to the medical psychotherapists' desire to draw from those fields beyond academic psychology which they believed were necessarily involved with psychotherapy as broadly conceived. Certainly the university psychologists of that time saw the Göring Institute's initiative with regard to the training of lay psychotherapists as advantageous to their own theoretical and professional claims in the field of medical psychology.

This projected competition has been realized recently in the Federal Republic, most notably in the dispute over the definition of behavioral therapy (*Verhaltenstherapie*). In 1980 the government planned to designate behavioral therapy as a medical mode so as to encourage its application by psychotherapeutically qualified physicians. Psychologists have by and large objected to this on the grounds that behavioral therapy is based on learning psychology and other psychological disciplines, and that doctors equipped only with the supplementary title of "psychotherapy" or "psychoanalysis" would therefore not possess the necessary expertise to use behavioral therapy; only psychologists with the degree of Dipl. Psych. should be allowed to practice it.[26] Clinical psychologists, beyond their professional desire not to be defined purely as a subspeciality of medicine, were obviously concerned about the traditional claims made on the realm of medical psychology by the medical profession. This was especially so since most psychotherapists and psychoanalysts have come out of the medical field and, in order to meet the challenge from "popular" psychotherapy and to further the use of *kleine* psychotherapy among general practitioners, have continuously promoted their belief that psychotherapy cannot be divorced from the practice of medicine.[27] At the same time, given the curative omnivorousness of the medical profession everywhere and especially its historically strong positivistic orientation in Germany, psychotherapists and psychoanalysts there have always been concerned about medical monopolization of psychotherapy. This concern has been at the heart of the opposition psychotherapists, psychoanalysts, and psychologists have expressed to the creation of a formal medical specialization in psychotherapy. Such a designation would not only undercut the ideal that every physician should be schooled in psychotherapy in order to improve his or her treatment of patients as whole human beings, it would also allow the medical profession to establish its own exclusive standards and regulations for the training and practice of medical psychotherapists. And, most distressing, such a development would mean the sacrifice of the training analysis, a keystone in the making of the nonmedical psychotherapist.[28]

The Socialist Version:
The German Democratic Republic

The conflicts we have described only underline the fact that psychotherapy as a collection of methods has achieved an acknowledged place in West German public and professional life that did not exist in Germany before 1933 or 1945. The same is true in East Germany, where psychotherapy has also become established, albeit without the proliferation of groups endemic to democracy. Since August 1978 the German Democratic Republic has recognized a specialist in psychotherapy (*Facharzt für Psychotherapie*), but only in combination with medical specialization in such fields as psychiatry/neurology, internal medicine, general medicine, and gynecology.[29] Thus the title is comparable to the supplementary specification in the Federal Republic. In the Democratic Republic, the medical profession, in conjunction with state authority, has remained much more in control of medical psychology than has its counterpart in the West.

Most practitioners of psychotherapy and psychoanalysis found their homes, professions, and a more congenial atmosphere in the Federal Republic. Müller-Hegemann was one of the few to settle in East Germany after the war, and he eventually emigrated because he found that the authorities were not sympathetic to the type of individual psychotherapy he wished to practice. Psychoanalysis, of course, was viewed, as in the Soviet Union, as an intolerably bourgeois creation unsuited for a socialist society, but the emphasis on the positive relationship of the individual to his environment that had been so prominent among German psychotherapists was particularly attractive to the builders of the new state in East Germany. Along with an emphasis on group therapy, this perspective has paved the way for psychotherapy to be incorporated into the medical establishment in the Democratic Republic. The group ideal extends even to the training of the candidates themselves: There is no training analysis, but instead a so-called "self-experience community" (*Selbsterfahrungskommunität*), consisting of approximately 120 hours of small-group meetings and around 50 hours of large-group sessions.[30]

Psychotherapy in the German Democratic Republic enjoys a considerably higher status than it does in other socialist countries in Eastern Europe, and East German doctors demonstrate a relatively high degree of appreciation for the psychological factors in human illness.[31] This fact most likely stems partly from the persistence of a medical tradition that did not exist in less developed Eastern Bloc countries (with the exception, perhaps, of more industrialized and Westernized

Czechoslovakia), and in particular from the development in the field of psychotherapy made possible by the Göring Institute and the elimination of many traditional bastions of authority, including medical, in the Soviet zone of occupation in Germany. East German psychotherapists and psychologists trace their own theoretical and practical heritage back to Oskar Vogt, the founder of modern hypnotic medicine. In 1949 the journal *Psychiatrie, Neurologie und medizinische Psychologie* was founded as the declared successor to Vogt's own *Zeitschrift für Hypnotismus* (1895–1902; 1902–42: *Journal für Psychologie und Neurologie*). This tradition of rational, suggestive medical psychology has been seen to combine nicely with dialectical materialism—as opposed to Freud's more passive and analytical method, and the Romantic indulgence of the irrational that was common to the nineteenth-century tradition in German psychotherapy—and found its chief twentieth-century expression in I. H. Schultz's autogenic training.[32]

In the immediate postwar period, psychotherapists from all the occupied sectors of Berlin took part in meetings, including one in the Soviet zone on 22–23 November 1946 in which eighty-five psychiatrists and neurologists from East Berlin took part, along with Kemper and Schultz-Hencke from the West. The theme of both Kemper's and Schultz-Hencke's remarks was that disputes among the various schools of psychotherapeutic thought must be overcome, an orientation which, in attenuating the overwhelming theoretical dominance of Freudian psychoanalysis, found favor among those physicians who, with various degrees of willingness, were structuring their vision of a future psychotherapeutic capacity on a Marxist basis. Kemper and Schultz-Hencke subsequently participated in the first scientific meeting of psychiatrists and neurologists from throughout Germany in the Soviet sector of Berlin on 27–29 May 1949, and both were original editorial board members of *Psychiatrie, Neurologie und medizinische Psychologie*.

Between 1950 and 1962 the institutionalization of psychotherapy in the new German Democratic Republic proceeded modestly yet steadily. The first outpatient clinic was founded in 1950 in Berlin, and training and clinical facilities were gradually introduced into the universities and municipalities of East Germany. During the early 1950s, however, most therapists continued to receive their training at Schultz-Hencke's Central Institute for Psychogenic Illness in West Berlin, while practice in great measure continued to be based on Schultz's autogenic training, alongside a certain interest in the application of Pavlovian theory. There was also a strong general emphasis on short-term therapy to meet what was described as an overload of patients. These efforts and others culminated in the founding, in Leipzig on 10 June 1960, of the Society for Medical Psychotherapy of the German Democratic Republic (Gesellschaft fur ärztliche Psychotherapie der DDR). Since 1963, in collaboration with the resolutions adopted by the Sixth Party Congress of the ruling Social Unity Party on the accelerated construction of socialism, psychotherapists in East Germany have been even more active in incorporating psychotherapy into a socialist system newly and vigorously committed to effectively mobilizing its citizens' talents and energies for achieving high social productivity in industry, agriculture, and sport. This has included the introduction of clinical psychologists as active psychotherapists, along roughly the same lines that prevailed in Nazi Germany after 1939 and in West Germany after 1949.[33]

The role the Göring Institute played in this process was more indirect than in the case of psychotherapy in the Federal Republic. Still, its influence has been acknowledged in the Democratic Republic, primarily in terms of the institute's outpatient clinic under the direction of Rittmeister and Kemper. Kemper, as we have seen, was actively involved in psychotherapy in Berlin after the war, while Rittmeister became a hero of the profession in East Germany because of his martyrdom at the hands of the Nazis on charges of espionage for the Soviet Union. Although other psychotherapists active in the early years of psychotherapy in the Democratic Republic, like Alexander Mette of Weimar, founding editor-in-chief of *Psychiatrie, Neurologie und medizinische Psychologie,* and Dietfried Müller-Hegemann, had been at the Göring Institute, the now-legendary figure of Rittmeister has remained the primary link between psychotherapy in the Third Reich and in the Democratic Republic. In 1979 the East German Society for Medical Psychotherapy created the John F. Rittmeister Medal for Psychotherapy; its first recipient was Rittmeister's widow, Eva Hildebrand.[34]

In 1933 the terminally morose Oswald Spengler admonished the enthusiasts of that year with the words "Woe to those who mistake mobilization for victory!" We have noted that many psychotherapists were among those for whom the warning was apropos, for the Nazis were not interested in knowledge in anything but its crudest and most utilitarian forms. The history of psychotherapy in the Third Reich is important as an heretofore missing segment of the larger history of medical psychology in the nineteenth and twentieth centuries. The tracing of some of these continuities in this field through the Hitler years has been the object of the foregoing study.

In Germany the evolution of medical psychology revolved to a great extent around the conflict between the materialist, positivist, and somaticist psychiatric establishment within the university clinics and those physicians and laypeople who were dedicated to reform on the basis of a holistic and therapeutic psychological approach to mental illness. The impulse of these reformers was drawn from the Romantic roots of nineteenth-century German natural philosophy and the discoveries of the twentieth-century psychodynamic movement pioneered by Freud's psychoanalytic school. Between 1920 and 1945 psychotherapy in Germany, as elsewhere, took a number of giant strides toward public and professional recognition and development. World War I witnessed dramatic demonstrations of the efficacy of psychoanalytic therapy in treating the war neurotics whose complaints had baffled and even enraged military psychiatrists. As a result, the 1920s was a time of renewed growth in the number of doctors and laypeople dedicated to the psychological appreciation and cure of mental disorders.

The decade following World War I had opened in Germany with political turmoil and economic catastrophe; the 1930s reversed the order of disaster, first with the Great Depression and then with the advent of the Nazis. The fate of those psychotherapists who could remain in Germany was nonetheless the same: After initial difficulties, there ensued continued individual and collective development. The chaos and accidents of the Nazis in power, even as they scattered and destroyed so many individuals, produced an unprecedented opportunity for professional advance for psychotherapists in Germany. Traditional psychiatrists, even favored as they were by the Nazi obsession with genetic factors in mental illness, were nevertheless forced to witness the growth in power and influence of a psychodynamic orientation in medical psychology, a development toward which most of them were skeptical and even hostile. And although the Göring Institute, along with everything else tangible occasioned by the Nazis, went to its final ruin in 1945, psychotherapy in central Europe after the war continued to advance according to the precedents and the position first established by psychotherapists during the Third Reich.

The evolution of psychotherapy in Germany from the end of World War I through 1945 was in harmony with a general psychodynamic trend in medicine in the Western world that became especially pronounced beginning in the 1940s. This trend had been given much of its impetus and direction as early as the 1920s by the works of medically trained psychoanalysts and psychotherapists in Europe and America who began to emphasize therapy over analysis and treatment over knowledge. For these individuals, psychoanalysis—which had dominated the psychodynamic movement in medical psychology since the turn of the century, and from which almost all of its theorists and practitioners drew significant inspiration and insight—presented significant limitations in the treatment of the great mass of neurotic patients clamoring for medical attention. Shorter-term therapies which could be integrated into general medical practice were increasingly proposed, adapted, and developed.

Complementing this therapeutic turn among psychoanalysts and psychotherapists was the parallel growth of laypeople's claims to expertise in medical psychology. Freud himself had vigorously defended the notion of lay analysis so as to prevent psychoanalysis from becoming a mere tool among the many others wielded by the traditional psychiatric specialist. Although most psychoanalysts and psychotherapists at the time advocated either restricting the field to medical doctors or placing all lay psychologists under various degrees of medical supervision, academic psychologists began during this period to claim a clinical capacity exclusive of medical training and practice. All of these trends came together under the roof of the Göring Institute. Psychotherapy in the Third Reich played a crucial role in preserving the process whereby the fields of medicine and psychology converged in their claims to the understanding and treatment of mental dysfunction.

These continuities with the past and present show that the society and the institute established by the psychotherapists in Nazi Germany were not simply fortuitous, or merely enforced, and thus meaningless, responses to the demands of National Socialism. Medical psychology in the Third Reich lost many great minds, most of them Jewish, but the resulting arrested advances in theory and practice were partially compensated for by the surprising opportunity of a period of officially sanctioned and funded practical development for the less prominent individuals who remained. While it is absurd and unseemly to argue that the departure of so many giants in the field of psychoanalysis and psychotherapy was somehow beneficial, it is accurate to say that the theoretical and practical unity imperiously demanded by the Nazis and anxiously displayed by the psychotherapists did allow for a chance to minimize differences and go about the tasks of systematizing, institutionalizing, and disseminating the training and practice of various modes of psychotherapy. This was of some benefit to patients as well as to the evolving profession itself.

Such gains to the profession and those it served must be balanced against the profound loss of skilled theoreticians and practitioners, especially from the psychoanalytic school. We must also continually acknowledge the ethical compromises and outright offenses that all psychotherapists committed to a greater or lesser degree through their very presence and professional activity inside the Third Reich. The early enthusiasms—and, in some cases, lasting allegiances—which blinded many of them to the true nature of Hitler and the Nazis stemmed partly from a Romantic cultural and intellectual tradition which placed the irrational and ineffable above the rational and the prosaic. It is an irony that this German Romantic tradition was also one of the vital philosophical bases for their professional campaign against "medicine without a soul," the phrase they used to characterize the practice of doctors and psychiatrists who were imbued with materialism. The composite of these beliefs, actions, inactions, choices, compromises, opportunisms, improprieties, and outrages presents a peculiarly human picture, devoid of either heroes or true villains.

If our evaluation of the motives and actions of psychotherapists during the Third Reich must remain morally ambiguous and our estimation of their individual and general effectiveness as therapists skeptical, our conclusion about the professional outcome of their collective fate is clear. Of course, common sense and the lack of evidence to the contrary must move us to conclude once more that psychotherapy, like any science or human service, could not flourish in theory or in practice under National Socialism; but we must also conclude, on the basis of the evidence presented in the foregoing study, that between 1933 and 1945 the discipline of psychotherapy made major strides toward an established professional and institutional status within the German medical profession and German society as a whole. This led after 1945 to further dynamic change in the evolving field of medical psychology in central Europe. In line with an international trend, various schools of psychotherapy and clinical psychology, which had been preserved and institutionally advanced during the Third Reich, challenged in the German successor states (though not in Austria) a psychiatric establishment disastrously compromised and demoralized by its association with Nazi racial biology. The result for psychotherapy has been an acceleration of the steps toward some degree of professional status, steps first taken under the aegis of the Göring Institute.

Psychotherapy anywhere has yet to achieve full professional status according to Blanck's criteria outlined in Chapter 1. Indeed, the very proliferation of psychotherapeutic and psychological applications in medicine and in a variety of other fields and disciplines has only aggravated the problem of the professional definition of psychotherapy. But the whole field of medical psychology in Germany has nonetheless been transformed, making it clear that in spite of all the difficulties and derelictions that comprised life under Hitler, the nature of Nazi goverance produced, on the institutional level, more opportunity than oppression for the evolving profession of psychotherapy and therefore allowed for a continuity of change that was of decided historical significance.

Notes

1. PSYCHOTHERAPY AND NATIONAL SOCIALISM: AN OVERVIEW

1. Felix Boehm, "Bericht über die Ereignisse von 1933 bis zum Amsterdamer Kongress im August 1951," p. 303. See also Regine Lockot, "Erinnern und Durcharbeiten," pp. 206–7, 240, 398–400.

2. See Helmut Thomä, "Some Remarks on Psychoanalysis in Germany, Past and Present"; Mary Henle, "One Man Against the Nazis—Wolfgang Köhler," *American Psychologist* 33 (1978): 939–44; and ibid. 34 (1979): 363–64.

3. Karl Jaspers, *Wesen und Kritik der Psychotherapie* (Munich: Piper, 1955), p. 46.

4. Andrew G. Whiteside, "The Nature and Origins of National Socialism," *Journal of Central European Affairs* 17 (1957): 48.

5. See Janet Caplan, "The Politics of Administration: The Reich Interior Ministry and the German Civil Service, 1933–1943," *The Historical Journal* 20 (1977): 707–36.

6. See, for example, Alexander Mitscherlich and Fred Mielke, *Doctors of Infamy: The Story of the Nazi Medical Crimes,* trans. Heinz Norden (New York: Henry Schuman, 1949); and Max Weinreich, *Hitler's Professors: The Part of Scholarship in Germany's Crimes Against the Jewish People* (New York: Yiddish Scientific Institute, 1946), pp. 27–36.

7. Philip Rieff, *Freud: The Mind of the Moralist,* 3rd ed. (Chicago: University of Chicago Press, 1979), p. 243.

8. Boris M. Segal, "The Theoretical Bases of Soviet Psychotherapy," *American Journal of Psychotherapy* 29 (1975): 503–23.

9. See Hans Buchheim, *Totalitarian Rule: Its Nature and Characteristics,* trans. Ruth Hein (Middletown, Conn.: Wesleyan University Press, 1968), pp. 35–36; and Joseph Nyomarky, *Charisma and Factionalism in the Nazi Party* (Minneapolis: University of Minnesota Press, 1967).

10. "Bericht über die 1. Tagung der Deutschen Gesellschaft für Kinderpsychiatrie und Heilpädagogik," *Zeitschrift für Kinderforschung* 49 (1941): 4. See also *Deutsche Wissenschaft. Arbeit und Aufgabe* (Leipzig: S. Hirzel, 1939), pp. 101–48.

11. See Charlotte Beradt, *The Third Reich of Dreams,* trans. Adrienne Gottwald (Chicago: Quadrangle, 1968). Psychoanalysts who emigrated from Germany and Austria during the Nazi period have firmly and consistently maintained that psychoanalysis could not have been practiced under the totalitarian order set up by Hitler. This would have been so, they have

asserted, not only because of the forced expulsion and oppression of its practitioners and the dissolution of its organization, but also because of the absence, due to the pervasive terror of such a regime, of the necessary bond of trust between analyst and analysand. This is a valid argument and supported by the experience of many of these analysts themselves.

But, as the history of the Göring Institute once again makes clear, Nazi Germany was not a perfect totalitarian order and it is possible to step away from the appalled and justified generalization of persecuted psychoanalysts to see that conditions did exist that could allow the practice of various modes of psychotherapy, including psychoanalysis, in the Third Reich. In any case, it is not the thesis of this book that psychoanalysis was successfully *practiced* in Nazi Germany on any sort of broad basis. It is of course impossible to determine the rate of "success" or "failure" of any such ventures even if we could document their frequency and course to any satisfactory degree. What this study seeks to document is the survival and professional development of the various modes of psychotherapy, including psychoanalysis, extant in Germany as of 1933. On psychoanalytic practice, cf. Arthur Feiner, "The Dilemma of Integrity"; Gerard Chrzanowski, "Psychoanalysis: Ideology and Practitioners," pp. 492–93; and Lutz Rosenkötter, "Schatten der Zeitgeschichte auf psychoanalytischen Behandlungen." See also Rose Spiegel, "Survival of Psychoanalysis in Nazi Germany"; and Lockot, "Erinnern und Durcharbeiten," pp. 288–89.

12. Martin Gumpert, *Heil Hunger!*, pp. 16, 41. See also idem, *Hölle in Paradies: Selbstdarstellung eines Arztes* (Stockholm: Bermann-Fischer, 1939), pp. 241–42.

13. Foreign Office and Ministry of Economic Warfare, "Public Health" (London, October 1944), pp. 229–56G. Wiener Library.

14. Richard Grunberger, *The 12-Year Reich*, p. 224.

15. Ernest Jones, *The Life and Work of Sigmund Freud*, 3:175.

16. See Franz Alexander, *The Western Mind in Transition: An Eyewitness Story* (New York: Random House, 1960), pp. 99–100; Richard I. Evans, *Dialogue with Erik Erikson* (New York: E. P. Dutton, 1969), p. 64; Robert Coles, *Erik H. Erikson: The Growth of His Work* (Boston: Little, Brown and Company, 1970), pp. 27–28, 30–31; Hannah S. Decker, *Freud in Germany*, p. 322; and H. Stuart Hughes, *The Sea Change: The Migration of European Social Thought, 1930–1965* (New York: Harper & Row, 1975), pp. 259–60.

17. Käthe Dräger, "Psychoanalysis in Hitler Germany: 1933–1949," p. 206. Cf. the restrictions on psychoanalysis adopted in 1939 by the Norwegian government and applauded in the German medical press: "Verbot bzw. Einschränkung psychoanalytischer Behandlung in Norwegen," *Deutsches Ärzteblatt* 69 (1939): 248. On the more benign atmosphere surrounding psychoanalysis in Mussolini's Italy until 1938, see Michel David, *La psicoanalisi nella cultura italiana* (Turin: Boringhieri, 1966), pp. 7–8, 18–24.

18. Anna Freud, "Report on the Sixteenth International Psycho-Analytical Congress," *Bulletin of the International Psycho-Analytical Association* 30 (1949): 186–87. See also Richard F. Sterba, *Reminiscences of a Viennese Psychoanalyst* (Detroit: Wayne State University Press, 1982), p. 156. The essentially "eclectic" nature of the medical response to, and incorporation of, the theories of Freud that has largely been ignored by psychoanalytic chroniclers

has of late drawn increasing historical attention. See Thomas F. Glick, "The Naked Science: Psychoanalysis in Spain, 1914–1948," *Comparative Studies in Society and History* 24 (1982): 533–71, especially pp. 535–36; Ilse N. Bulhof, "Psychoanalysis in the Netherlands," ibid.: 572–88; Hannah S. Decker, "The Reception of Psychoanalysis in Germany," ibid.: 589–602; and John C. Burnham, "Psychoanalysis in Western Cultures: An Afterword on Its Comparative History," ibid.: 603–10. For a recent orthodox history of psychoanalysis in central Europe, see Reuben Fine, *A History of Psychoanalysis* (New York: Columbia University Press, 1979), pp. 85, 87–113, 145–46.

19. Walter Theodor Winkler, "The Present Status of Psychotherapy in Germany," p. 288. See also idem, "50 Jahre AÄGP—ein Rückblick," pp. 76–77; and Hans Hoff and O. H. Arnold, "Germany and Austria," in Leopold Bellak, ed., *Contemporary European Psychiatry*, p. 92. Until recently, psychotherapists have been understandably reticent to discuss freely the activities of their discipline under Hitler. Some have stressed accounts of professional and political oppression while others have simply taken for granted their improved, if still imperfect, professional status. See, for example, H. Buder, "Der Zeitraum von 1933 bis 1945 und die Zeit nach dem Kriege," in Michael Fordham, ed., *Contact with Jung: Essays on the Influence of His Work and Personality* (Philadelphia: J. B. Lippincott, 1963), pp. 33–35.

20. Walter Cimbal, "Bericht des Geschäftführers über die Weiterführung des Zentralblattes und 'der allgemeinen ärztlichen Gesellschaft für Psychotherapie,' " *ZfP* 7 (1934) : 141. On a somewhat similar course of events among psychologists, see Ulfried Geuter, "Der Leipziger Kongress der Deutschen Gesellschaft für Psychologie 1933," *Psychologie- und Gesellschaftskritik* 3 (1979): 7–25.

21. Fritz Ringer, *The Decline of the German Mandarins;* and Fritz Stern, "The Political Consequences of the Unpolitical German," in Stern, *The Failure of Illiberalism: Essays on the Political Culture of Modern Germany* (New York: Alfred A. Knopf, 1972), pp. 3–25. See also Konrad H. Jarausch, *Students, Society and Politics in Imperial Germany: The Rise of Academic Illiberalism* (Princeton: Princeton University Press, 1982).

22. Werner Kemper, interview with the author, 28 November 1973.

23. Franz L. Neumann, "Introduction," in Daniel Lerner, *The Nazi Elite,* Hoover Institute Studies, Series B: Elite Studies, No. 3 (Palo Alto: Stanford University Press, 1951), p. iv.

24. Juan Linz, "Some Notes Toward a Comparative Study of Fascism in Sociological Historical Perspective," in Walter Laqueur, ed., *Fascism: A Reader's Guide* (Berkeley: University of California Press, 1976), p. 74.

25. Karl Schleunes, *The Twisted Road to Auschwitz: Nazi Policy Toward German Jews 1933–1939* (Chicago: University of Chicago Press, 1970).

26. Martin Broszat, *The Hitler State*, p. 360.

27. Klaus Epstein, "A New Study of Fascism," *World Politics* 16 (1964): 313.

28. Franz Baumeyer, "Zur Geschichte der Psychoanalyse in Deutschland," p. 208; Dräger, "Psychoanalysis in Hitler Germany," p. 207; and Gudrun Zapp, "Psychoanalyse und Nationalsozialismus," p. 26.

29. See, for example, Milton Mayer, *They Thought They Were Free: The Germans 1933–45* (Chicago: University of Chicago Press, 1955), p. 194.

30. Boehm, "Bericht über die Ereignisse," p. 303.

31. Edward N. Peterson, *The Limits of Hitler's Power*, p. xvii.

32. Amy R. Sims, "Intellectuals in Crisis: Historians Under Hitler," *Virginia Quarterly Review* 54 (1978): 246–52. Experimental psychologists in Germany underwent a similar experience in their desire for greater academic recognition. While psychotherapists battled against what they saw as the "materialism" of the German psychiatric establishment, experimental psychologists faced the charge of "materialism" leveled against them by the humanistic establishment within the philosophical faculties of the German universities. Indeed, academic critics of experimental psychology over time included some of the major inspirators of the psychotherapeutic movement in Germany, such as Wilhelm Dilthey and Eduard Spranger. See Mitchell G. Ash, "Academic Politics in the History of Science: Experimental Psychology in Germany, 1879–1941," *Central European History* 13 (1980): 255–86.

33. See Erich Jaensch, *Der Gegentypus. Psychologisch- anthropologisch Grundlagen deutscher Kulturphilosophie, ausgehend von dem was wir überwinden wollen,* Beiheft zur Zeitschrift für angewandte Psychologie und Charakterkunde, ed. Otto Klemm and Philipp Lersch, vol. 75 (Leipzig: Johann Ambrosius Barth, 1938). See also *Deutsche Wissenschaft*, pp. 46–48; Goodwin Watson, "Psychology in Germany and Austria," *Psychological Bulletin* 31 (1934); 755–56; Frederick Wyatt and Hans L. Teuber, "German Psychology Under the Nazi System 1933–1940"; E. Lerner, "A Reply to Wyatt and Teuber," *Psychological Review* 52 (1945): 52–54; and Ulfried Geuter, "Die Zerstörung wissenschaftlicher Vernunft," *Psychologie heute* 7 (1980): 40. On "inner emigration," see Hughes, *The Sea Change*, pp. 17–18.

34. Volker Losemann, *Nationalsozialismus und Antike: Studien zur Entwicklung des Faches Alte Geschichte 1933–1945* (Hamburg: Hoffmann und Campe, 1977).

35. Helmut Heiber, *Walter Frank und sein Reichsinstitut für Geschichte des neuen Deutschlands,* Quellen und Darstellungen zur Zeitgeschichte, vol. 13 (Stuttgart: Deutsche Verlags-Anstalt, 1966).

36. Alan D. Beyerchen, *Scientists Under Hitler,* pp. 203–6.

37. Howard M. Vollmer and Donald L. Mills, eds., *Professionalization,* p. 4.

38. Ronald M. Pavalko, *Sociology of Occupations and Professions* (Itasca, Ill.: F. E. Peacock, 1971), p. 21. Italics in original.

39. Nina Toren, "Semi-Professions and Social Work," p. 144.

40. William J. Goode, "Encroachment, Charlatanism and the Emerging Profession," p. 903.

41. Gertrude S. Blanck, "The Development of Psychotherapy as a Profession," pp. 160–61.

42. Ibid., pp. 229, 237.

43. Ibid., pp. 241–44.

44. Goode, "Encroachment," p. 910.

45. Blanck, "Psychotherapy as a Profession," p. 160; Goode, "Encroachment," pp. 910, 903.

46. See Harvey L. Smith, "Psychiatry in Medicine," pp. 285–86; and Karl Figlio, "The Historiography of Scientific Medicine: An Invitation to the Human Sciences," *Comparative Studies in Society and History* 19 (1977): 262–86, especially pp. 277–79.

47. Oswald Bumke, *Die Psychoanalyse und ihre Kinder,* p. 116. See also Geuter, "Der Leipziger Kongress," p. 19.

48. "Zum Geleit," *Allgemeine Ärztliche Zeitschrift für Psychotherapie* 1 (1928): 4.

49. Lockot, "Erinnern und Durcharbeiten," pp. 57, 92–94, 246, 321–35.

50. See Ulfried Geuter, "Die Professionalisierung der deutschen Psychologie im Nationalsozialismus"; and Ash, "Academic Politics," p. 286.

51. See Geuter, "Professionalisierung," pp. 330–73.

52. Rudolf Ramm, *Ärztliche Rechts- und Standeskunde,* pp. 32–62.

53. N. S. Timasheff, "Business and the Professions in Liberal, Fascist and Communist Society," in Vollmer and Mills, *Professionalization,* p. 60.

54. Broszat, *Hitler State,* pp. 43–44, 284, 348–49. See also Robert Koehl, "Feudal Aspects of National Socialism," *American Political Science Review* 54 (1960): 921–33.

55. Werner Achelis, "Psychologische Hygiene," p. 251.

56. David Schoenbaum, *Hitler's Social Revolution.*

2. PSYCHOTHERAPY AND MEDICINE: THE RISING CHALLENGE

1. Sigmund Freud, "The History of the Psychoanalytic Movement," in Freud, *Collected Papers,* trans. Joan Riviere (London: Hogarth, 1949), 1:319.

2. Heinz Hartmann, "Die k.u.k. Nervenklinik Graz im Dienste des Krieges," *Archiv für Psychiatrie* 59 (1918): 1162. On the other hand, the statistics on neurasthenia, a physiological nervous disorder, showed a marked stability after 1914 as the soldiers became more accustomed to the war environment. See Konrad Hummel, "Vergleichende Untersuchungen der psychogenen Störungen bei Kriegsteilnehmern des 1. und 2. Weltkrieges unter besonderer Berücksichtigung der Symptomatologie," (Medical dissertation, Tübingen, 1946).

3. See P. M. Awtokratowo, "Die Geisteskrankheiten im russischen Heere während des japanischen Krieges," *Allgemeine Zeitschrift für Psychiatrie* 64 (1907): 286–319.

4. Hummel, "Vergleichende Untersuchungen," pp. 26–27. For discussion of this among German psychiatrists and psychoanalysts between 1918 and 1945, see Gustav Störring, "Die Verschiedenheiten der psycho-pathologischen Erfahrungen im Weltkriege und im jetzigen Krieg und ihre Ursachen"; Robert Sommer, *Krieg und Seelenleben* (Giessen: O. Kindt, 1918); and Hilda Abraham and Ernst Freud, eds., *A Psychoanalytic Dialogue: The Letters of Sigmund Freud and Karl Abraham 1907–1926,* trans. B. Marsh and H. C. Abraham (New York: Basic Books, 1965), p. 265.

5. Gregory Zilboorg, *A History of Medical Psychology,* pp. 287–91, 319–41; Henri F. Ellenberger, *The Discovery of the Unconscious,* pp. 210–12.

6. Franz G. Alexander and Sheldon T. Selesnick, *The History of Psychiatry,* p. 163. See also Decker, *Freud in Germany,* pp. 47–54.

7. See Decker, *Freud in Germany,* pp. 36–72; and Robert Gaupp, "Psychiatrische Probleme der Gegenwart," *Zeitschrift für ärztliche Fortbildung* 38 (1941): 257–59.

8. Decker, *Freud in Germany,* pp. 77–81. See also Jan Goldstein, "The

Hysteria Diagnosis and the Politics of Anticlericalism in Late Nineteenth-Century France," *Journal of Modern History* 54 (1982): 209–39.

9. Zilboorg, *Medical Psychology*, pp. 494–95.

10. Thomas S. Kuhn, *The Structure of Scientific Revolutions* (Chicago: University of Chicago Press, 1962), p. 68.

11. C. Stanford Read, "A Survey of War Neuropsychiatry," *Mental Hygiene* 2 (1918): 360.

12. See Ernest Jones, *Papers on Psychoanalysis*, 5th ed. (London: Bailliere, Tindall & Cox, 1948), pp. 300–301.

13. Decker, *Freud in Germany*, pp. 46, 202, 324–28.

14. Robert Gaupp, "Some Reflections on the Development of Psychiatry in Germany."

15. See Jones, *Freud*, 2:197–98, 251–54; and Ernst Simmel, *Kriegs-Neurosen und psychische Trauma* (Berlin: O. Nemnich, 1918). See also Ernest Jones, ed., *Psychoanalysis and the War Neuroses* (Vienna: International Universities Press, 1921).

16. Abraham to Freud, 27 October 1918, in Abraham and Freud, *Psychoanalytic Dialogue*, pp. 279–80.

17. Quoted in Vincent Brome, *Freud and His Early Circle* (New York: Morrow, 1968), p. 31. See also Jack L. Rubins, *Karen Horney*, pp. 56–142.

18. See Decker, *Freud in Germany*; Johannes Heinrich Schultz, *S. Freud's Sexualpsychoanalyse: Kritische Einführung für Gerichtsärzte, Ärzte und Laien* (Berlin: Karger, 1917); and Carl Haeberlin, *Grundlinien der Psychoanalyse* (Munich: Otto Grülin, 1927). The same was true across the Atlantic Ocean; see Nathan G. Hale, *Freud and the Americans: The Beginnings of Psychoanalysis in the United States, 1876–1917* (New York: Oxford University Press, 1971).

19. J. A. C. Brown, *Freud and the Post-Freudians* (London: Penguin, 1972), p. 129.

20. Ibid., pp. 129–73. On the therapeutic turn within psychoanalysis, see Robert A. Harper, *Psychoanalysis and Psychotherapy: 36 Systems* (New York: Jason Aronson, 1974), pp. 44–81.

21. Rieff, *Moralist*, p. 35. See also Alexander and Selesnick, *Psychiatry*, pp. 234–48. On the crucial period from 1906 to 1914, see Sigmund Freud, *The Freud/Jung Letters: The Correspondence Between Sigmund Freud and C. G. Jung*, ed. William McGuire and trans. Ralph Manheim and R. F. C. Hull, Bollingen Series XCIV (Princeton: Princeton University Press, 1974).

22. Abraham and Freud, *Psychoanalytic Dialogue*, p. 382. See also Jones, *Freud*, 2:114–15; and Gerhard Maetze, ed., *Psychoanalyse in Berlin*.

23. Sigmund Freud, "Observations on 'Wild' Psychoanalysis," in Freud, *Collected Papers*, 2:297–304. See also Ellenberger, *Discovery*, p. 805.

24. Otto Fenichel, *The Psychoanalytic Theory of Neurosis* (New York: W. W. Norton, 1945), p. 565.

25. Decker, *Freud in Germany*, p. 187.

26. "Aktuelles," *ZfP* 16 (1944): 1. In 1910 Leonhard Seif had emerged at the first congress of Oskar Vogt's and Auguste Forel's International Society for Medical Psychology and Psychotherapy in Brussels as a vigorous young defender of Freud's ideas. See Ellenberger, *Discovery*, pp. 805–6.

27. Decker, *Freud in Germany*, p. 28.

28. Carl Haeberlin, "Die Bedeutung von Ludwig Klages and Hans Prinz-horn für die deutsche Psychotherapie," p. 39. See also idem, "Über das vital Unbewusste, Bewusstsein and Charakter mit Bemerkungen über die deutsche Seelenkunde von Goethe und Carus"; and Zilboorg, *Medical Psychology*, p. 39.

29. Alexander and Selesnick, *Psychiatry*, pp. 85–86. On this debate, see Zilboorg, *Medical Psychology*, pp. 180–200.

30. See David Stewart Hull, *Film in the Third Reich: A Study of the German Cinema, 1933–1945* (Berkeley: University of California Press, 1969), pp. 246–48; and Erich Otto, "Der Paracelsus Film: Zur Salzburger Uraufführung," *Deutsches Ärzteblatt* 73 (1943): 131.

31. M. H. Göring, quoted in Ilse Döhl, "Gottfried Wilhelm Leibniz als Entdecker des Unbewussten und als Psychotherapeut," in Döhl, Gustav Hans Graber and Fritz Mohr, *Leibniz, Carus und Nietzsche als Vorläufer unserer Tiefenpsychologie*, p. 8. See also the review by Josef Meinertz, *ZfP* 14 (1942): 175–77; and Döhl, *Bewusstseinsschichtung: Ein Beitrag zur Entwicklung ihrer Theorie, insbesondere durch Nachweis von Ursprüngen bei Leibniz* (Berlin: Collignon, 1935).

32. Zilboorg, *Medical Psychology*, p. 253. See also Ellenberger, *Discovery*; and Lynn L. White, *The Unconscious Before Freud* (Garden City, N.Y.: Doubleday, 1962).

33. See Siegfried Bernfeld, "Freud's Earliest Theories and the School of Helmholtz," *Psychoanalytic Quarterly* 13 (1944): 341–62, which places Freud in the tradition of the nineteenth-century German materialistic reaction to natural philosophy. See also Frank J. Sulloway, *Freud, Biologist of the Mind: Beyond the Psychoanalytic Legend* (New York: Basic Books, 1979).

34. C. G. Carus quoted in Haeberlin, "Unbewusste, Bewusstsein und Charakter," p. 285.

35. Gustav Graber, "Carl Gustav Carus als Erforscher des Unbewussten und Vorläufer unserer Seelenheilkunde," in Döhl et al., *Leibniz, Carus und Nietzsche*, p. 37. On Carus, see Ellenberger, *Discovery*, pp. 207–8; Alexander and Selesnick, *Psychiatry*, pp. 169–70; and Decker, *Freud in Germany*, p. 259.

36. Matthias Heinrich Göring, "Grundlagen der Psychotherapie." See also Ellenberger, *Discovery*, pp. 210–15; and Zilboorg, *Medical Psychology*, pp. 475–78.

37. Fritz Mohr, "Friedrich Nietzsche als Tiefenpsychologe und Küster eines neuen Arzttums," in Döhl et al., *Leibniz, Carus und Nietzsche*, p. 55. On Hartmann, see Kurt Gauger, "Die Lehre vom makrokosmischen Zweck-prozess bei Eduard v. Hartmann" (Inaugural dissertation, Rostock, 1922). For a critical view of the Romantics and science, see Charles Coulston Gillispie, *The Edge of Objectivity: An Essay in the History of Scientific Ideas* (Princeton: Princeton University Press, 1960), pp. 178–201.

38. John Rittmeister, "Der heutige Stand der Poliklinik und ihre künftigen Aufgaben," p. 88. See also, by name, BDC: Reichsärztekammer.

39. BDC: Reichsärztekammer. There is a problem of terminology here. Strictly defined, a neuropathologist is a specialist "in the laboratory and autopsic diagnosis of diseases of the nervous system." In German, *Nervenarzt* is synonymous with *Neurologe*, a neurologist, or general nerve specialist. The British translation of the German terms is "neuropathist," an obsolete

term in American usage replaced simply by "neurologist." In this study we have chosen to translate *Nervenarzt* as "neuropathologist" in order to distinguish physicians in this field whose specialty was the psychotherapeutic treatment of nervous disorders from the physicalist and positivist majority of German psychiatrists and neurologists. This word also has the more general advantage of recalling the evolving appreciation by doctors of the *psycho*-pathology of the nervous system, as in the work of the neuropathologist Meyer who in America had expanded his specialty's traditional concern with morphology and histology into the realm of human experience and motive. Without the necessity of such a distinction as obtains in this particular historical context, however, one may simply translate *Nervenarzt* as "neurologist" and/or "psychiatrist" and relegate "neuropathologist" to its more narrow definition, as we do in Chapter 7.

40. Ringer, *German Mandarins*, pp. 180–99.

41. Haeberlin, "Klages und Prinzhorn," p. 42.

42. Gustav Richard Heyer, "Lebenslauf" (Berlin, 29 February 1944), p. 3. BDC: Parteikorrespondenz.

43. Fritz Künkel, "Die dialektische Charakterkunde als Ergebnis der kulturellen Krise," p. 73.

44. Walter Cimbal, "Erinnerungen eines alten Arztes an die Frühzeit der Psychotherapie in Deutschland," p. 46. See also Johannes Heinrich Schultz, *Lebensbilderbuch eines Nervenarztes*, pp. 140–50.

45. Cimbal, "Frühzeit der Psychotherapie," p. 46.

46. Wladimir Eliasberg, "Allgemeine Ärztliche Gesellschaft für Psychotherapie, 1926–1931," pp. 738–39.

47. Ibid., p. 738. See also *Psychotherapie: Bericht über den 1. Allgemeinen Ärztlichen Kongress für Psychotherapie in Baden-Baden 17. bis 19. April 1926;* and Johannes Heinrich Schultz, "1. Allgemeiner Ärztlicher Kongress für Psychotherapie, Baden-Baden, 17.-19. IV. 1926," *Deutsche medizinische Wochenschrift* 52 (1926): 937.

48. August Friedländer, "Sozialmedizin und Politik," in Wladimir Eliasberg and Walter Cimbal, eds., *Bericht über den III. Allgemeinen ärztlichen Kongress für Psychotherapie in Baden-Baden 20. bis 22. April 1928,* p. 212.

49. "Zum Geleit," p. 2.

50. Ibid.

51. Schultz, *Lebensbilderbuch*, p. 150.

52. Johannes Heinrich Schultz, "Psychotherapie und Medizin," *Münchener medizinische Wochenschrift* 77 (1930) : 903–5. See also idem, *Taschenbuch der psychotherapeutischer Technik*, Fischer's Therapeutische Taschenbücher, vol. 12 (Berlin: Kornfeld, 1924); and idem, *Die seelische Krankenbehandlung, Psychotherapie; ein Grundriss für Fach und Allgemein Praxis*, 4th ed. (Jena: Fischer, 1930).

53. Henry Steele Commager, *The American Mind* (New Haven: Yale University Press, 1950), p. 100.

54. Wladimir Eliasberg, ed., *Bericht über den II. Allgemeinen ärztlichen Kongress für Psychotherapie in Bad Nauheim 27. bis 30. April 1927.*

56. Eliasberg and Cimbal, *Bericht.*

56. See Walter Cimbal, *Bericht über den IV. Allgemeinen ärztlichen Kongress für Psychotherapie in Bad Nauheim 11. bis 14. April 1929;* and Ernst Kretschmer, *Gestalten und Gedanken*, pp. 133–37.

57. See Ernst Kretschmer and Walter Cimbal, eds., *Bericht über den V. Allgemeinen ärztlichen Kongress für Psychotherapie in Baden-Baden 26. bis 29. April 1930;* and idem, *Bericht über den VI. Allgemeinen ärztlichen Kongress für Psychotherapie in Dresden 14. bis 17. Mai 1931.* On the psychotherapeutic interest in Oriental methods, see Heinrich Zimmer, "Indische Anschauungen über Psychotherapie," *ZfP* 8 (1935): 147–62.

58. As far as can be determined, of the twenty-two members of the "core group" within the General Medical Society for Psychotherapy, at least eleven were Lutheran, only two were Catholic, and two others (Boehm and Schultz-Hencke) were without religious affiliation (*konfessionslos*). Achelis, Gauger, and Heyer even changed their declared religious affiliation from Protestant (*evangelisch*) to the Nazi-approved "believer in God" (*gottgläubig*). See BDC: Reichsärztekammer. German Protestants at this time were by and large socially and politically conservative and were proportionally overrepresented among Nazi voters and activists. See also A. A. Friedländer, "Das erste jahrfünft des Allgemeinen Ärztlichen Kongresses für Psychotherapie," *Münchener medizinische Wochenschrift* 77 (1930): 992.

59. Michael H. Kater, "Hitlerjugend und Schule im Dritten Reich," *Historische Zeitschrift* 228 (1979): 609–10. See Walter Wuttke-Groneberg, "Leistung, Vernichtung, Verwertung," pp. 9–18. See also Louis Hagen, *Follow My Leader* (London: Allan Wingate, 1951), pp. 40–68. The popularity of Hitler with the German middle class and the social and professional elite in Germany has of late come under close historical scrutiny. See Richard F. Hamilton, *Who Voted for Hitler?* (Princeton: Princeton University Press, 1982); Gerhard Baader and Ulrich Schultz, eds., *Medizin und Nationalsozialismus. Tabuisierte Vergangenheit—Ungebrochene Tradition?* (Berlin: Verlagsgesellschaft Gesundheit, 1980); and, especially for Nazi proclivities among German physicians, Michael H. Kater, *The Nazi Party,* pp. 48, 67–68, 73, 110, 112–14, 134–37.

60. Dräger, "Psychoanalysis in Hitler Germany," p. 208.

61. BDC: NSDAP-Zentralkartei. Of these 47 psychotherapists, 8 (17 percent) were members of the NSV; 7 (14.9 percent), of the Nazi Physicians League; 5 (10.6 percent), of the Teachers League; 3 (6.4 percent) each, of the SA, the University Lecturers League and the Motor Corps; 2 (4.25 percent) each, of the Nazi Women's Organization and the Labor Front; and 1 (2.1 percent) each, of the Hitler Youth and the Student League. See also Geuter, "Professionalisierung," p. 153.

62. See Rubins, *Karen Horney,* pp. 113–41; Decker, *Freud in Germany,* p. 84; Schultz, *Lebensbilderbuch,* p. 164; and Lockot, "Erinnern und Durcharbeiten," pp. 72–101.

3. PSYCHE AND SWASTIKA

1. Fritz Künkel, *Grundzüge der politischen Charakterkunde,* p. vi.

2. Hans von Hattingberg, "Neue Richtung, Neue Bindung," pp. 98, 103.

3. C. G. Jung, "After the Catastrophe" (1945), in Jung, *Essays on Contemporary Events,* trans. Elizabeth Welsh, Barbara Hannah and Mary Briner (London: Kegan Paul, 1947), p. 58; and in idem, *Civilization in Transition,* p. 205.

4. Kurt Gauger, "Psychotherapie und politisches Weltbild," p. 167; idem, *Politische Medizin*, p. 17; and George Mosse, ed., *Nazi Culture*, p. 218. For another example of the professional confiscation of Hitler's name, see Dr. Stephen, "Adolf Hitler als Arzt des deutschen Volkes," *Volksgesundheitswacht* 2 (1935): 3–4. See also Walther Poppelreuter, *Hitler der politische Psychologe* (Langensalza: Beyer & Söhne, 1934).

5. Gustav Richard Heyer, *Praktische Seelenheilkunde*, p. 80.

6. Werner Zabel, *Grenzerweiterung der Schulmedizin*, pp. 130–31.

7. Carl and Sylvia Grossman, *The Wild Analyst: The Life and Times of Georg Groddeck* (New York: George Braziller, 1965), pp. 194–95, 204.

8. Matthias Heinrich Göring, "Eröffnungsansprache," in Rudolf Bilz, ed., *Psyche und Leistung*, p. 8.

9. Felix Scherke, "Lebenslauf" (Berlin, 4 November 1936). BDC: Kulturkammer.

10. Ludwig J. Pongratz, ed., *Psychotherapie in Selbstdarstellungen*, p. 292.

11. Those who joined the NSDAP in 1933 included Göring and his wife Erna, Otto Curtius, Walter Cimbal, Werner Achelis, Carl Haeberlin, Gustav Schmaltz, Franz Brendgen, and Eckart von Sydow. Gustav Richard Heyer, Ernst Speer, Hans Krisch, and Lene Credner joined in 1937. Heinrich von Kogerer, head of the Vienna branch of the Göring Institute, joined the party in 1938. See BDC: NSDAP-Zentralkartei. See also Hans Mommsen, *Beamtentum im Dritten Reich*, Schriftenreihe der Vierteljahreshefte für Zeitgeschichte, no. 12 (Stuttgart: Deutsche Verlagsanstalt, 1966), pp. 57–59; and Dietrich Orlow, *The History of the Nazi Party 1933–1945*, pp. 202–5. See also Broszat, *Hitler State*, p. 237, n. 35.

12. Ellenberger, *Discovery*, p. 608.

13. Fritz Künkel, Fragebogen für Mitglieder, Reichsverband Deutscher Schriftsteller, e.V., 20 December 1933, p. 1; idem, Fragebogen zur Bearbeitung des Aufnahmeantrages für die Reichsschriftumskammer, 25 May 1938, p. 2; BDC: Kulturkammer; and BDC: Reichsärztekammer.

14. See Kenneth D. Barkin, *The Controversy over German Industrialization, 1890–1902* (Chicago: University of Chicago Press, 1970), p. 278. See also Fritz Künkel, *Krisenbriefe. Die Beziehungen zwischen Wirtschaftskrise und Charakterkrise.* (Schwerin i. Meckl: F. Bahn, 1932).

15. Otto Kohlreutter quoted in Hubert Schorn, *Der Richter im Dritten Reich: Geschichte und Dokumente* (Frankfurt: Vittorio Klostermann, 1959), p. 81.

16. Fritz Künkel, "Die Lehrbarkeit der tiefenpsychologischen Denkweisen," p. 238. See also Hans Alfred Grunsky, *Seele und Staat. Die psychologischen Grundlagen des nationalsozialistischen Sieges über den bürgerlichen und bolschewistischen Menschen* (Berlin: Junker & Dünnhaupt, 1935), pp. 22, 65.

17. Helmut Fabricius, "Gemeinschaftspsychologie," pp. 11–12; and Wolfgang Kloppe, "Die Lebenskunst bei Carl Gustav Carus," *Medizinische Monatsschrift* 30 (1976): 499–506. See also Fritz Künkel, "Psychotherapie: Eine Übersicht."

18. Hans Prinzhorn, *Psychotherapie*, p. 15. On Prinzhorn, psychotherapy, and National Socialism, see Albert Moll, *Ein Leben als Arzt der Seele. Erinnerungen* (Dresden: Carl Reissner, 1936), pp. 64–66.

19. Fritz Künkel, "Individualpsychologie und Psychoanalyse," in Eliasberg,

Bericht, pp. 61–71. See also Johannes Heinrich Schultz, *Psychotherapie,* p. 180.

20. Ellenberger, *Discovery,* p. 627.

21. Prinzhorn, *Psychotherapie,* p. 16.

22. Charles Spearman, "German Science of Character II," *Character and Personality* 6 (1937): 48.

23. Fritz Künkel, *Charakter, Einzelmensch und Gruppe,* p. iii.

24. Künkel, "Die dialektische Charakterkunde," p. 74.

25. Fritz Künkel, *Psychotherapie und Seelsorge,* Arzt und Seelsorger, ed. Carl Schweitzer, no. 1 (Schwerin i. Meckl.: F. Bahn, 1926), pp. 7, 25.

26. Künkel, "Die dialektische Charakterkunde," p. 84.

27. Fritz and Elisabeth Künkel, *Die Erziehung deiner Kinder,* p. 7.

28. Fritz Künkel, "Seelenheilkunde," p. 396. Künkel's interest in child development, shared by his wife Elisabeth, is evidenced by the twelve editions of his study on adolescence, *Jugendcharakterkunde; Theorie und Praxis des Erwachsenswerdens* (Schwerin i. Meckl.: F. Bahn, 1930).

29. See Kemper's account in Pongratz, *Psychotherapie,* p. 282.

30. Matthias Heinrich Göring, "Individuum und Gemeinschaft im Reich der Psychologie," pp. 286–87.

31. Göring, "Grundlagen der Psychotherapie," p. 1445. Göring's text was originally given as an address to the Berlin Medical Society on 12 May 1937. See also *Zeitschrift für ärztliche Fortbildung* 34 (1937): 426; and ibid. 35 (1938): 49–50; and idem, "Der Einfluss der Religion bei Zwangsneurosen," in Kretschmer and Cimbal, *Bericht,* pp. 223–26. On Adler, goals, and *Gemeinschaft,* see "Generaldiskussion VIII. Allgemeiner ärztlicher Kongress für Psychotherapie in Bad Nauheim 1935," *ZfP* 8 (1935): 360–65. Cf. the complete rejection of Adler in favor of Nietzsche in Gerhard Eggert, "Nietzsche und die Individualpsychologie."

32. See Künkel, Fragebogen zur Bearbeitung des Aufnahmeantrages, p. 2; idem, Fragebogen für Mitglieder, p. 2; and idem to Reichsschriftumskammer, 25 May 1938; BDC: Kulturkammer. All publications in the field of medicine, as opposed to those written for a general audience, fell under the supervision of the Reich Physicians Chamber.

33. Elisabeth Künkel to Reichsschriftumskammer, 18 November 1939. BDC: Kulturkammer. Künkel's fascination with the American West was widely shared; see Ray Allen Billington, *Land of Savagery, Land of Promise: The European Image of the American Frontier* (New York: W. W. Norton, 1981).

34. See, among many others, Fritz Künkel, *God Helps Those . . . Psychology and the Development of Character* (New York: Washburn, 1931). Künkel eventually founded a short-lived institute in Los Angeles.

35. See *New York Times,* 2 April 1956, 23:5.

36. See "Dr. Leonhard Seif, geboren 15.1.1866," *ZfP* 12 (1941): 321–22; and Lene Credner, "Geleitwort zur Neuherausgabe," in Leonhard Seif, ed., *Wege der Erziehungshilfe. Ergebnisse und praktische Hinweise aus der Tätigkeit des Münchener Arbeitskreises für Erziehung,* 2nd ed. (Munich: J. F. Lehmanns, 1952), pp. 8–11. Both Freud and Jung, as well as Adler, seemed impressed by Seif's dedication and intelligence. See Freud, *Freud/Jung Letters,* pp. 214, 224, 226, 233, 257, 267, 280, 329, 410, 417, 420, 444, 513, 520, 521.

37. Leonhard Seif, "Volksgemeinschaft und Neurose," pp. 54, 60. Lene Credner, a member of Seif's circle, in 1940 correctly even if obsequiously de-

fined the interest of the Nazi leadership in what was known among the psychotherapists as psychagogy: "Our National Socialist state provides an example of this writ large: We are experiencing a conscious educational effort directed at the young, unparalleled in history." Lene Credner, "Vererbung und Erziehungsberatung," in Seif, *Erziehungshilfe* (1940), p. 81. On psychagogy as an agent of fascist political conditioning of the masses, see Serge Tchakotine, *Le Viol des foules par la propagande politique* (Paris: Gallimard, 1939). Tchakotine's definition and analysis of psychagogy was limited, however, by a Pavlovian perspective. See also George Frederick Kneller, *The Educational Philosophy of National Socialism* (New Haven: Yale University Press, 1941). For a succinct dismissal of Nazi pedagogues Alfred Bäumler and Ernst Krieck, see Ringer, *German Mandarins*, p. 442.

38. Leonhard Seif, "Erziehung der Erzieher," in Seif, *Erziehungshilfe*, p. 32. See also Matthias Heinrich Göring, "Erfolgsmöglichkeiten der Psychotherapie"; August Hanse, "Ärztliche Seelenführung"; and Fritz Künkel, *Das Wir*.

39. Seif, "Volksgemeinschaft und Neurose," p. 60. See also "Dr. Leonhard Seif," p. 321, wherein his differences with Adler are perhaps exaggerated by editors Göring and Bilz in the anti-Semitic spirit of a loyal Germanic psychotherapy. Cf. Credner, "Geleitwort zur Neuherausgabe," pp. 8–9.

40. BDC: Parteikorrespondenz.

41. Heyer, "Lebenslauf," p. 4.

42. Ibid., p. 6. See also BDC: Reichsärztekammer.

43. Gustav Richard Heyer, *Praktische Seelenheilkunde*, p. 113.

44. In 1932 Jung spoke positively of Heyer's "aggressive temperament." See C. G. Jung, *Letters*, p. 113. Heyer-Grote sees the branding of Heyer as a Nazi a function of his direct manner and jealousy over his favor in Jung's eyes. Göring's son, Ernst, was studying at the University of Munich at the same time Heyer was there and clashed with him. Carl Müller-Braunschweig's son, Hans, claims that Heyer was often in uniform at the institute. See Zapp, "Psychoanalyse und Nationalsozialismus," p. 65. Müller-Braunschweig did not say whether the uniform was that of a party organization or a military one. It was certainly the latter, since there is no record of Heyer being a member of any party organization that had a uniform, but he was a member of the military reserve and served as a physician at the Greater Berlin Reserve Military Hospital beginning in 1942. Zoe Heyer to the author, 1 March 1983.

Both of Heyer's wives have claimed that Heyer was no racist. Heyer-Grote asserts that he joined the Nazi party only to work within it for improvement, while Zoe Heyer (in a letter to the author of 19 April 1983) maintains that her husband joined only after long reflection, and then, as in his approach to everything, did it wholeheartedly. It is true that most intellectuals in Germany were probably too smart to believe genuinely in Nazi racist cant and in fact, were, as we have noted before, busily overestimating their influence and rationalizing their actions. But at the same time we cannot ignore an intellectual and cultural heritage that incorporated, among other things, an ethnocentric and anti-Semitic bias. We also cannot ignore the willingness of such individuals as Heyer to engage in racist rhetoric out of whatever combination of conviction, fear, and opportunism moved them to do so. Heyer, according to his second wife, considered joining the party as early as 1930. This fact, coupled with Heyer's anti-Semitic rhetoric during the Third Reich (see below, Chapter 4; and "Lebenslauf," pp. 6, 7), casts doubt on the assertion that Heyer was free of bias toward the Jews inside and outside of his profession. On Heyer and Hess, see Göring to Cimbal, 10 March 1934, Kl. Erw. 762; Bundesarchiv.

45. Gustav Richard Heyer, "Zur Psychologie des Ostraumes," *Zeitschrift für Geopolitik* 19 (1942): 309–15. Heyer's essay was studied by an undetermined Nazi organization concerned with the East and praised as a cultural jeremiad, but it was also criticized for its unsupported generalizations about the Russian character. See Miscellaneous German Records Collection, Microcopy T-84, Roll 294, frames 872–78; National Archives. See also BDC: Reichsärztekammer.

46. See, for example, Leonardo Conti, "Körperliche Erziehung als biologische Aufgabe des Staates," *Staatsmedizinische Abhandlungen* 6 (1935) : 17. In the new professional, political, and philosophical context, performance (*Leistung*) and productivity (*Leistungsfähigkeit*) became equated with happiness.

47. Harald Schultz-Hencke, "Lebenslauf" (Berlin-Wilmersdorf, 3 July 1944), p. 1. BDC: Parteikorrespondenz. See also BDC: Reichsärztekammer.

48. Ibid., pp. 1–2.

49. Harald Schultz-Hencke, "Die heutigen Aufgabe der Psychotherapie als Wissenschaft," *Allgemeine ärztliche Zeitschrift für Psychotherapie und psychische Hygiene* 1 (1928): 238–52.

50. Harald Schultz-Hencke, "Psychoanalyse und Individualpsychologie," in idem, *Psychoanalyse und Psychotherapie. Gesammelte Aufsätze,* pp. 11–14. See also Eliasberg, *Bericht,* p. 207.

51. See Ellenberger, *Discovery,* pp. 640–41. See also Harald Schultz-Hencke, *Der Gehemmte Mensch;* and Hans Kunz, "Der gehemmte Mensch: Bemerkungen zu dem gleichnamigen Buche von H. Schultz-Hencke," *Der Nervenarzt* 14 (1941): 201–14, 241–60.

52. Schultz-Hencke, "Lebenslauf," p. 1. See also idem, "Das Unbewusste in seiner mehrfachen Bedeutung," *ZfP* 12 (1941): 336–49; and idem, *Die Überwindung der Parteien durch die Jugend, Das Wollen der neuen Jugend: Eine Auseinandersetzung mit den Grundfragen der Zeit,* ed. Harald Schultz-Hencke, vol. 1 (Gotha: Perthes, 1921).

53. Harald Schultz-Hencke, "Die Tüchtigkeit als psychotherapeutisches Ziel," p. 85. See also Zapp, "Psychoanalyse und Nationalsozialismus," pp. 129–65.

54. Schultz-Hencke, "Die Tüchtigkeit als psychotherapeutisches Ziel," pp. 85, 91, 95–97. See comments in the review by R. Blum in *Ziel und Weg* 4 (1934): 466. After the war Schultz-Hencke came in for a great deal of criticism for having appropriated Nazified terms and ideals in his essay: Helmut Thomä, "Die Neo-Psychoanalyse Schultz-Henckes: Eine historische und kritische Betrachtung," *Psyche* 17 (1963): 44–128. See also Carl Müller-Braunschweig, "Skizze der Geschichte der 'Deutschen Psychoanalytischen Gesellschaft' von 1936 bis 1947," p. 25; Pongratz, *Psychotherapie,* pp. 318, 559–60; cf. Baumeyer, "Psychoanalyse in Deutschland," pp. 216–19; Chrzanowski, "Psychoanalysis," pp. 497–98; and Spiegel, "Survival," p. 484.

55. Werner Kemper, "John F. Rittmeister zum Gedächtnis," *Zeitschrift für psychosomatische Medizin und Psychoanalyse* 14 (1968): 147–49; Pongratz, *Psychotherapie,* pp. 276, 281. See also John Rittmeister, "Die mystische Krise

des jungen Descartes," *Zeitschrift für psychosomatische Medizin und Psycho-analyse* 15 (1969) : 206–24, the text of an address given at the Göring Institute early in 1942.

56. John F. Rittmeister, "Voraussetzungen und Konsequenzen der Jung-schen Archetypenlehre" [1936–37], *Psyche* 36 (1982): 1032–44. See also Ludger M. Hermanns, "John F. Rittmeister und C. G. Jung," p. 1026.

57. See Elisabeth Brainin and Isidor J. Kaminer, "Psychoanalyse und Na-tionalsozialismus," pp. 990, n. 3, 991, 996, n. 7. Wilhelm Reich was the most notorious example of this trend in his attempt to merge psychoanalysis with communism. From exile in Norway he condemned not only Jung but the psy-choanalysts for collaborating with the Nazis. See *Zeitschrift für politische Psy-chologie und Sexualökonomie* 1 (1934): 59. The same political persuasions and resultant difficulties also obtained among psychoanalysts in Austria. See Hans-Martin Lohmann and Lutz Rosenkötter, "Psychoanalyse in Hitler-deutschland," p. 972; and Marie Langer, "Psychoanalyse in wessen Dienst?" *Neues Forum* 18 (1971): 39–42. See also Wolfgang Huber, *Psychoanalyse in Österreich seit 1933*, pp. 26–28, 179–81; and Muriel Gardiner, *Code Name "Mary": Memoirs of an American Woman in the Austrian Underground* (New Haven: Yale University Press, 1983).

58. Ernst Bloch, *Erbschaft dieser Zeit* [1935] (Frankfurt a.M.: Suhrkamp, 1973), p. 344; and pp. 84, 345–51.

59. Hermanns, "Rittmeister und C. G. Jung," p. 1024. See also Manfred Schultz, "Dr. John Rittmeister. Nervenarzt und Widerstandskämpfer" (Medi-cal dissertation, Wilhelm Humboldt University, Berlin, 1981).

60. John F. Rittmeister, "Tagebuchblättern aus dem Gefängnis," p. 23.

61. Hermanns, "Rittmeister und C. G. Jung," p. 1024.

62. Heinz Höhne, *Codeword: Direktor. The Story of the Red Orchestra,* trans. Richard Barry (London: Secker & Warburg, 1971), p. 127.

63. Rittmeister, "Tagebuchblättern," p. 18.

64. Ibid., pp. 25, 18, 17.

65. Ibid., pp. 19, 25. For a definitive statement on his humanistic ideals, see John F. Rittmeister, "Die psychotherapeutische Aufgabe und der neue Humanismus," *Psyche* 22 (1968): 934–53. Kranefeldt claims he quit the insti-tute in 1943 after Göring told him of Rittmeister's execution.

66. See, for example, "In Memoriam: Aus den Tagebuchblättern des Dr. John Rittmeister, aufgezeichnet im Gefängnis in der Zeit vom 26.9.42 bis zum Tage seiner Hinrichtung am 13.5.43," *Zeitschrift für Psychoanalyse* 1 (1949): 60–66. This journal was edited by Carl Müller-Braunschweig. Many psycho-therapists have remained critical of Rittmeister on patriotic grounds, a ten-dency that was aggravated in the 1960s in West Germany when a number of books appeared "exposing" the notorious ties of the Schulze-Boysen group to the hated Kremlin. On his status in East Germany, see Chapter 7.

67. See Rittmeister, "Tagebuchblättern," pp. 2, 3, 4, 6, 10, 12, 31, 32.

68. Ibid., p. 4. See also pp. 3, 4, 15, 21.

69. Ibid., p. 26. Rittmeister, while studying in Munich in 1922, went to Hattingberg for psychotherapy and established a close relationship with him. This association ended abruptly and bitterly in 1930, presumably over philo-sophical and political differences. Eva Hildebrand to the author, 4 March 1983.

70. Hans von Hattingberg, "Lebenslauf" (Berlin, c. 1940), pp. 1–3.

71. "Aktuelles" (1944). See also Pongratz, *Psychotherapie,* p. 289.

72. Hans von Hattingberg, "Zur Problematik des Führertums," p. 142. See also Seif, "Volksgemeinschaft und Neurose," p. 60.

73. Hans von Hattingberg, *Über die Liebe,* p. 357.

74. Wladimir Eliasberg, *Arzt und Propaganda: ein Stück medizinische Soziologie aus der ärztlichen Wirklichkeit* (Vienna: Saturn-Verlag, 1936).

75. See Hattingberg, "Neue Richtung, Neue Bindung," p. 102.

76. See, for example, Hans von Hattingberg, "Der neue Weg der Psychoanalyse," *Medizinische Klinik* 21 (1925): 849–51; and idem, "Zur Analyse der analytischen Situation," *Internationale Zeitschrift für Psychoanalyse* 10 (1924): 34–56.

77. Hans von Hattingberg, "Zur Entwicklung der analytischen Bewegung."

78. Ibid., p. 330.

79. Pongratz, *Psychotherapie,* p. 287.

80. Decker, *Freud in Germany,* p. 78.

81. See Johannes Heinrich Schultz, *Hypnose-Technik; praktische Anleitung zum Hypnotisieren für Ärzte* (Jena: Gustav Fischer, 1935).

82. Schultz, *Lebensbilderbuch,* p. 106; and BDC: Reichsärztekammer.

83. Johannes Heinrich Schultz, "Seelische Schulung," p. 315. See also idem, "Der nervöse Zustand."

84. Johannes Heinrich Schultz, "Der Yoga und die deutsche Seele," pp. 67–69.

85. Johannes Heinrich Schultz, *Psychiatrie, Psychotherapie und Seelsorge, Arzt und Seelsorger,* ed. Carl Schweitzer, vol. 2 (Schwerin i. Meckl.: F. Bahn, 1926), p. 14. See also Eugen von Grosschopf, *Die seelische Behandlung kranker Menschen. Grundlagen und Grundfragen schöpferischer Psychotherapie* (Leipzig: O. Gmelin, 1940).

86. Johannes Heinrich Schultz, "Über kleine Psychotherapie," p. 72. See also Gerhart Scheunert, "Über Psychotherapie Kurzbehandlungen"; Klaus Wegscheider, "Psychotherapie bei Kassenpatienten"; and Schultz, "Die Bedeutung primitivaktiver Methoden in der Psychotherapie mit besonderer Berücksichtigung der Behandlung Alkoholkranker," *ZfP* 9 (1936): 193–200. Beyond their practical medical aims and effects, such processes are common to the "political reeducation" that occurs in totalitarian systems. Robert Jay Lifton describes four basic approaches to reeducation: coercion, exhortation, therapy, and realization. See Lifton, *Thought Reform and the Psychology of Totalism* (New York: W. W. Norton, 1961), pp. 458–61.

87. Fritz Mohr, "Brief an eine durch Fliegerangriff stillunfähig gewordene Mutter," p. 1016. See also Matthias Heinrich Göring, *Über seelisch bedingte echte Organerkrankungen;* idem, "Körperliche Erkrankungen als Auswirkungen seelischer Störungen"; and Rudolf Bilz, *Pars pro Toto. Ein Beitrag zur Pathologie menschlicher Affekte* (Leipzig: S. Hirzel, 1940). See also Lockot, "Erinnern und Durcharbeiten," p. 261.

88. Erik H. Erikson, "The Legend of Hitler's Childhood," in Erikson, *Childhood and Society,* 2nd ed. (New York: W. W. Norton, 1963), p. 30.

89. Johannes Heinrich Schultz, "Über tiefenpsychologische Kurzbehandlungen," p. 29.

90. See Hans Krisch, "Die Lehrbarkeit der psychotherapeutischen Wissen-

schaft"; Fritz Künkel, "Die Lehrbarkeit der tiefenpsychologischen Denk-weisen"; and I. H. Schultz, "Ist Psychotherapie lehr- und lernbar?" During the period, articles by physicians from throughout Germany and Austria reporting on the use of such methods of *kleine* psychotherapy appeared regu-larly in the medical journals. See, for example, W. Leschmann, "Psychother-apie in der Allgemeinpraxis," *Münchener medizinische Wochenschrift* 79 (1932): 1319–22; W. Enke, "Neurosenverhütung in der allgemeinen ärztlichen Praxis," in Otto Curtius, ed., *Psychotherapie in der Praxis,* pp. 175–89; and Ludwig Mayer, *Die Psychotherapie des praktischen Arztes* (Munich: J. F. Leh-mann, 1939).

91. See Johannes Heinrich Schultz, *Neurose, Lebensnot und ärztliche Pflicht,* a collection of essays from the *Deutsche medizinische Wochenschrift.*

92. See Johannes Heinrich Schultz, "Praktischer Arzt und Hypnose"; Hans von Hattingberg, *Neue Seelenheilkunde,* pp. 44–45; and Fritz Künkel, "Das Hausarzt und Psychotherapie."

93. Johannes Heinrich Schultz, *Die seelische Gesunderhaltung,* p. 48. This was the basis for Schultz's positive review of Roland Freisler's book on divorce law. See *ZfP* 11 (1939): 122.

94. BDC: Reichsärztekammer and Parteistatistische Erhebung. See Werner Achelis, *Das Problem des Traumes, eine philosophische Abhandlung,* Schriften zur Seelenforschung, ed. Carl Schneider, vol. 20 (Stuttgart: J. Püttmann, 1928).

95. Werner Achelis, "Psychologische Zivilisationsbilanz," p. 60. See Werner Hollmann's review of Karl Pintschovious and Heinrich Zeiss, eds., *Zivilisa-tionsschäden am Menschen,* which appeared in *ZfP* 14 (1942): 98–101. Achelis was inspired by Blüher's work on the homosexual bonds uniting young men's associations. On Blüher and the German Youth Movement as purveyors of a conservative and nationalist etherealization of homosexuality, see George Mosse, "Nationalism and Respectability: Normal and Abnormal Sexuality in the Nineteenth Century," *Journal of Contemporary History* 17 (1982): 237, 240.

96. Achelis, "Psychologische Zivilisationsbilanz," p. 73.

97. Achelis, "Psychologische Hygiene," pp. 263–64.

98. Hans Dietrich-Röhrs, "Biologischer Sozialismus," *Die Gesundheitsführ-ung* "*Ziel und Weg*" 4 (1942): 181–88.

99. See Werner Achelis, "Politische Schulung und die Frage der Gesin-nungsschulung als rassenpsychologisches Problem," in Otto Curtius, "Kongress der allgemeinen ärztlichen Gesellschaft für Psychotherapie," p. 358; and "Kongress für Psychotherapie in Breslau," p. 1067.

100. Buchholz, "Aufbau der Gesinnung und des Kameradschaftgeistes," ad-dress to the Breslau congress of the German General Medical Society for Psy-chotherapy in 1935. See Curtius, "Kongress," p. 359; and "Kongress für Psy-chotherapie in Breslau," p. 1067. See also Mosse, *Nazi Culture,* p. 349.

101. Gerhard Wagner, "Der Weg zu einer neuen deutschen Heilkunde," p. 5.

102. August Hanse, *Persönlichkeitsgefüge und Krankheit,* p. 146. See Wer-ner Kemper's review: *ZfP* 12 (1941): 361–62.

103. Franz Brendgen, "Vegetative Stigmatisation und Neurose," p. 91.

104. Helmut Peil, "Über die Hysterie," p. 6. See also J. Hobohm, "Der Nationalsozialismus als Überwinder des Zeitalters der Neurose."

105. Johannes Neumann, *Leben Ohne Angst,* pp. 8, 172. See also ibid., pp. 142–43.

106. See, for example, Leonardo Conti, "Mehr Vollkornbrot! Aufruf zur Mitarbeit an der Vollkornbrotaktion," *Deutsches Ärzteblatt* 70 (1940): 310; "Coca-Cola, das grosse Fragezeichen," *Volksgesundheitswacht* 6 (1939): 127–28; and the request by the NSDAP Main Office for National Health for information on the possible deleterious effects of Coke and other soft drinks in *Deutsches Ärzteblatt* 70 (1940): 142. See also Rudolf Hess, "Arzt und Heilweise," in Hess, *Reden* (Munich: Franz Eher, 1938), pp. 259–62, the text of an address to the twelfth international congress of homeopaths in Berlin on 9 August 1937; and Gerhard Wagner's introduction to Louis Grote and Alfred Brauchle, *Gespräche über Schulmedizin und Naturheilkunde* (Leipzig: P. Reclam, jun., 1935).

107. Carl Haeberlin, "Lebensrhythmus und Lebensführung"; idem, "Aus der Praxis der Konstitutionstherapie," *Hippokrates* 5 (1934): 469–74. See also Vogt, "Die Behandlung nervöser und seelischer Krankheiten in Bad und Kurorten," in "Kongress für Psychotherapie in Breslau," p. 1066; Adolf Hoff, "Gesundungshäuser für das deutsche Volk," *Hippokrates* 12 (1941): 435–37; and Walter Cimbal, *Naturgemässe Wege und Heilwege der Biochemie und Naturheilkunde* (Berlin: F. Duberow, 1940).

108. Gerhard Wagner, "Neue deutsche Heilkunde," pp. 419–20.

109. Hildegard Hetzer, "Ordnung als eine Frage der Gesundheit," *Die Ärztin* 15 (1939): 56–57. See also Hetzer and Gertrud Noelle, "Lebensordnung und Lebensrhythmus im Kindergarten," *Zeitschrift für Kinderforschung* 47 (1939): 271–93; and Hetzer, *Kindheit und Armut: Psychologische Methoden in Armutsforschung und Bekämpfung,* 2nd ed. (Leipzig: S. Hirzel, 1937).

110. Franz Wirz, "Lebensbeanspruchung und Lebensgestaltung," *Hippokrates* 10 (1939): 627–31. See also Heyer's review in *ZfP* 12 (1941): 358.

111. See Johannes Heinrich Schultz, *Das autogene Training. konzentrative Selbstentspannung. Versuch einer klinischpraktischen Darstellung,* 5th ed. (Leipzig: Georg Thieme, 1942); and idem, *Übungsheft für das autogene Training,* 5th ed. (Leipzig: Georg Thieme, 1943). See also Kretschmer, *Gestalten und Gedanken,* pp. 179–82.

112. BDC: NSDAP-Zentralkartei and Reichsärztekammer. His wife, Josephine, joined the Nazi party in 1932.

113. Rudolf Bilz, *Lebensgesetze der Liebe,* pp. 54, 74.

114. Ibid., p. 80.

115. Walter Cimbal, "Aufgaben und Wege einer deutschen Seelenheilkunde," p. 111.

116. BDC: NSDAP-Zentralkartei.

117. On family demographics in Nazi Germany, see Grunberger, *12-Year Reich,* pp. 235–50.

118. Cimbal, "Aufgaben und Wege," p. 111. See also Hans von Hattingberg, "Ehekrisen, ärztlich gesehen"; and idem, "Die Eheproblematik unserer Zeit und der Entwicklungsgedanke."

119. Cimbal, "Aufgaben und Wege," p. 117; Lockot, "Erinnern und Durcharbeiten," pp. 93–100, 103–5, 200–201, 356.

120. Stern, "Political Consequences," p. 18.

121. Carl Haeberlin, *Deutsche Einheit. Rede bei der von der Stadt Bad-*

Nauheim veranstalteten Reichsgründungsfeier am 18. Januar 1921 gehalten von Dr. med. Carl Haeberlin (Bad Nauheim: H. Burk, 1921).

122. BDC: Reichsärztekammer; BDC: NSDAP-Zentralkartei.

123. Haeberlin, "Klages und Prinzhorn," p. 44.

124. Prinzhorn, *Psychotherapie*, p. 25.

125. Ibid., p. 295.

126. As a philosopher and graphologist, Klages was a prominent figure in the revival of vitalism, which reached its height in Germany between 1895 and 1915. Klages celebrated life and instinct over civilization and reason, positing an equation of "mind as adversary of the soul" (*"Geist als Widersacher der Seele"*). Character for Klages was the innate but variable balance between spirit and soul before the modern emergence of the ego and personality. Thus he was in the tradition of that life philosophy (*Lebensphilosophie*), pioneered by his teacher Dilthey, which stressed cultural immediacy and the fullness of life. For a Nazi panegyric, see "Wir stehen zu Klages," *Wille und Macht* 6 (1938): 1–6.

127. Haeberlin, "Klages und Prinzhorn," p. 44.

128. Ibid., p. 49.

129. Ibid., p. 39.

130. Carl Haeberlin, *Lebensrhythmen und Heilkunde. Entwurf einer biozentrischen ärztlichen Betrachtung* (Stuttgart: Hippokrates, 1935).

131. Johannes Heinrich Schultz, *Die Schichksalsstunde der Psychotherapie,* Abhandlungen aus dem Gebiete der Psychotherapie und medizinische Psychologie, ed. Albert Moll, vol. 1 (Stuttgart: F. Enke, 1925). Ernest Jones notes that Schultz had made a "serious attempt" in 1909 to come to an understanding of psychoanalysis, but that his attitude remained "negative." Jones, *Freud,* 2:119–20. See Schultz's typically comprehensive and broad-minded essay, "Psychoanalyse, die Breuer-Freud'sche Lehre, ihre Entstehung und Aufnahme," *Zeitschrift für angewandte Psychologie* 2 (1909): 440–97; reprinted as "Psychoanalyse und ihre Kritik," in Curt Adam, ed., *Die Psychologie und ihre Bedeutung für die ärztliche Praxis. Acht Vorträge* (Jena: Gustav Fischer, 1921), pp. 73–103. See also Freud, *Freud/Jung Letters,* p. 209; and Schultz, *Lebensbilderbuch,* p. 58.

For a Roman Catholic review of the strengths and weaknesses of *"nationale deutsche Psychotherapie,"* see Albert Niedermeyer, *Handbuch der speziellen Pastoralmedizin,* 6 vols. (Vienna: Herder, 1952) 5:230–40.

4. PERIL AND OPPORTUNITY

1. "Die Psychoanalyse des Juden Sigmund Freud," p. 15. (Italics in original.) See Gumpert, *Heil Hunger!,* pp. 46–47; Baumeyer, "Psychoanalyse in Deutschland," p. 206; and Boehm, "Bericht," p. 2.

2. Christian Jansenn, "Die Reform der Psychoanalyse durch C. G. Jung," in "Wider die Psychoanalyse," *Kritische Gänge: Literaturblatt der Berliner Börsen-Zeitung,* 14 May 1933, p. 2.

3. Dietrich Aigner, *Die Indizierung "schädlichen und unerwünschten Schrifttums" im Dritten Reich,* Sonderdruck aus dem *Archiv für Geschichte*

des Buchwesens (Frankfurt a.M.: Buchhändler-Vereinigung, 1971), pp. 937, 999–1000. See also Zapp, "Psychoanalyse und Nationalsozialismus," p. 39.

4. Edmund Finke, "Siegmund Freud: Studien zum europäischen Nihilismus." See also H. Finck, "Volksgesundheit und Liebesleben."

5. Carl Müller-Braunschweig, "Psychoanalyse und Weltanschauung," p. 22, quoted in Elisabeth Brainin and Isidor J. Kaminer, "Psychoanalyse und Nationalsozialismus," p. 995; and Lohmann and Rosenkötter, "Psychoanalyse in Hitlerdeutschland," p. 964. See also Müller-Braunschweig, "Psychoanalyse und Weltanschauung" (1931); and *Psyche* 37 (1983): 1116–45.

6. Dräger, "Psychoanalysis in Hitler Germany," p. 205; and Spiegel, "Survival," p. 485.

7. Jones, *Freud*, 3:188.

8. Jung to Gauger, 14 May 1936. For an account of the Jungians in Munich and in Berlin, see Käthe Bügler, "Die Entwicklung der analytischen Psychologie in Deutschland," in Fordham, *Contact with Jung*, pp. 23–32.

9. See *Reichsärzteordnung* (Berlin & Vienna: Reichsgesundheitsverlag, 1944).

10. Heinrich Lammers, "Ergebnis des Vortrages beim Führer am 14. Juni 1937 in Gegenwart von Reichsleiter Bormann," R 43, II (Medizinalwesen) 733, p. 43. Bundesarchiv. On at least one occasion Hitler remarked to Wagner that among all academics doctors were most important to the state. See Hans-Dietrich Röhrs, *Hitlers Krankheit*, pp. 71–72.

11. "Wortlaut der 4. Verordnung des Führers und Reichskanzlers zum Reichsbürgergesetz," *Reichsgesetzblatt* (1938): 679–80; Lockot, "Erinnern und Durcharbeiten," pp. 232, 303.

12. See, for example, "Die Juden in der Berliner Ärzteschaft," *Deutsches Ärzteblatt* 66 (1936): 1046. See also Gerhard Wagner, "Anordnung betreffend Unterscheidung zwischen jüdischen und night-jüdischen Ärzte," *Reichsgesetzblatt* (1936): 237–38; and Siegfried Ostrowski, "Zur Lage der Berliner Jüdischen Ärzteschaft unter dem Hitlerregime von 1933–Ende August 1939," p. 2, File 01/16; Yad Vashem Archives (also as: "Vom Schicksal Jüdischer Ärzte im Dritten Reich. Ein Augenzeugenbericht aus den Jahren 1933–39," *Bulletin des Leo Baeck Instituts* 6 (1963): 313–51).

13. J. Tas, "Psychical Disorders Among Inmates of Concentration Camps," *Psychiatric Quarterly* 25 (1951): 679–90.

14. Herman Pineas to the author, 25 June 1981. See also "10. Verordnung zum Reichsbürgergesetz 4. Juli 1939," *Reichsgesetzblatt* (1939): 642–43; "Aufnahme jüdischer Geisteskranker in Heil- und Pflegeanstalten," *Reichsgesetzblatt* (1941): 37–38; and idem (1942): 906; and Raul Hilberg, *The Destruction of the European Jews* (Chicago: Quadrangle, 1961), pp. 122–24, 303–4.

15. Max Schur, *Freud: Living and Dying* (New York: International Universities Press, 1972), p. 496. See also Pongratz, *Psychotherapie*, pp. 275–76.

16. Jones, *Freud*, 3:217–26. See also Ronald W. Clark, *Freud: The Man and the Cause* (New York: Random House, 1980), p. 510; Anton Sauerwald, "Bericht" (Vienna, 21 March 1938); Gerhard Maetze, "Psychoanalyse in Deutschland," in *Die Psychologie des 20. Jahrhunderts*, vol. 2: *Freud und die Folgen (I)*, ed. Dieter Eicke (Zurich: Kindler, 1976), p. 1171; and Huber, *Psychoanalyse in Österreich*, pp. 52–56.

17. *Münchener medizinische Wochenschrift* 85 (1938): 1095. See also Der

Reichskommissar für die Wiedervereinigung Österreichs mit dem deutschen Reich, Stab Stillhaltekommissar für Vereine, Organisationen und Verbände, to Polizeidirektor Wien, 25 August 1938. Sigmund Freud-Gesellschaft, Vienna.

Richard Sterba, one of the few non-Jewish members of Freud's circle in Vienna, has a more critical view of Müller-Braunschweig's role in the German takeover of the Vienna Psychoanalytic Society. See Sterba, *Reminiscences,* p. 165. Sterba does report, however, that Müller-Braunschweig wanted him to return from Basel to help conduct the operations of the Vienna society, a recollection that is in line with Müller-Braunschweig's reported desire to maintain a psychoanalytic presence in the Austrian capital. Ernest Jones, according to Sterba (pp. 163–64, 165–66), had also wished him to remain in Vienna—because, as Sterba later learned from Helene Deutsch's autobiography, Jones wanted the psychoanalytic movement to be headquartered in London, with Sterba as the representative in Vienna who would be racially acceptable to the Nazis and thus able to perpetuate its existence. See Helene Deutsch, *Confrontations with Myself: An Epilogue* (New York: W. W. Norton, 1973), p. 170. See also Huber, *Psychoanalyse in Österreich,* pp. 54–55.

On the efforts of a number of foreign colleagues to help Austrian psychoanalysts in escaping from Austria after the *Anschluss,* see Walter C. Langer and Sanford Gifford, "An American Analyst in Vienna During the *Anschluss,* 1936–1938," *Journal of the History of the Behavioral Sciences* 14 (1978): 37–54.

18. Günter Grass, *The Tin Drum,* trans. Ralph Manheim (New York: Pantheon, 1961), p. 116.

The private circulation of Freud's works among members of the institute was not affected by Göring's lockup. See Lohmann and Rosenkötter, "Psychoanalyse in Hitlerdeutschland," p. 986; and Pongratz, *Psychotherapie,* p. 41. Moreover, in 1938 the institute also expressed the hope that some of the forty-five boxes of books that the SD had taken from the International Psychoanalytic Press in Vienna would find their way into the institute's library. It is not clear whether this happened. See "Tätigkeitsbericht 1938," p. 4. It was clearly the institute's understanding, apparently a correct one, that the books were not to be destroyed. See Huber, *Psychoanalyse in Österreich,* p. 181, n. 26. Only the books by August Aichhorn and Marie Bonaparte were not seized. See Huber, *Psychoanalyse in Österreich,* p. 179, n. 27. Werner Kemper claims that all but two copies of each book taken from the press were destroyed. See Pongratz, *Psychotherapie,* p. 276.

For a list of meetings and discussion topics of the DPG from 1935 to 1944, see Baumeyer, "Psychoanalyse in Deutschland," pp. 211–15.

19. *Ziel und Weg* 4 (1934): 464–67. See also Zapp, "Psychoanalyse und Nationalsozialismus," pp. 201–3, 212; and the review of *Deutsche Seelenheilkunde* by Heyer in *Hippokrates* 5 (1934): 432.

20. *Ziel und Weg* 8 (1938): 284. See also Zapp, "Psychoanalyse und Nationalsozialismus," p. 212.

21. Walter Cimbal, *Naturgemässe Wege zum seelischen Gleichgewicht,* p. 137. See also C. Luchsinger, "Psychotherapie."

22. See Victor Klemperer, *Die unbewältigte Sprache. Aus dem Notizbuch eines Philologen "LTI"* (Darmstadt: Joseph Melzer, 1966), pp. 279–80. See ibid., pp. 286–87.

23. Gustav Richard Heyer, "Leben und Erkennen: Gedanken zu einer deutschen Seelenkunde," *Suddeutsche Monatshefte* 33 (1936): 281.

24. Gustav Richard Heyer, *Der Organismus der Seele* (1932 and 1937), pp. 99, 100, 107, 108, 90–91, 81.

25. Bumke, *Psychoanalyse und ihre Kinder*, p. 2. Bumke also did not hesitate to sponsor a dissertation on psychoanalysis and criminality written by a member of a Nazi group that was studying "Jewish influence" in psychiatry and psychology. See Adolf Stelzle, *Das Verbrechen in der Auffassung der Psychoanalyse*, Hervorgegangen aus der Arbeitsgemeinschaft: Einfluss des Judentums in der Psychologie, Psychiatrie und in den Grenzgebieten zwischen Medizin und Rechtspflege (Dachau: Steinberger, 1940), p. 24. See *National-sozialistische Bibliographie* 7:11/12 (November/December 1942), p. 14, entry 63. And even a friend of psychotherapy like Hans Luxenburger could assert to his psychiatry colleagues that the teachings of Freud and Adler remained "Jewish" no matter how much "German" camouflage or decoration was applied. See Luxenburger, "Rückblick auf die wissenschaftlichen Sitzungen der II. Jahresversammlung der Gesellschaft Deutscher Neurologen und Psychiater in Frankfurt am Main, 22.–25. VIII, 1936," *Deutsche medizinische Wochenschrift* 62 (1936): 1702. See also Zapp, "Psychoanalyse und National-sozialismus," pp. 218–20.

26. Zilboorg, *Medical Psychology*, p. 497.

27. Jones, *Freud*, 2:111. See also Oswald Bumke, "Über Psychoanalyse," *ZfP* 3 (1930) : 650–64; and Decker, *Freud in Germany*, pp. 164–65.

28. Reichsleitung des Rassenpolitischen Amtes der NSDAP, "Richtlinien für die Beurteilung der Erbgesundheit des RMdI 18.7.40," quoted in Ernst Illing, "Asoziale Jugend," *Medizinische Zeitschrift* 1 (1944): 24.

29. Hans Reiter, "Dem neuen Jahrgang zum Geleit," *Monatsschrift für Kriminalbiologie* 28 (1937): 1–2.

30. See Gerald Reitlinger, *The Final Solution: The Attempt to Exterminate the Jews of Europe 1939–1945* (New York: A. S. Barnes, 1953), pp. 126–33. See also Heinz Boberach, ed., *Meldungen aus dem Reich. Auswahl aus den geheimen Lageberichten des Sicherheitsdienstes der SS 1939–1944* (Munich: Deutscher Taschenbuch Verlag, 1968), pp. 192–95, 214–15; and Hull, *Film in the Third Reich*, pp. 200–203.

31. Werner Hoffmann, "Die erbbiologischen Ergebnisse in der Neurosenlehre," in Ernst Rüdin, ed., *Erblehre und Rassenhygiene im völkischen Staat* (Munich: J. F. Lehmanns, 1934), p. 194n.

32. "Tätigkeitsbericht 1937," p. 205. See also Ludwig J. Pongratz, ed., *Psychiatrie in Selbstdarstellungen* (Bern: Hans Huber, 1977), pp. 304–5.

33. Johannes Heinrich Schultz, "Das Leib-Seele Problem in der Heilkunde," p. 292. See also idem, "Psychopathie und Neurose," *Forschungen und Fortschritte* 17 (1941): 228–29.

34. Matthias Heinrich Göring, "Eröffnungsansprache," in Curtius, *Psychotherapie in der Praxis*, p. 3. On Hattingberg's promotion, see Friedrich Wilhelm Universität, Personal- und Vorlesungsverzeichnis, Trimester 1941, p. 39; his "Lebenslauf" and Antrag zur Bearbeitung der Aufnahme als Mitglied der Reichsschriftumskammer, Gruppe Schriftsteller, 7 November 1940; BDC: Kulturkammer.

35. See Hans Luxenburger, "Die Indikation zur Psychotherapie der Neuro-

sen vom Standpunkt der Erbbiologie"; and Max Mikorey, "Über die Grenzen der Psychotherapie," *Medizinische Klinik* 35 (1939): 922–27. Mikorey worried about "Jewish influence" in criminal psychology. See Stelzle, *Das Verbrechen,* pp. 21–22; and Weinreich, *Hitler's Professors,* p. 40.

36. Otto Pötzl, "Hemmung und Ermüdung," in Bilz, *Psyche und Leistung,* pp. 156–73. See also Huber, *Psychoanalyse in Österreich,* pp. 12–14, 29, 52, 131–32, and 175, n. 21.

37. "Feierlicher Auftakt im Rudolf-Hess-Krankenhaus," *Ziel und Weg* 4 (1934): 447–49.

38. August Hanse, "Konstitution, Biozentrische Gesundheitsführung und Volksbezogenheit," p. 801.

39. Hattingberg, *Neue Seelenheilkunde,* pp. 42–43.

40. Achelis, "Psychologische Zivilisationsbilanz," p. 81. See also Scheunert, "Über Psychotherapie Kurzbehandlungen," p. 206, n. 2; and Schultz, *Lebensbilderbuch,* p. 131.

41. Carl Schneider, "Zukunft der psychiatrischen Therapien," p. 3.

42. Gumpert, *Heil Hunger!,* pp. 43–44.

43. Schneider, "Zukunft der psychiatrischen Therapien," p. 6. See also Ostmann, "Völkische Psychiatrie," *Deutsches Ärzteblatt* 63 (1933): 164–65.

44. Johannes Bresler, "Gibt es nationale Psychotherapie?"

45. Der Höhere SS- und Polizeiführer in Frankreich/SS Führer im Rasse- und Siedlungswesen, "Gedanken über eine SS-mässige Fürsorge: Fürsorge und Weltanschauung." BDC: SS-Führer.

46. Bormann to Himmler, October 1944, R 18, folder 2983. Bundesarchiv.

47. Wilhelm Schmitz and Gerhart Schramm, "Unfallneurose und Reichsgericht."

48. Rieff, *Moralist,* p. 241.

49. Herbert Marcuse, "Critique of Neo-Freudian Revisionism," in idem, *Eros and Civilization: A Philosophical Inquiry Into Freud* (Boston: Beacon, 1955), p. 257.

50. Paul Roazen, *Erik H. Erikson: The Power and Limits of a Vision* (New York: Free Press, 1976), p. 172. It was precisely the most radical social and political theoreticians in the Freudian movement who finally lost out to the "conservative" trend in psychoanalysis with the advent of Hitler. See Russell Jacoby, *The Repression of Psychoanalysis: Otto Fenichel and the Political Freudians* (New York: Basic Books, 1983), p. 77.

51. Erich Fromm, "The Social Philosophy of 'Will Therapy,'" *Psychiatry* 2 (1939): 233. See also Martin Birnbach, *Neo-Freudian Social Philosophy* (Stanford: Stanford University Press, 1961); and Isabel V. Hull, "The Bourgeoisie and its Discontents: Reflections on 'Nationalism and Respectability,'" *Journal of Contemporary History* 17 (1982): 255–57.

52. Ladislas Farago, ed., *German Psychological Warfare,* p. 270. See also Decker, *Freud in Germany,* pp. 245–46; and Freud, *Freud/Jung Letters,* p. 247. On Stransky's paper, see Zapp, "Psychoanalyse und Nationalsozialismus," pp. 105–6.

53. Erwin Stransky, "Rasse und Psychotherapie," pp. 23–24, 27. Viktor Frankl, a Viennese colleague of Stransky's, struck a different note on the same theme in an essay published in the *Zentralblatt* in 1937. Frankl argued that psychotherapy could never represent a world view, but that a world view

could serve as a means of therapy. See Viktor E. Frankl, "Zur geistigen Problematik der Psychotherapie," *ZfP* 10 (1937): 33–45; and Huber, *Psychoanalyse in Österreich,* pp. 31–32.

On the founding of the short-lived (1936–38) Austrian branch of the International General Medical Society for Psychotherapy, see *ZfP* 10 (1937): 7–8; and Huber, *Psychoanalyse in Österreich,* pp. 29–30, 32.

54. Matthias Heinrich Göring, "Die Bedeutung der Neurose in der Sozialversicherung," p. 46.

55. See Reichsinstitut für Psychologische Forschung und Psychotherapie im Reichsforschungsrat, "Richtlinien der Poliklinik," p. 7; Wegscheider, "Psychotherapie bei Kassenpatienten," pp. 57–58; Scheunert, "Über Psychotherapie Kurzbehandlungen," p. 219; Matthias Heinrich Göring, "Bericht über das Deutsche Institut für Psychologische Forschung und Psychotherapie vom 1. Oktober 1938 bis 30. September 1939," in Göring, ed., *1. Sonderheft des Deutschen Instituts für Psychologische Forschung und Psychotherapie,* p. 4; and "Tätigkeitsbericht 1938," p. 4.

56. Göring, "Neurose in der Sozialversicherung," pp. 49, 50.

57. Hans Hoske, *Die menschliche Leistung als Grundlage des totalen Staates,* p. 28. See review in *ZfP* 10 (1938): 195.

58. Viktor von Weizsäcker, "Über sogennante Unfallenneurosen," p. 222; and idem, "Ärztliche Aufgaben," pp. 85, 87, 88, 89. See also Paul Christian, "Rechtswissenschaft, Ursachenbegriff und Neurosenfrage," p. 319.

59. See F. Gl., "Das Arbeitspsychologische Institut der DAF," *Betriebsführer und Vertrauensrat* 9 (1942): 117–18; Friedrich Koch, "Über Arbeitsneurosen," *Münchener medizinische Wochenschrift* 86 (1939): 1161–64; and Franz Neumann, *Behemoth: The Structure and Practice of National Socialism 1933–1944* (Oxford: Oxford University Press, 1944), pp. 298–303.

60. See, for example, Harald Schultz-Hencke, "Das Problem der Psychopathie," in Schultz-Hencke, *Psychoanalyse and Psychotherapie,* pp. 236–45, a lecture given at the Göring Institute in April 1944. See also Decker, *Freud in Germany,* pp. 325–29.

61. Eric J. Leed, *No Man's Land: Combat and Identity in World War I* (London: Oxford University Press, 1979), pp. 63–92.

62. Matthias Heinrich Göring, "Abfassen von Zeugnissen und Gutachten," in "Jahresbericht 1940 des Deutschen Instituts für Psychologische Forschung und Psychotherapie," pp. 34–37; and R 18, folder 5585. The general professional and political care necessary was also reflected in Göring's observation that psychotherapists could diagnose cases for the military and for industry but under no circumstances render an opinion on the individual's fitness for military service or work. Ibid., p. 35.

63. Kretschmer, *Gestalten und Gedanken,* p. 158; Oswald Bumke, *Erinnerungen,* pp. 145–46; and Pongratz, *Psychotherapie,* pp. 191–92. See also Broszat, *Hitler State,* pp. 292–93, n. 57. When, in 1941, the SS research organization Ahnenerbe approached Rüdin's psychiatric research institute to aid in its research in racial biology, SD chief Reinhard Heydrich killed the offer with the judgment that Rüdin was not acceptable for membership in the SS. See Michael H. Kater, *Das "Ahnenerbe" der SS 1935–45. Ein Beitrag zur Kulturpolitik des Dritten Reiches* (Stuttgart: Deutsche Verlags-Anstalt, 1974), p. 206. See also Frankl, "Zur geistigen Problematik der Psychotherapie."

Among the psychotherapists, Ernst Göring claims there are documents proving his father's involvement with the protection of those slated for sterilization and execution, but these documents have not come to light. There is documentary evidence, however, that suggests the regime was unhappy with the attitude of the directors of the Bethel institution toward the state's program of sterilization and euthanasia. See Microcopy T-1021, Roll 11, frame 291; National Archives.

Recent research into the role of psychiatry in the Nazi attempt at euthanasia and sterilization of the incurably insane, while further documenting the cooperation and lack of opposition of many psychiatrists, has uncovered a number of instances of successful resistance by psychiatrists and relatives of those mental patients so threatened under Nazi law. See Dirk Blasius, "Psychiatrischer Alltag im Nationalsozialismus," in Detlev Peukert and Jürgen Reulecke, eds., *Die Reihen fest geschlossen. Beiträge zur Geschichte des Alltags unterm Nationalsozialismus.* (Wuppertal: Peter Hammer, 1981), pp. 367–80.

64. Robert Sommer, "Beziehungen der Psychotherapie zur Psychiatrie und psychischer Hygiene," in "Kongress für Psychotherapie in Breslau," p. 1064.

65. Matthias Heinrich Göring, "Die nationalsozialistische Idee in der Psychotherapie," p. 12; translation after Ralph Manheim.

66. Kurt Delius, "Ergänzungen zur Adgo und Preugo für das Gebiet des Facharztes für Neurologie und Psychiatrie" (Dortmund, September 1933), p. 4; and Delius to C. G. Jung, 18 October 1933.

67. See Hans Luxenburger, "Rückblick auf die wissenschaftliche Sitzungen der III. Jahresversammlung der Gesellschaft Deutscher Neurologen und Psychiater, München, 20.–23. IX 1937," *Deutsche medizinische Wochenschrift* 63 (1937): 1750–52.

68. "Tätigkeitsbericht 1935/36," p. 5. Rüdin, a friend of Göring's, had refused an early Nazi charge to dissolve the General Medical Society for Psychotherapy. Kretschmer briefly headed a section for psychotherapy in Rüdin's society. See Lockot, "Erinnern und Durcharbeiten," pp. 82–86, 100, 106–14, 242–43, 336–54.

69. Paul Schröder, "Kinderpsychiatrie und Heilpädagogik," *Zeitschrift für Kinderforschung* 49 (1941): 11–12.

70. See Ernst Rüdin to P. Nitsche, 6 February 1941, and Nitsche to Rüdin, 25 July 1941, T-1021, frames 368–69, 434. In 1941 eight of the eleven members of the society's board were psychiatrists; the other three were neurologists. See "Bericht 6.8.41," ibid., frame 459. Still, Rüdin worried about the threat to psychiatry even from neurology. See Rüdin to Linden, 24 July 1941, ibid., frames 450–51. On the problems in arranging the Munich meeting, see Rüdin to Linden, 28 March 1941, ibid., frame 366.

71. See "Tagesordnung," T-1021, frames 512–15; see also frame 507; and frame 474. Besides Schultz, the psychotherapists on the program were Gottfried Kühnel, Hattingberg, Mohr, Schultz-Hencke, and John Rittmeister. Schultz had also attended the 1939 congress in Wiesbaden, where he gave a lecture. See ibid., frames 522–23. It is significant that while twenty-two medical journals carried notices about the 1941 congress, the *Zentralblatt* did not. See ibid., frame 508.

72. See "Bericht über die 1. Tagung der Deutschen Gesellschaft für Kinderpsychiatrie und Heilpädagogik," pp. 1–118, published in book form under

the editorship of Werner Villinger by Julius Springer of Berlin in 1941. See Göring's review in *ZfP* 13 (1942): 382–83. Cf. Göring, "Eröffnungsansprache," p. 9.

73. See Rüdin to Reiter, 23 May 1941, T-1021, frame 386. See also ibid., frames 387–94, 450–51. Schröder died unexpectedly in the early summer of 1941, and Rüdin was actively involved through correspondence with Reiter and Linden in the selection of his successor in order to ensure, as he phrased it to Linden, that child psychiatry did not "slip away" from psychiatry. See ibid., frames 387–91.

74. Bumke, *Erinnerungen,* p. 123.

75. Dozentenführer der Universität Tübingen Dr. Usadel to Rektor Stickl, 6 January 1945. BDC: Parteikorrespondenz. There was, however, disagreement about Kretschmer's suitability for the chair of psychiatry and neurology at Tübingen. The rector and the medical faculty listed him as their first choice (Stickl to Kultusministerium, Stuttgart, 10 January 1945). A Lieutenant Bennhold of Karl Brandt's staff at Hitler's headquarters held the criticisms of Kretschmer's politics "totally unjustified" in light of his scientific contributions. See also Kretschmer, *Gestalten und Gedanken,* pp. 150–67; and Clark, *Man and Cause,* p. 492. Clark's brief observation that Kretschmer quit because of the imposition of Nazi control over psychoanalysis is true but incomplete and misleading.

76. Jung, *Letters,* p. 163. See also "Presidential Address to the 8th General Medical Congress for Psychotherapy, Bad Nauheim, 1935," in Jung, *Civilization,* pp. 554–56. Jung expressed the same sentiments in a letter to Kurt Gauger on 16 April 1936.

77. Quoted in Rüdin to Nitsche, frame 368.

78. Jung, *Letters,* p. 124. Eliasberg left for Vienna in 1933, fled to Prague in 1938, and to the United States the following year. Sommer remained as honorary president until his death in 1937.

79. See Matthias Heinrich Göring, "Mitteilung des Reichsführers der 'Deutschen allgemeinen ärztlichen Gesellschaft für Psychotherapie,'" *ZfP* 7 (1934): 140–41; and Cimbal, "Bericht des Geschäftsführers," pp. 141–44; and Lockot, "Erinnern und Durcharbeiten," pp. 89–90, 190. Cimbal, ill and in disfavor, was replaced as managing director of the German General Medical Society for Psychotherapy by Otto Curtius in 1935. Curtius became secretary of the body in 1937, its chief office now that the institute handled finances. Carl Haeberlin became Göring's deputy for the society the same year, but resigned that post in 1939, while Curtius stayed on until the society's last congress in 1940, retiring to Schliersee in Bavaria in 1944.

80. See Alexander and Selesnick, *Psychiatry,* p. 407; and Clark, *Man and Cause,* pp. 491–94. Cf. "Kongress für Psychotherapie in Breslau," p. 1068; Curtius, *Psychotherapie in der Praxis,* p. 4; and Curtius, *Psyche und Leistung,* p. 10. Schultz has said simply that the psychotherapists chose Göring under the pressure of circumstances in a secret meeting of representatives from the various groups of psychotherapists. See Schultz, *Lebensbilderbuch,* p. 131. Schultz would be loath to admit, of course, that the psychotherapists were ordered by the authorities to install Göring, but again there is no evidence that either the party or the government reached that deeply into the affairs of the psychotherapists.

81. Pongratz, *Psychotherapie*, pp. 273–74; Cimbal, "Bericht des Geschäftsführers," p. 142; and Lockot, "Erinnern und Durcharbeiten," pp. 86, 119–20, 186–87.

82. Joachim C. Fest, *The Face of the Third Reich*, p. 78. See also Roger Manvell and Heinrich Frankel, *Hermann Göring* (New York: Simon & Schuster, 1962), pp. 114–16, 268–69. On the clan gathering in Berlin in 1938, see Willi Frischauer, *The Rise and Fall of Hermann Göring* (Boston: Houghton Mifflin, 1951), p. 148.

83. Emmy Göring, *An der Seite meines Mannes* (Göttingen: K. W. Schütz, 1967), chart following p. 110.

84. C. G. Jung, Otto Curtius, and C. A. Meier, "Prof. Dr. M. H. Göring zum 60. Geburtstag," *ZfP* 11 (1939): 193–94. See Peter Göring, *Vorarbeit zu einer Geschichte der Sippe*, pp. 320–21.

85. Matthias Heinrich Göring, *Die Individualpsychologie als Werkzeug der Bibelbetrachtung*, p. 16. See also Cimbal, ed., *Bericht*, p. 161. On pietism, conservatism, and nationalism, see Koppel Pinson, *Pietism as a Factor in the Rise of German Nationalism* (New York: Columbia University Press, 1963).

86. Matthias Heinrich Göring, "Erfolgsmöglichkeiten der Psychotherapie," p. 227.

87. Matthias Heinrich Göring, "Die Kraft der Seele," p. 1076. See also idem, "Weltanschauung und Psychotherapie," (1936), p. 295, (1938), 1102; and idem, "Schlussansprache," in Curtius, *Psychotherapie in der Praxis*, p. 49. "Weltanschauung und Psychotherapie" was the text of an address given at the inaugural meeting of the Göring Institute membership and to the 1937 workshop of the German National Health League (Verein Deutsche Volksheilkunde) in Munich. See *Nationalsozialistische Bibliographie* 4:1/2 (January/February 1939), p. 64, entry 277. See also *Wiener medizinische Wochenschrift* 89 (1939) : 723–24.

88. Cimbal, *Bericht*, p. 161.

89. Göring, "Grundlagen der Psychotherapie," p. 1445.

90. Matthias Heinrich Göring, "Deutsche Seelenheilkunde." See *Nationalsozialistische Bibliographie* 4:1/2 (January/February 1939), p. 64, entry 276. See also "Neue Wege der Heilkunde. 2. Tagung der Deutschen Gesellschaft für Psychotherapie in Düsseldorf," *Völkischer Beobachter*, 2 October 1938, p. 5; and Herbert Gold, "Auch die ersten Kindheitseinflüsse bestimmen die Lebensgestaltung."

91. See "Mitteilung des Reichsführers," pp. 140–41; and "Bericht über den VII. Kongress für Psychotherapie," *ZfP* 7 (1934): 133. See also Hattingberg, "Fortschritte der Psychotherapie." Hattingberg did not attend this congress, as he was in Ann Arbor lecturing at the University of Michigan.

92. One former member of the institute, psychologist Wolfgang Hochheimer, recalls Göring making the demand for suspension of medical confidentiality at a meeting of the full membership in 1941 or 1942. Hochheimer claims that none of the psychotherapists voiced an objection. Wolfgang Hochheimer to the author, 30 September 1981. Assuming Hochheimer is correct, it is likely that Göring was responding to a Hitler decree of 1942 that ordered such a suspension in instances of treasonous statements or breaches of national security. Hochheimer's own inquiries after the war elicited from those who had been present the view that any objection would have meant the

threat of reprisal. This probably says less about Göring and the institute as a whole (even Hochheimer admits to Göring's general good-naturedness) than about the danger posed by some more radical Nazi members of the institute and the general wisdom of keeping one's own counsel in public on such matters. In addition, and in agreement with the eyewitness accounts of the 1944 meeting by Gerhard Maetze and Käthe Dräger, silence could also have meant opposition as well as a considerable degree of confidence that even in the unlikely event of Göring really pressing ahead for implementation of the Führer's order, such implementation would be impossible to enforce. We simply do not know what Göring did, or would have done, in such cases with his own patients. See Hitler's order on 23 December 1942 to "Ärzte, Heilpraktiker und Zahnärzte"; and the letter from Conti to Leiter der Gauämter für Volksgesundheit der NSDAP, "Führerordnung über Aufhebung der Schweigepflicht in besonderen Fällen," 9 January 1943; BDC: Reichsärztekammer, folder 213. The inclusion of the phrase "in special cases" indicates the resistance the Nazis recognized would be forthcoming from the medical profession. At the same time, the force of Hitler's decree was unqualified in intent, though compromised by the incomplete organizational and individual Nazification of the professions in Germany.

93. Baumeyer, "Psychoanalyse in Deutschland," p. 217; and Pongratz, *Psychotherapie*, p. 318.

94. Schultz, *Lebensbilderbuch*, p. 139.

95. Gerhard Adler to the author, 3 September 1980. See also Achelis, "Gesinnungsschulung als rassenpsychologisches Problem," in Curtius, "Kongress," p. 358; and "Kongress für Psychotherapie in Breslau," p. 1067.

96. "Satzungen der deutschen allgemeinen ärztlichen Gesellschaft für Psychotherapie," pp. 1–2.

97. Göring, "Mitteilung des Reichsführers," p. 140.

98. Review of Göring, *Über Seelisch bedingte echte Organerkrankungen*, in *Ziel und Weg* 9 (1939): 455–56. See also Zapp, "Psychoanalyse und Nationalsozialismus," p. 213; and Göring's reviews in *ZfP* 9 (1936): 297–98, 307–8; ibid. 10 (1938): 301.

99. Geuter, "Der Leipziger Kongress," pp. 9–10.

100. Microcopy T-84, Roll 6, frame 5303. National Archives. See also Lockot, "Erinnern und Durcharbeiten," p. 245.

101. See Schleunes, *Twisted Road*, pp. 128–29; and Hilberg, *Destruction*, pp. 50–53.

102. BDC: Parteikorrespondenz. See also Heinrich von Kogerer, *Psychotherapie* (Vienna: Maudrich, 1934).

103. Gauger, *Politische Medizin*, p. 27. See "Bericht" (1934), p. 129. See also the noncommital review of Gauger's book in *Der Öffentliche Gesundheitsdienst* 1 (1935): 618–19; and the excerpt in Mosse, *Nazi Culture*, pp. 215–17.

104. Kurt Gauger, "Lebenslauf" (Berlin, 27 June 1938), Reichsschriftumskammer Fragebogen/Anlage. BDC: Kulturkammer. See also the curriculum vitae in Gauger, "Über den Einfluss des Duodenalsaftes auf die Zuckervergärung" (Inaugural dissertation, Berlin, 1932).

105. See Sigmund Freud, "On Narcissism: An Introduction" (1914), in Freud, *Collected Papers*, 4:30–59.

106. Kurt Gauger, *Christoph: Roman einer Seefahrt*, p. 52.

107. Ibid., p. 60. But the surname Fählmann is even more revealing of Gauger's character since it translates as "failed" *(fehlen)*, with a suggestion of "able" *(fähig)*, "man."

108. Kurt Gauger, Personalfragebogen für die Auslegung der SA-Personalakte, Berlin, 12 January 1937, p. 4. BDC: SA. He dropped mention of this association the following year. See Fragebogen zur Bearbeitung des Aufnahmeauftrages für die Reichsschriftumskammer, Berlin, 26 June 1938. BDC: Kulturkammer.

109. See Alfred Bauer, *Deutscher Spielfilm Almanach 1929–1950* (Berlin: Filmblätter Verlag, 1950), pp. 273–74. The film is currently part of the Janus Collection, available in the United States through Films Incorporated. See also Lockot, "Erinnern und Durcharbeiten," p. 259.

110. See "Jahresbericht des Deutschen Instituts für Psychologische Forschung und Psychotherapie" (1941), p. 63; "Tätigkeitsbericht 1940," p. 3; and the review of *Christoph* in *ZfP* 14 (1942): 228–29.

111. Kurt Gauger, *Herz und Anker: Seemannsgeschichten* (Stuttgart: Hohenstaufen-Verlag, 1943), pp. 82–88. After the war, however, Gauger was able to establish a psychotherapy practice, first in Munich and then in Düsseldorf. See idem, *Die Dystrophie als psychosomatische Krankheitsbild* (Munich: Urban & Schwarzenberg, 1952); idem, *Psychotherapie und Zeitgeschehen. Abhandlungen und Vorträge* (Munich: Urban & Schwarzenberg, 1954); and idem, *Dämon Stadt* (Düsseldorf: Droste-Verlag, 1957).

112. Jung, *Letters*, pp. 131–32.

113. See "Grundversammlung der Überstaatlichen Allgemeinen Ärztlichen Gesellschaft für Psychotherapie," *ZfP* 7 (1934): 134–38; and Jung, *Letters*, p. 135. The international statutes made the president's decisions and actions contingent on the approval of the executive committee. See also Jung, *Civilization*, pp. 547–48. The eighth General Medical Congress for Psychotherapy was held in Bad Nauheim in 1935.

114. Jung, *Letters*, p. 156. See also "Circular Letter," in Jung, *Civilization*, pp. 545–46. See also Cimbal, "Bericht des Geschäftführers," p. 143; and Jung to James Krisch, 26 May 1934, in Jung, *Letters*, p. 161.

115. Kretschmer, *Gestalten und Gedanken*, pp. 133–36; Ellenberger, *Discovery*, p. 740, n. 57. See also Jung, *Letters*, pp. 160–61.

116. C. G. Jung, "An Interview on Radio Berlin," in Jung, *C. G. Jung Speaking*, p. 60.

117. Barbara Hannah, *Jung: His Life and Work*, p. 211. Franz Jung has also recalled this incident. It is possible, of course, that Göring had a hand in this. Hannah *thinks* it was Curtius but is not absolutely certain (p. 211n). She also implies that Curtius (or whoever) saw a chance that Jung might have been able to "cure" Goebbels of his obvious neuroses (p. 211n), but the more likely, or at the very least the more compelling, motivation was the protection of psychotherapy by using Jung.

118. Alfred A. Krauskopf, "Tiefenpsychologische Beiträge zur Rasenseelenforschung," p. 362.

119. Ibid., pp. 362n, 368. See *Nationalsozialistische Bibliographie* 4:5 (May 1939), p. 35, entry 131. See also *Nationalsozialistische Bibliographie* 8:6/8 (June/July/August 1943), p. 10, entry 51: Frederik Adama van Scheltema, "Mutter Erde und Vater Himmel in der germanischen Naturreligion," *ZfP* 14 (1943): 257–77.

120. Otto Curtius and C. A. Meier, "Prof. Dr. C. G. Jung zum 60. Geburtstag," *ZfP* 8 (1935): 146.

121. Jung, *Letters*, p. 184. See also Jung, "Votum C. G. Jung," *Schweizerische Ärztezeitung für Standesfragen* 16 (1935); and idem, "Contribution to a Discussion on Psychotherapy," in Jung, *Civilization*, pp. 557–60.

122. Jung, *Letters*, p. 188.

123. See Jung to Parelhoff, 17 December 1951, quoted in Paul Roazen, *Freud and His Followers* (New York: Alfred A. Knopf, 1973), p. 293.

124. Jung, "Interview on Radio Berlin," p. 65. See also Jung, *Wirklichkeit der Seele* (Zurich: Rascher, 1934), p. 1n.

125. C. G. Jung, "Geleitwort," *ZfP* 6 (1933): 139; and "Editorial (1933)," in Jung, *Civilization*, pp. 533–34.

126. Jung, *Letters*, p. 146.

127. Gustav Bally, "Deutschstämmige Psychotherapie," p. 2. Jung was widely criticized for his position. See B. Cohen, "Ist C. G. Jung 'gleichgeschaltet'?" *Israelitisches Wochenblatt für die Schweiz*, 16 March 1934; and Jung to Cohen, 26 March and 28 April 1934, in Jung, *Letters*, pp. 154–55, 159–60; see also pp. 156–72.

128. C. G. Jung, "Zeitgenössisches," *Neue Zürcher Zeitung*, 13 & 14 March 1934, p. 1; and "A Rejoinder to Dr. Bally," in Jung, *Civilization*, p. 536.

129. C. G. Jung, "Zur gegenwärtigen Lage der Psychotherapie," pp. 9–10; and "The State of Psychotherapy Today," in Jung, *Civilization*, pp. 157–73. In the translation by R. F. C. Hull, the word "Aryan" is capitalized and rendered in quotation marks (pp. 165–66), while in the original the word appears as a lowercase adjective (*arisch*) without quotation marks.

130. C. G. Jung, "Wotan," *Neue Schweizer Rundschau*, March 1936; and in Jung, *Civilization*, p. 185.

131. Jung, *Letters*, p. 276.

132. Ibid., p. 238; and C. A. Meier to the author, 12 July 1980.

133. Ibid., p. 130. See also Egon Freiherr von Eickstedt, *Grundlagen der Rassenpsychologie* (Stuttgart: F. Enke, 1936).

134. Göring, "Bericht," p. 5; idem, "Aktuelles," *ZfP* 12 (1940): 194–95; idem, "Bericht der internationalen Gesellschaft," *ZfP* 13 (1941): 1; and "Jahresbericht 1941," p. 74. In 1938 Göring wrote to Viennese psychoanalyst August Aichhorn that "German psychotherapy" was "neither something Jewish (Freud, Adler) nor something Alpine (Jung)." See Huber, *Psychoanalyse in Österreich*, p. 61.

135. Matthias Heinrich Göring, "Internationale allgemeine ärztliche Gesellschaft für Psychotherapie," *Deutsches Ärzteblatt* 67 (1937): 1099. See also the programs for the ninth congress printed in *ZfP* 10 (1937): 1–3, 65–68; Oluf Brüel, "Bericht über den IX. Internationalen ärztlichen Kongress für Psychotherapie in Kopenhagen, 2.–4. Oktober 1937," *ZfP* 10 (1938): 133–38; and Jung, "Presidential Address to the 9th International Medical Congress for Psychotherapy, Copenhagen, 1937," in Jung, *Civilization*, pp. 561–63. Göring's claims also held for the eighth congress held in Bad Nauheim in 1935, as shown in "Entwurf für den Aufbau des 8. psychotherapeutischen Kongresses in Bad Nauheim vom 11.–13. April 1935." On the "foreign policy" of Göring and the German psychotherapists, see Zapp, "Psychoanalyse und Nationalsozialismus," pp. 66–67; and Lockot, "Erinnern und Durcharbeiten," pp. 142–43, 355–88, 410–24.

136. Jung, *Letters,* p. 275. See also Jung to van den Hoop, 26 October 1940, ibid., pp. 286–88. On the last international congress, see Hans von Hattingberg, "Bericht über den X. Internationalen ärztlichen Kongress für Psychotherapie in Oxford," *ZfP* 11 (1939): 1–6; and "Vorläufige Mitteilung über den X. Internationalen ärztlichen Kongress für Psychotherapie," *ZfP* 10 (1938): 197–99; and, as an example of continuing intellectual contact, a translation of an article by E. A. Bennet in the *British Journal of Medical Psychology,* "Der Individualismus in der Psychotherapie," *ZfP* 11 (1939): 329–46. See also the "non-report" of the German General Medical Society for Psychotherapy for 1939, "Tätigkeitsbericht 1939."

5. BETWEEN PARTY AND STATE

1. See "Satzungen des Nationalsozialistischen Deutschen Ärztebund," (Nuremberg, 7 December 1940), Nationalsozialistischer Deutscher Ärztebund, NSDAP Hauptarchiv, Reel 83, folder 1702; Hoover Institution.

2. See Arthur Gütt, "Vorwort," *Der Öffentliche Gesundheitsdienst* 1 (1935): 1–2; *Deutsches Ärzteblatt* 63 (1933): 653; and Wilhelm Frick, *Aufbau und Aufgaben des Reichsausschusses für Volksgesundheitsdienst* (Berlin Reichsdrückerei, 1936).

3. August Fleck, "Wichtige Bekanntmachung," *N.S. Gesundheitsdienst* 2 (1934). 1.

4. "Der öffentliche Gesundheitsdienst," *Der Öffentliche Gesundheitsdienst* 1 (1935), chart following p. 326; and Fleck in *N.S. Gesundheitsdienst* 2 (1934): 1–3. See also Reichs- und Preussisches Ministerium des Innern, *Handbuch für das Deutsche Reich,* vol. 46 (Berlin: C. Heymann, 1936), pp. 132–33.

5. Frick to Lammers, September 1937, R 18, folder 5581. See also "Entwurf eines Gesetzes, betreffend Vereinheitlichung des Gesundheitswesens," II 1000a/28.10.33 IV, R 18, folder 5581. See also Heinz Spranger, "Übersicht über die Organisation und die Aufgaben der Reichsärztekammer," *Der Öffentliche Gesundheitsdienst* 2 (1936): 951.

6. "Vereinheitlichung des Gesundheitswesens—Begründung," (1 October 1934) R 43 II/717, pp. 40–43. For the Chancellery's position on Wagner's demands, see Lammers, "Aufzeichnung für die Besprechung über Fragen auf dem Gebiete des Gesundheitswesens am 18. Mai 1938," R 43 II/733, pp. 101–2. In 1937 the Foreign Ministry had complained to the Chancellery that Wagner's attempts to coordinate health policy with Italy represented an intolerable party intrusion into the Reich's foreign policy. See Staatssekretär von Mackensen to Lammers, 15 October 1937, and Lammers to Haedenkamp, 26 September 1937, R 43 II/717, p. 79. On the failure of "revolutionary foreign policy," see Broszat, *Hitler State,* pp. 215–21.

7. "Verbot impfgegnerischer Propaganda," *Reichs-Gesundheitsblatt* 9 (1934): 449–50; and *Deutsches Ärzteblatt* 65 (1935): 133–34.

8. See "Grundlagen einer Deutscher Volksgesundheit aus Blut und Boden. 12 Leitsätze," *Deutsche Volksgesundheit aus Blut und Boden* 1 (1933): 4; and "Die Deutsche Gesellschaft zur Bekämpfung des Kurpfuschertums—eines der dunkelsten Kapitel der seitherigen Medizinal-Politik," ibid. 2 (1934): 20.

9. "Mit vereinigten Kräften vorwärts!" *Deutsche Volksgesundheit aus Blut*

und Boden 3 (1935): 5–6; and Karl Kötschau, *Zum nationalsozialistischen Umbruch in der Medizin*, p. 7.

10. Wagner, "Neue deutsche Heilkunde," p. 419.

11. "Tätigkeitsbericht 1935/36," p. 4. Otto Curtius also participated in the meeting as a discussant. See "Reichsarbeitsgemeinschaft für eine neue deutsche Heilkunde," *Deutsches Ärzteblatt* 66 (1936): 357; and Walter Griesbeck, "Zur ersten Tagung der Reichsarbeitsgemeinschaft für eine neue deutsche Heilkunde," *Deutsches Ärzteblatt* 66 (1936): 421–22. Griesbeck was Hörmann's deputy in Munich.

12. Wagner and Göring, "Auflösung der Reichsarbeitsgemeinschaft für eine neue deutsche Heilkunde," *ZfP* 9 (1936): 258–59; see also *Hippokrates* 8 (1937): 1. Representatives of both Wagner (Dr. Peschke) and Reiter (Dr. Kresiment) had attended the first congress of the German General Medical Society for Psychotherapy in Breslau in 1935. Göring complained of the unscientific nature of the Reich Study Group. See Lockot, "Erinnern und Durcharbeiten," p. 243.

13. Stephen Roberts, *The House That Hitler Built* (New York: Harper & Row, 1938), pp. 85, 80.

14. See Gerhard Wagner, "Dienstanweisung Hauptamtes für Volksgesundheit der NSDAP" (Munich, 29 December 1934); BDC: Parteikorrespondenz; Fritz Bartels, "Die Gesundheitsführung des deutschen Volkes"; and Orlow, *Nazi Party*, pp. 67–70, 126, 149, 165.

15. Müller-Braunschweig, "Skizze der Geschichte," p. 17; Boehm, "Bericht," pp. 303–4; Jung, Curtius, and Meier, "M. H. Göring," p. 194; Pongratz, *Psychotherapie*, p. 273; and "Tätigkeitsbericht 1935/36," p. 5. Boehm does not identify the official within the Interior Ministry with whom he negotiated. He sets the official founding date of the institute as 14 June 1936. The society's report for 1935–36 declares May as the month of the institute's founding, as does Müller-Braunschweig; Jung, Curtius, and Meier say simply "summer 1936," while Kemper sets the date as 26 June. The role of Boehm (and Müller-Braunschweig) in the "coordination" of the DPG has been the subject of much controversy and debate. See, for example, Lohmann and Rosenkötter, "Psychoanalyse in Hitlerdeutschland," pp. 963–72, 976–78; Brainin and Kaminer, pp. 990–93, 996–97; and Müller-Braunschweig, "Skizze der Geschichte," pp. 17–22.

Geuter also sees 1936 as a dividing line between reform efforts and mobilization. Geuter, "Professionalisierung," pp. 98–100.

16. "Tätigkeitsbericht 1937," p. 201; Göring, "Bericht," p. 2.

17. "Tätigkeitsbericht 1935/36," p. 4. Until 1939, all institute teachers and administrators served without pay. See Gold, "Kindheitseinflüsse."

18. "Tätigkeitsbericht 1937," pp. 202–3.

19. See Felix Scherke, "Lebenslauf" (Berlin, 4 November 1936); BDC: Kulturkammer; Schultz, *Lebensbilderbuch*, pp. 130–34; August Vetter, "Testverfahren als Hilfsmittel der Psychologischen Diagnostik," in "Jahresbericht 1941," pp. 41–46; Erika Hantel, *Verborgenes Kräftespiel*; and, on Schmaltz, *Wer Leitet?*, p. 100.

20. Matthias Heinrich Göring, "Allgemeines," in "Jahresbericht 1940," p. 1.

21. Göring, "Eröffnungsansprache," p. 7. See also idem, "Allgemeines," p. 1; and idem, "Allgemeines," in "Jahresbericht 1941," p. 62. On the inade-

quacy of the Budapester Strasse offices, see Göring, "Bericht," p. 4. On DAF finances, see Timothy W. Mason, *Arbeiterklasse und Volksgemeinschaft,* p. 83.

22. See *Deutsches Ärzteblatt* 63 (1933): 685; and *Volksgesundheitswacht* 4 (1937): 256.

23. See "Gesetz über die berufsmässige Ausübung der Heilkunde ohne Bestallung (Heikpraktikergesetz)," *Reichsgesetzblatt* (1939): 251–52, 259–62; Bernhard Hörmann, "Kampf der Gefahr!" *Volksgesundheitswatcht* 3 (1936): 3; Ramm, *Standeskunde,* pp. 59–63; the article by Health Practitioner Leader (Heilpraktikerführer) Ernst Kees, "Wer fällt unter das Heilpraktikergesetz?" *Deutsches Ärzteblatt* 69 (1939) : 275; I. H. Schultz, "Die Aufhebung der Kurierfreiheit," ibid., pp. 151–57; and Kurt Blome, *Arzt im Kampf. Erlebnisse und Gedanken* (Leipzig: Barth, 1942), pp. 295–303. For Achelis's obsequious review of Blome, see *ZfP* 15 (1943): 58.

24. Martin Bormann, "Vorwort," in Leonardo Conti, ed., *Reden und Aufrufe Gerhard Wagners,* p. iii. See also Röhrs, *Hitlers Krankheit,* pp. 80, 126.

25. *Der Öffentliche Gesundheitsdienst* 5 (1939): 313; and *Deutsches Ärzteblatt* 69 (1939): 321.

26. Leonardo Conti, Fragebogen für kommunalpolitische Fachredner der Partei, Berlin, 25 January 1938. BDC: SS-Führer.

27. Röhrs, *Hitlers Krankheit,* p. 64. Röhrs was Conti's representative in Munich and with the Reich Physicians Chamber.

28. Akten des Obersten Parteigerichts I. Kammer: Conti 4339–34, 22 November 1934. BDC: Oberstes Parteigericht. See also Emil Ketterer, SA-Führerfragebogen, Munich, 22 May 1935; BDC: SA and Reichsärztekammer. On the Stennes putsch, see Heinz Höhne, *The Order of the Death's Head: The Story of Hitler's SS,* trans. Richard Barry (New York: Coward-McCann, 1970), p. 66. The SS was originally part of the SA, and Conti's membership in the SS dated from 1927; BDC: SS-Führer.

29. "Übersichtsdarstellung der Ereignisse im Falle Villain" (Berlin, 12 March, 2 June 1934); and Das Landgericht. 13. grosse Strafkammer, Beschluss, Berlin, 23 April 1934. BDC: Oberstes Parteigericht.

30. Villain's membership card, held in party files, notes with grim bureaucratic nonchalance that he had left (*ausgetreten*) the party on 30 June 1934; BDC: NSDAP-Zentralkartei. According to Siegfried Ostrowski, Villain was particularly brutal in his actions toward Jewish doctors. Ostrowski also reports as common knowledge among physicians that Villain had assaulted Conti with his riding crop, as well as the widespread belief that, as a result, Villain had died in the melee of 30 June at the hands of Conti. See Ostrowski, "Berliner Jüdischen Ärzteschaft," p. 9. On Adolf Wagner, see Peterson, *Limits,* pp. 163–64, 166–68.

31. Wagner to Reichsleiter Gusnier, 24 January 1935. BDC: Oberstes Parteigericht.

32. On the articulation and implementation of his medical views, see Leonardo Conti, "Gesundheitsführung–Volksschicksal" (28 March 1942), text of an address to the NSDAP Main Office for National Health; BDC: SS-Führer; and idem, "Die Bedeutung der Wissenschaft, insbesondere der kinderärztlichen, in der Gesundheitsführung," *Deutsche medizinische Wochenschrift* 68 (1942): 53–59. Conti's wife, Elfriede, was Reich Leader for Midwives (Reichshebammenführerin). See Leonardo Conti, "Geburtshilfe und Hebammen-

wesen in Deutschland," *Deutsches Ärzteblatt* 68 (1938) : 4–8, 26–29. On Conti's aversion toward alcohol and tobacco, see Röhrs, *Hitlers Krankheit,* p. 101. Although he was not as radical as some within the party who wanted to change the health system root and branch, Conti did conduct a campaign against Pervitin, an amphetamine in wide use in both military and civilian circles. Various adverse effects resulting from prolonged or intensive use of the drug had been reported in the medical literature, and Conti wished to place it under the same degree of control as opium. According to Röhrs, he was defeated in this move by the combined forces of the military and the Berlin Medical Society. See Röhrs, *Hitlers Krankheit,* pp. 96–104.

33. Kater, *Das "Ahnenerbe" der SS,* p. 100. See also Jill Stephenson, *The Nazi Organisation of Women* (Totowa, N.J.: Barnes & Noble, 1981), pp. 46–49.

34. See *Deutsches Ärzteblatt* 69 (1939): 561; "Das Gesundheitswesen von Partei und Staat," *Deutsches Nachrichtenbüro,* 1 April 1940, p. 1; and R 18, folder 5583.

35. Ley to Hess, 12 December 1939, R 18, folder 5572. Ley had been asking Hess to ensure the Labor Front's sovereignty over the health field. See Ley to Hess, 3 June 1939; BDC: Parteikorrespondenz Franz Wirz.

36. See *Reichsband: Adressenwerk der Dienststellen der NSDAP* (1939), pp. 377–78.

37. A protégé of Bormann's, Conti was nonetheless supplanted by Bormann's archenemy Karl Brandt, finally hanging himself on 6 October 1945 while awaiting trial at Nuremberg. See Burton C. Andrus, *I Was the Nuremberg Jailer* (New York: Coward-McCann, 1969), pp. 87–88; and Airey Neave, *On Trial at Nuremberg* (Boston: Little, Brown, 1978), p. 76.

38. Orlow, *Nazi Party,* p. 53.

39. Broszat, *Hitler State,* pp. 348–49.

40. Fest, *Face,* p. 147.

41. Ibid., p. 117. See also Albert Speer, *Infiltration,* trans. Joachim Neugroschel (New York: MacMillan, 1981).

42. Thomas Pynchon, *Gravity's Rainbow* (New York: Viking, 1973), p. 373. See also Broszat, *Hitler State,* pp. 357–59.

43. Orlow, *Nazi Party,* p. 488.

44. Broszat, *Hitler State,* pp. 348–49.

45. Höhne, *Death's Head,* pp. 63, 67–69, 76–77; and Broszat, *Hitler State,* p. 65.

46. On Conti, see "Lebenslauf und Amtseinführung," *Deutsches Ärzteblatt* 69 (1939): 324–25.

47. Röhrs, *Hitlers Krankheit,* pp. 126–27.

48. Göring, "Eröffnungsansprache," p. 8. See also idem, "Bericht," p. 2.

49. See *Deutsches Ärzteblatt* 74 (1944): 99; and *Die Gesundheitsführung "Ziel und Weg"* 6 (1944): 107. Conti's party deputy, Franz Bunz, was also involved in meetings with psychotherapists during the early years of the Third Reich. See "Stadtrat Dr. med. Franz Bunz 50 Jahre," *Deutsches Ärzteblatt* 69 (1939) : 391.

50. BDC: Parteikorrespondenz; Kurt Seelmann to the author, 15 October 1980. See also Seelmann, "Lebenslauf" (Munich, 1 November 1942); BDC: Parteikorrespondenz.

51. BDC: Parteikorrespondenz. Seif had, of course, been a member of the young avant garde who, among other things, supported Freud against the assaults of the medical establishment. See Ellenberger, *Discovery,* pp. 805–6. On Bavaria and the Reich, see Peterson, *Limits,* pp. 149–233.

52. BDC: Parteikorrespondenz.

53. BDC: Parteikorrespondenz. See also "Dr. Leonhard Seif," p. 322; Göring's review in *ZfP* 13 (1942): 310; and *Nationalsozialistische Bibliographie* 5:12 (December 1940), p. 20, entry 114.

54. *Nationalsozialistische Bibliographie* 8:4/5 (April/May 1943), p. 23, entry 164. See also Seelmann to Reichsschriftumskammer, 1 November 1942; BDC: Parteikorrespondenz. Seelmann said he did not know that he needed a special permit to publish the book; all he had done originally was to send a copy through Göring to the Propaganda Ministry.

55. *Nationalsozialistische Bibliographie* 7:7/8 (July/August 1942), p. 32, entry 165. Ibid., 7:3/4 (March/April 1942), p. 28, entry 149.

56. Beyerchen, *Scientists Under Hitler,* pp. 205–7.

57. Göring, "Weltanschauung und Psychotherapie" (1936), p. 295; (1938), p. 1102.

58. Johanna Herzog-Dürck to the author, 28 April 1980. See also Göring, "Allgemeines" (1940), p. 3. On Kris, see Wyatt and Teuber, "German Psychology," pp. 235–36; and Farago, *German Psychological Warfare,* p. 33.

59. Felix Kersten, *The Kersten Memoirs 1940–1945,* trans. Constantine Fitzgibbon and Jameson Oliver (New York: Macmillan, 1957), p. 58.

60. Larry V. Thompson, "Lebensborn and the Eugenics Policy of the Reichsführer-SS," *Central European History* 6 (1971) : 56–57. See also Kater, *Das "Ahnenerbe" der SS,* p. 205.

61. Fritz Mohr, "Die Behandlung der Neurosen durch Psychotherapie," p. 67. See also "Tätigkeitsbericht 1937," p. 201; and Künkel, "Psychotherapie. Eine Übersicht," pp. 1363–64. For the text of her address to the DPG in 1936, see Karen Horney, "Das neurotische Liebesbedürfnis," *ZfP* 10 (1937): 69–82.

62. Göring, "Bericht," p. 2. Thirteen tri-seminars took place in 1936–37, while during 1938–39 there were sixty-two scientific meetings, including tri-seminars. See ibid., p. 3; and "Tätigkeitsbericht 1937," p. 201. For a summation of the postwar debate on the tri-seminars, see Zapp, "Psychoanalyse und Nationalsozialismus," pp. 42–43.

63. Hans von Hattingberg, "Forschung und Bücherei," in "Jahresbericht 1940," pp. 4–5. See also idem, "Arbeitsplan der Forschungsabteilung," in Göring, *1. Sonderheft,* pp. 16–20; and idem, "Die Willensstörung in der Neurose," p. 33.

64. Kemper to the author, 2 March 1974.

65. Deutsches Institut für Psychologische Forschung und Psychotherapie, "Thesen zur Neurosenlehre," p. 28.

66. *ZfP* 14 (1943): 300. On the psychoanalysts, see Müller-Braunschweig, "Skizze der Geschichte," p. 19; and Pongratz, *Psychotherapie,* pp. 41, 279. Jung was editor-in-chief of the *Zentralblatt* from 1933 to 1940, and Göring from 1936 to 1944. Managing editors were Cimbal (1933–34), Meier and Curtius (1934–1939), Bilz and Meier (1940), and Bilz (1940–44). See "Tätigkeitsbericht 1935/36," p. 6.

67. *ZfP* 14 (1942): 173. See also ibid., pp. 205–6. On Horney, see *ZfP* 10

(1937): 51–55; *ZfP* 13 (1941): 61–64; and Rubins, *Karen Horney,* pp. 128, 133. Schultz also visited Horney in New York in 1936. See Schultz, *Lebensbilderbuch,* p. 111. See also S. Morita, "Der Begriff der Nervosität," *ZfP* 12 (1940): 38–53; Syuzo Naka, "Psychotherapie in Japan," in Curtius, *Psychotherapie in der Praxis,* pp. 144–47; and Nikiti Okumura, "Japanische Psychotherapie und Zen," in Bilz, *Psyche und Leistung,* pp. 183–205. See "Tätigkeitsbericht 1940," p. 4. Müller-Braunschweig also published an essay in the *Zentralblatt* in 1939; see Carl Müller-Braunschweig, "Forderungen an eine die Psychotherapie unterbauende Psychologie," *ZfP* 11 (1939) : 168–76.

68. Baumeyer, "Psychoanalyse in Deutschland," p. 209. On the Jungians and the Freudians, see the institute's "(Ankündigung der) Veranstaltungen"; and Lockot, "Erinnern und Durcharbeiten," p. 258. On Erna Göring, see BDC: Parteistatistische Erhebung and Parteikorrespondenz.

69. Johannes Heinrich Schultz, "Leistung und Psyche."

70. "Berliner Akademie für ärztliche Fortbildung," *Deutsches Ärzteblatt* 74 (1944): 181–82. See also Johannes Heinrich Schultz, "Rundschau Psychotherapie 1935/36"; idem, "Was kann die Psychotherapie in der Behandlung des Hochdruckes leisten?" *Zeitschrift für ärztliche Fortbildung* 41 (1944): 305–8; and idem, "Arbeitsplan für ärztliche Fortbildung," in Göring, *1. Sonderheft,* pp. 6–8. On a series of lectures Schultz gave at the Berlin Medical Society, see *Deutsches Ärzteblatt* 73 (1943): 151. Schultz also reported on the use in psychotherapy of the popular amphetamine Pervitin to the 1943 meeting of the German Society for Internal Medicine in Vienna. See *Deutsche medizinische Wochenschrift* 70:3/4 (21 January 1944): 52.

71. Höhne, *Codeword: Direktor,* p. 127.

72. Ibid., pp. 132, 134, 136.

73. Ibid., p. 203.

74. As the net began to close around the Schulze-Boysen ring, its members desperately sought to dispose of incriminating evidence. One radio set was dumped into the River Spree, while another found its way in a suitcase to the house of a pianist who had ties to the Rittmeister circle. See Höhne, *Codeword: Direktor,* p. 155. Ernst Göring, no doubt reflecting the attitude of his father, recounted the tale of the transmitter in the suitcase as proof of the Rittmeisters' complicity in the group's espionage activities. The truth seems more complex: that Rittmeister's group was in fact not involved so much in espionage for the Kremlin (if at all) as in intellectual resistance to the Nazis. Their connection with the radio transmitter and receiver, in sum, seems to have been brief and indirect. See also Lockot, "Erinnern und Durcharbeiten," pp. 123–24.

75. Höhne, *Codeword: Direktor,* pp. 182, 202.

76. Orlow, *Nazi Party,* p. 418. See also Albert Speer, *Inside the Third Reich,* pp. 254–55.

77. Mason, *Arbeiterklasse,* p. 129.

78. Anon. to Ministerialrat Klingelhofer, 23 June 1942; and DFG Registratur 1942. BDC: Personalakten Prof. Göring.

79. Kurt Zierold, *Forschungförderung in drei Epochen,* pp. 215–24. See also Beyerchen, *Scientists Under Hitler,* pp. 155–56.

80. Speer, *Inside the Third Reich,* p. 225. See "Erlass des Führers über den Reichsforschungsrat vom 9. Juni 1942," *Reichsgesetzblatt* (1942): 389.

81. Zierold, *Forschungsförderung*, pp. 225–26, 251–52.

82. Ferdinand Sauerbruch, *Master Surgeon*, pp. 227–28, 237. See also Zierold, *Forschungsförderung*, pp. 220, 244.

83. Scherke to Kemper, 20 October 1970.

84. Dräger, "Psychoanalysis in Hitler Germany," p. 210.

85. DFG Registratur 1943. BDC: Personalakten Prof. Göring.

86. Ernst Göring, interview with Rose Spiegel, 10 November 1974. Salary figures are from Baumeyer, "Psychoanalyse in Deutschland," p. 218. These salaries were based on the requisite civil service rankings.

87. Willi Boelcke, ed., *The Secret Conferences of Dr. Goebbels: The Nazi Propaganda War 1939–43*, trans. Ewald Osers (New York: E. P. Dutton, 1970), p. 326. On the Göring style of leadership, see Peterson, *Limits*, pp. 72–76.

88. Zierold, *Forschungsförderung*, pp. 248–53.

89. "Reichsinstitut für Psychologische Forschung und Psychotherapie," *Deutsches Ärzteblatt* 74 (1944): 60.

90. Luise Albertz, Deutscher Bundestag Petitions-Ausschuss Vorsitzende, to Frau E. Göring, 6 December 1956.

91. Göring to Brandt, 18 February 1944; and Göring to Paulus Rostock, Der Bevollmächtigte für das Sanitäts- und Gesundheitswesen (Medizinische Wissenschaft und Forschung), 18 March and 31 May 1944. BDC: Parteikorrespondenz Heyer.

92. DFG Registratur 1944. BDC: Personalakten Prof. Göring.

93. See Amt W: Medizinische Fakultäten und Gesellschaften, Medizinalstudium, Fachzeitschriften, Psychologie (Handakten Prof. de Crinis) 1942–1945; R 21, folders 475–76; Bundesarchiv. On de Crinis and Westphal, see de Crinis to Sergius Breuer, 6 September 1940; Universität Berlin: Psychiatrische/Nervenklinik Charité 1941/4; Geheimes Staatsarchiv. But Westphal was in fact not Jewish. De Crinis poisoned himself on 1 May 1945. See Werner Forssmann, *Experiments on Myself: Memoirs of a Surgeon in Germany*, trans. Hilary Davies (New York: Saint Martin's Press, 1974), p. 240.

94. Max de Crinis, "Denkschrift" (n.d.). BDC: Korrespondenz Wi. See also "Tagung der Dekane der med. Fakultäten in Reichserziehungsministerium" (6 May 1941), pp. 17–20; BDC: Korrespondenz Wi Rudolf Mentzel.

95. Heyer, *Praktische Seelenheilkunde*, pp. 82, 58.

96. De Crinis to Rostock, 3 April 1944. BDC: Personalakten des Prof. de Crinis.

97. De Crinis to Rostock. Kemper sees this as proof of the known influence of psychoanalysts at the Göring Institute, but it indicates only that de Crinis was condemning psychotherapy as a whole by associating it again in the minds of the authorities with Freud.

98. Gustav Richard Heyer, "Bericht über die Ausbildung der Behandelnden Psychologen," in Göring, *1. Sonderheft*, pp. 9–11.

99. De Crinis to [Gustav] Frey, 11 July 1944, R 21, folder 475. On psychologists and psychotherapy in the Third Reich, see Chapter 6.

100. Rostock to Brandt, 15 April 1944. BDC: Parteikorrespondenz Heyer.

101. De Crinis to Rostock. The same balance between the professional and the political is less easily discernible in de Crinis's nevertheless interesting evaluation of psychiatrist and psychotherapist Ernst Speer, whose nephew was Albert Speer: "As far as Speer is concerned, we are well aware of his work

and I value him in spite of my attitude toward psychotherapy." De Crinis to
B. Kihn, 5 February 1945. BDC: Korrespondenz Wi K. Mardersteig.

102. Anon. to Ministerialrat Klingelhofer.

103. By way of contrast, Johannes Stark and Philip Lenard, the two major
spokesmen for an "Aryan" physics, did not enjoy the advantages of a potent
name like Göring, the practical Nazi attraction to the therapeutic expertise
offered by psychotherapists, or the unity within a discipline whose members
were determined to achieve professional recognition and advancement. See
Beyerchen, *Scientists Under Hitler*, pp. 86–91, 125–26, 141–67, 203–7.

6. THE INSTITUTE AT WORK

1. These statistics are to be found in the institute's yearly reports for 1937
through 1941. Stuttgart psychoanalyst Graber and psychiatrist Beetz were
elected by the local membership to succeed Roemer. To the extent that
Göring governed the affairs of the branch *"kommissarisch,"* as the 1941 report put it, this arose only from the close ties to Berlin that characterized all
the branches, as well as from the fact that Beetz, like Roemer before him, was
overloaded with hospital work. Graber, as managing director, recalls having
a good working relationship with Göring.

2. See Göring, "Bericht," pp. 4–5; Werner Achelis, "Arbeitsplan der liter-
arischen Abteilung," in Göring, *1. Sonderheft*, pp. 21–27; "Jahresbericht
1940," p. 3; and Baumeyer, "Psychoanalyse in Deutschland," p. 218.

3. "Tätigkeitsbericht 1937," pp. 201–2.

4. Johannes Heinrich Schultz, "Poliklinische Aufgaben und Pflichten," in
"Jahresbericht 1940," pp. 12–13.

5. "Tätigkeitsbericht 1937," pp. 204–5.

6. "Tätigkeitsbericht 1938," pp. 4–6.

7. "Jahresbericht 1941," pp. 65–67; and Felix Boehm, "Erhebung und
Bearbeitung von Katamnesen," in "Jahresbericht 1940," p. 20.

8. Felix Boehm, "Poliklinische Erfahrungen," p. 71. See also Reichsinstitut
für Psychologische Forschung und Psychotherapie im Reichsforschungsrat,
"Richtlinien der Poliklinik," pp. 2, 8–9.

9. Boehm, "Poliklinische Erfahrungen," p. 75. See also Scheunert, "Kurzbehandlungen," pp. 218–20.

10. "Richtlinien der Poliklinik," pp. 4–5.

11. Johannes Heinrich Schultz, "Vorschlag eines Diagnosen-Schemas," pp.
99–100. See also ibid., pp. 157–60; and "Klinisches Diagnosen-Schema der
Poliklinik und Psychodiagnostischen Abteilung," in "Richtlinien der Poliklinik," pp. 11–15.

12. Rittmeister, "Stand der Poliklinik," pp. 90–93.

13. Scheunert, "Kurzbehandlungen," pp. 208–9, 213–14.

14. Wegscheider, "Psychotherapie bei Kassenpatienten," pp. 61–67.

15. Ibid., p. 65.

16. Kretschmer, *Gestalten und Gedanken*, pp. 180–181. See also Schultz,
Lebensbilderbuch, p. 160.

17. Alexander and Selesnick, *Psychiatry*, p. 175.

18. Schultz, *Psychotherapie*, pp. 41–62.

19. Ibid., pp. 101–6.

20. See Schultz's discussion remarks included in Göring, "Neurose in der Sozialversicherung," pp. 60–61.

21. Schultz, *Lebensbilderbuch*, p. 164. See also idem, "Über kleine Psychotherapie in der allgemeinen Praxis."

22. Olga von König-Fachsenfeld, "Erziehungshilfe," in "Jahresbericht 1940," pp. 25–34; idem, "Arbeitsplan der Abteilung für Erziehungshilfe," in Göring, *1. Sonderheft*, pp. 23–27; Elisabeth Künkel, "Die Bedeutung des Spieles in der Erziehungshilfe," in ibid., pp. 56–58; and Gerdhild von Staabs, "Spieltherapie beim Kleinkind," in ibid., pp. 59–60. See also "Jahresbericht 1941," pp. 67–70; "Jahresbericht 1938," p. 3; Göring, "Bericht," p. 4; and Rittmeister, "Stand der Poliklinik," p. 92. Rittmeister incorrectly names Fritz and Elisabeth Künkel as directors of the subdivision. See "Berichtigung," *ZfP* 12 (1940): 273. Elisabeth Künkel, Fritz Künkel's second wife, operated a private clinic at her summer home east of Berlin, where the Künkels had moved in 1938. She was occasionally in Berlin during the war and in 1947, with her two children, joined Fritz in America.

23. Elisabeth Künkel, "Zur Auswertung der Erfahrungen in der Erziehungshilfe des 'Instituts' in Berlin," in Matthias Heinrich Göring, ed., *Erziehungshilfe*, p. 14.

24. Olga Freiin von König-Fachsenfeld, "Die Erziehungshilfe in Berlin," in Göring, *Erziehungshilfe*, p. 12. See also idem, "Erziehungshilfe," *Die Ärztin* 17 (1941): 350–52. On psychologists in the NSV, see Geuter, "Professionalisierung," pp. 429–36, 480.

25. See Else Wildfang, "Erziehungshilfe der Berlin Verkehrsbetriebe (BVG)," in Göring, *Erziehungshilfe*, pp. 18–19; and Adelheid Fuchs-Kamp, "Sozial Betreute Kinder im psychotherapeutischen Heim," in ibid., pp. 25–27.

26. Adolf von Weizsäcker, "Heim-Erziehung," p. 95; and Pongratz, *Psychotherapie*, p. 207. See also von Weizsäcker, "Die tiefenpsychologische Behandlung von Kinderneurosen," versus Hans Eyferth, "Kinderpsychotherapie und Heilerziehung," *Zeitschrift für Kinderforschung* 49 (1941): 143–51.

27. F. Winkelmayr, "Die Erziehungshilfe in der Stadt Wien," in Göring, *Erziehungshilfe*, pp. 22–24. See also Richard Seyss-Inquart, "Aus der psychotherapeutischen Praxis in der Anstalt für Erziehungsbedürftige Kaiser-Ebersdorf in Wien," *ZfP* 14 (1942): 129–49; and Otto Schürer von Waldheim, "Arbeitstherapie als Mittel zur Besserung verwöhnter Jugendlicher," *ZfP* 13 (1941): 208–19. Richard Seyss-Inquart was the elder brother of Austrian Nazi Artur Seyss-Inquart. See Wolfgang Rosar, *Deutsche Gemeinschaft. Seyss-Inquart und der Anschluss* (Vienna: Europa, 1971), pp. 15–16.

28. On Aichhorn's career in general, see George J. Mohr, "August Aichhorn," in Franz Alexander, Samuel Eisenstein and Martin Grotjahn, eds., *Psychoanalytic Pioneers* (New York: Basic Books, 1966), pp. 348–59; and Alexander and Selesnick, *Psychiatry*, pp. 378–79. See also August Aichhorn, *Verwahrloste Jugend, die Psychoanalyse in der Fürsorgeerziehung. Zehn Vorträge zur ersten Einführung* (Leipzig: Internationale Psychoanalytische Bibliothek, 1925); and the letter from Göring to Sauerwald reprinted in *Neues Oesterreich*, 13 October 1948, p. 3, in which Göring expresses the hope that this book can be spared banning by the removal of Freud's foreword. Aichhorn's namesake was a strongly Catholic and anti-German member of

Dollfuss's Fatherland Front and spent a year in Dachau. Ernst Federn to the author, 9 August 1982. See also Anna Freud, "Obituary: August Aichhorn, July 27, 1878–October 17, 1949," *International Journal of Psychoanalysis* 32 (1951): 51–56. Aichhorn himself was a Christian Socialist but, according to his Jewish psychoanalytic colleague, Hermann Nunberg, was not an anti-Semite. See Nunberg, *Memoirs, Recollections, Ideas, Reflections* (New York: Psychoanalytic Research and Development Fund, 1969), p. 20.

It is clear from Aichhorn's correspondence between 24 March and 6 June 1938 with Müller-Braunschweig, Kemper, and Göring in Berlin that he saw membership in the Göring Institute as a means to free his son from captivity. Aichhorn's desire in this respect complemented Müller-Braunschweig's own desire to recruit Viennese psychoanalysts for the Göring Institute. See Huber, *Psychoanalyse in Österreich,* p. 60. Aichhorn gave his first lecture as a member of the institute on 22 June 1938 in Berlin. See ibid., p. 61; and a review of a 1936 Aichhorn work on youth counseling in *ZfP* 10 (1937): 62–63. On Aichhorn's work in Vienna from 1938 to 1944, see Huber, *Psychoanalyse in Österreich,* pp. 61–67, 242–46. On von Gebsattel, see ibid., p. 191, n. 35; see also his *Not und Hilfe. Prologomena zu einer Wesensehre der geistig-seelischen Hilfe* (Colmar: Alsatia-Verlag, 1944).

29. "Auszug aus der Statistik der Beratungsstelle," in Seif, *Erziehungshilfe,* pp. 209–11; "Jahresbericht 1941," p. 76.

30. Kurt Seelmann, "Vorbedingungen für die Errichtung einer Erziehungs-beratungsstelle," in Seif, *Erziehungshilfe,* pp. 117–27; and Margarete Krause-Ablass, "Auswirkungen auf NS-Mutterdienst," in ibid., pp. 293–95. See also Hildegard Hetzer, "Die Zusammenarbeit von Kindertagesstätte und Erziehungsberatung der NSV-Jugendhilfe," *Nationalsozialistischer Volksdienst* 9 (1942): 133–38.

31. See Lene Credner, "Die körperliche und erbbiologische Untersuchung," in Seif, *Erziehungshilfe,* pp. 140–50; and Göring, "Bericht," p. 1.

32. Marie Kalau vom Hofe, "Kriminalpsychologie," in "Jahresbericht 1940," pp. 37–41; "Jahresbericht 1941," pp. 70–71. See also Göring, "Allge-meines" (1940), p. 3; and idem, "Kriminalpsychologie," in Gustav Kafka, ed., *Handbuch der vergleichenden Psychologie,* vol. 3: *Die Funktion des abnor-men Seelenlebens* (Munich: Reinhardt, 1922), pp. 155–229.

33. "Tätigkeitsbericht 1937," p. 202.

34. Deutsches Institut für Psychologische Forschung und Psychotherapie e.V. in Berlin, "Richtlinien für die Ausbildung," p. 5. See also ibid., pp. 4–6. It is impossible to gauge the degree to which such racial and biological points of view were included by the various instructors in their courses, but it seems logical to suppose that the psychotherapists concentrated on instruction in the subject matter of their discipline. See the author's dissertation, "Psyche and Swastika," pp. 372–84; Geuter, "Professionalisierung," pp. 226–31, 289–329; and the institute's "(Ankündigung der) Veranstaltungen."

35. "Tätigkeitsbericht 1937," p. 203; Göring, "Allgemeines" (1940), p. 1.

36. "Richtlinien für die Ausbildung," p. 2; Göring, "Bericht," pp. 3, 5.

37. "Richtlinien für die Ausbildung," pp. 1, 7–8; Edgar Herzog, "Arbeits-plan der Abteilung 'Beratende Psychologen,'" in Göring, *1. Sonderheft,* pp. 12–15; and Göring, "Bericht," pp. 3, 5.

38. See "Tätigskeitbericht 1937," p. 203; Göring, "Bericht," p. 1; and Kl.

Erw. 762. It is hardly surprising that there was some initial confusion among nonmedical psychotherapists about their legal status and obligations. Immediately following the promulgation of the Health Practitioners Law in 1939, for example, at least two members of the Göring Institute, August Aichhorn in Vienna and Lucy Heyer-Grote in Berlin, applied for registration as health practitioners. Aichhorn nonetheless opined that his duties did not place him under the authority of the law since as an attending psychologist and a member of the German Institute for Psychological Research and Psychotherapy and the "General German Medical Society" he practiced in close cooperation with physicians. Aichhorn to Polizei Präsidium, Abt. V, Wien, 28 March 1939. See also *Amtsblatt des Polizeipräsidiums in Wien* 2:6 (15 March 1939), p. 3. On Heyer-Grote, see BDC: Parteikorrespondenz. See also the training and professional guidelines for attending psychologists drawn up by Göring and Heyer: Deutsches Institut für Psychologische Forschung und Psychotherapie e.V., "Richtlinien für das Arbeitsgebiet 'Behandelnde Psychologen' " (Berlin, n.d.); Geuter, "Professionalisierung," pp. 262–63; and "Gesetz zur Ordnung der Krankenpflege," *Reichsgesetzblatt* (1938): 1309–15.

39. "Jahresbericht 1941," p. 65.

40. Ibid., p. 63. See Oswald Kroh, "Bedeutsamer Fortschritt in der deutschen Psychologie"; Schultz's review in *ZfP* 14 (1942) : 89–91; Gustav Richard Heyer, "Ausbildungs- und Berufsfragen," in "Jahresbericht 1940," p. 11; and Geuter, "Professionalisierung," pp. 347–48 and 511, n. 12. See also Kroh, "Missverständnisse um die deutsche Psychologie"; and Arthur Hoffmann, "Erziehungs-Psychologie—Aufgaben und Wege," *ZfP* 13 (1941): 177–207. Hoffman's article was the text of a report given at the Munich branch of the institute on 19 June 1941. See also Walter Stets, "Freiheit der Berufswahl," *Das Reich,* 13 December 1942, p. 6.

41. "Diplomprüfungsordnung für Studierende der Psychologie," *Deutsche Wissenschaft, Erziehung und Volksbildung* 7 (1941): 256.

42. Ibid., p. 258.

43. See Nitsche to Rüdin, 17 July 1941; and Rüdin to de Crinis, 21 July 1941, T-1021, frames 424–27; and Otto Wuth to Oswald Bumke, 23 February 1942; Bumke to Wuth, 27 February 1942; and Wuth to Bumke, 3 March 1942; H 20/480 (Heeres-Sanitätsinspekteur, Beratender Psychiater); Bundesarchiv-Militärarchiv.

44. Der Reichsminister für Wissenschaft, Erziehung und Volksbildung to die Unterrichtsverwaltungen der Länder mit Hochschulen (ausser Preussen), die Herren Vorsteher der nachgeordneten Reichs- und Preussischen Dienststellen der Wissenschaftsverwaltung, 20 August 1942, R 21, folder 469. Bundesarchiv.

45. See Oswald Kroh, "Zum Ausbau der Prüfungsordnung für Diplom-Psychologen," *Zeitschrift für Psychologie* 155 (1943): 1–16.

46. Wolfgang Hochheimer to the author, 30 September 1981.

47. "Richtlinien für die Ausbildung," p. 1; Göring, "Allgemeines" (1940), p. 1.

48. "Richtlinien für die Ausbildung," p. 7; "Jahresbericht 1941," p. 65.

49. De Crinis to Frey.

50. Ibid.

51. Kroh, "Zum Ausbau der Prüfungsordnung," p. 12. On the evolution of the regulations concerning the certification of psychologists, see Geuter, "Pro-

fessionalisierung," pp. 74, 261–65, 286–88, 347–413, 438; on the work of psychologists in German industry, see pp. 265–74.

52. "Jahresbericht 1941," pp. 62–63; Göring, "Bericht," p. 3. See also Max de Crinis's memorandum of 15 February 1941, R 21, folder 476.

53. "Richtlinien für die Ausbildung," p. 7.

54. See Mason, *Arbeiterklasse*, pp. 1–16.

55. Broszat, *Hitler State*, pp. 145–146, 151. See also Schoenbaum, *Hitler's Social Revolution*, pp. 73–112.

56. Mason, *Arbeiterklasse*, pp. 123–42. See also R. J. Overy, "The German Pre-War Aircraft Production Plans: November 1936–April 1939," *English Historical Review* 90 (1975): 792–93.

57. Mason, *Arbeiterklasse*, p. 93; Arthur Schweitzer, *Big Business in the Third Reich*, pp. 179–84. See also Willy Müller, *Das soziale Leben im neuen Deutschland*, pp. 164–69; and Otto Marrenbach, ed., *Fundamente des Sieges. Die Gesamtarbeit der Deutschen Arbeitsfront von 1933 bis 1940*, 2nd ed. (Berlin: Verlag der DAF, 1941), pp. 278–92.

58. See Karl Arnhold, *Leistungsertüchtigung*, pp. 28–55.

59. Robert Brady, *The Spirit and Structure of German Fascism* (New York: Victor Gollancz, 1937), pp. 161–74. See also Neumann, *Behemoth*, pp. 429–31, 515; and Rolf Seubert, *Berufserziehung und Nationalsozialismus. Das berufspädagogische Erbe und seine Betreuer*, Berufliche Bildung und Berufsbildungspolitik, ed. Klaus W. Döring, Helga Thomas, Wilfried Voigt and Walter Volpert, vol. 1 (Weinheim, Basel: Beltz, 1977), pp. 59–138.

60. Karl Arnhold, "Umrisse einer deutschen Betriebslehre," in idem, *Der Deutsche Betrieb*, p. 24.

61. Arnhold, *Leistungsertüchtigung*, p. 12. On DINTA, see "Arbeitswissenschaft im Dienst der Volksgemeinschaft," *NS Sozialpolitik* 1 (1934): 235–39.

62. E. Gründger, "Die Sicherung der Schaffenskraft. Aufbau und Aufgaben des DAF Amtes für Volksgesundheit," *Monatshefte für N.S. Sozialpolitik* 7 (1940): 9–11.

63. See Mason, *Arbeiterklasse*, p. 918. See also Wuttke-Groneberg, "Leistung, Vernichtung, Verwertung," pp. 22–31.

64. Herzog, "Arbeitsplan," p. 12; Göring, "Allgemeines" (1940), p. 3; and Göring, "Bericht," p. 1.

65. Hattingberg, "Forschung und Bücherei," p. 9. Arnhold reassumed his post until 26 November 1942, when Herbert Steinwarz took over. Arnhold claimed after the war that he had resigned his post because of personal differences with Ley. See Gerhard P. Bunk, *Erziehung und Industriearbeit. Modelle betrieblicher Lernens und Arbeitens Erwachsener* (Weinheim, Basel: Beltz, 1972), p. 259, n. 3. Bremhorst could recall no differences between Arnhold and Ley, while another of Arnhold's colleagues saw his dissociation from Ley as a prudent move in expectation of a Nazi defeat. Ulfried Geuter to the author, 30 May 1981. Whatever the truth with regard to Arnhold's motives, it is reasonable to suppose that disenchantment and disillusionment with the increasingly flabby and stumbling Labor Front influenced his decision.

66. Gustav Richard Heyer, "Aus der psychotherapeutischen Praxis," p. 556; Hans H. Meyer-Mark, "Neurotiker der Wirtschaft," p. 246.

67. Karl Arnhold, "Psychologische Kräfte im Dienste der Berufserziehung und Leistungssteigerung." See idem, "Arbeitspsychologie."

68. Matthias Heinrich Göring, "Aktuelles," *ZfP* 13 (1941): 130. See also

Ferruccio Banissoni, "Leistungssteigerung durch psychische Energieentfaltung,"
in Bilz, *Psyche und Leistung*, pp. 128–55.

69. See "Jahresbericht 1941," p. 73. See also Grunberger, *12-Year Reich*,
pp. 193–94, 201; and Gumpert, *Heil Hunger!*, pp. 59–71.

70. Marrenbach, *Fundamente des Sieges*, p. 272. See also Müller, *Das soziale
Leben*, pp. 100, 159–69; Arbeitswissenschaftliches Institut der Deutschen Arbeitsfront, *Jahrbuch* (Berlin: Verlag der DAF, 1937), pp. 376–84; and Der
Reichsorganisationsleiter der DAF, ed., *Organisationsbuch der NSDAP* (Munich: Eher, 1937), pp. 205, 234–38.

71. Karl Arnhold, *Wege zur Leistungssteigerung in der Textilindustrie*
(Berlin: Lehrmittelzentrale der DAF, 1942), p. 55. See also "Querschnitt durch
die wichtigsten körperlichen und seelischen Krankheiten bei weiblichen Tex-
tilarbeiterinnen" (24 June 1940), N 5, I/21, Bundesarchiv; "Jahresbericht
1941," p. 74; and Hans Kellner, "Betriebsarzt und Psychotherapie."

72. Göring to Brandt. See also Ludwig J. Pongratz, Werner Traxel, and
Ernst G. Wehner, eds., *Psychologie in Selbstdarstellungen* (Bern: Hans Huber,
1972), pp. 345–47.

73. Friedrich Schulze-Maier, "Gesundheitspflege der Seele," p. 26. See *Nationalsozialistische Bibliographie* 6:7/8 (July/August 1941), p. 31, entry 194.

74. Collection Himmler, Box 1, Reels 37A and 38A: Terminbücher, entries
for 10 January and 18 December 1939. Hoover Institution. On Göring's son,
see Peter Göring, R.u.S.-Fragebogen, Potsdam, 27 March 1938, BDC: SS-Unterlagen; and Parteistatistische Erhebung.

75. Göring, "Allgemeines" (1940), p. 3.

76. William Telling, "Reconditioning the Maimed," *The Listener* 18
(1937): 1003. See also Höhne, *Death's Head*, p. 363; and Helmut Heiber, ed.,
Reichsführer! Briefe an und von Himmler (Munich: Deutscher Taschenbuch
Verlag, 1970), pp. 130–33.

77. Göring to Rostock, 31 May 1944.

78. See Göring to Himmler, 10 May 1939, BDC: SS-Führer; and NS 21,
folder 336/C 1; Bundesarchiv.

79. Der Beauftragte für das Forschungswerk "Wald and Baum in der
arisch-germanischen Geistes- und Kulturgeschichte," Gilbert Trathnigg, to
Walter Wüst, 11 July 1939, NS 21, folder 336/C 1; Himmler to Göring, 27
May 1939. BDC: SS-Unterlagen. See also Gustav Schmaltz, "Einige Bemerkungen zur Praxis der Psychotherapie," *ZfP* 10 (1938): 141–49.

80. See Eckart von Sydow to "Das Ahnenerbe," e.V., 26 June 1939, BDC:
SS-Unterlagen; DFG-Registratur, BDC: Personalakten von Sydow; and BDC:
Parteistatistische Erhebung. Sydow, born in 1885 in Dobberpfuhl, was a 1933
party member and a member of the Nazi University Lecturers League and the
NSV. See BDC: Parteistatistische Erhebung and NS-Lehrerbund. See also Paul
Kühne, "Dr. Felix Boehm. Ein halbes Jahrhundert psychoanalytischer Ge-
schichte" (1958), in Boehm, *Schriften*, p. 313.

81. Franz Alfred Six to Wolfram Sievers, 24 June 1942. BDC: SS-Ahnenerbe.
See Eckart von Sydow, "Zukunftsaussichten der negerischen Kunst," *Kolo-
niale Rundschau* 33 (1942): 26–31.

82. Wolff to Göring, 4 February 1942; and Fitzner to Wolff, 5 February
1942. BDC: Personalakten Prof. Göring. See also Microcopy T-175, Roll R76
(Persönlicher Stab Reichsführer-SS, Schriftgutverwaltung), folder 107; Na-

tional Archives. On Himmler, see Peter Bleuel, *Sex and Society in Nazi Germany*, pp. 201–7; and Peter Loewenberg, "The Unsuccessful Adolescence of Heinrich Himmler," *American Historical Review* 76 (1971): 612–41. See also "Bericht" (16 January 1942); and Wolff to Amtsgericht Berlin, 4 February 1942; BDC: Personalakten Prof. Göring.

83. Amtsgerichtsrat Dannenberg to Himmler, 28 February 1942. BDC: Personalakten Prof. Göring.

84. Matthias Heinrich Göring and Marie Kalau vom Hofe, "Fachärztliche Stellungnahme," to Wolff, 30 July 1942; and Fitzner to Göring, 14 September 1942. BDC: Personalakten Prof. Göring.

85. Fitzner to Heckenstaller, 6 August 1942; and Heckenstaller to Fitzner, 2 September 1942. BDC: Personalakten Prof. Göring.

86. Wolff to Göring, 7 September 1942. BDC: Personalakten Prof. Göring.

87. Göring to Fitzner, 11 September 1942. BDC: Personalakten Prof. Göring.

88. Fitzner to Wolff, 28 October 1942. BDC: Personalakten Prof. Göring.

89. "Homosexualität und Kunst," *Das Schwarze Korps,* 11 March 1937, p. 6. See also Bleuel, *Sex and Society*, pp. 23–24, 96–101, 118–19, 217–25; Heinrich Himmler, *Geheimreden 1933 bis 1945,* ed. Bradley F. Smith and Agnes F. Peterson (Franfurt a.M.: Propylaen, 1974), pp. 93–104, 120; and Hans-Georg Stümke and Rudi Finkler, *Rosa Winkel, Rosa Listen. Homosexuelle und "Gesundes Volksempfinden" von Auschwitz bis Heute* (Reinbek: Rowohlt, 1981).

90. See Arthur Schindler, "Die Umfrage der *Deutschen medizinischen Wochenschrift* betreffend den Satz 175 StGB," *ZfP* 3 (1930): 68–70. See also Ernst Kretschmer, *Psychiatry*, pp. 177, 262–65; and James D. Steakley, *The Homosexual Emancipation Movement in Germany* (New York: Arno, 1975), pp. 9–10, 13, 21, 30–40, 84–85, 106, 110–11.

91. See Fritz Mohr, "Einige Betrachtungen über Wesen, Entstehung und Behandlung der Homosexualität," pp. 1, 13, 16, 17, 19, 20; Hattingberg, *Über die Liebe,* pp. 67–82; Harald Schultz-Hencke, "Über Homosexualität," *Zeitschrift für die gesamte Neurologie und Psychiatrie* 140 (1932): 300–312; Johannes Heinrich Schultz, "Bemerkungen zur Arbeit von Th. Lang über die genetische Bedingtheit der Homosexualität," ibid. 157 (1937): 575–78; Herbert Linden, "Bekämpfung der Sittlichkeitsverbrechern mit ärztlichen Mitteln," *Allgemeine Zeitschrift für Psychiatrie* 112 (1939): 405–23; and Schultz's review essay in *ZfP* 12 (1940): 180–83. On the cultural bias against homosexuals in Germany, see Mosse, "Nationalism and Respectability"; and Hull, "Bourgeoisie and Its Discontents."

In 1932 Oswald Bumke had written to Munich publisher J. F. Lehmann regarding the danger to Germany's youth if homosexuals such as Röhm should assume power. Lehmann reportedly showed the letter to Hitler, who dismissed it with an affirmation of his loyalty to Röhm. Bumke, *Erinnerungen,* pp. 163–66.

92. Reichsjugendführung, ed., "Sonderrichtlinien. Die Bekämpfung gleichgeschlechtlicher Verfehlungen im Rahmen der Jugenderziehung," *Arbeitsrichtlinien der Hitler-Jugend* 4/43 (Berlin, 1 June 1943), p. 6, R 22, folder 1196. Bundesarchiv. See also Jugendführer des Deutschen Reichs, ed., *Kriminalität und Gefährdung der Jugend. Lagebericht bis zum Stande vom 1.*

Januar 1941 (Berlin: Limpert, 1941), pp. 87–120; Hans Büsing, "Erfahrungen mehrjährigen jugendärztlicher Tätigkeit im Rahmen eines ländlichen Gesundheitsamtes in Hinblick auf die Neuausrichtung der HJ-ärztlichen Tätigkeit," *Der Öffentliche Gesundheitsdienst* 6 (1940): 405–20; and Peter D. Stachura, *The German Youth Movement 1900–1945* (London: Macmillan, 1981), pp. 132, 161–62.

93. Kersten, *Memoirs*, p. 59.

94. Heiber, *Reichsführer!*, pp. 271–73; T-175, Roll 55, frames 0024–27. See also ibid., pp. 55, 199–200. Ellen Bartens, a secretary at the Göring Institute from 1939 to 1945, remembers Schultz telling her he treated an SS man for homosexuality who had been sent by his family after his being threatened with execution by his superiors. For accounts of homosexuality in the SS, see Kersten, *Memoirs*, pp. 56–64; Himmler, *Geheimreden*, pp. 97–98; and Höhne, *Death's Head*, pp. 142–43.

95. Vaernet to Himmler, 30 October 1944. BDC: SS-Führer.

96. Martin Broszat, "The Concentration Camps 1933–45," in Helmut Krausnick et al., *The Anatomy of the SS State*, trans. Richard Barry, Marian Jackson, and Dorothy Long (New York: Walker, 1968), pp. 446–47.

97. Johannes Heinrich Schultz, "Anweisung für Trüppenärzte," p. 19. On the 1938 survey, see Boehm's review of Rudolf Lemke, *Über Ursache und strafrechtliche Beurteilung der Homosexualität* (1940), in *ZfP* 14 (1942): 123.

98. Peter Johannes Thiel, "Die Selbstbefleckung (Onanie!)." See also Bleuel, *Sex and Society*, p. 23.

99. See John Knodel, *The Decline of Fertility in Germany 1871–1939* (Princeton: Princeton University Press, 1974); Richard Korheer, *Gebürtenrückgang. Mahnruf an das deutsche Volk* (Munich: Suddeutsche Monatshefte, 1935); "Die Fruchtbarkeitszunahme des deutschen Volkes," *Deutsches Ärzteblatt* 72 (1942): 118–19; and Erich Nehse, "Die Frauenfrage vom eugenischen Standpunkt aus betrachtet," ibid. 63 (1933): 704–5. On women in the Third Reich, see Mosse, *Nazi Culture*, pp. 39–47; Bleuel, *Sex and Society*, pp. 34–37, 54–68, 76–85, 120–27, 148–73; Grunberger, *12-Year Reich*, pp. 251–66; and Jill Stephenson, *Women in Nazi Society* (New York: Barnes & Noble, 1975).

100. "Polizeiverordnung über Verfahren, Mittel und Gegenstände zur Unterbrechung und Verhütung von Schwangerschaften vom 21. Januar 1941," *Die Gesundheitsführung "Ziel und Weg"* 3 (1941): 7.

101. F. Rott, "Die Unfruchtbarkeit der Frau als Krankheit im Sinne der Reichsversicherung," *Reichs-Gesundheitsblatt* 11 (1936): 738–42; "Beseitigung der Unfruchtbarkeit bei Frauen," *Deutsches Ärzteblatt* 67 (1937): 833. See also G. Haselhorst, "Weibliche Sterilität," *Deutsches Ärzteblatt* 65 (1935): 1259–61.

102. Johannes Heinrich Schultz, "Seelische Gründe der Unfruchtbarkeit," p. 22. See also Fritz Mohr, "Die seelischen Faktoren bei der Entstehung und Behandlung der Unfruchtbarkeit der Frau," *ZfP* 7 (1934): 208–20.

103. Heyer to Hasselbach, 29 December 1943. BDC: Parteikorrespondenz. Kemper's book was reprinted in 1943, 1967, and 1972. See also "Anordnung Reichsgesundheitsführers—Arbeitsgemeinschaft 'Hilfe bei der Kinderlosigkeit in der Ehe,' " *Reichs-Gesundheitsblatt* 17 (1942): 761.

104. See Werner Kemper, "Der seelische Anteil an der Sterilität"; D. Kleff,

"Das Problem der Sterilität," *Deutsches Ärzteblatt* 72 (1942): 368–70; H. Stieve, "Nervös bedingte Unfruchtbarkeit," ibid. 74 (1944): 3–8; and A. Meyer, "Über die seelischen Ursachen der unfreiwilligen weiblichen Sterilität," ibid., pp. 219–25.

105. Himmler to Ernst Grawitz, 8 June 1942. BDC: SS-Führer. See Günther von Wolff, "Weibliche Unfruchtbarkeit: ihre Ursachen und die Möglichkeiten ihrer Verhütung" (Berlin, n.d.), BDC: SS-Führer; and Kemper, "Der seelische Anteil an der Sterilität," p. 397. See also Grawitz to Himmler, 25 May 1941, BDC: SS-Führer; Heiber, *Reichsführer!*, pp. 151, 159–60, 170–71; and Günter K. F. Schultze, "Der gegenwärtige Stand der Bekämpfung der weiblichen Unfruchtbarkeit," *Deutsche medizinische Wochenschrift* 68 (1942): 997–1002, 1027–32.

106. Ebner to Sollmann, 6 March 1944, NS 19/201, folder 1152. Bundesarchiv. On Lebensborn, see Thompson, "Lebensborn"; Bleuel, *Sex and Society*, pp. 161–66; and Marc Hillel and Clarissa Henry, *Of Pure Blood* (New York: McGraw-Hill, 1970).

107. Meyer, "Vorschläge zur Behandlung und Heilung der Empfängnisunfähigkeit der Frau und der Zeugungsunfähigkeit des Mannes," pp. 11–12. On Himmler and natural health, see Kersten, *Memoirs*, pp. 38–51; Kater, *Das "Ahnenerbe" der SS*, pp. 99–100; and Fest, *Face*, p. 116.

108. Erika Hantel, "Beginenwesen—ohne Romantik," in Hantel, *Brücken von Mensch zu Mensch*, pp. 90–94. Frederik Adama van Scheltema of Munich struck the same note in his *Zentralblatt* article, "Mutter Erde und Vater Himmel in der germanischen Naturreligion," which was listed in the *National-sozialistische Bibliographie* (see above, Chapter 4, n. 120). At the conclusion of his article, Scheltema asked rhetorically what the use of a psychological study of German mythology was in a time of grave national crisis. The answer, he averred, was that the myths showed how the warrior always wished to return for reinvigoration to the homeland, a lesson of great importance to Germany in 1944.

Hildegard Hetzer, a public health official and child psychologist who had dealings with the Göring Institute, worked for the SS Race and Settlement Main Office conducting psychological examinations of European children racially eligible for enforced transplantation into German families under the Lebensborn program. See Hillel and Henry, *Of Pure Blood*, pp. 183, 198.

109. Jung, *Letters*, p. 405n. Bonhoeffer's activities in 1938 were related to the author by Klaus Hoppe.

110. See Pongratz, *Psychotherapie*, p. 46n; Walter Schellenberg, *The Schellenberg Memoirs*, ed. Louis Hagen (London: Deutsch, 1956), pp. 86–87, 90–91, 112, 265, 284, 391, 438, 440; and Kersten, *Memoirs*, pp. 165–71. On similar squirmings in 1945, see Höhne, *Death's Head*, pp. 571–72. Barbara Hannah reports that Jung was involved in a plot, which she places in the summer of 1942, involving a German psychiatrist and some Swiss psychiatrists. Since the plot (and its outcome) is similar to that recounted by Bitter and Schellenberg, it is likely that it was the same one described by those sources for 1943. See Hannah, *Jung*, pp. 273–74.

111. Glenn Infield, *Eva and Adolf* (New York: Grossett & Dunlap, 1974), p. 147.

112. Orlow, *Nazi Party*, p. 335.

113. Albert Speer to the author, 31 August 1979.

114. Gert Buchheit, *Richter in roter Robe: Freisler Präsident des Volksgerichtshofes* (Munich: List, 1968), pp. 274–75.

115. Marc Bloch, *Strange Defeat: A Statement of Evidence Written in 1940*, trans. Gerard Hopkins (New York: W. W. Norton, 1968), pp. 36, 60.

116. See Karl Pintschovious, *Die seelische Widerstandskraft im modernen Krieg*, pp. 13–56. See also Wladimir Eliasberg, "German Philosophy and German Psychological Warfare," *Journal of Psychology* 14 (1942): 207.

117. Farago, *German Psychological Warfare*, pp. ix–x; John Laffin, *Jackboot: The Story of the German Soldier* (London: Cassell, 1965), pp. 154–59, 166–67, 176–77, 180–81.

118. Farago, *German Psychological Warfare*, pp. 13–33; and Ulfried Geuter to the author, 5 May 1981. See also Max Simoneit, *Deutsches Soldatentum 1914 und 1939* (Berlin: Junker & Dünnhaupt, 1940).

119. See E. Tiling and Max Simoneit, "Der Psychiater auf der Psychologischen Prüfstelle," *Der deutsche Militärarzt* 3 (1938): 509–14; ibid. 4 (1939): 201–5; and ibid., pp. 205–6.

120. "Propagandamöglichkeiten in der Farbigenarmee Frankreichs," Völkerpsychologischen Untersuchungen Nr. 8. H 1/661 (Generalstab des Heeres, 2. Abteilung), Bundesarchiv-Militärarchiv; and Microcopy T-78, Roll 440. National Archives.

121. Felix Scherke and Ursula Vitzhun, eds., *Bibliographie der geistigen Kriegsführung* (Berlin: Bernard & Graefe, 1938), p. 10. See also William Ebenstein, *The Nazi State* (New York: Farrer & Rinehart, 1943), p. 108. On psychology in the German military, see Geuter, "Professionalisierung," pp. 203–9, 274–86, 414–50.

122. Störring, "Die Verschiedenheiten der psychopathologischen Erfahrungen"; Hummel, "Vergleichende Untersuchungen"; Schultz, *Lebensbilderbuch*, p. 136; and Decker, *Freud in Germany*, pp. 194, 207–9, 225, 236–39.

123. See Heinrich Wietfeldt, *Kriegsneurose als psychisch-soziale Mangelkrankheit* (Leipzig: Georg Thieme, 1936), pp. 12–13, 25; Viktor von Weizsäcker, "Soziologische Bedeutung der nervösen Krankheiten und der Psychotherapie."

124. Pintschovious, *Seelische Widerstandskraft*, p. 24.

125. See Simon, "Das Problem der Psychopathen in der Wehrmacht," *Der deutsche Militärarzt* 3 (1938): 33–35. See also Otto Wuth, "Die Psychopathen in der Wehrmacht nebst Besprechung einiger einschlägigen Fragen."

126. Schultz, "Anweisung für Trüppenärzte," p. 20.

127. A. Eichberg, "Der nervöse Mensch als Soldat." Cf. the somewhat grudging acknowledgment of psychotherapy's usefulness in Werner Villinger, "Psychiatrie und Wehrmacht."

128. Schultz, *Lebensbilderbuch*, pp. 135–36. See also Otto Brosius, "Methode und Auswertung Kurzer zum Zwecke des Menschenerkennens durchgeführter Aussprachen," *Soldatentum* 4 (1937): 130–34; and Lockot, "Erinnern und Durcharbeiten," pp. 123, 280.

129. Heinrich Knoche, "Die Entwicklung und Organisation des Sanitätswesens der deutschen Luftwaffe 1935–1945" (Medical dissertation, Düsseldorf, 1974); and Heinz Knoche to the author, 22 December 1982. By 1944 Göring

was addressed by a fellow medical staff officer as an *Oberfeldarzt,* a rank equivalent to lieutenant-colonel. See Wolfgang Driest, *Richtlinien über Menschenführung in der Truppe,* p. 4.

130. Kemper to the author, 20 February 1974. See A. Briegel, "Psychiatrie in der Luftfahrtmedizin," in Kretschmer, *Psychiatry,* pp. 276–88; Immo von Hattingberg, Fragebogen, 19 August 1939, BDC: Parteikorrespondenz; and Schultz, *Lebensbilderbuch,* p. 143. See also Heinrich Lottig, "Neurologische und psychologische Erfahrungen aus der Luftfahrtmedizin," *Fortschritte der Neurologie* 11 (1939): 441–54.

131. P. Würfler, "Zum Verständnis der Neurose."

132. Erich Hippke, "Anweisung für die Truppenärzte über gesundheitliche Betreuung der jugendlichen Lw-Helfer und Lw-Helferinnen." On the particular importance of the psychological care of young air force auxiliaries, see also Schultz, "Anweisung fur Trüppenärzte," p. 20.

133. Immo von Hattingberg, "Medical Care for Flying Personnel," pp. 1059, 1060–64, 1067–68. See also Hans Luxenburger, "Seelische Wehrhygiene, insbesondere bei der Luftwaffe," in Siegfried Handloser and Wilhelm Hoffmann, eds., *Wehrhygiene* (Berlin: Springer-Verlag, 1944), pp. 530–32; and Pongratz, *Psychiatrie,* pp. 377–78.

It is uncertain how many of the doctors and psychologists ("medical assistants with special training") had been trained at the Göring Institute. Given its short lifespan, the institute did not produce a huge number of graduates and, given their duties, the supervising psychotherapists there did not have the opportunity to serve the Luftwaffe in this capacity. It is likely, however, that some of those in this realm of Luftwaffe medical service received some or all of their training at the Göring Institute.

134. *ZfP* 10 (1938): 186. See Clemens Laar (pseud.), . . . *reitet für Deutschland. Carl-Friedrich von Langen: ein Kämpferschicksal* (Hanover: A. Sponholtz, 1936).

135. BDC: Reichsärztekammer and Parteikorrespondenz. See also Briegel, "Psychiatrie in der Luftfahrtmedizin," pp. 283–85.

136. See Heinrich Grunwaldt, "Über die psychischen Bedingungen des Luftschutzes," p. 39.

137. Johannes Heinrich Schultz, "Seelische Reaktionen auf die Verdunkelung."

138. Schultz, *Die seelische Gesunderhaltung,* pp. 31–34.

139. Pongratz, *Psychotherapie,* p. 260; and Heyer to Hasselbach. Schultz likewise intervened for Riemann; see ibid., p. 360.

140. See, for example, Günter Elsässer, "Erfahrungen an 1400 Kriegsneurosen (Aus einem neurologisch-psychiatrischen Reserve-Lazarett des 2. Weltkrieges)," in Hans Walter Gruhle et al., eds., *Psychiatrie der Gegenwart. Forschung und Praxis* (Berlin: J. Springer, 1960–), vol. 3: *Soziale und Angewandte Psychiatrie,* ed. E. K. Cruickshank et al. (1961), p. 696; and Richard Jung, "Einleitung zur Kriegspsychiatrie," in ibid., pp. 568–73. Jung, drawing from Elsässer's report, argues (p. 570) that neuroses in World War II were less common because, given the distance from home and the frequent savagery of the fighting (especially on the eastern front), men were less likely to break down when they were fighting for survival without prospect of leave. Yet it is clear that some psychiatrists (like Elsässer) were using psychotherapeutic

methods, a practice that conflicted with the official military and party line that any mental dysfunction was physiological and/or hereditary. Such theses were easier to assert at home during peacetime: See, for example, Adolf Heidenhain, *Die Psychiatrie im Dienste der Wehrmacht* (Leipzig: Georg Thieme, 1938).

141. Beratender Psychiater beim Heeresgruppenarzt D, "Vierteljährlicher Erfahrungsbericht für die Zeit vom 1.4. bis 30.6.1944" (Paris, 10 July 1944), pp. 1–2, H 20/122 (Beratender Psychiater), Bundesarchiv-Militärarchiv; and T-78, Roll 192.

142. Dr. Wilke, Beratender Psychiater beim Armeearzt Panzer A.O.K. 4— i.A. Heeresgruppenarztes Nord-Ukraine, "Erfahrungsbericht über die Zeit vom 1. April bis 30. Juni 1944"; H 20/122.

143. Wuth to Bumke, 23 February 1942; Bumke to Wuth, 27 February 1942; and Wuth to Bumke, 3 March 1942.

144. Briegel, "Psychiatrie in der Luftfahrtmedizin," p. 276.

145. *Luftwaffeverordnungsblatt* no. 1209 (1943): 636. See Otto Paust, "Gegen jeder Kriegspsychose," *Das Schwarze Korps,* 25 August 1938, p. 1.

146. Verfügung Chef des Oberkommandos der Wehrmacht 14 n 19 WR (II) 58/43 q vom 19.5.1943; Der Chef des Sanitätswesens der Luftwaffe, "Anweisung für Trüppenärzte zur Beurteilung gleichgeschlechtlicher Handlungen," Az. 49 a Nr. 28500/44 (2 G) vom 7.6.44., cited in Schultz, "Anweisung für Trüppenärzte," p. 19.

147. Max de Crinis, Beratender Psychiater beim Heeres-Sanitätsinspekteur, "Sammelbericht Nr. 10" (Berlin, December 1944), p. 26, H 20/90, Bundesarchiv-Militärarchiv; and T-78, Roll 190.

148. Oberkommando des Heeres (Gen z b V/H Wes Abt), "Unterlagen zur wehrgeistigen Führung der Truppe," no. 2 (January 1943), H 34/21, Bundesarchiv-Militärarchiv; and Microcopy T-77, Roll 135. See also Volker R. Berghahn, "NSDAP und 'Geistige Führung' der Wehrmacht 1939–1943," *Vierteljahreshefte für Zeitgeschichte* 17 (1969): 17–72.

149. Driest, *Menschenführung,* p. 4.

150. OKW Chef W. San Nr. 3696/44 H S In/Wi G Ib vom 30. Juni 1944, cited in Schultz, "Anweisung für Trüppenärzte," p. 2. Immo von Hattingberg maintains that this terminology was used because of medical dissatisfaction with the vagueness of the word "neurosis." Hattingberg flatly rejects the notion that the diagnosis of hysteria or neurosis was banned on political grounds by the Nazis and that physicians responded by ignoring such disorders or diagnosing them as organic diseases. For Hattingberg, the matter was simply one of evolving and using more specific and meaningful terms. See Hattingberg, "Medical Care for Flying Personnel," p. 1063.

This is most likely true as far as it goes. The development of medical psychology over the first three decades of the twentieth century had brought with it a great deal of experience and knowledge that was beginning to break the bounds established by the now popular term "neurosis." Schultz himself, in his Luftwaffe directive, referred to the insufficiency of the term. Such a concern was a natural one in light of psychotherapy's recently elevated professional status, and there was every reason for psychotherapists to take proud proprietary interest in the scientific development of their field as reflected in its concepts and terms. In addition, as we have seen, the Nazis did not ban the word "neurosis" in 1933 or destroy medical psychology in Germany. But the pressures of war did lead them to demand much more from individual citizens and soldiers and from the various professions. It is thus clear to any student of the German army, the Third Reich, or the Total War program that the notion of "war hysterics" or "war neurotics" was intolerable to the political and military authorities. This was especially the case when the Allied noose tightened around the Nazis' necks in the wake of the Normandy invasion of June 1944. Schultz in his directive refers to the OKW *prohibition* of such terms and not just to the official prescription of the more specific terms to replace the word "neurosis." There can be no doubt that there was an important political element in this order that stemmed from the leadership's concern about morale and the desire to justify brutal measures against those who "fled" into illness.

151. Otto Nitzsche, "Kriegswichtiges in der ärztlichen Praxis," p. 170. The hard line adopted in the fervor for total war applied to the civilian work force as well. In 1944 Conti announced an order by slave labor boss Fritz Sauckel on behalf of Goebbels, dated 28 July, that outlined punishments for physicians who allowed patients to duck work. See *Deutsches Ärzteblatt* 74 (1944): 147.

152. Störring, "Die Verschiedenheiten der psychopathologischen Erfahrungen," p. 29. See also Otto Wuth, "Über den Selbstmord bei den Soldaten," *Soldatentum* 3' (1936): 84–90.

153. Pongratz, *Psychotherapie,* pp. 290–91.

154. Edward Shils and Morris Janowitz, "Cohesion and Disintegration in the Wehrmacht in World War II," *Public Opinion Quarterly* 12 (1948): 281. (Italics in original.) See also Henry Dicks, "Psychological Foundations of the Wehrmacht," Directorate of Army Psychiatry Research Memorandum Nr. 11/02/9a (1944), Wiener Library; idem, "Personality Traits and National Socialist Ideology," *Human Relations* 3 (1950): 111–55; M. S. Gurfein and Morris Janowitz, "Trends in Wehrmacht Morale," *Public Opinion Quarterly* 10 (1946): 78–84; and Erik H. Erikson, "Hitler's Imagery and German Youth," *Psychiatry* 5 (1942): 475–93.

155. Regine Lockot to the author, 30 April 1980.

156. Adolf Martin Däumling to the author, 18 August 1980.

157. Anon. to Kemper, 14 July 1964; Pongratz, *Psychotherapie,* p. 291.

158. Nitzsche, "Kriegswichtiges in der ärztlichen Praxis," p. 169. For Müller-Hegemann's own account, see Jochen Köhler, *Klettern in der Grossstadt. Volkstümliche Geschichten vom Überleben in Berlin 1933–1945* (Berlin: Das Arsenal, 1979), pp. 139–40, 246–48.

159. Der Bevollmächtige für das Sanitäts- und Gesundheitswesen/Der Beauftragte für medizinische Wissenschaft und Forschung, "Medizinische Zeitschriften, die nach dem 1.I.1944 bestehen bleiben sollen," (Berlin: n.d.), p. 4, R 18, folder 5572, p. 4.

160. Pongratz, *Psychotherapie,* p. 290; and Heyer to Hasselbach.

161. Reichsinstitut für Psychologische Forschung und Psychotherapie im Reichsforschungsrat, "Ankündigung der Veranstaltungen des Sommer-Semesters 1944," pp. 16–20; and idem, "Ankündigung der Veranstaltungen des Winter-Semesters 1944/45," pp. 16–20.

162. According to Kemper, the institute must have been destroyed in one

of the last big air raids. See Pongratz, *Psychotherapie,* p. 293. According to Schultz-Hencke, however, the institute was burned to the ground by the Russians after a Russian officer was shot by SS men harbored in the building by Göring; for this reason Göring was taken prisoner. See Lockot, "Erinnern und Durcharbeiten," pp. 125, 281.

7. PSYCHOTHERAPY IN THE POSTWAR GERMANIES

1. Werner Kemper, *Die Seelenheilkunde in unserer Zeit,* p. 7. This book is based on a series of lectures given in a university extension course in Berlin-Charlottenburg during the autumn of 1945. See also ibid., pp. 66–68.

2. Pongratz, *Psychotherapie,* pp. 59, 72.

3. Gordon Wright, *The Ordeal of Total War 1939–1945,* The Rise of Modern Europe, ed. William Langer, vol. 20 (New York: Harper & Row, 1968), p. 246.

4. Lohmann and Rosenkötter, "Psychoanalyse in Hitlerdeutschland," p. 983; Pongratz, *Psychotherapie,* p. 277; and Schultz, *Lebensbilderbuch,* p. 148.

5. Pongratz, *Psychotherapie,* pp. 64, 264–99, 303–6; Dräger, "Psychoanalysis in Hitler Germany," p. 212; and Annemarie Dührssen, "Das Institut für psychogene Erkrankungen der AOK Berlin," Beilage zum Geschäftsbericht der Allgemeinen Ortskrankenkasse Berlin, pp. 3–6.

6. Pongratz, *Psychotherapie,* pp. 41–49, 56–59, 63–66, 302–3, 309; Credner, "Geleitwort," p. 11.

7. Pongratz, *Psychotherapie,* pp. 59–63, 303. See also Friedrich Domay, ed., *Handbuch der Deutschen Wissenschaftlichen Gesellschaften* (Wiesbaden: Steiner, 1964), pp. 543–50; and Thomä, "Psychoanalysis in Germany," pp. 685–88.

8. See Baumeyer, "Psychoanalyse in Deutschland," pp. 220–33; Boehm, "Bericht," pp. 306–10; Müller-Braunschweig, "Skizze der Geschichte," pp. 22–35; Dräger, "Psychoanalysis in Hitler Germany," pp. 213–14; Pongratz, *Psychotherapie,* pp. 279–80, 312, 321–22; and Edith Kurzweil, "The (Freudian) Congress of Vienna," *Commentary* 52 (1971): 80–83. On Mitscherlich, see also Frederick Wyatt, "Psychoanalysis Abroad: Observations on Image and Practice in Europe, and particularly in the German Federal Republic," paper presented to the Michigan Psychoanalytic Society, 25 May 1984.

9. See Pongratz, *Psychotherapie,* p. 323n; Domay, *Handbuch,* p. 543; and Schultz, *Lebensbilderbuch,* p. 161. Heyer, along with Curtius, was denied membership in the C. G. Jung Society after the war because of Nazi party membership. Hannah, *Jung,* p. 289n. Jung himself rejected Heyer's protestations of political innocence and loyalty to Jung. See Jung to van den Hoop, 14 January 1946, in Jung, *Letters,* p. 406.

10. Albert Wellek, "Deutsche Psychologie und Nationalsozialismus," *Psychologie und Praxis* 4 (1960): 177–82; Pongratz, *Psychotherapie,* p. 49. See also Ulfried Geuter, "Institutionelle und professionelle Schranken der Nachkriegsauseinandersetzungen über die Psychologie im Nationalsozialismus," *Psychologie- und Gesellschaftskritik* 4 (1980): 5–39.

11. Walter Seitz, "Die Lage der Psychotherapie in Deutschland."

12. See Domay, *Handbuch,* p. 542; and Winkler, "50 Jahre AÄGP," p. 79.

13. Seitz, "Lage der Psychotherapie," p. 400.

14. Bundesministerium der Verteidigung to the author, 15 May 1981. See also Ulfried Geuter and Bernhard Kroner, "Militärpsychologie," in Gunter Rexilius and Siegfried Grübitsch, eds., *Handbuch psychologischer Grundbegriffe* (Reinbek b. Hamburg: Rowohlt, 1981), pp. 672–89. On the academic and professional activity of psychotherapists in West Germany, see Marlies von Hattingberg, "Über Psychotherapie," *Medizinische Monatsschrift* 3 (1949): 385–88; Schultz, *Psychotherapie,* pp. 173–79; and idem, *Lebensbilderbuch,* p. 160.

15. Winkler, "Present Status of Psychotherapy"; and idem, "50 Jahre AÄGP," p. 79.

16. Raoul Schindler, "The Development of Psychotherapy in Austria Since 1945," in Fromm-Reichmann and Moreno, *Progress in Psychotherapy 1956,* pp. 267–76; and Wolfgang Huber, *Psychoanalyse in Österreich,* pp. 71–172.

17. Winkler, "Present Status of Psychotherapy," p. 288.

18. Winkler, "50 Jahre AÄGP," pp. 76–79; Domay, *Handbuch,* p. 542. The German and Austrian societies were members of the International Society for Medical Psychotherapy, which, after World War II, succeeded Jung's International General Medical Society for Psychotherapy (1934–40).

19. See Johannes Hirschmann, "Psychotherapie," in Kretschmer, *Psychiatry,* pp. 203–14; Baumeyer, "Psychoanalyse in Deutschland," pp. 219–20; and Pongratz, *Psychotherapie,* pp. 308–9. See also Ernst Kretschmer, *Medizinische Psychologie,* 9th ed. (Stuttgart: Georg Thieme, 1947).

20. Pongratz, *Psychotherapie,* pp. 51–56; Jung, *Letters,* pp. 542–44.

21. Ernst Kretschmer, "Organisationsfragen der deutschen Psychotherapie," pp. 378–79; Pongratz, *Psychotherapie,* p. 61; "Gesetz zur Ordnung der Krankenpflege"; Göring, "Bericht," p. 1; "Vereinbarung über die Ausübung von tiefenpsychologisch fundierter und analytischer Psychotherapie in der kassenärztlichen Versorgung," *Deutsches Ärzteblatt–Ärztliche Mitteilungen* 73 (1976): 1769; and Kurt Höck, "Das abgestufte System der Diagnostik und Therapie neurotischer Störungen," p. 91.

22. Winkler, "50 Jahre AÄGP," pp. 80–82.

23. Pongratz, *Psychotherapie,* p. 54. Even some of Kretschmer's assistants secretly sought training analyses from Marzinowski in Tübingen. See Pongratz, *Psychiatrie,* p. 67.

24. Winkler, "50 Jahre AÄGP," p. 82.

25. Annemarie Dührssen, "Zu den neuen Psychotherapie-Richtlinien," *Die Ortskrankenkasse* 23/24 (1976): 836; Seitz, "Lage der Psychotherapie," p. 401.

26. See the "open letters" published in *Report Psychologie Sonderheft der Landesgruppe Berlin* (1980): 9–11.

27. Cf. Michael Hockel, "Der Beruf des Diplom-Psychologen," *Report Psychologie* 4 (1979): 19–73; and Carl Nedelmann and Klaus Horn, "Gesellschaftliche Aufgaben der Psychotherapie," *Psyche* 30 (1976): 827–53.

28. Seitz, "Lage der Psychotherapie," p. 401; "Erläuterungen zum Konzept des 'Klinischen Psychologen,'" *Report Psychologie Sonderheft der Landesgruppe Berlin,* pp. 15–18; and Nedelman and Horn, "Gesellschaftliche Aufgaben," p. 840.

29. Kurt Höck to the author, 21 September 1979.

30. Ibid.

31. Höck, "System der Diagnostik und Therapie," p. 90.

32. Kurt Höck, "Psychotherapie in der DDR," p. 7; see also idem, "Entwicklung und Aufgaben der Psychotherapie in der DDR."

33. Höck, "Psychotherapie in der DDR," pp. 8–23; and Adolf Kossakowski, "Psychology in the German Democratic Republic," *American Psychologist* 35 (1980): 450–60.

34. Höck, "Psychotherapie in der DDR," p. 7; and Höck to the author.

Bibliography

I. INTERVIEWS

Franz Baumeyer, West Berlin, 1 November 1973
Käthe Dräger, West Berlin, 25 October 1973
Ernst Göring, Waibstadt/Baden, 21, 22, and 23 November 1979
Gustav Graber, Berne, 12 February 1974
Erika Hantel, Alstädten/Allgäu, 16 March 1974
Lucy Heyer-Grote, Schlangenbad, 21 January 1974
Eva Hildebrand (Rittmeister), Reckenberg/Schwarzwald, 10 February 1974
Franz Jung, Küsnacht/Zurich, 7 June 1974
Marie Kalau vom Hofe, Neuhaus am Schliersee, 11 January 1974
Werner Kemper, West Berlin, 11 October, 28 November, and 3 December 1973
Olga von König-Fachsenfeld, Aalen Fachsenfeld, 25 May 1974
Wolfgang Kranefeldt, West Berlin, 23 October 1973
John Kunkel, Ann Arbor, 23 April 1983
Gerhard Maetze, West Berlin, 11 November 1973
Dietfried Müller-Hegemann, Essen, 30 January 1974
Fritz Riemann, Munich, 8 January 1974
Gerhart Scheunert, Hamburg, 10 July 1974
Kurt Seelmann, Munich, 7 January 1974
August Vetter, Ammerland am Starnberger See, 10 January 1974
Kurt Zierold, Bad Godesberg, 27 January 1974

II. UNPUBLISHED MATERIAL

1. Archives

Berlin Document Center
    Korrespondenz W:
    Kulturkammer
    NS-Lehrerbund
    NSDAP-Zentralkartei
    Oberstes Parteigericht
    Parteikorrespondenz
    Parteistatistische Erhebung 1939 (Berlin)
    Reichsärztekammer

SA
SS-Ahnenerbe
SS-Führer

Bundesarchiv
K1Erw.762   Deutsches Institut für Psychologische Forschung und Psycho-
             therapie
  NS 5   Deutsche Arbeitsfront
  NS 19   Persönlicher Stab des Reichsführer-SS
  NS 21   Das Ahnenerbe
  R 18   Reichsministerium des Innern
  R 21   Reichsministerium für Wissenschaft, Erziehung und Volksbild-
             ung
  R 22   Reichsjustizministerium
  R 36   Deutscher Gemeindetag
  R 43   Reichskanzlei
  R 96   Öffentliche Einrichtungen der Gesundheits- und Wohlfahrts-
             pflege

Bundesarchiv-Militärarchiv
  H 1   Generalstab des Heeres
  H 20   Heeres-Sanitätsinspekteur
  H 34   OKW
  RW 2   OKW, Chef des Wehrmachtsanitätswesens

National Archives
  T-77   Records of the Headquarters of the German Armed Forces High
             Command
  T-78   Records of the Headquarters of the German Armed Forces High
             Command
  T-84   Miscellaneous German Records Collection
  T-175   Records of the Reich Leader of the SS and Chief of the German
             Police
  T-321   Records of Headquarters of the German Air Force High
             Command
  T-1021   German Documents Among the War Crimes Records of the
             Judge Advocate Division, Headquarters, United States Army,
             Europe

2. *Papers, Documents, and Dissertations*

Blanck, Gertrude S. "The Development of Psychotherapy as a Profession: A
    Study of the Process of Professionalization." Ph.D. dissertation, New York
    University, 1963.
Cocks, Geoffrey Campbell. "Psyche and Swastika: 'Neue Deutsche Seelenheil-
    kunde' 1933–1945." Ph.D. dissertation, University of California, Los An-
    geles, 1975.
Deutsches Institut für Psychologische Forschung und Psychotherapie e.V. in
    Berlin, "Ankündigung der Veranstaltungen." Berlin, Summer 1941 to
    Winter 1943–44.

————. "Richtlinien für die Ausbildung." Berlin, n.d.

————. "Thesen zur Neurosenlehre." Berlin, n.d.

————. "Veranstaltungen." Berlin, Winter 1936–37 to Winter 1940–41.

Geuter, Ulfried. "Die Professionalisierung der deutschen Psychologie im-Nationalsozialismus." Inaugural dissertation, Free University of Berlin, 1982.

Hippke, Erich. "Anweisung für die Trüppenärzte über gesundheitliche Betreuung der jugendlichen Lw.-Helfer und Lw.-Helferinnen." Sanitätsinspekteur der Luftwaffe, 21 December 1942. H 20/122 (Heeres-Sanitätsinspekteur, Beratender Psychiater). Bundesarchiv-Militärarchiv. Records of the Headquarters of the German Army High Command, T-78, Roll 92. National Archives.

Höck, Kurt. "Psychotherapie in der DDR. Eine Dokumentation zum 30. Jahrestag der Republik, Teil I." Berlin, 1979.

Lockot, Regine. "Erinnern und Durcharbeiten. Zur Geschichte der Psychoanalyse und Psychotherapie im Nationalsozialismus." Inaugural dissertation, Free University of Berlin, 1984.

Meyer, Dr. "Vorschläge zur Behandlung und Heilung der Empfängnisunfähigkeit der Frau und der Zeugungsunfähigkeit des Mannes." The Hague: SS-Lebensborn, Abteilung Gesundheitswesen, n.d. NS 19 (Persönlicher Stab der Reichsführer-SS) 291, folder 1152. Bundesarchiv. Records of the Reich Leader of the SS and Chief of the German Police, T-175, Roll 20. National Archives.

Müller-Braunschweig, Carl. "Skizze der Geschichte der 'Deutschen Psychoanalytischen Gesellschaft' von 1936 bis 1947." In Deutsche Psychoanalytische Gesellschaft, e.V. "Dokumente zur Geschichte der Psychoanalyse in Deutschland 1933–1951."

Reichsinstitut für Psychologische Forschung und Psychotherapie im Reichsforschungsrat, "Ankündigung der Veranstaltungen." Berlin, Summer 1944 to Winter 1944–45.

————. "Richtlinien der Poliklinik und Psychodiagnostischen Abteilung." Berlin, 1 April 1944.

[Rittmeister, John F.] "Tagebuchblätter aus dem Gefängnis von Dr. med. John Rittmeister geb. 22.8.1898 hingerichtet am 13.5.1943," Akten der Staatsanwaltschaft am Landgericht Lüneburg Strafsache gegen Dr. Manfred Roeder, Nds 721 Acc. 69/76 Lüneburg, vol. 10, pp. 126–57. Niedersächsisches Hauptstaatsarchiv, Hanover.

"Satzungen der deutschen allgemeinen ärztlichen Gesellschaft fur Psychotherapie." Berlin, 15 September 1933.

[Schneider, Carl.] "Schlussbemerkungen: Wissenschaftliche, wirtschaftliche und soziale Bedeutung und Zukunft der psychiatrischen Therapien." Berlin, 1941. R 96 (Öffentliche Einrichtung der Gesundheits- und Wohlfahrtspflege) I 9 (Reichsarbeitsgemeinschaft Heil- und Pflegeanstalten: Denkschriften und wissenschaftliche Veröffentlichungen). Bundersarchiv.

Schultz, Johannes Heinrich. "Anweisung für Trüppenärzte über Erkennung und Behandlung von abnormen seelischen Reaktionen (Neurosen)." Berlin, n.d. RW 2 (OKW, Chef des Wehrmachtsanitätswesens) v. 251. Bundesarchiv-Militärarchiv. Records of the Headquarters of the German Armed Forces High Command, T-77, Roll 857. National Archives.

Wuth, Otto. "Psychopathen in der Wehrmacht nebst Besprechung einiger einschlägigen Fragen." Berlin: Reichsluftfahrtsministerium, 9–10 March 1939. H 20/128. Bundesarchiv-Militärarchiv. Records of the Headquarters of the German Army High Command, T-78, Roll 192, frames 6135877–6135898. National Archives.

Zapp, Gudrun. "Psychoanalyse und Nationalsozialismus. Untersuchungen zum Verhältnis Medizin/Psychoanalyse während des Nationalsozialismus." Medical dissertation, Kiel, 1980.

III. PUBLISHED PRIMARY SOURCES

1. Nazi Medicine and Health Administration

Bartels, Fritz. "Die Gesundheitsfuhrung des deutschen Volkes." *Deutsches Ärzteblatt* 66 (1936): 334–37.

Blome, Kurt. "Das öffentliche Gesundheitswesen im nationalsozialistischen Staate." *Deutsches Ärzteblatt* 66 (1936): 341–43.

Bockhacker, Werner. "Die betriebliche Gesundheitsführung." *Monatshefte für Nationalsozialistische Sozialpolitik* 10 (1943): 28–29.

Bonhoeffer, Karl. *Die psychiatrische Aufgaben bei der Ausführung des Gesetzes zur Verhütung erbkranken Nachwuchses.* Berlin: Karger, 1934.

Conti, Leonardo, ed., *Reden und Aufrufe Gerhard Wagners.* Berlin: Reichsgesundheitsverlag, c. 1944.

Finck, H. "Volksgesundheit und Liebesleben." *Ziel und Weg* 4 (1934): 287–94.

Finke, Edmund. "Siegmund Freud: Studien zum europäischen Nihilismus." *Deutsche Ostmark* 24 (1938): 41–45.

Haag, Friedrich Erhard. *Die geistige Gesundheit des Volkes und ihre Pflege.* 2nd ed. Munich: J. F. Lehmanns, 1935.

———. "Gesundheitsführung." *Münchener medizinische Wochenschrift* 86 (1939): 180–84.

Hobohm, J. "Der Nationalsozialismus als Überwinder des Zeitalters der Neurose." *Ziel und Weg* 4 (1934): 41–44.

Hoske, Hans. *Die menschliche Leistung als Grundlage des totalen Staates.* Leipzig: S. Hirzel, 1936.

Kötschau, Karl. *Zum nationalsozialistischen Umbruch in der Medizin.* Stuttgart: Hippokrates, 1936.

Krauskopf, Alfred A. "Tiefenpsychologische Beiträge zur Rassenseelenforschung." *Rasse* 5 (1939): 362–68.

Löhr, Hanns. *Über die Stellung und Bedeutung der Heilkunde im nationalsozialistischen Staate.* Berlin: "Die medizinische Welt," 1935.

Müller, Willy. *Das soziale Leben im neuen Deutschland unter besonderer Berücksichtigung der Deutschen Arbeitsfront.* Berlin: E. S. Mittler, 1938.

Nitzsche, Otto. "Kriegswichtiges in der ärztlichen Praxis." *Deutsches Ärzteblatt* 74 (1944): 169–71.

Peil, Helmut. "Über die Hysterie: Ein Beitrag zur Krise der Medizin." *Volksgesundheitswacht* 2 (1935): 4–7.

Pfotenhauer, Gerhard. "'Aufnordnung' und 'vorgeburtliche Erziehung'— 'Rassenhygiene' eines Psychoanalytikers." *Der Öffentliche Gesundheitsdienst* 2 (1936): 184–87.

Pintschovious, Karl, and Zeiss, Heinrich, eds. *Zivilisationsschäden am Menschen.* 2nd ed. Munich: J. F. Lehmanns, 1944.

"Die Psychoanalyse des Juden Sigmund Freud." *Deutsche Volksgesundheit aus Blut und Boden* 1 (1933): 15–16.

Ramm, Rudolf. *Ärztliche Rechts- und Standeskunde. Der Arzt als Gesundheitserzieher.* 2nd ed. Berlin: Walter de Gruyter, 1943.

Reichsministerium des Innern, *Der öffentliche Gesundheitsdienst im 3. Reich.* Berlin: Schoetz, 1939.

Reiter, Hans. *Ziele und Wege des Reichsgesundheitsamtes im 3. Reich.* Leipzig: Barth, 1936.

Schulze-Maier, Friedrich. "Gesundheitspflege der Seele." *Der Hoheitsträger* 5 (1937): 26–27.

Thiel, Peter Johannes. "Die Selbstbefleckung (Onanie!)." *Deutsche Volksgesundheit aus Blut und Boden* 2 (1934): 10.

Wagner, Gerhard. "Die Aufhebung der Kurierfreiheit." *Deutsches Ärzteblatt* 63 (1933): 650–51.

———. "Neue deutsche Heilkunde." *Deutsches Ärzteblatt* 66 (1936): 419–20.

———. *Reden und Aufrufe.* Edited by Leonardo Conti. Berlin: Reichsgesundheitsverlag, 1943.

———. "Der Weg zu einer neuen deutschen Heilkunde." *Völkischer Beobachter,* 17 April 1936, p. 5.

2. Psychotherapy

a. BOOKS

Arnhold, Karl, *Der Deutsche Betrieb: Aufgaben und Ziele Nationalsozialistischer Betriebsführung.* 2nd ed. Leipzig: Bibliographisches Institut, 1942.

———. *Leistungsertüchtigung.* Berlin: Lehrmittelzentrale der DAF, 1942.

Bilz, Rudolf. *Lebensgesetze der Liebe. Eine anthropologische Studie über Gefühlselemente, Bewegungen und Metaphern menschlicher Liebe. ZfP* Supplement no. 4, Leipzig: Hirzel, 1942.

———. ed. *Psyche und Leistung. Bericht über die 3. Tagung der deutschen allgemeinen ärztlichen Gesellschaft für Psychotherapie in Wien am 6. und 7. September 1940.* Stuttgart: Hippokrates, 1940.

Bumke, Oswald. *Die Psychoanalyse und ihre Kinder. Eine Auseinandersetzung mit Freud, Adler und Jung.* 2nd ed. Berlin: Julius Springer, 1938.

Cimbal, Walter, ed. *Bericht über den IV. Allgemeinen ärztlichen Kongress für Psychotherapie in Bad Nauheim 11. bis 14. April 1929.* Leipzig: S. Hirzel, 1929.

———. *Naturgemässe Wege zum seelischen Gleichgewicht, eine natürliche Seelenkunde.* Berlin: F. Duberow, 1941.

Curtius, Otto, ed. *Psychotherapie in der Praxis. Ein Gesamtüberblick über die 2. Tagung der deutschen Allgemeinen ärztlichen Gesellschaft für Psychotherapie zu Düsseldorf September 1938.* Düsseldorf: Knorsch, 1939.

Detmar, Bernhard. *Die natürliche Behandlung und Heilung der Nervenkrankheiten.* Stuttgart: Hippokrates, 1939.

Döhl, Ilse; Graber, Gustav; and Mohr, Fritz. *Leibniz, Carus und Nietzsche als Vorläufer unserer Tiefenpsychologie. ZfP* Supplement no. 3. Leipzig: S. Hirzel, 1940.

Driest, Wolfgang. *Richtlinien über Menschenführung in der Truppe. Seelische Wehrbetreuung.* 2nd ed. Berlin: F. Vogtmann, 1944.

Eliasberg, Wladimir, ed. *Bericht über den II. Allgemeinen ärztlichen Kongress
für Psychotherapie in Bad Nauheim 27. bis 30. April 1927.* Leipzig: S. Hirzel, 1927.

————, and Cimbal, Walter, eds. *Bericht über den III. Allgemeinen ärztlichen
Kongress für Psychotherapie in Baden-Baden 20. bis 22. April 1928.* Leipzig:
S. Hirzel, 1929.

Gauger, Kurt. *Christoph. Roman einer Seefahrt.* Stuttgart: Hohenstaufen,
1940.

————. *Politische Medizin. Grundriss einer deutschen Psychotherapie.* Hamburg: Hanseatische Verlagsanstalt, 1934.

Göring, Matthias Heinrich, ed. *Deutsche Seelenheilkunde. Zehn Aufsätze zu
den seelenärztlichen Aufgaben unserer Zeit.* Leipzig: S. Hirzel, 1934.

————. ed. *1. Sonderheft des Deutschen Instituts für Psychologische Forschung
und Psychotherapie, ZfP.* Leipzig: S. Hirzel, 1940.

————. ed. *Erziehungshilfe. 2. Sonderheft des Deutschen Instituts für Psychologische Forschung und Psychotherapie, ZfP.* Leipzig: S. Hirzel, 1940.

————. *Die Individualpsychologie als Werkzeug der Bibelbetrachtung.* Wuppertal-Elberfeld: J. H. Born, 1933.

————. *Über seelisch bedingte echte Organerkrankungen.* Stuttgart: Hippokrates, 1938.

Hanse, August. *Persönlichkeitsgefüge und Krankheit.* Stuttgart: Hippokrates,
1938.

Hantel, Erika. *Brücken von Mensch zu Mensch. Erfahrungen einer Betriebs-
psychologin.* Stuttgart: Hippokrates, 1953.

————. *Verborgenes Kräftespiel. Die Pflege des Menschlichen als Aufgabe für
Industrie und Wirtschaft.* 2nd ed. Stuttgart: Ernst Klett, 1947.

Hattingberg, Hans von. *Neue Seelenheilkunde.* Berlin: Bucholz, 1943.

————. *Über die Liebe. Eine ärztliche Wegweisung.* Munich: J. F. Lehmanns,
1936.

Heyer, Gustav Richard. *Der Organismus der Seele. Eine Einführung in die
analytische Seelenheilkunde.* 2nd ed. Munich: J. F. Lehmanns, 1937.

————. *Menschen in Not.* Stuttgart: Hippokrates, 1943.

————. *Praktische Seelenheilkunde.* Munich: J. F. Lehmanns, 1935.

————, and Seifert, Friedrich, eds. *Reich der Seele. Arbeiten aus dem Münchener Psychologischen Arbeitskreis,* 2 vols. Munich: J. F. Lehmanns, 1937.

Jung, Carl Gustav. *C. G. Jung Speaking, Interviews and Encounters.* Edited
by William McGuire and translated by R. F. C. Hull. Princeton: Princeton
University Press, 1977.

————. *Collected Works.* Edited by Herbert Read, Michael Fordham and
Gerhard Adler. Translated by R. F. C. Hull. Vol. 10, *Civilization in Transition.* Bollingen Series XX. New York: Pantheon, 1964.

————. *Letters.* Edited by Gerhard Adler and Aniela Jaffe and translated by
R. F. C. Hull, Vol. 1, *1906–1950.* Bollingen Series XCV: 1. Princeton:
Princeton University Press, 1973.

Kemper, Werner. *Die Seelenheilkunde in unserer Zeit. Ihre Entwicklung, Ihr
Stand, Ihr Anspruch, Ihre Aufgaben.* Stuttgart: Ernst Klett, 1947.

————. *Die Störungen der Liebesfähigkeit beim Weibe. Klinik, Biologie und*

Psychologie der Geschlechtsfunktion und des Orgasmus. Leipzig: Georg Thieme, 1942.

Kretschmer, Ernst, sr. auth. *Psychiatry.* Field Information Agencies Technical Review of German Science 1939–1946, no. 83. Wiesbaden: Dietrich'sche Verlagsbuchhandlung, 1948.

Kretschmer, Ernst, and Cimbal, Walter, eds. *Bericht über den V. Allgemeinen ärztlichen Kongress für Psychotherapie in Baden-Baden 26. bis 29. April 1930.* Leipzig: S. Hirzel, 1930.

———. *Bericht über den VI. Allgemeinen ärztlichen Kongress für Psychotherapie in Dresden 14. bis 17. Mai 1931.* Leipzig: S. Hirzel, 1931.

Künkel, Fritz. *Charakter, Einzelmensch und Gruppe.* Leipzig: S. Hirzel, 1933.

———. *Grundzüge der politischen Charakterkunde.* 2nd ed. Berlin: Junker & Dünnhaupt, 1934.

———. *Das Wir. Die Grundbegriffe der Wir-Psychologie.* 3rd ed. Schwerin: Bahn, 1939.

———, and Künkel, Elisabeth. *Die Erziehung deiner Kinder.* Berlin: Falken-Verlag, 1936.

Meinertz, Josef. *Psychotherapie—eine Wissenschaft! Untersuchungen über die Wissenschaftsstruktur der Grundlagen seelischer Krankenbehandlung.* Berlin: Julius Springer, 1939.

Neumann, Johannes. *Leben ohne Angst. Psychologische Seelenheilkunde.* Stuttgart: Hippokrates, 1941.

Pintschovious, Karl. *Die seelische Widerstandskraft im modernen Krieg.* Berlin: Stalling, 1936.

Prinzhorn, Hans. *Psychotherapie. Voraussentzungen, Wesen, Grenzen.* Leipzig: Georg Thieme, 1929.

Psychotherapie. Bericht über den 1. Allgemeinen ärztlichen Kongress für Psychotherapie in Baden-Baden 17. bis 19. April 1926. Halle: Carl Marhold, 1926.

Schultz, Johannes Heinrich. *Geschlecht, Liebe, Ehe. Die Grundtatsachen des Liebes- und Geschlechtslebens in ihrer Bedeutung für Einzel- und Volksdasein.* 2nd ed. Munich: Reinhardt, 1941.

———. *Neurose, Lebensnot und ärztliche Pflicht: klinische Vorlesungen über Psychotherapie für Ärzte und Studierende.* Leipzig: Georg Thieme, 1936.

———. *Psychotherapie. Leben und Werk grosser Ärzte.* Stuttgart: Hippokrates, 1952.

———. *Die seelische Gesunderhaltung unter besonderer Berücksichtigung der Kriegsverhältnisse.* Berlin: E. S. Mittler, 1942.

Schultz-Hencke, Harald. *Der gehemmte Mensch. Grundlagen einer Desmologie als Beitrag zur Tiefenspsychologie.* Leipzig: Georg Thieme, 1940.

———. *Psychoanalyse und Psychotherapie. Gesammelte Aufsätze.* n.p., n.d.

Seelmann, Kurt. *Kind, Sexualität und Erziehung.* Munich: Reinhardt, 1942.

Seif, Leonhard, ed. *Wege der Erziehungshilfe. Ergebnisse und praktische Hinweise aus der Tätigkeit des Münchener Arbeitskreises für Erziehung.* Munich: J. F. Lehmanns, 1940.

Speer, Ernst. *Die Liebesfähigkeit (Kontaktpsychologie).* Munich: J. F. Lehmanns, 1937.

Zabel, Werner. *Grenzerweiterung der Schulmedizin.* Stuttgart: Hippokrates, 1934.

b. ARTICLES

Achelis, Werner. "Psychologische Hygiene." In Pintschovious and Zeiss, *Zivilisationssachäden am Menschen*, pp. 247–67.

———. "Psychologische Zivilisationsbilanz." In Pintschovious and Zeiss, *Zivilisationsschäden am Menschen*, pp. 53–81.

———. "Zivilisation und Gesundheit." *Die Gesundheitsführung "Ziel und Weg"* 3 (1941): 381–86.

Arnhold, Karl. "Arbeitspsychologie." *Deutsches Ärzteblatt* 64 (1934): 155–57.

———. "Psychologische Kräfte im Dienste der Berufserziehung und Leistungssteigerung." In Bilz, *Psyche und Leistung*, pp. 105–27.

Bally, Gustav. "Deutschstämmige Psychotherapie." *Neue Zürcher Zeitung*, 27 February 1934, p. 2.

Becker, Werner. "Psychotherapie bei Geisteskranken." *Psychiatrisch-Neurologische Wochenschrift* 45 (1943): 275–77.

Boehm, Felix. "Erhebung und Bearbeitung von Katamnesen." *ZfP* 14 (1942): 17–25.

———. "Poliklinische Erfahrungen." *ZfP* 12 (1940): 65–87.

Brauchle, Alfred. "Seelische Beeinflussung in der Gemeinschaft." *Münchener medizinische Wochenschrift* 87 (1940): 317–20.

———. "Seelische Naturheilkunde." *Volksgesundheitswacht* 1 (1934): 10–16.

Brendgen, Franz. "Vegetative Stigmatisation und Neurose." *ZfP* 11 (1939): 84–112.

Bresler, Johannes. "Geisteskrankheit als Kampf." *Psychiatrisch-Neurologische Wochenschrift* 42 (1940): 466–69.

———. "Gibt es nationale Psychotherapie?" *Psychiatrisch-Neurologische Wochenschrift* 42 (1940): 12–14.

———. "Unfallneurose und Reichsgericht." *Psychiatrisch- Neurologische Wochenschrift* 41 (1939): 453–55.

Christian, Paul. "Rechtswissenschaft, Ursachenbegriff und Neurosenfrage. Zum gleichnamigen Heft der sozialmedizinischen Schriftenreihe aus dem Gebiete des Reichsarbeitministeriums." *Der Nervenarzt* 14 (1941): 315–20.

Cimbal, Walter. "Aufgaben und Wege einer deutschen Seelenheilkunde." In Göring, *Deutsche Seelenheilkunde*, pp. 108–12.

———. "Gedanken zu einer vergleichenden Psychotherapie." *ZfP* 7 (1934): 304–12.

———. "Volksgemässe und wissenschaftliche Heilkunst nicht als Gegensatz, sondern als notwendige Ergänzung." *Hippokrates* 4 (1933): 277–87.

Curtius, Otto. "Das Kollektiv Unbewusste C. G. Jungs, seine Beziehung zur Persönlichkeit und Gruppenseele." *ZfP* 8 (1935): 265–79.

———. "Kongress der deutschen allgemeinen ärztlichen Gesellschaft für Psychotherapie 3. bis 6. Oktober 1935 in Breslau." *Zeitschrift für angewandte Psychologie* 9 (1935): 358–65.

de Crinis, Max, and Veit, Gertrud. "Stand der heutigen Psychiatrie in Deutschland." *Forschungen und Fortschritte* 19 (1943): 347–50.

Eggert, Gerhard. "Nietzsche und die Individualpsychologie." *ZfP* 11 (1939): 195–205.

Eichberg, A. "Der nervöse Mensch als Soldat." *Der Truppendienst* 4 (1939): 329–31.

Gauger, Kurt. "Psychotherapie und politisches Weltbild." *ZfP* 7 (1934): 158–68.

Gold, Herbert. "Auch die ersten Kindheitseinflüsse bestimmen die Lebensgestaltung." *Völkischer Beobachter,* 14 May 1939, p. 5.

Göring, Matthias Heinrich. "Die Bedeutung der Neurose in der Sozialversicherung." *ZfP* 11 (1939): 36–56.

————. "Deutsche Seelenheilkunde." *Völkischer Beobachter,* 3 December 1938, p. 5.

————. "Erfolgsmöglichkeiten der Psychotherapie." *ZfP* 8 (1935): 219–27.

————. "Grundlagen der Psychotherapie." *Deutsche medizinische Wochenschrift* 63 (1937): 1442–46.

————. "Individuum und Gemeinschaft im Reich der Psychologie." *Suddeutsche Monatshefte* 33 (1936): 286–88.

————. "Der Internationale und Deutsche Kongress für Psychotherapie." *Deutsches Ärzteblatt* 68 (1938): 868–69.

————. "Körperliche Erkrankungen als Auswirkungen seelischer Störungen." *Hippokrates* 5 (1934): 848–90.

————. "Die Kraft der Seele." *Hippokrates* 10 (1939): 1074–76.

————. "Die nationalsozialistische Idee in der Psychotherapie." In Göring, *Deutsche Seelenheilkunde,* pp. 11–16.

————. "Weltanschauung und Psychotherapie." *ZfP* 9 (1936): 291–96; and *Hippokrates* 9 (1938): 1097–1103.

————. "Zur Neurosenlehre." *Deutsches Ärzteblatt* 66 (1936): 562–63.

Grunwaldt, Heinrich. "Über die psychischen Bedingungen des Luftschutzes." *Wissen und Wehr* 6 (1937): 39–49.

Haeberlin, Carl. "Die Bedeutung von Ludwig Klages und Hans Prinzhorn für die deutsche Psychotherapie." *ZfP* 7 (1934): 38–51.

————. "Lebensrythmus und Lebensführung." *Hippokrates* 9 (1938): 826.

————. "Über das vital Unbewusste, Bewusstsein und Charakter mit Bemerkungen über die deutsche Seelenkunde von Goethe und Carus." *ZfP* (1935): 279–95.

Hanse, August. "Ärztliche Seelenführung." *Ziel und Weg* 6 (1936): 440–43.

————. "Konstitution, Biozentrische Gesundheitsführung und Volksbezogenheit." *Hippokrates* 6 (1936): 701–11.

————. "Zur volksbiologischen und wertphilosophischen Begründung einer deutschen Psychotherapie." *Medizinische Klinik* 30 (1934): 286–88.

Hantel, Erika. "Beginenwesen—ohne Romantik." *Frankfurter Zeitung,* 24 October 1942, p. 4.

Hattingberg, Hans von. "Ehekrisen, ärztlich gesehen." *Deutsche medicinische Wochenschrift* 66 (1940): 909–12.

————. "Die Eheproblematik unserer Zeit und der Entwicklungsgedanke." *Europäischer Wissenschaftsdienst* 3 (1943): 11–13.

————. "Fortschritte der Psychotherapie." *Fortschritte der Neurologie* 7 (1935): 85–105.

————. "Neue Richtung, Neue Bindung." *ZfP* 7 (1934): 98–107.

————. "Weltfrömmigkeit. Ein Vortrag von Eduard Spranger." *ZfP* 13 (1942): 278–82.

————. "Die Willensstörung in der Neurose." In Curtius, *Psychotherapie in der Praxis,* pp. 42–59.

————. "Zur Entwicklung der analytischen Bewegung (Freud, Adler, Jung)." *Deutsche medizinische Wochenschrift* 59 (1933): 328–33.

————. "Zur Problematik des Führertums." *Zeitschrift für Menschenkunde* 7 (1932): 142–56.

————. "Zur Psychologie des Glaubens. Ein Vortrag von Eduard Spranger." *ZfP* 15 (1943): 130–36.

Hattingberg, Immo von. "Medical Care for Flying Personnel." In *German Aviation Medicine. World War II*, 2:1059–68. Washington: Department of the Air Force, 1950. Reprint. Pelham Manor, New York: Scholium International, 1971.

Herzog, Edgar. "Psychotherapie und Erziehungshilfe." In Göring, *Erziehungshilfe*, pp. 5–7.

Heyer, Gustav Richard. "Aus dem psychotherapeutischen Praxis. Eine Reihe von Briefen." *Hippokrates* 11–14 (1940–43).

————. "Die Polarität, ein Grundproblem in Werden und Wesen der deutschen Psychotherapie." *ZfP* 7 (1934): 17–23.

————. "Prognose in der Psychotherapie." In Curtius, *Psychotherapie in der Praxis*, pp. 110–25.

————. "Sigmund Freud." *Münchener medizinische Wochenschrift* 77 (1930): 1551–52.

Höck, Kurt. "Das abgestufte System der Diagnostik und Therapie neurotischer Störungen." In *Psychotherapie in sozialistischen Ländern. Bericht über die 1. Symposium Sozialistischer Länder über Psychotherapie in Prag von 13.3.-15.3.1973*. Edited by Milan Hausner, Stanislav Kratochvil and Kurt Höck, pp. 89–92. Leipzig: Thieme VEB, 1975.

————. "Entwicklung und Aufgaben der Psychotherapie in der DDR." In *Psychotherapie in sozialistischen Ländern*, pp. 51–55.

"Jahresbericht des Deutschen Instituts für Psychologische Forschung und Psychotherapie und Hinweise für die Weiterarbeit anlässlich der Mitgliederversammlung am 28. März 1942." *ZfP* 14 (1942): 62–77.

"Jahresbericht 1940 des Deutschen Instituts für Psychologische Forschung und Psychotherapie." *ZfP* 14 (1942): 1–62.

Jung, Carl Gustav. "Grundsätzliches zur praktischen Psychotherapie." *ZfP* 8 (1935): 66–82.

————. "Zur gegenwärtigen Lage der Psychotherapie." *ZfP* 7 (1934): 1–16.

Kellner, Hans. "Betriebsarzt und Psychotherapie?" *ZfP* 11 (1939): 220–28.

Kemper, Werner. "Die Indikation zur Psychotherapie bei Neurosen." In Curtius, *Psychotherapie in der Praxis*, pp. 9–26.

————. "Der seelische Anteil an der Sterilität." *Deutsches Ärzteblatt* 72 (1942): 397–99.

————. "Weniger bekannte Aufgaben ärztlicher Eheberatung." *Deutsches Ärzteblatt* 74 (1944): 166–69.

"Kongress für Psychotherapie in Breslau." *Deutsches Ärzteblatt* 65 (1935): 1064–68.

Kranefeldt, Wolfgang. "Freud und Jung." *ZfP* 7 (1934): 24–38.

Kretschmer, Ernst. "Organisationsfragen der deutschen Psychotherapie." *Deutsche medizinische Wochenscrift* 75 (1950): 377–79.

Krisch, Hans. "Die Lehrbarkeit der psychotherapeutischen Wissenschaft." *ZfP* 8 (1935): 227–34.

———. "Die Psychologie des Unbewussten von Carus." *ZfP* 9 (1936): 283–90.

Kroh, Oswald. "Bedeutsamer Fortschritt in der Psychologie." *Zeitschrift für Psychologie* 151 (1941): 1–32.

———. "Missverständnisse um die Psychologie." *Deutschlands Erneuerung* 27 (1943): 21–37.

Künkel, Fritz. "Die dialektische Charakterkunde als Ergebnis der kulturellen Krise."*ZfP* 7 (1934): 69–84.

———. "Das Hausarzt und Psychotherapie." *Deutsche medizinische Wochenschrift* 64 (1938): 1730–33.

———. "Die Lehrbarkeit der tiefenpsychologischen Denkweisen." *ZfP* 8 (1935): 235–48.

———. "Psychotherapie. Eine Übersicht über die Neuerscheinungen der letzten Jahre." *Hippokrates* 10 (1939): 1361–69.

———. "Seelenheilkunde." *Suddeutsche Monatshefte* 33 (1936): 294–300.

———. "Vorbeugung der Neurose." In Curtius, *Psychotherapie in der Praxis,* pp. 190–94.

Luchsinger, C. "Psychotherapie." *Volksgesundheitswacht* 3 (1936): 3–6.

Luxenburger, Hans. "Die Indikation zur Psychotherapie der Neurosen vom Standpunkt der Erbbiologie aus gesehen." In Curtius, *Psychotherapie in der Praxis,* pp. 20–32.

Meyer-Mark, Hans H. "Neurotiker der Wirtschaft." *ZfP* 11 (1939): 228–46.

Mohr, Fritz. "Die Behandlung der Neurosen durch Psychotherapie." In Curtius, *Psychotherapie in der Praxis,* pp. 60–82.

———. "Betrachtung über Wesen, Entstehung und Behandlung der Homosexualität." *ZfP* 15 (1943): 1–20.

———. "Brief an eine durch Fliegerangriff stillunfähig gewordene Mutter." *Hippokrates* 11 (1940): 1016.

———. "Das Leib-Seele Problem (vom Standpunkt der Psychotherapie aus)." *Münchener medizinische Wochenschrift* 86 (1939): 61–64.

Müller-Braunschweig, Carl. "Psychoanalyse und Weltanschauung." *Almanach der Psychoanalyse* 6 (1931): 102–16.

———. "Psychoanalyse und Weltanschauung." *Reichswart,* 22 October 1933, p. 22.

Rittmeister, John. "Der augenblickliche Stand der Poliklinik und ihre künftigen Aufgaben." *ZfP* 12 (1940): 88–96.

Scheunert, Gerhart. "Über Psychotherapie Kurzbehandlungen." *ZfP* 11 (1939): 206–20.

Schmitz, Wilhelm, and Schramm, Gerhart. "Unfallneurose und Reichsgericht." *Münchener medizinische Wochenschrift* 86 (1939): 1387–90.

Schultz, Johannes Heinrich. "Ist Psychotherapie lehr- und lernbar?" *ZfP* 7 (1934): 146–58.

———. "Das Leib-Seele Problem in der Heilkunde." *Suddeutsche Monatshefte* 33 (1936): 289–94.

———. "Leistung und Psyche." *Das Reich,* 14 February 1943, pp. 5–6.

———. "Der nervöse Zustand." In Pintschovious and Zeiss, *Zivilisationsschäden am Menschen,* pp. 82–102.

———. "Neurosenbekämpfung als Mittel der Leistungssteigerung. Grundsätzliches über Neurosenformen." *Die Gesundheitsführung "Ziel und Weg"* 7 (1945): 19–21.

———. "Poliklinische Aufgaben und Pflichten." *ZfP* 14 (1942): 12–17.

———. "Praktischer Arzt und Hypnose." *Deutsche medizinische Wochenschrift* 67 (1941): 1032–34.

———. "Psychopathie und Neurose." *Forschungen und Fortschritte* 17 (1941): 228–29.

———. "Rundschau. Psychotherapie 1935/36." *Jahreskurse für ärztliche Fortbildung* 5 (1936): 37–44.

———. "Seelische Gründe der Unfruchtbarkeit." *Europäischer Wissesschaftsdienst* 2 (1942): 22–24.

———. "Seelische Reaktionen auf die Verdunkelung." *Deutsche medizinische Wochenschrift* 66 (1940): 564–67.

———. "Seelische Schulung, Körperfunktion und Unbewusstes." *ZfP* 8 (1935): 304–18.

———. "Der seelische Schutz des Gesunden in den verschiedenen Lebensaltern." *Medizinische Klinik* 36 (1940): 213–16.

———. "Über kleine Psychotherapie in der allgemeinen Praxis und Kurzverfahren in der Psychotherapie." *ZfP* 11 (1939): 69–84.

———. "Über den Schutz seelisch Gefährdeter." *Medizinische Klinik* 36 (1940): 699–703.

———. "Über tiefenpsychologische Kurzbehandlungen." *Europäischer Wissenschaftsdienst* 4 (1944): 6–8.

———. "Vom Seelenleben der Jugend." *Die Gesundheitsführung "Ziel und Weg"* 5 (1943): 88–92.

———. "Vorschlag eines Diagnosen-Schemas." *ZfP* 12 (1940): 97–161.

———. "Der Yoga und die deutsche Seele." *ZfP* 7 (1934): 61–69.

Schultz-Hencke, Harald. "Die Tüchtigkeit als psychotherapeutisches Ziel." *ZfP* 7 (1934): 62–97.

Seelman, Kurt. "Die Erziehung des Schulkindes in Hinblick auf seine Lebensaufgaben." In Bilz, *Psyche und Leistung*, pp. 29–56.

Seif, Leonhard. "Prophylaxe gegen Neurose." In Curtius, *Psychotherapie in der Praxis*, pp. 165–74.

———. "Volksgemeinschaft und Neurose." *ZfP* 7 (1934): 52–61.

Seitz, Walter. "Die Lage der Psychotherapie in Deutschland." *Medizinische Klinik* 46 (1951): 399–402.

Speer, Ernst. "Ergebnisse aus der psychotherapeutischen Praxis zum Typenproblem." *ZfP* 7 (1934): 24–54.

Störring, Gustav E. "Die Verschiedenheiten der psychopathologischen Erfahrungen im Weltkriege und im jetzigen Krieg und ihre Ursachen." *Münchener medizinische Wochenschrift* 89 (1942): 25–30.

Stransky, Erwin. "Rasse und Psychotherapie." *ZfP* 10 (1937): 9–29.

"Tätigkeitsbericht 1935/36." *ZfP* 10 (1937): 4–6.

"Tätigkeitsbericht 1937." *ZfP* 10 (1938): 200–209.

"Tätigkeitsbericht 1938." *ZfP* 12 (1940): 2–9.

"Tätigkeitsbericht 1939." *ZfP* 13 (1941): 2.

"Tätigkeitsbericht 1940." *ZfP* 13 (1941): 2–4.

Thomä, Helmut. "Some Remarks on Psychoanalysis in Germany, Past and Present." *International Journal of Psycho-Analysis* 50 (1969): 683–92.

Villinger, Werner. "Psychiatrie und Wehrmacht." *Münchener medizinische Wochenschrift* 88 (1941): 437–43.

Wegscheider, Klaus. "Psychotherapie bei Kassenpatienten." *ZfP* 11 (1939): 56–69.

Weizsäcker, Adolf von. "Heimerziehung (Beobachtungen und Gedanken über den Austausch zwischen Psychotherapie und Heilerziehung)." In Bilz, *Psyche und Leistung*, pp. 88–104.

———. "Die tiefenpsychologische Behandlung von Kinderneurosen und ihr Verhältnis zur Heilerziehung." *Zeitschrift für Kinderforschung* 49 (1942): 255–83.

Weizsäcker, Viktor von. "Ärztliche Aufgaben." *Volk im Werden* 2 (1934): 80–90.

———. "Soziologische Bedeutung der nervösen Krankheiten und der Psychotherapie." *ZfP* 8 (1935): 295–304.

Winkler, Walter Theodor. "50 Jahre AÄGP—ein Rückblick." *Zeitschrift für Psychotherapie und medizinische Psychologie* 27 (1977): 74–84.

———. "The Present Status of Psychotherapy in Germany." In *Progress in Psychotherapy 1956*. Edited by Frieda Fromm-Reichmann and J. L. Moreno, pp. 288–305. New York: Grune & Stratton, 1956.

Würfler, P. "Zum Verständnis der Neurose, auch im Hinblick auf militärische Verhältnisse." *Der deutsche Militärarzt* 4 (1939): 124–28.

IV. AUTOBIOGRAPHIES AND MEMOIRS

Baumeyer, Franz. "Zur Geschichte der Psychoanalyse in Deutschland. 60 Jahre Deutsche Psychoanalytische Gesellschaft." *Zeitschrift für Psychosomatische Medizin und Psychoanalyse* 17 (1971): 203–40.

Boehm, Felix. "Bericht über die Ereignisse von 1933 bis zum Amsterdamer Kongress im August 1951." In Boehm, *Schriften zur Psychoanalyse*. Edited by Deutschen Psychoanalytischen Gesellschaft, pp. 301–10. Munich: Ölschläger, 1978.

Bumke, Oswald. *Erinnerungen und Betrachtungen. Der Weg eines deutschen Psychiaters*. Munich: Richard Pflaum, 1952.

Cimbal, Walter. "Erinnerungen eines alten Arztes an die Frühzeit der Psychotherapie in Deutschland." n.p., n.d.

Dräger, Käthe. "Psychoanalysis in Hitler Germany: 1933–1949." Translated by Jeanette Friedeberg. *American Imago* 29 (1972): 199–214.

Eliasberg, Wladimir. "Allgemeine ärztliche Gesellschaft für Psychotherapie, 1926–31: History of the Six Congresses." *American Journal of Psychiatry*, 112 (1956): 738–40.

Kretschmer, Ernst. *Gestalten und Gedanken. Erlebnisse*. Stuttgart: Georg Thieme, 1963.

Maetze, Gerhard, ed. *Psychoanalyse in Berlin. Beiträge zur Geschichte, Theorie und Praxis*. Meisenheim: Hain, 1971.

Pongratz, Ludwig J., ed. *Psychotherapie in Selbstdarstellungen*. Berne: Hans Huber, 1973.

Sauerbruch, Ferdinand. *Master Surgeon*. Translated by Fernand G. Renier and Anne Cliff. New York: Thomas Y. Crowell, 1954.

Schultz, Johannes Heinrich. *Lebensbilderbuch eines Nervenarztes. Jahrzehnte in Dankbarkeit*. Stuttgart: Georg Thieme, 1964.

Speer, Albert. *Inside the Third Reich: Memoirs.* Translated by Richard and Clara Winston. New York: Macmillan, 1970.

V. PUBLISHED SECONDARY SOURCES

Alexander, Franz G., and Selesnick, Sheldon T. *The History of Psychiatry: An Evaluation of Psychiatric Thought and Practice from Prehistoric Times to the Present.* New York: Harper & Row, 1966.

Bellak, Leopold, ed. *Contemporary European Psychiatry.* New York: Grove, 1961.

Beyerchen, Alan D. *Scientists Under Hitler: Politics and the Physics Community in the Third Reich.* New Haven: Yale University Press, 1979.

Bleuel, Hans Peter. *Sex and Society in Nazi Germany.* Translated by J. Maxwell Brownjohn. Philadelphia: J. B. Lippincott, 1973.

Brainin, Elisabeth, and Kaminer, Isidor J. "Psychoanalyse und Nationalsozialismus." *Psyche* 36 (1982): 989–1012.

Broszat, Martin. *The Hitler State: The Foundation and Development of the Internal Structure of the Third Reich.* Translated by John W. Hiden. London: Longman, 1981.

Chrzanowski, Gerard. "Psychoanalysis: Ideology and Practitioners." *Contemporary Psychoanalysis,* 11 (1975): 492–500.

Cocks, Geoffrey. "C. G. Jung and German Psychotherapy, 1933–1940: A Research Note." *Spring* 10 (1979): 221–27.

———. "Psychoanalyse, Psychotherapie und Nationalsozialismus." Translated by Michael Schröter. *Psyche* 37 (1983): 1057–1106.

———. "Psychotherapy in the Third Reich: A Research Note." *Journal of the History of the Behavioral Sciences* 14 (1978): 33–36.

Decker, Hannah S. *Freud in Germany: Revolution and Reaction in Science 1893–1907.* Psychological Issues Monograph 41. New York: International Universities Press, 1977.

Ellenberger, Henri F. *The Discovery of the Unconscious: The History and Evolution of Dynamic Psychiatry.* New York: Basic Books, 1970.

Fabricius, Helmut. "Gemeinschaftspsychologie—Adler-Seif-Künkel (1889–1956)." *Schwestern Revue* 11 (1975): 11–14.

Farago, Ladislas, ed. *German Psychological Warfare.* New York: G. P. Putnam's Sons, 1942.

Feiner, Arthur H. "The Dilemma of Integrity." *Contemporary Psychoanalysis* 11 (1975): 500–509.

Fest, Joachim C. *The Face of the Third Reich: Portraits of the Nazi Leadership.* Translated by Michael Bullock. New York: Pantheon, 1970.

Gaupp, Robert. "Some Reflections on the Development of Psychiatry in Germany." *American Journal of Psychiatry* 108 (1952): 721–23.

Goode, William J. "Encroachment, Charlatanism and the Emerging Profession: Psychology, Sociology and Medicine." *American Sociological Review* 25 (1960): 902–14.

Göring, Peter. *Vorarbeit zu einer Geschichte der Sippe.* Munich: n.p., 1911.

Grunberger, Richard. *The 12-Year Reich: A Social History of Nazi Germany.* New York: Holt, Rinehart & Winston, 1971.

Gumpert, Martin. *Heil Hunger! Health Under Hitler.* Translated by Maurice Samuel. New York: Alliance, 1940.

Hannah, Barbara. *Jung: His Life and Work. A Biographical Memoir.* New York: G. P. Putnam's Sons, 1976.

Hermanns, Ludger M. "John F. Rittmeister und C. G. Jung," *Psyche* 36 (1982): 1022–31.

Huber, Wolfgang. *Psychoanalyse in Österreich seit 1933.* Veröffentlichungen des Ludwig Boltzmann-Instituts für Geschichte der Gesellschaftswissenschaften, edited by Erika Weinzierl and Wolfgang Huber, vol. 2. Vienna: Geyer, 1977.

Jones, Ernest. *Sigmund Freud: Life and Work.* 3 volumes. London: Hogarth, 1957.

Kater, Michael H., *The Nazi Party: A Social Profile of Members and Leaders 1919–1945.* Cambridge: Harvard University Press, 1983.

Lohmanns, Hans-Martin, and Rosenkötter, Lutz. "Psychoanalyse in Hitlerdeutschland. Wie war es wirklich?" *Psyche* 36 (1982): 961–88.

Mason, Timothy W. *Arbeiterklasse und Volksgemeinschaft. Dokumente und Materialen zur deutschen Arbeiterpolitik 1936–1939.* Opladen: Westdeutscher Verlag, 1975.

Mosse, George, ed. *Nazi Culture: Intellectual, Cultural and Social Life in the Third Reich.* Translated by Salvator Attanasio et al. New York: Grossett & Dunlap, 1966.

Orlow, Dietrich. *The History of the Nazi Party 1933–1945.* Pittsburgh: University of Pittsburgh Press, 1973.

Peterson, Edward N. *The Limits of Hitler's Power.* Princeton: Princeton University Press, 1969.

Ringer, Fritz. *The Decline of the German Mandarins: The German Academic Community, 1890–1933.* Cambridge: Harvard University Press, 1969.

Röhrs, Hans-Dietrich, *Hitlers Krankheit. Tatsache und Legende. Medizinische und psychische Grundlagen seines Zusammenbruchs.* Zeitgeschichtliche Streitfragen, vol. 1. Neckargemünd: Kurt Vowinckel, 1966.

Rosenkötter, Lutz. "Schatten der Zeitgeschichte auf psychoanalytischen Behandlungen." *Psyche* 33 (1979): 1024–38.

Rubins, Jack L. *Karen Horney: Gentle Rebel of Psychoanalysis.* New York: Dial, 1978.

Schoenbaum, David. *Hitler's Social Revolution: Class and Status in Nazi Germany 1933–1939.* Garden City, N.Y.: Doubleday, 1966.

Schweitzer, Arthur. *Big Business in the Third Reich.* Bloomington: University of Indiana Press, 1964.

Smith, Harvey L. "Psychiatry in Medicine: Intra- or Inter-Professional Relationships?" *American Journal of Sociology* 63 (1957): 285–89.

Spiegel, Rose. "Survival of Psychoanalysis in Nazi Germany." *Contemporary Psychoanalysis* 11 (1975): 479–92.

Toren, Nina. "Semi-Professionalism and Social Work." In *The Semiprofessions and Their Organization.* Edited by Amitai Etzioni, pp. 142–62. New York: Free Press, 1969.

Vollmer, Howard M., and Mills, Donald L., eds. *Professionalization.* Englewood Cliffs, N.J.: Prentice-Hall, 1966.

Wuttke-Groneberg, Walter. "Leistung, Vernichtung, Verwertung. Überlegungen zur Struktur der Nationalsozialistischen Medizin." In *Volk und Ge-sundheit. Heilen und Vernichten im Nationalsozialismus.* Edited by Projekt-gruppe "Volk und Gesundheit," pp. 9–59. Tübingen, Schloss: Tübinger Vereinigung für Volkskunde e.V., 1982.

Wyatt, Frederick, and Teuber, Hans L. "German Psychology Under the Nazi System 1933–1940." *Psychological Review* 31 (1944): 229–47.

Zierold, Kurt. *Forschungsförderung in drei Epochen.* Wiesbaden: Steiner, 1968.

Zilboorg, Gregory. *A History of Medical Psychology.* New York: W. W. Norton, 1941.

INDEX

319